DOS/VSE

ICCF

System and editing commands •
VSE job management •
Interactive partition processing •

Steve Eckols

Mike Murach & Associates, Inc.

4697 West Jacquelyn Avenue
Fresno, California 93722
(209) 275-3335

Development team

Editors:	Anne Prince
	Doug Lowe
Designer and production director:	Steve Ehlers
Production staff:	Carl Kisling
	Norene Foin
	Lori Davis

Related books

DOS/VSE JCL, by Steve Eckols

DOS/VSE Assembler Language, by Kevin McQuillen and Anne Prince

20 19 18 17 16 15 14 13 12 11 10 9 8 7 6 5 4 3 2 1

Library of Congress Catalog Card Number: 86-61650

ISBN: 0-911625-36-4

Contents

Preface

If you're a programmer or an operator in an IBM mainframe computer facility that uses the DOS/VSE operating system, it's likely that much of the work you do will be through VSE/ICCF, IBM's Interactive Computing and Control Facility. As its name implies, ICCF lets you *interact* with your DOS/VSE system to use its resources. From your display station, you use ICCF to enter text (like source programs and job streams), run programs, and manage DOS/VSE jobs. Because ICCF is your window to the system, you have to know how to use it. And the more you know about it, the better and more efficiently you'll be able to do your job.

Why you should have this book

Frankly, it's not difficult to learn the bare minimum to use ICCF for text entry. There are two typical ways to learn ICCF. First, you can try to pick up what you need to know from IBM's reference manuals. Or, second, you can try to learn ICCF from your co-workers. Unfortunately, there are problems with both approaches.

Although all the information you need to use ICCF is in IBM's reference manuals, the way the manuals are structured actually gets in the way of learning. The manuals seldom present material so you can tell what's essential, what's useless, and what's in between. As a result, if you try to learn ICCF from the manuals, you can count on wasting time and having a frustrating experience.

There are also problems with learning ICCF from your co-workers. After a few minutes of looking over a co-worker's shoulder, you'll know enough about ICCF to enter source programs and job streams. However, when you learn like that, you're exposed only to a small subset of ICCF's features. Not only will you probably miss out on some

v

advanced features that are likely to be ones you'd use often, but you also might not learn some basic features you really should know.

ICCF's editing facilities are powerful, and, although you're not likely to use them all, you do need to know what's available. This book presents ICCF text editing features (1) so you can learn a complete and appropriate working subset of them and (2) so you can augment that subset with the advanced features that will be most useful for you. Because you'll spend most of your ICCF time doing text editing, that alone makes this book worth reading.

However, ICCF is much more than just a text editor. You should also know how to use ICCF's advanced features for VSE job management and interactive partition processing. With the former, you can transfer jobs from ICCF to the batch VSE environment, monitor their progress, and handle their output. And with the latter, you can run programs completely within ICCF. These are features that are even harder to learn from IBM's manuals, but you'll need to use one or both. This book teaches you how both work and what processing options they provide. As a result, when you've finished this book, you'll be able to make better use of ICCF than you could before.

Required background

ICCF and DOS/VSE are interrelated. ICCF runs in the VSE environment, and most of the ICCF work you do will ultimately use VSE facilities. However, if you're new to the DOS/VSE environment, don't panic. Chapter 1 presents conceptual background for readers who are new to IBM mainframes and/or the DOS/VSE operating system. If IBM systems are new to you, you should read both topics in chapter 1. However, if you have IBM mainframe experience, you can probably skip topic 1, which describes hardware devices. (However, if you're not familiar with 3270-type terminals, look over the part of chapter 1 that describes how to use them.) If you have DOS/VSE experience, you can probably also skip topic 2, which presents VSE concepts and components. In either case, review the objectives and terminology lists at the end of the topics; if you feel comfortable with them, you don't need to read the topics.

Although you can learn almost all of the features this book presents with just the background chapter 1 gives you, you must have a thorough understanding of DOS/VSE to use ICCF for practical work at your installation. For that background, I recommend the companion to this book, *DOS/VSE JCL*. As with ICCF, it's difficult, inefficient, and frustrating to learn DOS/VSE facilities from the IBM manuals. As a result, it would be worth the investment for you to get a copy of *DOS/VSE JCL*; you can use the order form at the end of this book to do so. (By the way, if you've read chapters 1 and 2 of *DOS/VSE JCL*, you don't need to read chapter 1 of this book, except perhaps for the section that describes how to use 3270-type display stations.)

How to use this book

The chapters in this book are organized in what I consider the most logical, effective sequence. As a result, I suggest you start with chapter 1 and read the book through to the end. However, I'm aware that your time is limited and that you may not want to read the entire book in that way.

I've already described how to decide whether you should skip the material chapter 1 presents. Regardless of whether you read chapter 1, you should read chapters 2 and 3. Chapter 2 presents the ICCF concepts and terminology you need to know, and chapter 3 shows you how to use basic ICCF system and editing commands.

After you've finished chapter 3, you can move directly to the chapters that you're immediately interested in. Most of the chapters that follow stand alone, and you can read them in whatever order you like. However, there are two exceptions. First, you need to have a conceptual understanding of the VSE spooling program VSE/POWER (provided in chapter 7) before you can learn how to use ICCF's facilities for VSE job management (chapter 8). And second, you need to know how to write jobs for execution in interactive partitions (described in chapter 9) before you can learn how to write typical procedures (chapter 11).

In addition to teaching you how to use ICCF, I think this book will also be your primary reference as you use ICCF. As a result, I've included a reference summary in an appendix. It includes the syntax of the system and editing commands and of the procedure and macro command lines the text presents. For each, it provides a chapter reference you can use to look up more detailed information on an item, if you need to.

Related reference manuals

Although you'll be able to use this book to answer most of your reference questions, you'll occasionally need to refer to an IBM reference manual. Depending on the release of ICCF that's installed on your system, the order numbers for manuals vary. However, their titles are consistent, so it should be easy for you to find the appropriate manual.

The manual you'll use most often is *VSE/Interactive Computing and Control Facility Terminal User's Guide*. It describes all the features of all the commands, procedures, macros, and statements ICCF supports. At points in this book, I'll refer you to this manual for details on infrequently used features; when I do, I'll usually call it *VSE/ICCF Terminal User's Guide*.

There are two other manuals you might be interested in. One, *VSE/Interactive Computing and Control Facility Installation and Operations Reference*, is designed primarily for systems programmers who are responsible for keeping ICCF running on your system. However, it contains technical information on ICCF's relationship to the VSE environment and on some ICCF features that you might like to read. The other, *VSE/Interactive Computing and Control Facility Messages* contains descriptions of all the messages ICCF can generate. Usually, ICCF messages are self-explanatory, but there may be times when you'll need to look one up.

Conclusion   I'm confident that this book will help you use ICCF more effectively. Even so, I'd like to know what you think about this book. So if you have any comments, please feel free to drop me a line using the postage-paid comment form at the back of this book. I look forward to hearing from you!

Steve Eckols
Fresno, California
May, 1986

Section 1

Required background

This section's two chapters give you the conceptual background you need to understand and use ICCF. Chapter 1 introduces the elements that make up the ICCF environment. It emphasizes IBM mainframe computer system hardware and the DOS/VSE operating system and the program products that typically operate under it. Chapter 2 turns specifically to ICCF. It describes how ICCF fits into the batch operating system environment, how data is stored by ICCF, and how ICCF itself uses processor storage.

Chapter 1

IBM mainframe system hardware
and the DOS/VSE operating system

ICCF runs on IBM mainframe computer systems that are controlled by the DOS/VSE operating system. This chapter gives you the background you need to understand both the hardware and software elements that make up ICCF's environment. Topic 1 covers mainframe hardware components, and topic 2 introduces DOS/VSE.

If IBM mainframe systems and DOS/VSE are new to you, you should certainly read this chapter. Even though some of the concepts and terms may be familiar to you from experience or previous study, you'll benefit from reading about them as they apply specifically to DOS/VSE. On the other hand, if you're already familiar with IBM systems, much of the material in this chapter will be review. If that's the case, you might want to skip one or both topics. To find out if you should, review the terminology and objectives at the end of each topic. If you're comfortable with them, you can probably skip the topic.

TOPIC 1   Mainframe hardware components

A *mainframe system* is a large collection of computer equipment. Just what "large" is, though, is debatable. Usually, mainframe systems support many applications and require staffs to operate and maintain them. In contrast, minicomputer and microcomputer systems usually support a smaller number of applications and often don't require staffs for operations and systems troubleshooting. The terminology is imprecise—the smallest mainframe systems are smaller than the largest minicomputer systems. In general, however, a mainframe system is expandable upward to create a large configuration, while minicomputer systems are more limited.

For mainframe systems, IBM manufactures dozens of hardware devices. Moreover, most are available in different models and with a variety of features. This topic won't teach you about all the specific devices that can be part of an IBM mainframe system. Instead, it approaches mainframe hardware at three levels.

First, it briefly describes the major components of a mainframe system: the processor and input/output equipment. Then, it presents the components of data communication networks, through which ICCF terminals are attached to mainframe systems. Finally, it describes a particular group of terminal types: the 3270 Information Display System. Since almost all ICCF users work at 3270 terminals, this section presents not only the components of a 3270 system, but it also shows you how to use a 3270-type terminal.

PROCESSORS The center of a mainframe system is the *processor*; all the other devices that make up the system configuration attach in some way to it. Although it's a simplification, you can think of the processor as consisting of two main parts: the central processing unit and main storage. The *central processing unit* (or *CPU*) is a collection of circuits that perform machine service functions and execute program instructions for calculation and data manipulation. *Main storage* (or *main memory*) is the high-speed, general-purpose electronic storage area that contains both the data the CPU operates upon and the program instructions it executes.

DOS/VSE (and, as a result, ICCF) runs on processors that are members of the *System/360-370* family. The System/360-370 family is a group of general-purpose processors that has developed over a 20-year span, beginning with the System/360 models of the mid-1960s, and continuing with the System/370 and 3030 series models of the 1970s. The 3080 and 4300 series models are current today.

Of course, as IBM has developed new System/360-370 processors, it has used contemporary technologies to create better, faster, and cheaper machines. Although the mainframe processors IBM manufactures today are direct descendants of the System/360s of the mid-1960s, those older machines are all but obsolete. In fact, DOS/VSE doesn't even run on them.

Processors that do support DOS/VSE are the System/370, 3030, 3080, and 4300 series processors. Models in the 4300 series are the most common type of DOS/VSE processor. The typical growth path for a DOS/VSE shop is to replace an older System/370 with a newer 4300. Although there are significant technical differences in the ways these processors operate, it doesn't matter much which one your shop uses. DOS/VSE and ICCF are essentially the same regardless of the processor on which they run.

INPUT/OUTPUT EQUIPMENT

The other broad group of mainframe devices consists of the *peripheral equipment* connected to the processor. Collectively, they're called *input/output devices*, or just *I/O devices*. Input devices provide data to the processor, and output devices receive data from it. Some machines can perform both functions. Basic types of I/O units on IBM mainframes are (1) printers, (2) card devices, (3) magnetic tape devices, (4) direct-access storage devices, and (5) terminal devices.

Direct-access storage devices (DASDs) have become key components of all mainframe systems because they allow direct and rapid access to large quantities of data. The most common type of DASD is the *disk drive*, a unit that reads and writes data on a *disk pack*. A disk pack is a stack of metal platters that are coated with a metal oxide material. Data is recorded on both surfaces of most of the platters in concentric circles called *tracks*. Although disk drives vary in capacity and "architecture," they're all organized in this basic way.

With such variety in the types of IBM mainframe processors and input/output devices, the number of possible *system configurations* is practically limitless. As a result, one installation's configuration is almost certain to differ from another, even if the two systems do similar processing.

Figure 1-1 represents a small 4300 system configuration. This configuration is smaller than the average installation's—in fact, it's nearly the smallest system that can be configured under DOS/VSE. At the center of the system is a 4331 Model 1 with 1M (M is the abbreviation for *megabyte*, about one million bytes) of main memory. Attached to the processor is a collection of I/O devices you might find on a small DOS/VSE system.

I particularly want you to notice one group of devices in figure 1-1: the four 3178 terminals. These are *local terminals*. A local terminal is one that's located at or near the central computer facility and doesn't require extensive telecommunications services to access the system. ICCF users on the system in figure 1-1 would work at those terminals.

Most DOS/VSE systems have some local terminals. However, terminal users who work in locations far from the central site have to use *remote terminals*. In either case, terminals are attached to the system through a *data communications network*.

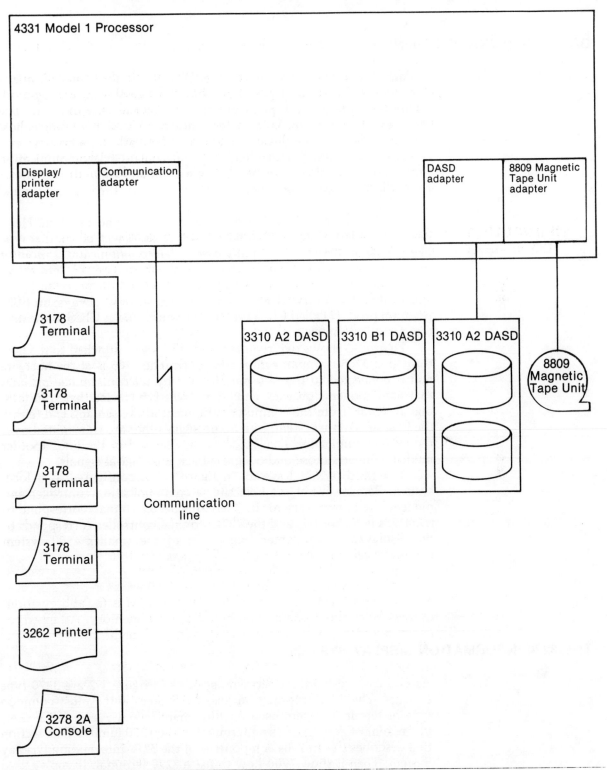

Figure 1-1   A small 4300 system configuration

DATA COMMUNICATIONS NETWORKS

A data communications network (often called a *telecommunications network*) lets terminal users access a *host computer* (or *host system*). Figure 1-2 represents a typical telecommunications network; here, one local and two remote 3270 systems are connected to a single host system. Basically, five elements make up a network: (1) a host system, (2) a communication controller, (3) modems, (4) telecommunication lines, and (5) terminal systems. A single *terminal system* can be one or more display stations, connected to the network through a terminal controller.

At the center of the network in figure 1-2 is the host system. Here, its processor is a System/370 model, but it could as well be another type like a 4300 or 3080 model. In any case, a *telecommunications monitor* program runs in the host system processor to control interactive application programs and to manage data base and file processing. For ICCF, that telecommunications monitor is almost always an IBM program product called CICS; you'll learn more about CICS in the next topic and in chapter 2.

Figure 1-2 shows two remote terminal systems attached to the host through a 3705 *communication controller*. The 3705 is at the host site and is connected to the two remote sites by *telecommunication lines* that have modems on each end. A *modem* is a device that translates digital signals from the computer equipment at the sending end (either the host or remote system) into audio signals that are transmitted over the telecommunication line. At the receiving end of the line, another modem converts those audio signals back into digital signals.

The third terminal system in figure 1-2 is configured as a local system. Because it's at the host site, a communication controller and modems aren't necessary for it. (Here, the 3278 terminals correspond to the 3178s in figure 1-1, and the 3274 terminal controller corresponds to the display/printer adapter that's part of the smaller 4300 system configuration.)

THE 3270 INFORMATION DISPLAY SYSTEM

As you can see, all three terminal systems in figure 1-2 are 3270-type systems. The 3270 Information Display System is the most common type of terminal system used on IBM mainframes. As an ICCF user, you're almost certain to use a terminal in the 3270 family. This section first describes the various components of the 3270 Information Display System. Then it shows you how to use a 3270 terminal. If you've used 3270-type terminals before, feel free to skip this section.

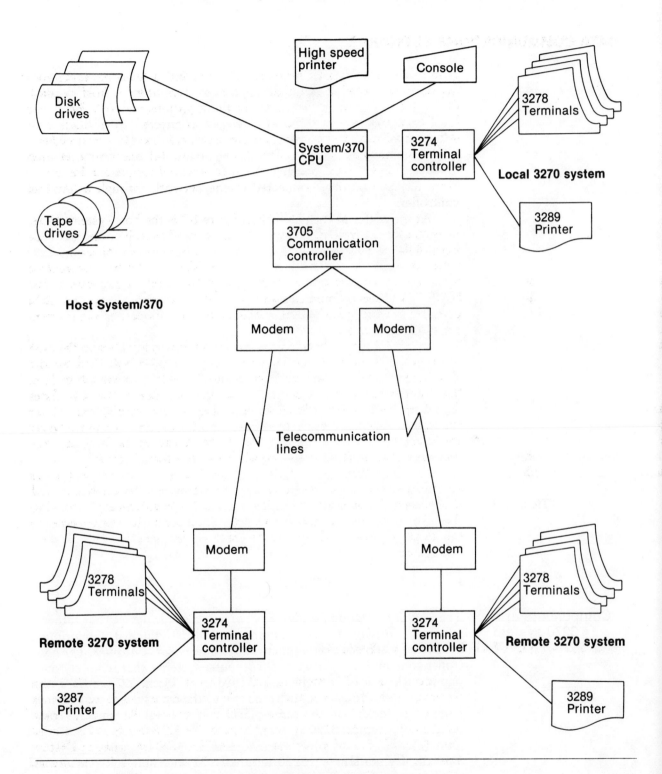

Figure 1-2   A typical telecommunications network

Figure 1-3   Components of a typical 3270 terminal system

**Components of a
3270 system**

The *3270 Information Display System* isn't a single device, but rather a system of *display stations* (commonly called terminals) and printers connected to a piece of equipment called a *terminal controller*. The controller communicates with a host computer system either remotely over phone lines or directly by being attached to a CPU. In other words, the terminals and printers use the resources of the host system, whether or not they're located in the same place. Figure 1-3 illustrates the components of a typical 3270 system.

3270 display stations   3270 terminals are available in a variety of configurations that display anywhere from 12 lines of 40 characters each to 43 lines of 80 characters, with one model that displays 27 lines of 132 characters. One advanced 3270-type terminal, the 3290, can serve as four separate display stations at the same time. However, the most common 3270-type terminals (like the 3278 Model 2 and the 3178) have screens with 24 usable display lines, each with 80 characters, for a total screen size of 1920 characters. (Notice that the usual screen width is 80 characters: the same as a standard punched card.) In addition, there's a special status line at the bottom of the 3270 screen.

3270 display stations can be configured with a variety of options, including alternate keyboard configurations for special applications or foreign languages. Less common features are a selector light pen that lets the operator communicate with the host system without using the keyboard, a magnetic slot reader or magnetic hand scanner, color display, extended highlighting capabilities (including underscore, blink, and reverse video), and graphics.

3270 printers   In addition to display stations, printers can be attached to a 3270 system. Many 3270 systems have a local-print feature that allows the data on the screen of a 3270 display station to be transferred to the terminal controller and then printed by one of the 3270 printers. Since this operation doesn't involve transmission of data between the 3270 system and the host, it's an efficient way to print. (You'll see plenty of examples of this sort of print output throughout this book.)

3270-compatible devices and emulators   Because of the enormous popularity of the 3270 system, many manufacturers besides IBM offer compatible terminals, controllers, and printers. And most manufacturers of minicomputers and microcomputers offer *emulator programs* that allow their computers to behave as if they were 3270 devices. Because of cost advantages and additional benefits, it's becoming more and more common to see such products in 3270 networks.

How to use a 3270 display station

To use ICCF, you need to know how to operate a 3270 display station. In this section, I'm just going to describe the way the screen is used by the terminal and what the keyboard keys do. For information about your system's specific terminal configurations and log-on procedures, you should check with your system administrator.

Characteristics of the 3270 display screen   As I've already mentioned, most 3270 terminals display 24 lines of 80 characters each. To control the way data is displayed, the 3270 treats its screen as a series of *fields*, each of which has various characteristics. For example, some screen fields allow the operator to key data into them, while others are protected from data entry.

Data-entry fields are called *unprotected fields* because they are *not* protected from operator entry. As a result, an operator can key data into an unprotected field. In contrast, display-only fields—such as captions and data displayed by a program—are called *protected fields* because they're protected from operator entry.

There is one more detail of how the 3270 handles data on its screen that I want you to know about. When you enter data into an unprotected field, character positions that follow the last characters you key in appear to contain spaces. However, they usually contain a special character called a *null character*. This helps the 3270 system optimize telecommunication line usage; null characters aren't transmitted between the terminal system and the host, while spaces are. As you'll see in a moment, whether an unprotected field contains trailing spaces or trailing null characters affects how you can enter data into the field.

Functions of the 3270 keys   The 3270 display station's keyboard is similar to a typewriter keyboard, with the addition of a few special keys. Although 3270 keyboards are available in many configurations, the layout in figure 1-4 is typical. The keyboard contains five types of keys: (1) data-entry keys, (2) cursor-control keys, (3) editing keys, (4) attention keys, and (5) miscellaneous keys. Each keyboard in figure 1-4 highlights one of the five categories of keys.

The data-entry keys include the letters, numerals, and special characters (÷ , @, and so on) usually found on a typewriter keyboard. You use these keys for normal text and data entry. The shift and shift-lock keys work just as they do on a typewriter. Some keyboards, but not this one, include a numeric keypad to speed entry of numeric data.

The cursor-control keys are used to change the location of the cursor on the terminal's screen. The *cursor* is a special character—an underscore or a solid block—that shows the screen location where the terminal will display the next character the user enters at the keyboard. The basic cursor-control keys are the four keys with arrows that point up, down, right, and left. When you press one of these keys, the cursor moves in the indicated direction.

The double-headed arrows on the left and right cursor-control keys are express functions. If you press and hold the ALT key, then press either the left or right arrow key, the cursor moves the indicated direction twice as quickly as it otherwise does. When a symbol appears on the front of a key rather than on its top, you have to press and hold the ALT key, then press the desired key to have the display station perform the function you request.

Although you can move the cursor to any position on the screen using only the four arrow keys, the 3270 keyboard includes other keys that let you move the cursor around more quickly and efficiently than the arrow keys allow. These keys include the tab key, the back-tab key, the new-line key, and the home key. The tab key moves the cursor to the beginning of the next unprotected field on the screen; it's heavily used in data-entry applications. The back-tab key moves the cursor to the previous unprotected field. The new-line key moves the cursor to the first unprotected field on a subsequent line. Finally, the home key

Data-entry keys

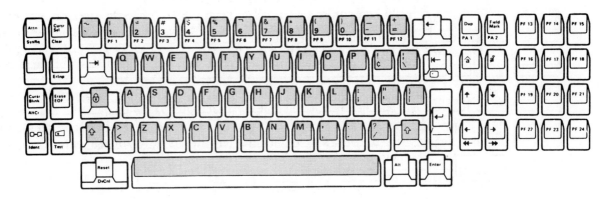

Cursor-control keys

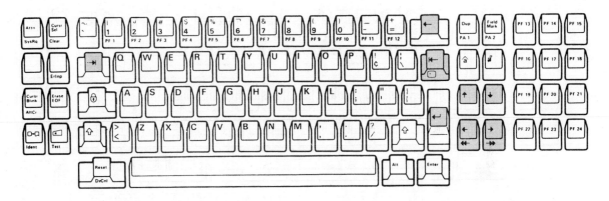

Editing keys

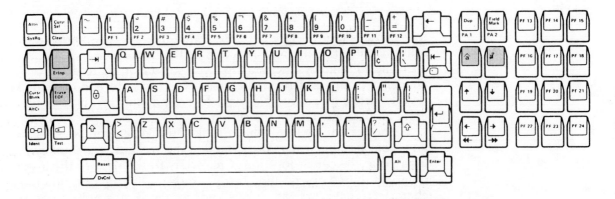

Figure 1-4   A typical 3270 keyboard arrangement (part 1 of 2)

Attention keys

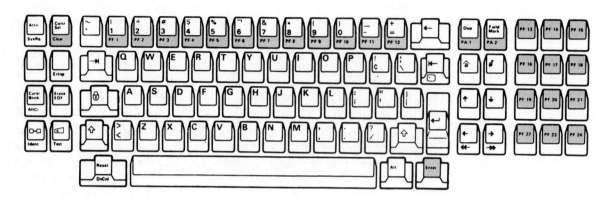

Miscellaneous keys

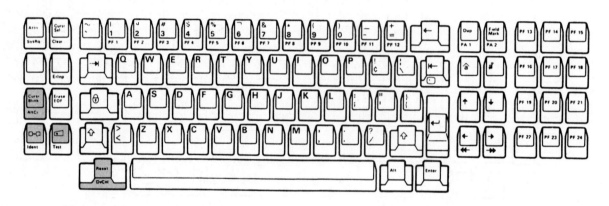

Figure 1-4   A typical 3270 keyboard arrangement (part 2 of 2)

moves the cursor to the first unprotected field on the screen. (Incidentally, home is the alternate function of the back-tab key.)

The editing keys include the delete key (🖊, used to delete a single character from the screen; the erase-EOF (erase to end-of-field) key, used to delete an entire field; and the erase-input (ErInp) key, used to erase all data entered on the screen.

Another editing key is the insert key (â). When you press the insert key, your terminal enters insert mode. Then, characters you key in are inserted at the cursor location. Characters to the right of the insertion point are shifted one position farther to the right each time you insert a character. That works as long as there are remaining null characters at the end of the field. However, if the field is full of trailing spaces, the insert function causes your keyboard to lock. (Then, you have to press the reset key to release it; I'll have more to say about the reset key in a moment.)

The attention keys let your terminal communicate with the system. For example, when you press the enter key, ICCF processes the data you've entered on the screen. Other attention keys are the PF and PA keys.

The *program function keys* (or *PF keys*) are attention keys you can use to invoke pre-defined ICCF functions. A 3270 display station can have up to 24 PF keys, but most have 12. The PF keys are labelled PF1, PF2, and so on up to PF24. In figure 1-4, PF1 through PF12 are located along the top row of the keyboard, on the same keys as the numerals. To use them, you first depress and hold ALT, then you press the correct PF key. In contrast, PF13 through PF24 in figure 1-4 are separated from the main keyboard; you don't have to press ALT to use them.

A 3270 keyboard also has two or three *program access keys* (or *PA keys*), labelled PA1, PA2, and PA3. (Note that the keyboard in figure 1-4 doesn't have PA3.) The PA keys work like the PF keys except that no data is sent to the system when they're used. Instead, just an indication of which PA key was pressed is sent. PA2 is widely used as a cancel key for many ICCF features. In other words, when you press PA2, the ICCF function currently operating is immediately terminated. However, this is installation-dependent, so PA2 may not work this way on your terminal.

The *clear key* works like a PA key, except that it causes the screen to be erased, and any data that was on the screen is lost. As a result, you shouldn't normally use the clear key.

As you can see in figure 1-4, there are several other keys on a 3270 keyboard. But with the exception of the *reset key*, you don't use them often. You use the reset key whenever the terminal "locks up"—that is, when you make an entry error and the terminal freezes the keyboard to prevent further data entry. In this case, the keyboard is released when you press the reset key. (The insert situation I described a moment ago is a case in which you have to use the reset key.)

Terminology	
	mainframe system
	processor
	central processing unit
	CPU
	main storage
	main memory
	System/360-370
	peripheral equipment
	input/output device
	I/O device
	direct-access storage device
	DASD
	disk drive

disk pack
track
system configuration
megabyte
local terminal
remote terminal
data communications network
telecommunications network
host computer
host system
terminal system
telecommunications monitor
communication controller
telecommunication line
modem
3270 Information Display System
display station
terminal controller
emulator program
field
unprotected field
protected field
null character
cursor
program function key
PF key
program access key
PA key
clear key
reset key

Objectives

1. List the types of components that make up:
    a. a typical IBM mainframe computer system
    b. a data communications network
    c. the 3270 Information Display system

2. Find the data-entry, cursor-control, editing, PF, PA, and reset keys on your keyboard, and describe how to use each.

TOPIC 2   DOS/VSE concepts and terminology

This topic introduces you to *DOS/VSE*, IBM's *Disk Operating System/Virtual Storage Extended*, (or just VSE, as I'll frequently call it from now on) and the other programs that make up a VSE system. First, it describes how the VSE system control programs manage processor storage. Then, it describes the VSE library structure and introduces you to the complete set of components that make up a production VSE system. Because ICCF runs in this environment and relates to these facilities and components, you need to understand them to use ICCF effectively.

HOW VSE MANAGES PROCESSOR STORAGE

Although VSE performs a variety of functions, probably the most important is processor storage management. This section introduces you to VSE by describing how it manages processor storage. First, it describes multiprogramming; then it presents virtual storage.

Multiprogramming

A common feature of mainframe computer systems, VSE systems included, is *multiprogramming*. When a system provides multiprogramming, it allows a single processor to execute more than one program at the same time. Actually, that's somewhat misleading, because although multiple programs are present in storage at the same time, only one is executing at a given instant. Nevertheless, it looks like multiple programs are executing at one time.

Multiprogramming improves the overall productivity of a computing installation. As you should know, internal processing speeds are far greater than input and output operation speeds. Because most business applications do relatively little processing between I/O operations, a processor that only executes one program at a time is idle a large percentage of the time while the program waits for an I/O operation to finish. To make better use of this wasted time, multiprogramming allows additional programs to be in storage so their instructions can be executed while the first program waits for its I/O operations to be completed.

The central component of VSE, the *supervisor program*, or just *supervisor*, determines what program should be executing at any moment. A program that's executing is said to be in control of the system. When the program that's in control of the system must wait for an I/O operation to complete, it gives up control to the supervisor. Then, the supervisor passes control to another program.

The supervisor uses a scheme of priorities to determine what program should execute next. *Priority* is a "rank" that determines a program's eligibility for receiving system services. If several programs are waiting to resume execution, the supervisor passes control to the one with the highest priority. This process of passing control among programs of different priorities is called *task selection*. Actually, priority isn't associated directly with a program, but rather with the partition the program executes in.

Partitions   VSE implements multiprogramming by dividing available processor storage (that is, storage not required by the VSE system control programs) into 2 to 12 *partitions*. Each partition may contain a user program. Under VSE, multiprogramming isn't an option: The storage available for user programs *must* be divided into partitions.

On a system with only two partitions, one is the *background partition* and the other is the *foreground partition*. Lower priority programs run in the background partition, and higher priority programs run in the foreground partition.

Frankly, a system that requires only two partitions is probably being underutilized; it's more common for a VSE system to use several partitions. When your VSE system was generated, your systems programmer decided how many partitions should be configured. The decision was based on the kind and number of programs that would be run on the system. Although the number of partitions varies up to 12 from one VSE system to another, the number on your system is probably fixed.

Figure 1-5 illustrates the maximum number of partitions a single VSE processor can support. Just as with a two-partition system, one partition is the background. All of the other partitions are foreground partitions. As the figure indicates, the background partition (BG) is for the lowest priority processing and the foreground partitions (F1 through FB) are for higher priority processing. Among the foreground partitions, Foreground-1 is usually for the highest priority jobs, and Foreground-11 is usually for the lowest priority jobs.

Address space organization   All programs, including the supervisor, execute in the processor's *address space*. You can think of the address space as a string of bytes as long as the amount of storage on the system. For example, a 16M address space would begin at byte 0 (numbering begins with 0, not 1) and extend to byte 16,777,215. Locations within the address space are identified by their displacement from its beginning.

Figure 1-6 illustrates the address space layout for a 16M four-partition system. The supervisor resides in the lowest portion of the address space. In other words, the supervisor area begins at 0K and extends upward. A typical VSE supervisor requires 222K; its address range would be 0K to 222K. (The exact size of the supervisor depends on options specified when the system was generated.)

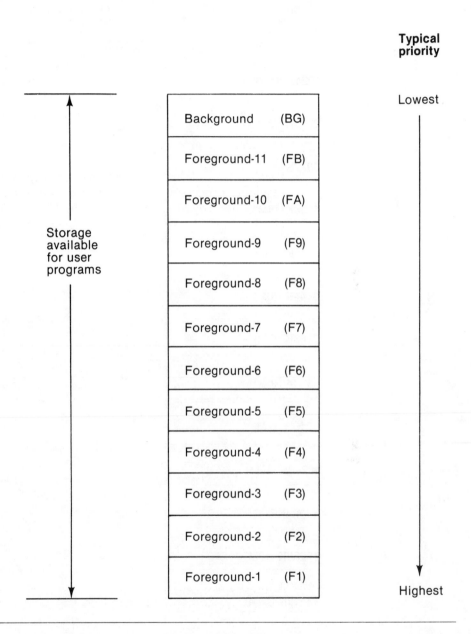

Figure 1-5   VSE partitions

After the supervisor comes the storage available to user programs, divided into partitions. This is the space that corresponds to figure 1-5. However, in figure 1-6, the system is configured with only four partitions. The background partition immediately follows the supervisor, and the three foreground partitions follow the background partition. As you can see, partition sizes vary. The systems programmer decides how much of the total address space to allocate to a partition based on

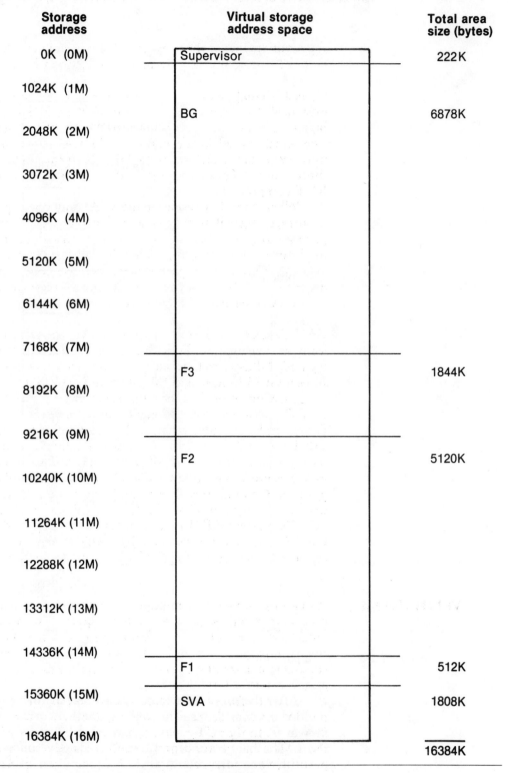

Storage address	Virtual storage address space	Total area size (bytes)
0K (0M)	Supervisor	222K
1024K (1M)		
	BG	6878K
2048K (2M)		
3072K (3M)		
4096K (4M)		
5120K (5M)		
6144K (6M)		
7168K (7M)		
	F3	1844K
8192K (8M)		
9216K (9M)		
	F2	5120K
10240K (10M)		
11264K (11M)		
12288K (12M)		
13312K (13M)		
14336K (14M)		
	F1	512K
15360K (15M)	SVA	1808K
16384K (16M)		
		16384K

Figure 1-6   VSE address space usage on a four-partition system

the requirements of the programs that will run in it. For example, in this case, F2's programs require more storage than F1's.

Shared Virtual Area   The area available for user programs doesn't extend all the way to the high end of the address space. Instead, the highest address range is occupied by the *SVA*, or *Shared Virtual Area*. The word shared in the name should help you remember the SVA's most important function: It contains program modules that are shared throughout the system. Most of these are I/O modules, but some are ICCF components.

When a module resides in the SVA, only one copy of it needs to be in storage, regardless of how many partitions use it. In contrast, if each partition required its own copy, more storage would be required for the duplicates. As a result, the SVA helps optimize storage usage. The SVA also improves system performance because commonly used modules don't have to be retrieved from DASD and loaded into storage each time they're needed; they're already there.

GETVIS areas   Often, programs need to acquire storage dynamically as they execute. To let programs do this, VSE uses *GETVIS areas*. Figure 1-7 illustrates the locations of the two types of GETVIS areas: the system GETVIS area and the partition GETVIS areas.

Each partition has its own *partition GETVIS area*. A partition's GETVIS area occupies the highest address range within the partition. For example, in figure 1-7, the GETVIS area for F1 occupies the highest 48K bytes of storage within F1. (The minimum, and usual, size for a partition GETVIS area is 48K.) The maximum size of a program that may execute in a partition is the full partition size, minus the size of the partition GETVIS area. For example, in figure 1-7, the largest program that may execute in F3 is 1796K bytes (1844K − 48K).

The *system GETVIS area* occupies the high-address range within the SVA. It's used exclusively by VSE's system control programs. In figure 1-7, the system GETVIS area occupies 464K bytes.

Virtual storage   As you can imagine, a multiprogramming system with a dozen active programs requires a large address space. To provide the storage required to support a large address space, VSE uses virtual storage. *Virtual storage* is a technique that allows a large amount of storage to be simulated in a smaller amount of *real storage* by using DASD storage as an extension of internal storage.

The advantage of virtual storage is that more programs can be multiprogrammed, thus increasing the efficiency of the computer system. Although the operating system itself is less efficient because of the additional virtual storage control functions it must perform, the productivity of the system as a whole increases. Fortunately, from the application programmer's point of view, virtual storage appears to be real storage.

Storage address	Virtual storage address space	Total area size (bytes)	GETVIS area size (bytes)
0K (0M)	Supervisor	222K	
1024K (1M)			
	BG	6878K	48K
2048K (2M)			
3072K (3M)			
4096K (4M)			
5120K (5M)			
6144K (6M)			
7168K (7M)	BG GETVIS area		
	F3	1844K	48K
8192K (8M)			
9216K (9M)	F3 GETVIS area		
	F2	5120K	48K
10240K (10M)			
11264K (11M)			
12288K (12M)			
13312K (13M)			
	F2 GETVIS area		
14336K (14M)	F1	512K	48K
	F1 GETVIS area		
15360K (15M)	SVA	1808K	464K
	System GETVIS area		
16384K (16M)		16384K	

Figure 1-7   Partition and system GETVIS areas on a four-partition system

The idea behind virtual storage is that, at any instant, only the single program instruction being executed and the data areas it accesses need to be in real storage. The parts of the program that aren't currently executing don't need to reside in real storage. Instead, they can reside outside real storage on a disk drive. As additional portions of the program are required, parts that are no longer needed are written to the disk, and new ones from the disk replace them in real storage. Because it would be inefficient to transfer program instructions, along with the data they require, back and forth from main memory one by one, transfer takes place in blocks. Those blocks are 2K program segments called *pages*.

When a program requires data or instructions that aren't in real storage, a *page fault* occurs. Then, the supervisor transfers a page that isn't immediately needed in real storage to the disk and fetches the page that contains the required data or instructions. The process of transferring pages to and from disk is called *paging, page swapping,* or just *swapping*. Real storage is divided into 2K byte areas called *page frames* that are grouped together in the *page pool*. The DASD area that contains the pages is called the *page data set*. (Obviously, the DASD that contains the page data set must be operational at all times on a VSE system.)

Figure 1-8 illustrates virtual storage and should help you better understand this terminology. This example uses the 16M virtual storage address space from figures 1-6 and 1-7. As you can see, the page data set contains an image of the virtual storage address space. The page data set must be the same size as the virtual storage address space (16M). Real storage—only 1M in this example—contains the resident parts of the supervisor and the page pool. The page pool contains all of the system's available page frames; each page frame contains a page from the page data set.

Although a program occupies a continuous range of virtual storage address space, it doesn't necessarily occupy a continuous group of page frames in the page pool. That's what the patchwork of page frames in the real storage section of figure 1-8 illustrates. The supervisor keeps track of what program pages are in what page frames by maintaining tables that reflect the current status of virtual storage.

COMPONENTS OF A COMPLETE VSE SYSTEM

This section describes the software elements that make up a complete VSE system. First, you'll learn about VSE libraries: specialized DASD files whose main purpose is to store programs in various forms. Then, I'll give you quick descriptions of the other software products that supplement VSE on typical production systems.

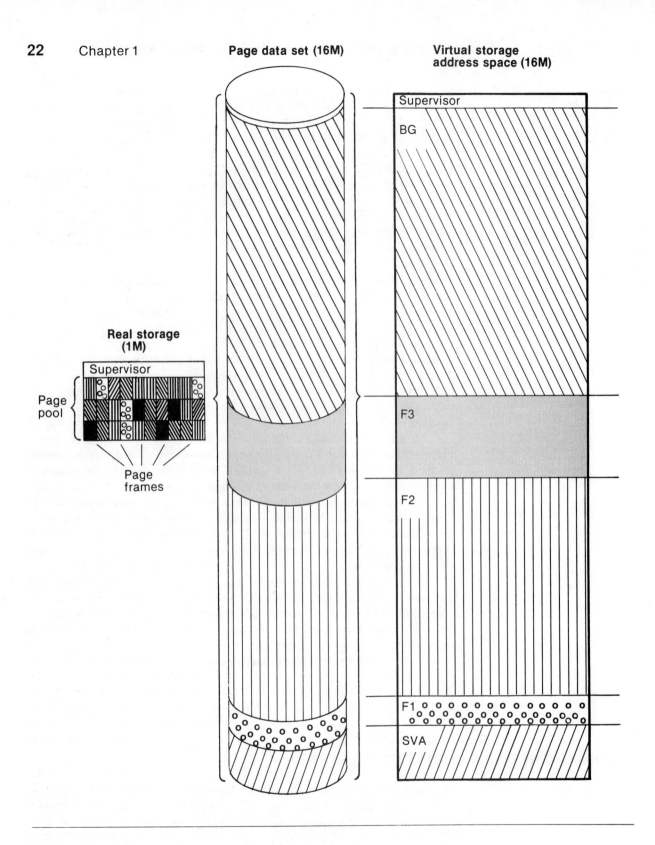

Figure 1-8 Virtual storage under VSE

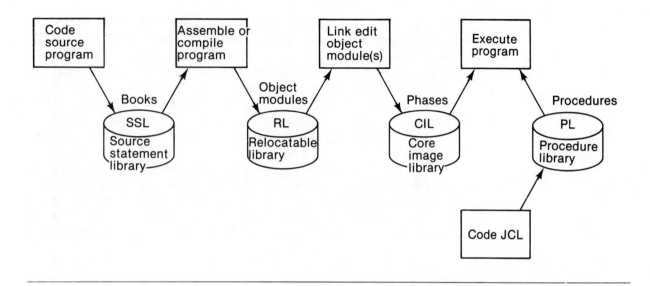

Figure 1-9   Program development and VSE libraries (through release 1.3)

VSE libraries   The software components that make up a complete VSE system number in the hundreds, and they're all stored on DASD. As you can imagine, managing all of them as separate DASD files would be inefficient and could easily get out of control. To help systems personnel keep track of program components, VSE components are stored in special files called libraries. In addition, you can use libraries to store user-written applications.

A VSE *library* is a DASD file that contains a collection of related sub-files, or *members*. For example, one library (or set of libraries) may contain the programs for a particular application subsystem, like general ledger. All of a library's members are listed in the library's *directory*. The directory specifies each member's name, DASD location, and size.

When you're developing a program on a VSE system, you go through a standard series of steps before you can execute the program. First, you code the program. Second, you compile (or assemble) it. Third, you link edit the program. And fourth, you code the control statements that will invoke it. The four main types of data VSE libraries contain correspond to the results of each of these four steps, as figure 1-9 shows.

Figure 1-9 illustrates the library structure VSE used up through release 1.3. As you can see, this older library structure uses four different kinds of libraries. The output of the coding step is a source program (or a segment of a source program) in whatever language you use (such as COBOL, assembler, or PL/I) which can be stored in a *source statement library*, or *SSL*. A member in an SSL is called a *book*.

The output of the compilation (or assembly) step is a relocatable module. A relocatable module is stored in a *relocatable library* (or *RL*) and is called an *object module*. An object module can't be executed directly; it has to be processed by the linkage editor program first. The output of the linkage editor is an executable module called a *phase*. Phases are stored as members in *core image libraries*, also called *CILs*. Finally, when a program is complete, you use job control statements to invoke it. Job control statements can be stored in a *procedure library*, or *PL*. A member in a PL is a *procedure*.

In contrast to the rather cumbersome library structure of older VSE releases, VSE 2.1 uses a simpler, more flexible scheme. Even so, the four main kinds of data that are stored in libraries remain the same. Under VSE 2.1, any combination of books, object modules, phases, and procedures can be stored in the same library. So, under the new library structure, a single library can replace the four libraries (SSL, RL, CIL, and PL) that were required under the old structure to store the programs and procedures for an application. Thus, the distinctions between the kinds of older VSE libraries is shifted to an emphasis on the *type* of a particular library member. In addition, a VSE 2.1 library can also contain storage dumps and even user data.

I've gone into some detail discussing VSE libraries because one of the most confusing parts of learning about ICCF and VSE is that they both use the term "library" extensively. And, it's easy to confuse the VSE terms and the ICCF terms. When I describe ICCF libraries in the next chapter, I want to be sure you already understand VSE libraries so you can avoid that kind of confusion.

VSE software components

In addition to these library files, a production VSE system also uses a variety of related software products. Some are components of the operating system itself; others are separately licensed products. The practical distinction between programs in the two groups isn't clear. A fully functioning VSE system must use some separately licensed products and may not use all of the facilities of the basic operating system. The point is that you need to be familiar with both the critical components of VSE itself and the other IBM software products that make up a complete system.

VSE/AF　At the heart of a VSE system's software is *VSE/Advanced Functions* (or *VSE/AF*). You've already been introduced to VSE storage management (multiprogramming and virtual storage) and VSE libraries. Other services the programs of VSE/AF provide are system start-up, job control, data access methods (which I'll describe in a moment), operator communication, and some utility functions.

To use and understand some of the advanced features this book presents, you need a thorough understanding of VSE job control language. However, it's well beyond the scope of this book to teach you JCL. As a result, if you need to learn how to use job control language, I recommend the companion to this book: *DOS/VSE JCL*. Ordering information is at the end of this book.

One characteristic of VSE JCL that I particularly want you to be aware of is that it's card-oriented. That's because the earliest versions of the DOS/VSE program that interprets control statements required that they be supplied on cards. Although DOS/VSE has been enhanced extensively, job control statements still must be supplied on cards or, and this is important, *appear* to be supplied on cards. One of the components of a complete VSE system, VSE/POWER, can supply card images rather than cards to a VSE partition.

VSE/POWER   *VSE/POWER*, or just *POWER*, provides a function required for a VSE system to operate efficiently: *spooling*. Spooling manages card devices and printers for application programs by intercepting program I/O requests for those devices and routing them to or from disk files instead. For example, if a processing program tries to print a line on a printer, the line is spooled to a disk file. Because DASDs are faster than printers, spooling lets the processing program resume execution more rapidly. Later, when the processing program has finished execution, the print lines temporarily stored on DASD are actually printed.

The same spooling technique is used in reverse for card input files. As cards pass through the reader, the data from them isn't immediately processed by the application program. Instead, it's stored on disk until all of the cards have been read. Then, the processing program begins execution. Records are supplied to it not from the card reader, but rather from the DASD file.

The result is a two-fold benefit. First, programs can execute more rapidly because their I/O requests are satisfied at DASD rather than printer or card device speeds. Second, and probably more important, several programs that would otherwise require exclusive control of the same card devices and printers can execute at the same time. Without spooling, a program that writes to a printer has complete control of the device until it has finished executing; other programs that need to do printer output have to wait.

POWER stands for Priority Output Writers, Execution processors, and input Readers. It runs in a high priority partition and can provide spooling services for all lower priority partitions. POWER not only provides spooling services for program input and output, but it's also a job scheduler. It uses a scheme of classes and priorities to determine when and in what partition a program should execute. POWER also routes output to appropriate devices and is used to control those devices.

Because POWER performs such useful system functions, you need to understand how it works and how to use it. If you want to run a batch VSE job from ICCF, you have to use a special ICCF feature that lets it pass a job stream to POWER. Then, POWER treats the job just as if it had been read in from a physical card reader. You'll learn more about POWER and how to use it through ICCF in chapters 7 and 8.

Data access methods   To process files, a VSE system uses *data access methods*. An access method is an interface between application programs and the operations of physical I/O devices. When an application program executes an I/O instruction, an access method is invoked to satisfy the request. Access methods relieve you of having to handle the complex technical details of using I/O devices.

The access methods available as a part of VSE are called *native access methods*. There are three of them: SAM, DAM, and ISAM. *SAM*, the *Sequential Access Method*, is used to store and retrieve data sequentially. When you access data on cards or tape, or write data to cards, tape, or a printer, you invoke SAM services. Similarly, sequential files stored on DASDs can be processed by SAM. *DAM*, the *Direct Access Method*, can be used only for DASD files that have direct organization. *ISAM*, the *Indexed Sequential Access Method*, is used to process DASD files that have indexed sequential organization.

Another data access method is an integral part of a VSE system: *VSAM*, the *Virtual Storage Access Method*. Although it's not part of VSE itself, it's a required component of a VSE system. VSAM can support DASD files with any of the organizations supported by SAM, DAM, or ISAM. Because VSAM offers more functions than the native access methods and simplifies data management, it's the most heavily used data access method in typical VSE shops.

Telecommunications access methods   Just as the native access methods and VSAM serve as interfaces between application programs and I/O devices, *telecommunication (TC) access methods* are interfaces between programs and communications devices. For a system to support any terminal devices, local or remote, it must include a telecommunications access method. TC access methods provide facilities for building and operating data communications applications. Although it's possible to write assembler language programs that use TC access methods directly, it's more common for them to be used through other IBM program products, such as CICS/VS. (I'll describe CICS/VS in a moment.) On a VSE system, two TC access methods are available: *BTAM* and *VTAM*.

On smaller VSE systems, the TC access method most likely to be used is *BTAM-ES* (*Basic Telecommunications Access Method -Extended Support*). BTAM-ES provides routines that programmers can use to code telecommunications applications in assembler language.

On larger systems with heavier communications workloads, you're more likely to find VTAM in use. VTAM is part of IBM's *System Network Architecture*, or *SNA*. Actually, VTAM is available in two versions. *ACF/VTAM* runs on most VSE-compatible processors, while *ACF/VTAME* runs only on 4331-type machines. (The acronyms stand for *Advanced Communications Function for Virtual Telecommunications Access Method* and *ACF/VTAM Entry*).

CICS/VS   *CICS/VS (Customer Information Control System/Virtual Storage)* is a sophisticated *data base/data communications (DB/DC) system* that serves as an interface between interactive application programs and VSE, with its TC access methods. CICS can support a large network of both local and remote terminals that run a wide variety of interactive applications. It controls communications between the central processor and terminals, manages concurrently executing application programs for all terminal users, and controls access to files by those programs.

As an ICCF user, you need to have a basic understanding of CICS because in almost all cases, ICCF and CICS execute together in the same VSE partition. ICCF almost always uses CICS to control its terminals. You'll learn more about the relationship between ICCF and CICS in the next chapter.

Language translators and linkage editor   *Language translators* are the programs that convert source programs into object modules. One language translator, the assembler, is supplied as a part of VSE. Other language translators, the COBOL, PL/I, RPG II, and FORTRAN IV compilers, are separate products. The purpose of the language translators is to reduce the programming time required to prepare a working object program. As a result, they all print diagnostic (error) listings to help the programmer correct clerical errors. In addition, they also often provide debugging statements to help the programmer test the program. The *linkage editor* program, supplied as part of VSE, converts object modules into executable phases and combines multiple object modules into a single phase.

Library maintenance programs   Not only does the linkage editor combine modules to create phases, but it's also used to add (or *catalog*) phases to core image libraries. In addition to the linkage editor, older VSE releases include several other specialized programs that perform library maintenance functions. Collectively, they're called the *VSE Librarian*. Under VSE 2.1, a single multi-function Librarian program is used.

Utility programs   Certain routine processing functions are common to most computer installations, such as copying files and sorting and merging records from one or more files. As a result, most shops use a set of general-purpose *utility programs* (like Sort/Merge, VSE/DITTO, and the multi-function VSAM utility program Access Method Services) to perform these functions. With utility programs, specialized programs don't have to be created to perform common functions. Instead, you can supply parameters to a general-purpose utility program to specify the exact processing it should do.

DISCUSSION   Figure 1-10 should help you better understand the material this chapter has presented. It shows the address space I described earlier in this topic, but illustrates the software products that typically execute in its partitions. The spooling product POWER executes in F1, the highest priority partition. As a result, it can provide spooling and job scheduling services for the other partitions. The SVA contains modules that might be used throughout the system, such as SAM and VSAM components. F3 and BG are reserved for other batch applications. (The only reason BG is so large is because no other partitions are configured. For example, if this system included F4 and F5, the size of BG would be reduced accordingly.) Finally, F2 is used for CICS and ICCF. As you can see, CICS and ICCF require a large partition. In the next chapter, you'll learn why.

As you can tell by now, a VSE system is a complex collection of many components. Don't worry at this point if you're confused by the large number of terms and acronyms. They'll become second nature to you as you work with your system. As I've already mentioned, this topic is just an introduction to VSE facilities. There's plenty more to learn, particularly about access methods and job control language. As a result, if you feel overwhelmed by this material, I encourage you to get a copy of *DOS/VSE JCL*.

Terminology   DOS/VSE
Disk Operating System/Virtual Storage Extended
multiprogramming
supervisor program
supervisor
priority
task selection
partition
background partition
foreground partition
address space
SVA
Shared Virtual Area
GETVIS area
partition GETVIS area
system GETVIS area
virtual storage
real storage
pages
page fault
paging
page swapping
swapping
page frame
page pool

Storage address	Virtual storage address space	
0K (0M)	Supervisor	
1024K (1M)		
	BG	Available for low priority batch jobs
2048K (2M)		
3072K (3M)		
4096K (4M)		
5120K (5M)		
6144K (6M)		
7168K (7M)		
8192K (8M)	F3	Available for high priority batch jobs
9216K (9M)		
	F2	
10240K (10M)		ICCF and CICS
		Available for interactive program execution and time-sharing by multiple users
11264K (11M)		
12288K (12M)		
13312K (13M)		
14336K (14M)		
	F1	POWER Spooling program
15360K (15M)	SVA	Common phases (e.g. VSAM components)
16384K (16M)		

Figure 1-10   Partition usage on the sample system

page data set
library
member
directory
source statement library
SSL
book
relocatable library
RL
object module
phase
core image library
CIL
procedure library
PL
procedure
VSE/Advanced Functions
VSE/AF
VSE/POWER
POWER
spooling
data access methods
native access methods
SAM
Sequential Access Method
DAM
Direct Access Method
ISAM
Indexed Sequential Access Method
VSAM
Virtual Storage Access Method
telecommunications access methods
TC access methods
BTAM
VTAM
BTAM-ES
Basic Telecommunications Access Method - Extended Support
System Network Architecture
SNA
ACF/VTAM
ACF/VTAME
Advanced Communications Function for Virtual
    Telecommunications Access Method
ACF/VTAM Entry
CICS/VS
Customer Information Control System/Virtual Storage
data base/data communications system
DB/DC system

language translators
linkage editor
catalog
VSE Librarian
utility program

Objectives

1. Describe how VSE implements multiprogramming.

2. Describe the function of the SVA.

3. Describe the function of GETVIS areas.

4. Describe how VSE implements virtual storage.

5. List the four types of VSE libraries, through release 1.3, (when classified by contents) and describe how they fit in the sequence of program development for a typical application.

6. Describe the functions of:

    a. POWER
    b. data access methods
    c. telecommunications access methods
    d. CICS

Chapter 2

ICCF concepts

Much of the work you do on a VSE system requires that you key in text and data. On early systems, that entry work was almost exclusively done by keypunching. However, keypunching is all but a thing of the past. Instead of using a keypunch, you're likely to do text entry interactively at a display station. On VSE systems, the IBM program product that lets you do keyed entry at a display station is *VSE/ICCF*, or just *ICCF*, the *Interactive Computing and Control Facility*. In this book, you'll learn all of ICCF's important features. First, though, you need to have a general understanding of what ICCF is, what you can use it for, and how it performs some of its functions. That's what this chapter presents.

This chapter has three topics. Topic 1 describes how ICCF lets VSE, a card-oriented operating system, operate without card devices. Topic 2 describes how the data you key in using ICCF is stored and organized. And, topic 3 introduces the processing you can do under ICCF, either in ICCF's foreground or background.

TOPIC 1   ICCF and the cardless system

In the last chapter, you learned about the complete DOS/VSE environment in which ICCF operates. Now, I want to focus more directly on ICCF itself. As I pointed out in chapter 1, DOS/VSE is a card-oriented operating system. This topic describes what that means and how ICCF alters the apparent nature of DOS/VSE.

DOS/VSE is a card-oriented system

In the simplest cases, units of work on a DOS/VSE system (called *jobs*) are initiated by supplying a series of control statements on a deck of punched cards. As you can see in figure 2-1, the deck of cards for a job is read by a card device associated with the DOS system logical unit *SYSRDR* (which stands for system card reader). Similarly, data cards required by the job can be supplied by another card reader which is associated with the DOS system logical unit *SYSIPT* (which stands for system input). SYSRDR and SYSIPT can be assigned to the same physical device so job control statements and input data can be mixed in a single input deck. That combined logical unit is called *SYSIN*. Output is directed to the device associated with the system logical units *SYSPCH* (for punch output) and *SYSLST* (for print output).

This is the way the earliest DOS systems had to operate, and even today, it's the still the underlying way VSE functions. However, as DOS/VSE has evolved, additional layers of software, like the VSE library structure I described in the last chapter, have been added to change the way the system seems to work. Another example is the spooling subsystem, VSE/POWER.

With VSE/POWER, card input isn't read directly from the card reader by the batch partition. Instead, the card input is first read by POWER, which stores it on disk in a queue. Then, when the entire deck has been stored, data from it can be supplied to the batch partition much more rapidly than if it were read directly from a card reader. As a result, partition usage and overall system performance are enhanced. Figure 2-2 illustrates the path spooled input data follows. Here, SYSRDR and SYSIPT input *appear* to the batch partition to be coming directly from a card reader, but actually they aren't.

Figure 2-2 doesn't illustrate output spooling, but it's easy enough to understand. Both punch and print output from the batch partition are intercepted by POWER; they're not written directly to a card punch or printer. Then, when all of the job's output has been produced and an appropriate device is free, POWER can route the output to it.

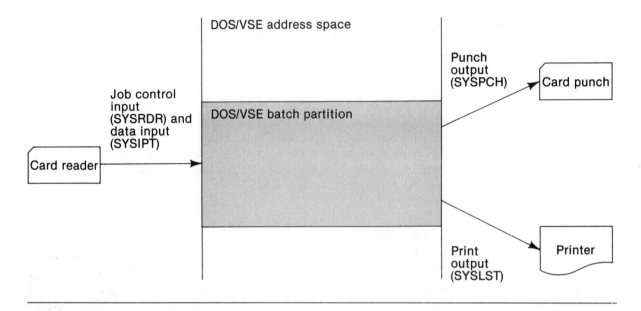

Figure 2-1   Basic DOS/VSE batch input and output

ICCF eliminates the need for punched cards

Notice in figure 2-2 that even with spooling, the *original* source of input to a batch partition is still a card device. As a result, to get away from punched cards, a typical VSE shop uses still another layer of system software: ICCF. To understand, consider figure 2-3. As you can see here, the original source of input is no longer a deck of cards read by a card reader, but data entered by an operator at a terminal.

A primary function of ICCF is supporting keyed entry by display station users. Basically, what would have been keypunched before is now entered at a terminal and stored not as a deck of punched cards, but rather as a group of *card images* in a disk file called the ICCF library file. (In chapters 3 and 4, you'll learn how to use ICCF's powerful text entry and editing features.) ICCF manages data organization and storage in its library file, as you'll learn in topic 2. Also, topic 2 shows you how the ICCF library file and VSE libraries differ.

If a user has entered and stored a VSE job stream, he can transfer it to POWER. (Chapters 7 and 8 present the conceptual background and specific commands you need to know to do this.) Because the records in the ICCF library file were stored as card images, they seem to POWER as if they were submitted from a card reader. POWER stores those card images in its queue. Then, at the appropriate time, it supplies that card-image data to a batch partition.

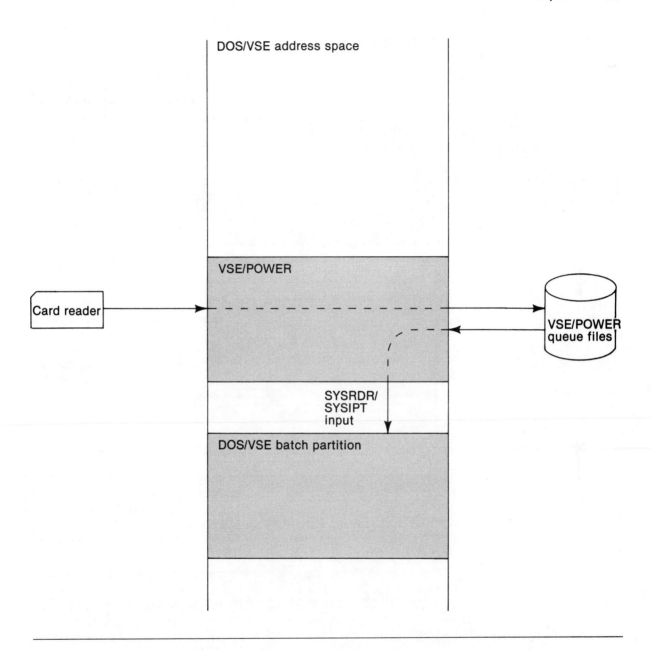

Figure 2-2   Spooled input to a DOS/VSE batch partition

In addition to providing a way to get rid of card input on a system, ICCF also works with POWER to retrieve output data (punch or print) that was produced by programs running in batch partitions and which POWER intercepted and stored in its queue files. This output data can then be viewed at the user's terminal. As a result, hard copy output is no longer required for all jobs.

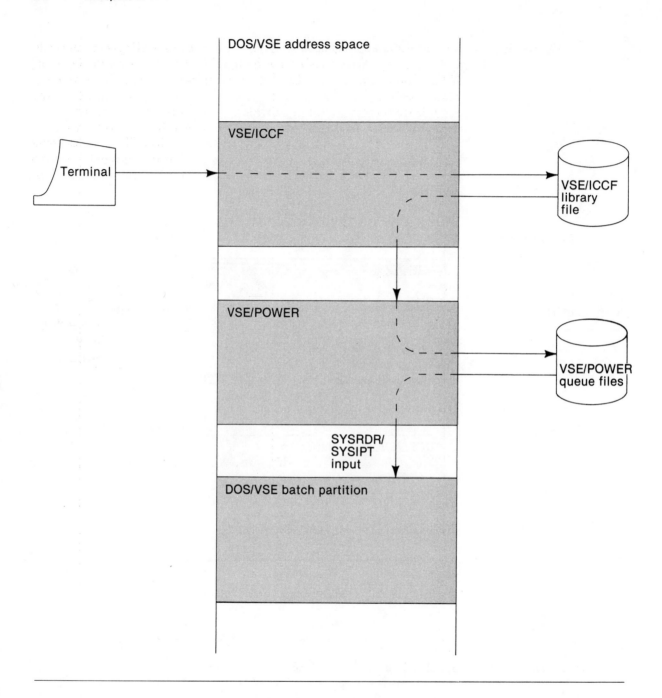

Figure 2-3   Spooled input to a DOS/VSE batch partition from an ICCF user

Discussion   As you can see, ICCF reduces the dependence of a VSE system on cards. In fact, many current systems don't have card readers or punches at all; ICCF combined with POWER has replaced them. In summary, remember that ICCF eliminates the need for card devices in two ways. First, it frees users from keypunching by supporting terminal entry and disk storage of text. And second, it provides a facility to transfer job streams (stored not in punched cards but in a disk file in card-image format) to the spooling subsystem for execution in the batch environment. Much of the content of this book describes how to use these features.

Terminology   VSE/ICCF
ICCF
Interactive Computing and Control Facility
job
SYSRDR
SYSIPT
SYSIN
SYSPCH
SYSLST
card image

Objectives   1. Describe how DOS/VSE is a card-oriented system.

2. Describe how ICCF eliminates the need for card devices and reduces the use of printed output.

TOPIC 2   ICCF libraries

A critical component of an ICCF system is the *ICCF library file*. Because the library file, also called *DTSFILE* (DTS is the VSE prefix for ICCF), is central to the functions of ICCF, you must understand what it is and how it's used. Frankly, one of the most confusing parts of ICCF terminology is the use of the term "library." As a result, I want to be sure you understand how it's used before I show you how to use ICCF's features. First, I'll describe how the ICCF library file is similar to and different from VSE libraries. Then, I'll describe how the term "library" is used within the ICCF environment itself.

VSE libraries and the ICCF library

In chapter 1, you learned that VSE libraries store four main kinds of data: source statement books, relocatable object modules, core image phases, and job control procedures. In each of these cases, data is stored in 80-character card-image format.

Similarly, you can store card-image data in the ICCF library file. Most often that data will be program source statements and job streams. Sometimes, though, you'll also want to store an object module in the ICCF library file. (There's no reason to store a core image phase in the ICCF library file.)

As you can see, the same kinds of data can be stored in a set of VSE libraries and in the ICCF library file. Since that's the case, you might well ask, for example, where the source code for a group of programs that make up an application subsystem might reside. It could be either in one or more VSE libraries, in the ICCF library file, or in both.

In practice, it's most common for data that needs to be accessed and updated frequently to be stored in the ICCF library file. For example, during the development of the programs for an application subsystem, it's likely that the source code for them will be stored in the ICCF library file so programmers can edit them easily.

However, the ICCF library file simply isn't large enough to contain the source code for all the programs at a typical installation. In theory, it might be, but in practice, the result would be an ICCF library file that's too large to use efficiently. As a result, when an application has been developed, it's likely that its source code will be stored as books in a VSE library and deleted from the ICCF library file. Although you can't directly edit a member in a VSE library from ICCF, it's always possible to retrieve a member from a VSE library and transfer it to the ICCF library file so it can be edited.

There are other differences between VSE libraries and the ICCF library file. VSE libraries are processed by the VSE Librarian program(s); the ICCF library file is processed only by the components of ICCF. Also, there can be any number of VSE libraries on a system; only one ICCF library file can be in use at one time.

With this background, it should be easy for you to distinguish between the ICCF library file and VSE libraries. However, how the term "library" is used within the ICCF environment itself can also be confusing.

Libraries within the ICCF environment

The ICCF library file is a single data set that's stored on a DASD; figure 2-4 shows schematically how it's organized. The DTSFILE data set contains a number of logical internal divisions that themselves are called *ICCF libraries*, or just *libraries*. When you read the term "library" within the context of ICCF, it almost always refers to one of these subdivisions. These ICCF libraries, identified by numbers, don't exist as independent data sets; they're all contained within the ICCF library file.

For example, on the ICCF system I use, there are 99 libraries, identified by the numbers 1 to 99. The actual number of libraries on your system may be different. The upper limit, which is never reached, is 32,767. When the ICCF file is created, the systems programmer specifies how many libraries should be used. For each, a record describing library characteristics is stored in the library file. Then, as users add permanent data to the ICCF library file, it's associated with one of the libraries.

ICCF stores data in *library members*, or just *members*, that are subordinate to one of the ICCF libraries. You can store a variety of data in a library member: program source code, job streams, test data, or object code. The only restriction is that the data stored in a library member has to be in 80-character card-image format.

For example, in figure 2-4, library 1 contains 12 members: four are job streams, five are program source code, one is test data, one is an object module, and one simply contains text (perhaps program documentation or notes). Although all of the library members in figure 2-4 seem to be the same size, that's not really the case. A library member uses only as much space as it needs.

An ICCF library member is identified by an eight-character name you give it when it's created. In addition, you can supply a four-character password to protect the member. If you use a password, you have to supply it along with the name to access the member. Within a library, each member must have a unique name. However, you can use the same name for two or more members as long as they reside in different libraries.

As you create members, they're recorded in the library's *directory*. Although ICCF was designed to allow an unlimited number of directory entries in each library, it's practical for performance reasons to limit the number that can actually be used. IBM recommends that the maximum number of directory entries be between 100 and 200. However, for

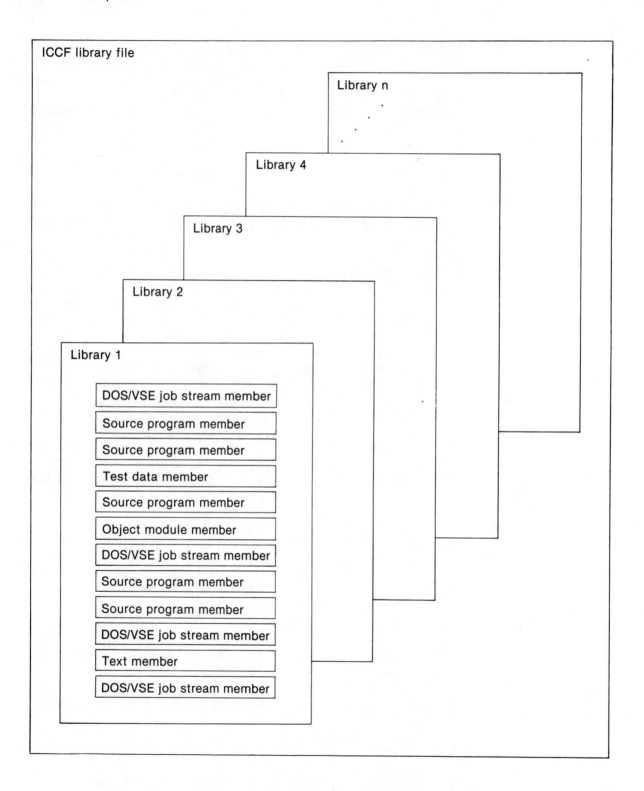

Figure 2-4   Libraries and members within the ICCF library file

libraries with intensive use, the number might be smaller, and for relatively inactive libraries, the number might be greater.

Kinds of ICCF libraries   One way to characterize an ICCF library is by whether or not you need explicit authorization to use it. If a library is defined as a *public library*, any user can access data stored in it by issuing the proper ICCF commands (which you'll learn in the next chapter). On the other hand, if a library is defined as a *private library*, you must be explicitly authorized by the system administrator to use it. Otherwise, you can't access the data stored in it.

As an ICCF user, one of the ICCF libraries will be designated as your *main library*. Other libraries to which you have access (any public library or any authorized private library) are considered your *alternate libraries*. Because different users will have different authorized private libraries, one user's set of alternate libraries will probably differ from another's.

When you start to use the ICCF system, your main library is considered to be your *primary library*. Your primary library is where ICCF will look for members you want to retrieve and where it will store members you want to save. By issuing the proper ICCF command, you can change your primary library to be any of your alternate libraries. As a result, you can access and update data throughout your authorized subset of the ICCF library file.

Also, you can "connect" to another of your authorized libraries and make it your *secondary library*. When you try to access a library member that isn't in your primary library, ICCF automatically searches for it in your secondary library.

Another type of library is the *common library*. There's only one common library on the system, and it's usually library 2. Data stored in the common library can be read by all users, but can only be updated by authorized users. As a result, it's a combination of a private library (one that's protected from indiscriminate updating) and a public library (one that's accessible to all users).

The common library usually contains data that all users might need to use, like model jobs for compiles and special procedures used to perform ICCF functions. If ICCF can't find a member you want in your primary or secondary library, it looks in the common library. Keep in mind that this chaining of libraries works only for retrieving data from the ICCF file. You can change data only in your primary library, not in your secondary library or the common library.

This combination of libraries isn't as complex as it sounds. Basically, you can access three libraries at the same time. One is always the common library, so you have two libraries you can change to suit your immediate needs. For example, figure 2-5 shows the libraries I'm authorized to use, the libraries available to me when I start a terminal session, and all of the possible combinations of primary and secondary libraries I can access. Here, you can see that my main library is library 9, and my alternate libraries are 8, 10, 11, 12, 14, 82, and 83. That

Authorized libraries

Main library: 9
Alternate libraries: 8 10 11 12 14 82 83

Active libraries at log on

Primary library: 9
Secondary library: none
Common library: 2

Possible libraries

Primary	Secondary	Common	Primary	Secondary	Common
8		2	12		2
8	9	2	12	8	2
8	10	2	12	9	2
8	11	2	12	10	2
8	12	2	12	11	2
8	14	2	12	14	2
8	82	2	12	82	2
8	83	2	12	83	2
9		2	14		2
9	8	2	14	8	2
9	10	2	14	9	2
9	11	2	14	10	2
9	12	2	14	11	2
9	14	2	14	12	2
9	82	2	14	82	2
9	83	2	14	83	2
10		2	82		2
10	8	2	82	8	2
10	9	2	82	9	2
10	11	2	82	10	2
10	12	2	82	11	2
10	14	2	82	12	2
10	82	2	82	14	2
10	83	2	82	83	2
11		2	83		2
11	8	2	83	8	2
11	9	2	83	9	2
11	10	2	83	10	2
11	12	2	83	11	2
11	14	2	83	12	2
11	82	2	83	14	2
11	83	2	83	82	2

Figure 2-5   An example of possible current library combinations

means that when I start to use ICCF, it will look in library 9 for members I request. However, I can make any of these other libraries my primary library. Also, I can make any of these libraries other than my current primary library my secondary library. As you can see in the figure, there are many possible combinations. Which combination I decide to use depends on my immediate system needs.

Private libraries can be further characterized. For example, you might be given exclusive use of a private library. When that's the case, no other users can access your library, and it's called an *owned library*. For example, in a typical shop, library 1 is usually owned by the systems programmer responsible for maintaining ICCF (the *ICCF administrator*), and no other users can access the data stored in it. It's more typical for a group of users to be authorized to use the same private library, which is then called a *shared library*. It's practical to use a shared library when the members of a programming team are working on the same project and need access to the same library members, but when access to the data in the library needs to be otherwise restricted.

Kinds of library members   Just as ICCF libraries can be protected from unauthorized use by defining them as private or public and by controlling which users can access them, individual users can control access to their own library members by protecting them. Depending again on a user's authorizations, library members he creates may automatically be *public data* (accessible to all users who can assess the library in which they reside) or *private data* (accessible only by their creator or the ICCF administrator). However, by issuing the proper ICCF commands, you can change the protection of a library member. I'll show you how to do that in chapter 5.

Also, it's possible to store data that's formatted for printing in a *print type member*. When that's the case, each print line is split in two parts and is stored in two library member records. (Remember, an ICCF library member can only be 80 characters in length.) It's an ICCF convention that a print type member's name end with .P; for example, PROJ32.P is a valid name for a print type member.

The structure of the ICCF library file

The ICCF library file has three main areas: the fixed area, the permanent area, and the temporary area. The *fixed area* contains records that identify all ICCF users and that name and locate all the ICCF libraries. You can think of the fixed area as being at the start of the ICCF file. It's created when the ICCF file is defined, and its structure can't be altered.

The *permanent area* contains all of the library members and directory records for all the libraries. Within the permanent area, a system of pointers is used to relate directory entries to members. As new library members are added in free sections of the file, their records become part of the permanent area.

Competing with the permanent area for total space in the ICCF library file is the *temporary area*. When an ICCF user starts a terminal session, four different temporary areas are allocated for his use out of the free space in the library file. (In the next topic, I'll describe the four kinds of temporary areas and show you how they're used.) A user's temporary areas are active only as long as he is working; when the user ends the terminal session, his temporary areas are freed. Then, they can be used either for temporary work areas for other users or for data that will be stored permanently.

In all three areas of the library file, data is stored in 88-byte records. In addition to 80 bytes of card-image data, a record also contains pointers that relate it to the records before and after it in a member. Although the structure of the ICCF file is more complicated than this, this is all you really need to know.

Terminology	ICCF library file
	DTSFILE
	ICCF library
	library
	library member
	member
	directory
	public library
	private library
	main library
	alternate library
	primary library
	secondary library
	common library
	owned library
	ICCF administrator
	shared library
	public data
	private data
	print type member
	fixed area
	permanent area
	temporary area

Objectives   1. Distinguish between:

  a. a VSE library and the ICCF library file
  b. a VSE library and an ICCF library (within the ICCF library file)
  c. the ICCF library file and an ICCF library

2. List the kinds of data that can be stored in an ICCF library file member.

3. Distinguish between:
  a. public and private libraries
  b. main and alternate libraries
  c. primary, secondary, and common libraries
  d. owned and shared libraries

4. Distinguish between:
  a. a private library and private data
  b. public data and private data

5. Describe the basic structure of the ICCF library file.

TOPIC 3 ICCF foreground and background processing

Although ICCF executes in a VSE partition, the way it uses the virtual storage in its partition is more complex than the way a typical application program uses storage. This topic describes how the ICCF partition is organized and, at the same time, describes the two kinds of ICCF processing: foreground and background.

You can think of the program area of the ICCF partition as being divided into four parts: (1) the terminal control program (almost certainly CICS), (2) the main ICCF control program, (3) ICCF command processors, and (4) interactive partitions.

CICS as ICCF's terminal control program

As you learned in the last chapter, CICS lets many application program users at display stations run a variety of interactive programs at the same time. To run a CICS program, a terminal user enters a four-character *transaction-identifier*, or *trans-id*. Then, CICS loads the program that's associated with that trans-id, formats the user's display station screen, and allows data entry. The data the operator enters is passed to the program, which then does appropriate processing.

To use ICCF when terminal control services are provided by CICS, the user enters the trans-id ICCF. Then, CICS transfers control to ICCF. Although it's practical to think of ICCF as running as a typical CICS transaction, that's not strictly accurate. ICCF is more complicated than a typical CICS transaction and operates semi-independently. Even so, ICCF is like a simple transaction because you invoke it through CICS, CICS manages ICCF terminal operations, and ICCF and CICS execute together in the same DOS/VSE partition, as figure 2-6 shows.

As a sidelight, you should know that not all ICCF installations run ICCF and CICS together. In smaller, older ICCF installations, a separate component of ICCF called *TTF*, the *Terminal Transaction Facility*, provides terminal control. However, TTF's functions are limited. And with newer releases of ICCF, TTF isn't provided at all. As a result, most ICCF shops use ICCF together with CICS. And from the other point of view, CICS can run without ICCF when an installation needs to support interactive programs, but doesn't need ICCF's text-entry and editing features.

Although figure 2-6 stresses the relationship between ICCF and CICS, it simplifies the organization of the ICCF partition. Figure 2-7 more accurately represents how ICCF uses storage. It shows the other main parts of the ICCF partition: the main control program, the command processors, and the interactive partitions.

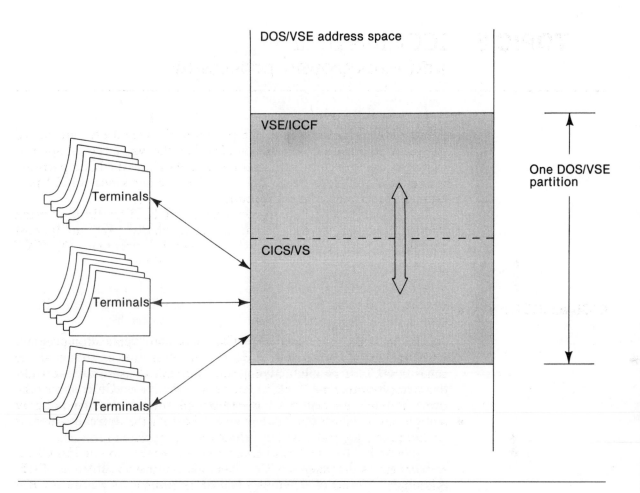

Figure 2-6   VSE/ICCF and CICS/VS share the same DOS/VSE partition

Foreground processing: ICCF's main control program and command processors

Part of the storage ICCF uses is occupied by its *main control program*, which manages functions other than terminal control, and its *command processors*, which interpret and handle commands you issue. When you enter commands or text, the main control program, the terminal control program (CICS), and the command processors work together to fulfill your requests.

In ICCF terms, this type of processing is called *foreground processing*. However, don't confuse this with a VSE foreground partition. ICCF foreground processing takes place within the ICCF partition, which itself is a VSE foreground partition.

ICCF foreground processing is relatively fast because typical interactive requests that users make take little processor time. Because human work speeds are so much slower than computer speeds, a single system can support many on-line users. As a result, many ICCF users can share system resources, yet all can seem to have exclusive use of the system. This is called *time sharing*. (Another time-sharing system you may know about is TSO, which provides services for IBM's OS systems that are similar to the services ICCF provides for DOS systems.)

Background processing: interactive partitions

You might assume that if you can do foreground processing within ICCF, then you might also be able to do *background processing*. You can. While ICCF foreground processing is characterized by continuous interaction with you at your terminal, basic background processing is essentially independent of your terminal. In fact, it's even possible to detach your terminal from a background execution and do foreground work while it runs. As you can imagine, then, ICCF background processing has a lower priority than foreground processing.

Background processing takes place in *interactive partitions*, which are actually contained within the larger ICCF partition. Although ICCF can support up to 35 interactive partitions, only three are configured in the example in figure 2-7. Don't let the "interactive" in "interactive partition" confuse you. An ICCF interactive partition is used to do batch work entirely within the ICCF environment; it's not typically used to run programs that interact with the user.

Interactive partitions have some characteristics in common with VSE partitions. For example, they have their own GETVIS areas. Also, ICCF includes a set of statements (called *job entry statements*) you use to write jobs to control ICCF background processing. Job entry statements for interactive partitions parallel VSE job control statements for batch partitions. You'll learn how to write jobs for interactive partitions in chapter 9.

Just as VSE partitions need to have devices associated with the system logical units SYSRDR, SYSIPT, SYSLST, and SYSPCH, interactive partitions also need some mechanism to accept typical input and to produce print and punch output. Within the ICCF environment, temporary user areas serve this function, as figure 2-8 shows.

In the last topic, I mentioned that four temporary areas are allocated dynamically for each user. They're the input area, the print area, the punch area, and the log area. For an ICCF background job, the *input area* is the logical equivalent of a card reader. As a result, when you run a job in an interactive partition, input is retrieved from your input area. Job entry statements for interactive partition processing are processed via the input area.

For output, the *punch area* is the logical equivalent of a card punch, and the *print area* is the logical equivalent of a printer. After a background job has executed, you can display output stored in these

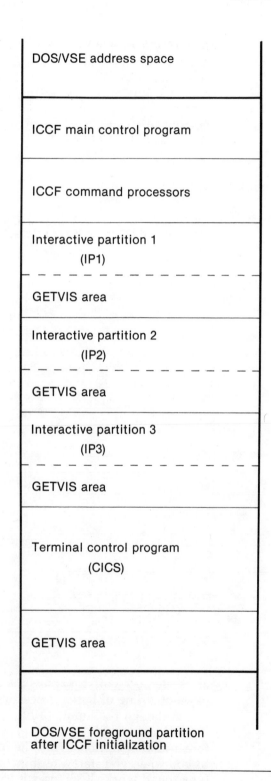

Figure 2-7   ICCF storage usage

Unit record I/O in a VSE partition

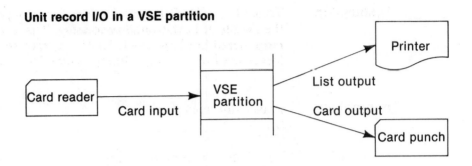

Unit record I/O in an ICCF interactive partition

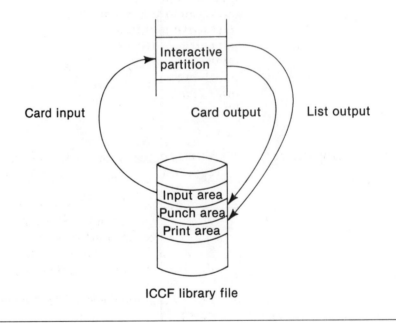

ICCF library file

Figure 2-8   Unit record I/O in a VSE partition and an ICCF interactive partition

areas. Because you can access the output at your terminal, much of the paper-shuffling of batch processing is eliminated.

Although the input, print, and punch areas are used heavily for ICCF background processing, you can also use them for some foreground operations. And the fourth temporary area that's allocated to you when you start a terminal session, the *log area*, is primarily for foreground work. ICCF uses it to record commands you enter; you'll learn how to use it in chapter 5.

Discussion   To use basic ICCF entry and editing facilities you don't need to know all the details of background processing. That's why I don't describe it in more detail until section 4. First, you need to learn how to use ICCF's foreground processing features, which I'll cover in the next section.

Terminology   transaction identifier
trans-id
TTF
Terminal Transaction Facility
main control program
command processor
foreground processing
time sharing
background processing
interactive partition
job entry statement
input area
punch area
print area
log area

Objectives   1. Describe the organization of the VSE partition in which ICCF executes.

2. Distinguish between any two of the following:
    a. VSE foreground processing
    b. VSE background processing
    c. ICCF foreground processing
    d. ICCF background processing

3. Distinguish between a VSE partition and an ICCF interactive partition.

4. List and briefly describe the functions of the four kinds of temporary user areas ICCF provides.

Section 2

System and editing commands

This section contains four chapters that present most of the ICCF system and editing commands you're likely to use. Chapter 3 is the most important chapter in the book. In it, you'll learn how to use the essential commands to work with the system and the editor. After you've finished chapter 3, you'll know enough to use ICCF for typical text entry and library management functions. Then, you can turn to any of the other chapters in this section. Chapters 4 and 5 present, respectively, advanced editor commands and advanced system commands. And chapter 6 shows you how to group commands to create macros.

Chapter 3

A basic subset of ICCF system and editing commands

This chapter introduces you to the ICCF elements you need to know to do simple terminal work. After you've finished this chapter, you'll be able to use ICCF to enter job streams and program source code and store them in the ICCF library file. Then, you can turn to the chapters that follow for more information on functions like using advanced editing features (chapter 4), using advanced system commands (chapter 5), or using the facilities of VSE/POWER through ICCF (chapters 7 and 8).

This chapter has two topics. The first presents the ICCF system commands you must know. In it, you'll learn how to log on and log off the ICCF system, how to manage your current libraries, and how to issue commands to do basic operations on library members. Topic 2 presents the ICCF editing commands you need to know. After you've finished topic 2, you'll be able to use the ICCF full-screen editor to enter a wide variety of text.

TOPIC 1   Basic ICCF system commands

This topic will teach you the basic commands you need to know to use ICCF. Specifically, you'll learn how to log on and log off the system, how to code system commands properly, how to find out what members are stored in your current libraries, how to change your current libraries (that is, your primary and secondary libraries and the common library), how to view the contents of library members, and how to delete and rename library members.

A simple ICCF terminal session

Before I describe the details of the system commands, I want to show you a simple terminal session. To begin an ICCF terminal session, you clear your terminal screen, key in

        I C C F

and tap the enter key. Then, you have to log on to work on the system. You do this using the log-on screen ICCF displays, shown in part 1 of figure 3-1.

Logging on   To log on, you have to identify yourself to ICCF. You do that by supplying two items of information: your user-id and your password. Both are assigned to you by the ICCF administrator and are stored in your *user profile*. (In addition to your user-id and password, your user profile contains information about what ICCF features you're authorized to use, lists your authorized libraries, and specifies limits on how much of certain system resources you can use. I'll point out these elements when appropriate throughout this book.)

Logging on is a two-step process. First, you enter a /LOGON command followed by your user-id. You enter the /LOGON command, like all other ICCF system commands, by keying it in on the top line of the screen, called the *command line*, and tapping the enter key. For example, to log on, I entered

        / LOGON STEV

in part 2 of figure 3-1. /LOGON is the ICCF command and STEV is my user-id. ICCF only accepts user-ids that have already been defined in a user profile. So if you try to log on with a user-id that isn't defined in a user profile, ICCF doesn't let you continue. Since STEV is defined in my user profile, ICCF accepts my user-id.

The second step in the logon process is to enter your password. Once your user-id has been entered and accepted, ICCF prompts you for your password, as you can see in part 3 of the figure. Then, you just

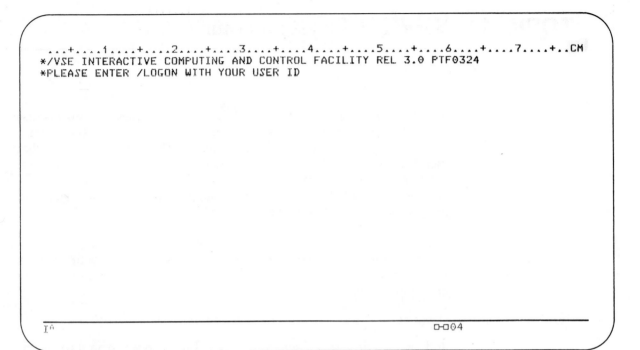

Figure 3-1   Logging on to ICCF (part 1 of 4)

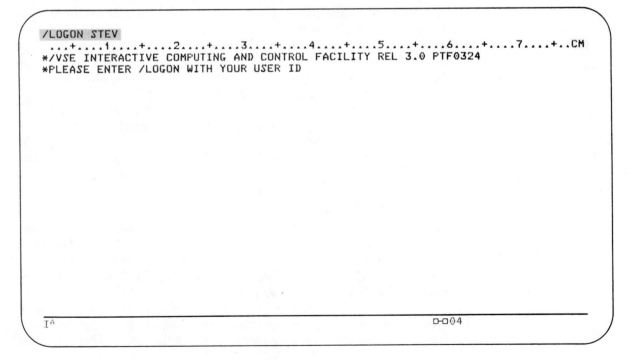

Figure 3-1   Logging on to ICCF (part 2 of 4)

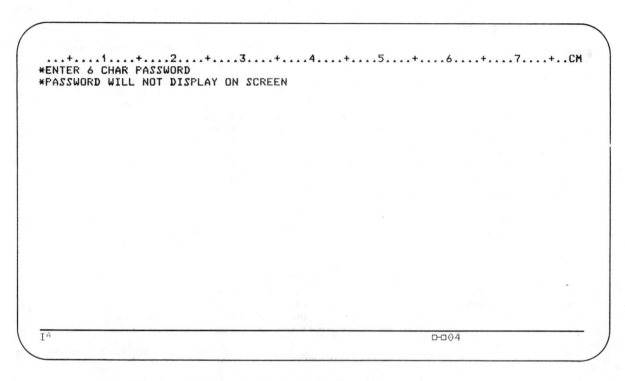

Figure 3-1   Logging on to ICCF (part 3 of 4)

```
    ...+....1....+....2....+....3....+....4....+....5....+....6....+....7....+..CM
*LOGON COMPLETE - DATE 04/10/86   TIME 13:09
*READY




I^                                                    □-□04
```

Figure 3-1   Logging on to ICCF (part 4 of 4)

Command: /LIBRARY

```
...+....1....+....2....+....3....+....4....+....5....+....6....+....7....+..LS
LIBRARY NO. - 0009          04/10/86   13/11/03    DIR ENTRIES = 0201

LOADCR    ********    FILES     ********    DLIFUNC   ********
EREP1     ********    RRTEST    ********    INV2300   ********
CONDS     ********    TEMP      ********    OAMHIDAM  ********
ICCF4-1   ********    TESTDBD   ********    ICCF4-9   ********
CICSTST   ********    TEMP1     ********    DCTST     ********
ICCF4-10  ********    OAMHSAM   ********    TESTA     ********
IMSJOB    ********    TESTB     ********    LISTCAT   ********
TESTC     ********    LISTUIB   ********    VSAMTST   ********
CCTEST    ********    TESTD     ********    EXECDLI   ********
SETSCREX  ********    MODCALL   ********    SQTEST    ********
GNPTEST   ********    SQTESTD   ********    SITEST1   ********
LTSTVEN   ********    GATEST    ********    DTS.P     ********
OAMHISAM  ********    EX10-1    ********    DEFCATSP  ********
EX10-4    ********    LISTCR    ********    COPYMEM2  ********
CCIL      ********    COPYMEM1  ********    DLIFIGS   ********
F10-3     ********    STEP15    ********    PSERVIPL  ********
LOGTEST1  ********    PSERV2    ********    APPC      ********
AMS1      ********    DBDSPSBS  ********    LOGTEST2  ********

IA                                              0-004
```

Figure 3-2   Sample output of the /LIBRARY command

type it in and press the enter key. For security reasons, your password isn't displayed as you key it in. After ICCF validates the password you entered against your user profile, the log on process is complete and you can start work. That's what part 4 of figure 3-1 shows.

Using the ICCF commands   During and just after your log on, ICCF is in *command mode*. (That's what the CM in the upper right corner of the screen in part 4 of figure 3-1 means.) In command mode, you can issue system commands or enter other modes for particular functions.

A system command you'll use often is /LIBRARY. In its simplest form, it displays a directory list of the members in your primary library. Figure 3-2 shows what the output of the /LIBRARY command looks like. The first line identifies the library, gives the current date and time, and shows how many directory entries are available in the library.

Not all of the available directory entries have to be used. Each row of asterisks in figure 3-2 represents an available directory entry in my library. As you can see, there's plenty of room for me to add more members to my library. As new members are added to this library, these available directory entries are used, then new directory entries are created as they're needed. (The alternating arrangement of free and

Command: /LIST INV2300

```
...+....1....+....2....+....3....+....4....+....5....+....6....+....7....+..LS
// JOB     INV2300
// OPTION LIST,ERRS,CATAL,SXREF,NOSYM
   PHASE INV2300,*
   INCLUDE DLZBPJRA
// EXEC FCOBOL
 CBL VERB
       IDENTIFICATION DIVISION.
       *
       PROGRAM-ID.  INV2300.
       *
       ENVIRONMENT DIVISION.
       *
       INPUT-OUTPUT SECTION.
       *
       FILE-CONTROL.
       *
          SELECT PRTOUT ASSIGN TO SYS006-UR-1403-S
                       ACCESS IS SEQUENTIAL.
       DATA DIVISION.
       *

 IA                                           0-004
```

Figure 3-3   Sample output of the /LIST command

used library directory entries in the figure is due to the fact that the
ICCF library file was reorganized just before my terminal session; in a
typical situation, free entries are distributed more randomly.)

Notice the member names in figure 3-2. When you create a member
in an ICCF library, you have to name it. You should recall from the last
chapter that the name can be from one to eight characters long. Also, it
must begin with a letter.

To view the contents of a library member, you can use the /LIST
command. For example, if I key in

    /LIST INV2300

and tap the enter key, ICCF displays the screen in figure 3-3. As you can
see, the library member INV2300 contains VSE JCL and COBOL source
code. If the member is too long to be displayed on one screen, as in
figure 3-3, your terminal goes into *list mode*. (That's what the LS in the
upper right corner of the screens in both figure 3-2 and 3-3 means.)
When your terminal is in list mode, you tap the enter key to display the
next section of text.

To page through the member, I'd tap the enter key repeatedly until
I found the section I was interested in. I can continue to tap the enter

key until I reach the end of the member, when the terminal returns to command mode. Alternatively, I can press the PA2 key at any time to end list mode and return immediately to command mode. (Still another way to end a listing and return to command mode is to issue the /CANCEL command, which I'll present later in this topic. But I think it's easier to use PA2.)

Logging off   To end your terminal session, all you do is key in the system command

    /LOGOFF

and press the enter key. Be sure to log off when you're finished with a terminal session to prevent other users from working under your user-id.

The syntax of ICCF system commands

As you can tell from the examples you've just seen, an ICCF system command consists of a slash followed by a brief *operation code* that indicates the command's function. You can abbreviate most operation codes, as long as you provide enough information for ICCF to determine what command you mean. For example, /LIB is an acceptable abbreviation for the /LIBRARY command, but /LI isn't because it could mean /LIBRARY or /LIST.

Usually, you can also enter *operands* on a system command that provide more specific information about what the command should do. For example, in the command I entered to log on, /LOGON is the operation code and STEV, the user-id, is the operand.

Some commands may require a series of operands. When that's the case, you can separate them from one another by spaces, commas, or parentheses. When used in this context, these characters are called delimiters. I recommend you use the delimiter that's the easiest to key in, which is a single space. However, if you prefer commas, parentheses, or multiple spaces, feel free to use them.

Basic system commands to manage current libraries

You should remember from the last chapter that during an ICCF terminal session you can access data in as many as three different libraries: your primary library, your secondary library, and the common library (which is usually library 2). In this section, I'll show you how to use the commands to find out what your current libraries are, to find out what libraries you're authorized to use, and to change your current libraries. Figure 3-4 lists the commands you'll learn in this section.

The /SHOW LIBRARIES command

```
/SHOW LIBRARIES
```

The /USERS LIBRARIES command

```
/USERS LIBRARIES
```

The /CONNECT command

```
/CONNECT {library-number}
        {OFF           }
```

The /SET COMLIB command

```
/SET COMLIB {ON }
            {OFF}
```

The /SWITCH command

```
/SWITCH {library-number}
        {RESET         }
        {LIBS          }
```

Figure 3-4   Commands to display library information and set current libraries

How to display your current libraries: the /SHOW LIBRARIES command   To find out what your current libraries are (in other words, what libraries are accessible to you at a given time), you can enter the command

```
/SHOW LIBRARIES
```

or any abbreviation down to

```
/SH LIB
```

(The /SHOW command has a variety of options that you can enter to display different details about ICCF; I'll describe them at the appropriate points throughout this book.) When you enter this command, ICCF displays your current libraries in this format:

```
LIBS: MAIN = 0009 CONN = NONE COMMON = 0002
```

Here, library 9 is my primary (main) library, and library 2 is the common library. There is no active secondary (or connected) library. You'll see sample output of the /SHOW LIBRARIES command throughout this section.

How to display the libraries you're authorized to use: the /USERS LIBRARIES command To find out what libraries you're authorized to use, you can issue the command

`/USERS LIBRARIES`

which displays a line like this:

`MAIN = 9 ALT = 8 10 12 13 14 81 82 83 COMM = 2`

Here, I'm authorized to use libraries 8, 10, 12, 13, 14, 81, 82, and 83, as well as my main library, 9 and the common library, 2. If I were to try to access any other private library using the commands I'll show you in a moment, ICCF would deny access to it and display this message:

`*INVALID OR UNAUTHORIZED LIBRARY`

How to access a secondary library: the /CONNECT command To activate a secondary library, you use the /CONNECT command. For example, to make library 83 my secondary library, I'd enter

`/CONNECT 83`

or the abbreviated form

`/CONN 83`

(You need to key in two N's when you use the abbreviated form; if you don't, ICCF interprets it as the /CONTINU command.) After I enter the /CONNECT command above, the /SHOW LIBRARIES command indicates that I have access to all three libraries (9, 83, and 2):

`LIBS: MAIN = 0009 CONN = 0083 COMMON = 0002`

You can change your connected library by just entering another /CONNECT command with the right library number. Remember, though, that you can only be connected to one secondary library at a time. And you can only connect to public libraries or private libraries you're authorized to use. If you don't want to have a secondary library, you can disconnect the current one by entering

`/CONNECT OFF`

How to access the common library: the /SET command Depending on your user profile, you may or may not automatically have access to the common library when you log on. Usually, you'll want to keep the common library accessible because at the least it contains procedures and macros that you'll want to run. (More about this later.) However, if you want to make the common library inaccessible, you can issue the command

```
/SET COMLIB OFF
```

If I issued this command then inquired about my current libraries by issuing the command

```
/SHOW LIBS
```

ICCF would display

```
LIBS: MAIN = 0009 CONN = NONE COMMON = OFF
```

To restore access to the common library, all I have to do is issue the command

```
/SET COMLIB ON
```

Then, the common library is again part of the search chain for library members. (By the way, like the /SHOW command, the /SET command has a variety of operands to set many system options; I'll describe them where they're relevant.)

How to change your primary library: the /SWITCH command
Although you can access data stored in your connected library or the common library, you can't update it. Updates are restricted to members stored in your primary, or main library. To change your main library, you use the /SWITCH command (abbreviated /SW).

The /SWITCH command is easy to use. For example, all I have to do to change my primary library from 9 to 83 is enter

```
/SW 83
```

Then, library 83 is my primary library, as the /SHOW LIBRARIES command indicates:

```
LIBS: MAIN = 0083 CONN = NONE COMMON = 0002
```

If I had still been connected to library 83 (as my secondary library) when I issued the /SWITCH command, ICCF would have displayed this message:

```
*LIB ALREADY PRIMARY OR CONNECTED
```

Because ICCF's designers realized you'd sometimes want to make your connected library your primary library, they provided a special option of the /SWITCH command to let you swap your primary and secondary libraries with one command. To do that, just enter

```
/SWITCH LIB
```

The alternative is to disconnect your secondary library by entering /CONN OFF, then switch to that library with the basic form of the

The /LIBRARY command

```
/LIBRARY [{CON}] [{FULL      [ALL]}]
         [{COM}] [{*abcdefg      }]
```

The SDSERV procedure

```
SDSERV [{*abcdefg}] [{NAME}]
       [{CONN    }] [{USER}]
       [{COM     }] [{DATE}]
```

The /PURGE command

```
/PURGE member-name [password]
```

The /RENAME command

```
/RENAME old-member-name new-member-name [password]
```

Figure 3-5   Commands and procedures to manage library members

/SWITCH command, and finally connect to your original main library with the /CONNECT command.

If you want to restore your basic primary and secondary library configuration (that is, the one specified in your user profile), you can enter the /SWITCH command with the RESET or OFF options. For example, the command

```
/SW RESET
```

would cause my current libraries to be set like this:

```
LIBS: MAIN = 0009 CONN = NONE COMMON = 0002
```

However, if you've disabled access to the common library, /SWITCH with RESET won't reenable access; you have to do that by issuing the /SET command with COMLIB ON.

Basic system commands to manage library members

I've already introduced you to the basic operation of the /LIBRARY command. In this section, I'll show you how to use some of its more powerful features, as well as how to get information about your connected library and the common library in addition to your main library. Also, I'll show you how to use commands to rename and delete library members. Figure 3-5 lists the commands this section presents.

How to display directory listings: the /LIBRARY command I've already shown you how to use the /LIBRARY command to list the members in your main library. You can also use it to list members in your connected library by entering

```
/LIB CON
```

or in the common library by entering

```
/LIB COM
```

When you use the basic form of the /LIBRARY command, all you see are member names. Often, that's sufficient. However, sometimes, you need more information. To display full member data, you can specify the FULL operand on the /LIBRARY command. For example, to display complete information for members in your current secondary library, you can enter

```
/LIB CON FULL
```

Figure 3-6 shows the output of the /LIB CON command, both with and without FULL, when library 83 is my secondary library.

In the output of the /LIB command with FULL, there are nine columns of data. The last three (compressed, generation data group, and flagging) are for advanced functions I'll describe later. For now, you only need to be concerned with the information in the first six columns. The first column contains the directory entry number of the member, and the second contains the name of the member. The third column, which is only one character wide, contains either a blank or a P. If the value is P, the member is password protected; if it's blank, no password protection is in effect. (You'll learn about password protection in chapter 5.) The next column contains the date the member was last modified (or, if it hasn't been modified, the date it was created). The fifth column contains the user-id of the member's owner. In figure 3-6, all the members were created by me, so the user-id for each is STEV. Finally, the sixth column indicates the ownership status of the member. If the column contains blanks, the member is public, but if it contains PRIV, the member is private.

To display selected library members, you can code an asterisk followed by from one to seven characters. Then, only members whose names begin with the characters you specify will be displayed. For instance, to display members whose names begin with the characters J8 in my connected library, I'd enter

```
/LIB CON *J8
```

The output produced by this command is in figure 3-7. Notice that when you use this technique to display specific library members, you get detailed information, just as if you had specified FULL.

Command: /LIB CON

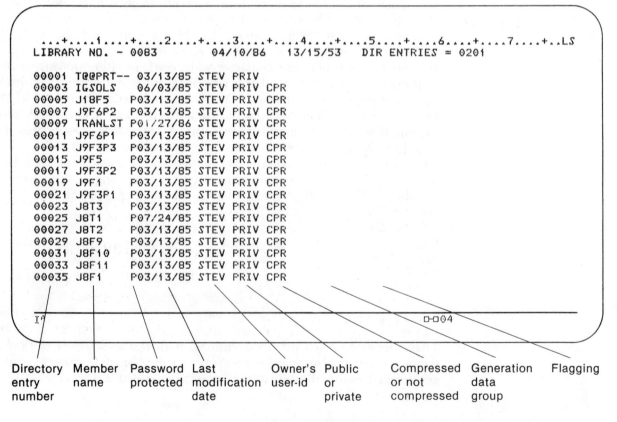

```
...+....1....+....2....+....3....+....4....+....5....+....6....+....7....+..LS
LIBRARY NO. - 0083          04/10/86   13/14/00   DIR ENTRIES = 0201

T@@PRT--  ********  IGSOLS   ********  J18F5    ********
J9F6P2    ********  TRANLST  ********  J9F6P1   ********
J9F3P3    ********  J9F5     ********  J9F3P2   ********
J9F1      ********  J9F3P1   ********  J8T3     ********
J8T1      ********  J8T2     ********  J8F9     ********
J8F10     ********  J8F11    ********  J8F1     ********
J6T1      ********  J7F6     ********  J6F9     ********
J6F6      ********  J6F7     ********  J6F14    ********
J6F12     ********  J6F13    ********  J6F11    ********
J5F7      ********  J5F9     ********  J5F12    ********
J4T3      ********  J4T2     ********  J4T1     ********
J4F19     ********  J4F23    ********  J4F14    ********
J3F6      J3F9      J3F5     J3F2      J3F4     J3F12
J3F10     J3F11     J2F4     J18F9     J18T1    J18F7
J18F4.P   J18F5.P   J18F4    J18F3     J18F3.P  J18F2.P
J18F16.P  J18F2     J18F16   J18F15    J18F15.P J18F14.P
J18F13    J18F14    J18F12   J17T7     J17T99   J17T6
J17T4     J17T5     J17T3    J17F7.P   J17T2    J17F7
```
```
I^                                                      □-□04
```

Command: /LIB CON FULL

```
...+....1....+....2....+....3....+....4....+....5....+....6....+....7....+..LS
LIBRARY NO. - 0083          04/10/86   13/15/53   DIR ENTRIES = 0201

00001  T@@PRT-- 03/13/85 STEV PRIV
00003  IGSOLS   06/03/85 STEV PRIV CPR
00005  J18F5   P03/13/85 STEV PRIV CPR
00007  J9F6P2  P03/13/85 STEV PRIV CPR
00009  TRANLST P01/27/86 STEV PRIV CPR
00011  J9F6P1  P03/13/85 STEV PRIV CPR
00013  J9F3P3  P03/13/85 STEV PRIV CPR
00015  J9F5    P03/13/85 STEV PRIV CPR
00017  J9F3P2  P03/13/85 STEV PRIV CPR
00019  J9F1    P03/13/85 STEV PRIV CPR
00021  J9F3P1  P03/13/85 STEV PRIV CPR
00023  J8T3    P03/13/85 STEV PRIV CPR
00025  J8T1    P07/24/85 STEV PRIV CPR
00027  J8T2    P03/13/85 STEV PRIV CPR
00029  J8F9    P03/13/85 STEV PRIV CPR
00031  J8F10   P03/13/85 STEV PRIV CPR
00033  J8F11   P03/13/85 STEV PRIV CPR
00035  J8F1    P03/13/85 STEV PRIV CPR
```
```
I^                                                      □-□04
```

Directory entry number	Member name	Password protected	Last modification date	Owner's user-id	Public or private	Compressed or not compressed	Generation data group	Flagging

Figure 3-6   Sample output of the /LIBRARY command without and with FULL

Command: /LIB CON *J8

```
....+....1....+....2....+....3....+....4....+....5....+....6....+....7....+..CM
LIBRARY NO. - 0083          04/10/86   13/16/40   DIR ENTRIES = 0201

00023 J8T3      P03/13/85 STEV PRIV CPR
00025 J8T1      P07/24/85 STEV PRIV CPR
00027 J8T2      P03/13/85 STEV PRIV CPR
00029 J8F9      P03/13/85 STEV PRIV CPR
00031 J8F10     P03/13/85 STEV PRIV CPR
00033 J8F11     P03/13/85 STEV PRIV CPR
00035 J8F1      P03/13/85 STEV PRIV CPR
*END PRINT
*READY




I^A                                               ▭-▭04
```

Figure 3-7   Selective /LIBRARY output

When you use either of the forms of the /LIBRARY command that produce full output, you typically see only details for library members that you own (in other words, those that you created). That's why all of the members in figures 3-6 and 3-7 show STEV for the user-id. If you want to see detailed data for all members in the library, specify ALL as the last operand on the command. For example, the command

```
/LIB CON *J8 ALL
```

would display all of the members in my connected library whose names begin with the characters J8, regardless of who owns them.

How to display sorted directory listings: the SDSERV procedure   If you want a detailed, sorted listing of the contents of a library, you can run an ICCF-supplied procedure called SDSERV; figure 3-5 gives its format. A *procedure* is a series of statements that are processed in the ICCF background; in chapter 11, you'll learn how to write procedures of your own. For now, just realize you use SDSERV, and a number of other ICCF supplied procedures, much as you use commands. Note, though, that you typically invoke a procedure by specifying its name on the command line; you don't precede it with a slash like you do a system command.

With the SDSERV procedure, you can display the contents of your primary or secondary library or the common library. And you can have the display sorted by member name (the default), user-id, or modification date. For example, if I enter

```
SDSERV CONN DATE
```

The members in my connected library are listed in sequence by date of last modification.

The SDSERV procedure is useful when you're looking for particular members in a large library. However, because SDSERV is a procedure, not a command, it takes longer to run than /LIB.

How to delete a member from your primary library: the /PURGE command   To delete a member from your primary library, you enter the /PURGE command. Its format is simple: It's just the operation code followed by the member name and, if one is required, the member password. For instance, the command

```
/PURGE PR4300 P52Q
```

deletes the member PR4300 (protected with the password P52Q) from my primary library.

How to rename a member in your primary library: the /RENAME command   If you want to change the name of a library member, you enter the /RENAME command. Just code the operation code followed by the old name, then the new name. If the member is password protected, key in the password after the new name on the command line. You can change only the member name with this command; the original password is retained. For instance, I could change the name of PR4300 to OLDPR43 with this command:

```
/RENAME PR4300 OLDPR43 P52Q
```

Basic system commands to list library members

In the brief terminal session that I presented at the beginning of this chapter, I showed you how to use a simple form of the /LIST command to display the contents of a library member. In this section, I'll show you some additional ICCF features that let you look at the contents of a library member. Figure 3-8 shows the formats of the commands this section presents.

How to display data in your input area or a library member: the /LIST command   The simplest command you can use to display data is /LIST. If you simply enter

The /LIST, /LISTX, and /DISPLAY commands

```
/LIST     [start [end]] [member-name [password]]
/LISTX    [start [end]] [member-name [password]]
/DISPLAY  [start [end]] [member-name [password]]
```

The /CANCEL command

```
/CANCEL
```

The /SKIP command

```
/SKIP operand
```

Values you can code for the operand on the /SKIP command

In each case, n is a number between 0 and 99999.

n	Skip forward n lines from the last line listed.
−n	Skip backward n lines from the last line listed.
S+n	Skip forward n lines from the top of the 3270 display screen.
S−n	Skip backward n lines from the top of the 3270 display screen.
P+n	Skip forward n pages in list output from an interactive partition.
P−n	Skip backward n pages in list output from an interactive partition.
TOP	Skip to the first line.
BOTTOM	Skip to the last line.
END	Skip to the last line.

Figure 3-8   Commands to list library members

```
/LIST
```

ICCF displays the contents of your input area. On the other hand, if you specify the name of a library member like

```
/LIST INV2300
```

/LIST displays its contents.

If you want to display just part of the data in the input area or a library member, you can specify a beginning and ending line number for the display. For example, to display lines 100 through 150 of the member INV2300, I'd enter

```
/LIST 100 150 INV2300
```

If you only enter one line number, ICCF assumes it's the position in the member where you want the display to start. Then, it displays data through the end of the member. However, you can press the PA2 key, as I described earlier, to terminate a list operation at any time.

Also, you can use the /LIST command to display the contents of your punch area (if you specify $$PUNCH as the member name) or your print area (if you specify $$PRINT). You may want to use these forms when you retrieve output produced by a job run in an interactive partition. For example, the output of the SDSERV procedure is stored in the print area. As a result, you could issue the command

```
/LIST $$PRINT
```

to review it. Also, you can display the contents of your log area if you specify $$LOG.

How to display the hexadecimal values of data in your input area or a library member: the /LISTX command   If you need to see the hexadecimal values of the data in either the input area or a library member, you can use the /LISTX command. I suspect the only time you'll need to use this command is if you have to look at a source program that contains literals that are entered not as characters from the standard character set, but rather as hex values. Figure 3-9 compares the output of the /LIST and /LISTX commands.

How to display data in your input area or a library member with line numbers: the /DISPLAY command   /DISPLAY works like /LIST, only it displays line numbers with each line; /LIST doesn't. Figure 3-10 compares the output the two commands produce. Generally, I think you'll use /LIST for a quick look at a small member and /DISPLAY for a more lengthy examination of a larger member in which you might want to use the /SKIP command to move forward and backward.

How to scroll through a listing: the /SKIP command   When your terminal is in list mode, you can use the /SKIP command to scroll the text forward or backward a specified number of lines. It's effective when you entered list mode either with the /LIST or /DISPLAY command. However, because it uses relative line numbers to move, I think you're more likely to use it with /DISPLAY than with /LIST. That's because /DISPLAY shows the line numbers along with the data from the member. Figure 3-8 shows the operands you can use when you issue the /SKIP command.

Command:　/LIST INV2300

```
...+....1....+....2....+....3....+....4....+....5....+....6....+....7....+..LS
// JOB     INV2300
// OPTION LIST,ERRS,CATAL,SXREF,NOSYM
   PHASE INV2300,*
   INCLUDE DLZBPJRA
// EXEC FCOBOL
 CBL VERB
       IDENTIFICATION DIVISION.
     *
       PROGRAM-ID.  INV2300.
     *
       ENVIRONMENT DIVISION.
     *
       INPUT-OUTPUT SECTION.
     *
       FILE-CONTROL.
     *
         SELECT PRTOUT ASSIGN TO SYS006-UR-1403-S
                       ACCESS IS SEQUENTIAL.
       DATA DIVISION.
     *
```
```
Iᴬ                                                    ▫▫04
```

Command:　/LISTX INV2300

```
...+....1....+....2....+....3....+....4....+....5....+....6....+....7....+..LS
// JOB     INV2300
664DDC44444CDEFFFF44444444444444444444444444444444444444444444444444444444444
11016200000955230000000000000000000000000000000000000000000000000000000000000
// OPTION LIST,ERRS,CATAL,SXREF,NOSYM
664DDECDD4DCEE6CDDE6CCECD6EEDCC6DDEED44444444444444444444444444444444444444444
11067396503923B5992B31313B27956B562840000000000000000000000000000000000000000
   PHASE INV2300,*
444DCCEC4CDEFFFF65444444444444444444444444444444444444444444444444444444444444
00078125095523008C0000000000000000000000000000000000000000000000000000000000
   INCLUDE DLZBPJRA
444CDCDECC4CDECDDDC44444444444444444444444444444444444444444444444444444444444
00095334450439271910000000000000000000000000000000000000000000000000000000000
// EXEC FCOBOL
664CECC4CCDCDD444444444444444444444444444444444444444444444444444444444444444
11057530636263000000000000000000000000000000000000000000000000000000000000000
 CBL VERB
4CCD4ECDC444444444444444444444444444444444444444444444444444444444444444444444
03230559200000000000000000000000000000000000000000000000000000000000000000000
       IDENTIFICATION DIVISION.
4444444CCCDECCCCCECDD4CCECECDD44444444444444444444444444444444444444444444444
000000094553969313965049592965B000000000000000000000000000000000000000000000
```
```
Iᴬ                                                    ▫▫04
```

Figure 3-9   Sample output of the /LIST and /LISTX commands

Command: /LIST INV2300

```
...+....1....+....2....+....3....+....4....+....5....+....6....+....7....+..LS
// JOB     INV2300
// OPTION LIST,ERRS,CATAL,SXREF,NOSYM
   PHASE INV2300,*
   INCLUDE DLZBPJRA
// EXEC FCOBOL
 CBL VERB
      IDENTIFICATION DIVISION.
      *
      PROGRAM-ID.  INV2300.
      *
      ENVIRONMENT DIVISION.
      *
      INPUT-OUTPUT SECTION.
      *
      FILE-CONTROL.
      *
          SELECT PRTOUT ASSIGN TO SYS006-UR-1403-S
                      ACCESS IS SEQUENTIAL.
      DATA DIVISION.
      *
```
```
IA                                                    □-□04
```

Command: /DISPLAY INV2300

```
...+....1....+....2....+....3....+....4....+....5....+....6....+....7....+..LS
00001 // JOB     INV2300
00002 // OPTION LIST,ERRS,CATAL,SXREF,NOSYM
00003    PHASE INV2300,*
00004    INCLUDE DLZBPJRA
00005 // EXEC FCOBOL
00006  CBL VERB
00007      IDENTIFICATION DIVISION.
00008      *
00009      PROGRAM-ID.  INV2300.
00010      *
00011      ENVIRONMENT DIVISION.
00012      *
00013      INPUT-OUTPUT SECTION.
00014      *
00015      FILE-CONTROL.
00016      *
00017          SELECT PRTOUT ASSIGN TO SYS006-UR-1403-S
00018                      ACCESS IS SEQUENTIAL.
00019      DATA DIVISION.
00020      *
```
```
IA                                                    □-□04
```

Figure 3-10   Sample output of the /LIST and /DISPLAY commands

How to terminate a listing: the /CANCEL command   You can issue the /CANCEL command when your terminal is in list mode to terminate the listing and return to command mode. However, an easier alternative for most terminal users is to use the PA2 key, which has the same effect and requires fewer keystrokes.

Discussion

To use ICCF effectively, you must understand libraries and the system commands this topic introduced. Most of these commands are used to manipulate the members you create and maintain using ICCF's text editing facilities. As an ICCF user, you'll spend most of your terminal time entering text using the full-screen editor. That's what the next topic teaches you.

Terminology

user profile
command line
command mode
list mode
operation code
operand
procedure

Objectives

1. Given your user-id and password, log on and log off ICCF at your terminal.

2. Describe the syntax of an ICCF system command.

3. Use the /SHOW, /SWITCH, /CONNECT, /USERS, and /SET commands as described in this topic to manage your current libraries.

4. Use the /LIBRARY command and the SDSERV procedure as described in this topic to list the members in any of your current libraries.

5. Use the /PURGE command to remove a member from your primary library.

6. Use the /RENAME command to assign a new name to a member in your primary library.

7. Use the /LIST, /LISTX, or /DISPLAY command, as appropriate, to display the contents of a member.

8. Use the /SKIP command to control list mode output.

TOPIC 2   Basic ICCF editing commands

If you're a typical user, you'll spend most of your ICCF time working with the *full-screen editor*. It's the ICCF component that lets you enter new data and store it in a library member. In addition, it lets you retrieve data from an existing library member and make changes to it. First in this topic, I'll briefly compare the full-screen editor with ICCF's other facility for text entry, the *context editor*. Then I'll show you how to use the basic editing functions you must be familiar with.

ICCF'S TWO TEXT EDITORS: THE CONTEXT EDITOR AND THE FULL-SCREEN EDITOR

The context editor is ICCF's basic editor. It's a line editor, which means it requires you to position the text you're working on at a specific line, then issue a command to operate on that line. Because the context editor has such a strong line orientation, it's cumbersome to use. But even worse, you have to key in some commands so they specify details from the current line that give the command a context in which to operate. (That's why it's called the "context" editor.)

To run the context editor, you enter the system command

```
/EDIT member-name
```

When you do, your terminal enters *edit mode*, indicated by ED in the upper right corner of the screen. Then, you can make changes to any of the lines stored in the library member you specified. Alternatively, if you issue the /EDIT command without a member-name, you'll be editing the input area.

You can work in the context editor in two *sub-modes*: edit sub-mode and input sub-mode. In *edit sub-mode*, you can only make changes to existing lines. (The line on which you can operate, the *current line*, is marked by the *line pointer*.) In *input sub-mode*, you can add new lines of data.

For installations that used old teletypewriter terminals, the context editor, with its line-by-line approach, was appropriate. Today, however, teletypewriter terminals are virtually museum pieces. It's almost certain that text editing you do under ICCF will be at a 3270-type display station. Because a typical 3270 displays 24 lines at a time and can accept changes to any of them in one transmission, it's a waste of the power of the device to use the context editor. And more importantly, it's a waste of your time. So instead of doing text editing with the context editor, you'll want to use the more sophisticated full-screen editor.

The full-screen editor, which I'll often refer to simply as the "editor," provides all the capabilities of the context editor, and it packages them in a way that makes them easier to use. For example, to change text with the full-screen editor, all you have to do is move the cursor to the right line and type in your change over the existing data. There's usually no need to enter contextual commands with the full-screen editor, although it does provide them.

In addition to letting you make changes directly on multiple lines, the full-screen editor also uses the facilities of the 3270 to make editing easier. For example, you can define program function keys to perform functions you do over and over. And you can actually work on two or more library members at the same time on the same screen. Alternatively, you can edit different parts of the same library member at the same time.

In practice, you can think of the full-screen editor and the context editor as separate ICCF functions. For example, you invoke them in different ways and use them differently. Actually, though, the full-screen editor is a third sub-mode of the context editor, which is called *full-screen edit sub-mode*. So although the full-screen editor differs from the context editor in that it provides a variety of significant and useful enhancements, the two editors are similar because they provide many identical functions. As you learn to use the full-screen editor, you'll find that some of the commands you use have a line orientation. In other words, they affect only the current line. That's because the command is really from the underlying context editor.

THE BASIC FEATURES OF THE FULL-SCREEN EDITOR

Now that you understand the relationship between the two ICCF editors, you're ready to learn the basic features of the full-screen editor. When you've finished this topic, you won't know all of the full-screen editor commands, but you will be able to use the full-screen editor to enter and change practically any kind of text.

How to invoke the full-screen editor

You invoke the editor with the ICCF-supplied macro called ED. (A *macro* is a series of ICCF commands stored in a library member. When you run a macro, the commands it contains are processed by ICCF one by one, just as if you'd entered them at the terminal interactively. However, you only need to enter the macro name to invoke them. This is similar to a procedure, which I introduced in the last topic; the difference is that a procedure is processed in ICCF's background, while the commands in a macro are all processed in ICCF's foreground.)

The full-screen editor macro, ED, should be stored in your system's common library. As a result, you should be able to access it from your terminal. To run a macro under the most current releases of ICCF, just enter its name (without a slash), like this:

```
ED
```

If you're using a release of ICCF before 1.3 modification level 5, you have to precede the macro name with an at-sign, like this:

```
@ED
```

The "@" is required under older releases to indicate to ICCF that you want to run a macro. Although @ is no longer required by the more current releases of ICCF, you can still use it if you wish.

When you use the full-screen editor, you can process text in two ways. First, you can work on text stored in your input area. That's what happens if you invoke the ED macro like I just showed you, without a member name. (ICCF uses the input area for a variety of functions, so depending on what you've already done during your terminal session, the input area may or may not already contain data.) When you edit the input area, you can add new text to it or you can copy text into it from an existing library member. Then, when you've finished your editing session, you can transfer the contents of the input area to a new library member or you can replace the contents of an existing library member with it. Or, you can leave the text in the input area so it can be processed by another ICCF command that uses the input area.

The other way you can use the full-screen editor is to work directly on an existing library member. When you do, any changes you key in are recorded in the library member immediately as you work. To invoke the full-screen editor to edit an existing library member, you enter a command in this format:

```
@ED [member-name [password]]
```

For example,

```
@ED INV2300
```

causes the full-screen editor to begin using the member INV2300 in your primary library.

ICCF also supplies two specialized versions of the ED macro: EDPUN and EDPRT. They let you edit the contents of the punch and print areas. However, I suspect that you'll use these macros infrequently, if you use them at all; almost all of your full-screen editor work will be done on data stored in the input area or a library member. If you do use these macros, you'll find that members with strange looking names (T@@PUN-- and T@@PRT--) appear in your library; the macros create them.

Regardless of whether you decide to edit the input area or an existing library member, the format of the screen ICCF displays when you enter the full-screen editor is the same. So now, I want to describe the format of the screen and how you use it.

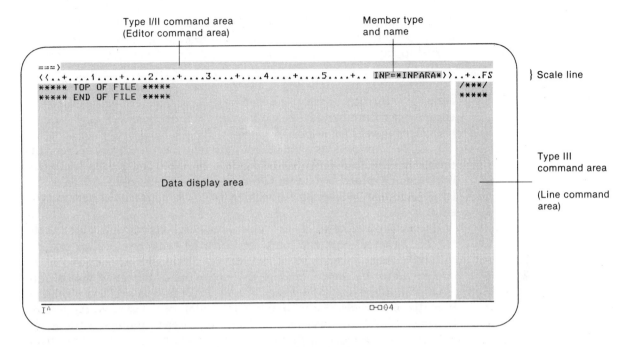

Figure 3-11   The format of the full-screen editor display

The format of the full-screen editor display

Figure 3-11 presents the ICCF full-screen editor display. In this example, I invoked the editor without specifying a member name, so I'm editing the input area. You can tell in this case that the input area is empty because the indicators for the top and the end of the file are together; if the input area had contained text, the text would appear between those indicators.

I want you to notice the parts of figure 3-11 I've labelled and shaded. The second line of the screen contains a *scale line* you can use to identify column positions within the text you edit. Embedded in the scale line is a field that displays what you're editing. In this figure, the value

    INP=*INPARA*

indicates that I'm editing the input area. If I were editing a library member, it would look something like this:

    MEM=INV2300

where INV2300 is the member name. The FS on the right side of the scale line indicates that ICCF is in the full-screen editor. The paired greater than and less than signs in the scale line mark the editor zone; I'll describe it in the next chapter.

The largest part of the full-screen editor screen is the *data display area*. In it, ICCF displays the text you're editing. You can move the cursor to any position in the data display area and key data directly into it.

The other two labelled areas in figure 3-11 are command entry areas. The top line of the screen can be used to enter commands like you enter system commands. This is the *type I/II command area*, or simply the *editor command area*.

Type I commands, which you enter at the top of the screen, are unique to the full-screen editor. Some of them replace and enhance functions provided by similar context editor commands, while others let you control advanced full-screen editor functions like split-screen editing.

On the other hand, *type II commands*, which you also enter at the top of the screen, are the same for both the full-screen editor and the context editor. Most type II commands obviously have roots in the context editor because they depend heavily on the current line position.

In all, there are more than 20 type I commands and more than 60 type II commands. From a practical point of view, the distinction between type I and type II commands doesn't matter. And in the manuals for the most current releases of ICCF, the distinction has been dropped and they're collectively called *editor commands*.

The area on the right side of the screen can be used to enter special full-screen editor commands. This is the *type III command area*, also called the *line command area*. The most commonly used *type III commands*, also called *line commands*, let you add, delete, copy, and move the lines you indicate.

Notice also that the line command area in the first line in figure 3-11 begins with a slash. The slash indicates that the line is the current line. You need to be aware of this because some of the commands of the full-screen editor are actually context editor commands which operate on the current line. For most ICCF users, the default is for the current line to be the first line of the data display area, but it doesn't have to be.

To help you understand how you use these areas, I want to illustrate a simple full-screen editor session. Then, I'll describe the basic full-screen editor commands you need to know.

A simple full-screen editor session

Figure 3-12 shows seven screens from a brief session with the full-screen editor in which I entered the first few lines of a COBOL program, then stored them in a library member. As I describe this session, I'm not going to focus on the details of the commands themselves. Instead, I just want to give you a sense for how the editor works.

I invoked the full-screen editor with the command line

@ED

and ICCF displayed the same screen as in figure 3-11. Because I didn't specify a member name when I invoked the editor, I'm editing the input area.

So I could begin entering text, I decided to add some blank lines to the input area. To do that, I keyed in the line command

    A100

as you can see in part 1 of figure 3-12. This command told the editor to add (A) 100 lines to the text.

After I pressed the enter key, ICCF displayed the screen in part 2 of figure 3-12. As you can see, the editing area was expanded, and the end-of-file indicator was no longer on the screen. What you see here are the first 21 of the 100 blank lines I added to the input area.

To enter text, I simply keyed it in where I wanted it in the data display area. Part 3 of figure 3-12 shows the screen after I entered data for the first lines of my COBOL program. All I did was key in text where I wanted it, but because my 3270 treats character positions in empty lines as nulls, I also had to enter leading spaces in each line.

Because the editor only displays 21 lines at a time on my terminal, I had to *scroll* the text up to be able to enter more lines. The slash I entered in the line command area in part 3 of the figure tells ICCF that line should be made the current line on the next screen that's displayed. As you can see in part 4 of the figure, that's what happened.

Although a typical editing session to enter a COBOL source program would be longer than this, I'm going to show you how I'd end this session. First, I wanted to get rid of the blank lines I added to the input area but didn't use. To do that, I keyed in the line command

    D100

to delete the 100 lines that follow the last line I coded, as you can see in part 4 of the figure. Since there were only 100 lines in the input area when I began entering text, there were fewer than 100 blank lines remaining. However, I didn't have to specify the exact number of blank lines that remained. By specifying more lines than I knew were present, all of them were deleted, as you can see in part 5.

In the editor command area in part 5, I entered a SAVE command to cause the text I had entered in the input area to be stored in a library member named TRANLST. SAVE causes a new member to be created with the name specified.

After ICCF had processed the SAVE command, the member I was editing was changed from the input area to the library member I named: TRANLST. You can tell that from the display

    MEM=TRANLST

in the editor scale line in part 6 of figure 3-12. Also in part 6, you can see that I keyed in the QUIT command to terminate the full-screen editor.

```
===>
<<...+....1....+....2....+....3....+....4....+....5....+.. INP=*INPARA*>>..+..FS
***** TOP OF FILE *****                                              A100/
***** END OF FILE *****                                              *****
```

```
I^                                              □-□04
```

Figure 3-12   A simple full-screen editor session (part 1 of 7)

```
===>
<<...+....1....+....2....+....3....+....4....+....5....+.. INP=*INPARA*>>..+..FS
***** TOP OF FILE *****                                              /**/
                                                                     *===*
                                                                     *===*
                                                                     *===*
                                                                     *===*
                                                                     *===*
                                                                     *===*
                                                                     *===*
                                                                     *===*
                                                                     '*===*
                                                                     *===*
                                                                     *===*
                                                                     *===*
                                                                     *===*
                                                                     *===*
                                                                     *===*
                                                                     *===*
                                                                     *===*
                                                                     *===*
                                                                     *===*
```

```
I^                                              □-□04
```

Figure 3-12   A simple full-screen editor session (part 2 of 7)

```
===>
<<..+....1....+....2....+....3....+....4....+....5....+.. INP=*INPARA*>>..+..FS
***** TOP OF FILE *****                                              /***/
        IDENTIFICATION DIVISION.                                     *====*
      *                                                              *====*
        PROGRAM-ID.   TRANLST.                                       *====*
      *                                                              *====*
        ENVIRONMENT DIVISION.                                        *====*
      *                                                              *====*
        CONFIGURATION SECTION.                                       *====*
      *                                                              *====*
        INPUT-OUTPUT SECTION.                                        *====*
      *                                                              *====*
        FILE-CONTROL.                                                *====*
            SELECT ARTRANS   ASSIGN TO SYS005-UR-2540R-S.            *====*
            SELECT TRANLIST ASSIGN TO SYS006-UR-1403-S.              *====*
      *                                                              *====*
        DATA DIVISION.                                               /====*
      *                                                              *====*
        FILE SECTION.                                                *====*
      *                                                              *====*
        FD  ARTRANS                                                  *====*
            LABEL RECORDS ARE OMITTED                                *====*
            RECORD CONTAINS 80 CHARACTERS.                           *====*
IA                                                    D-D04
```

Figure 3-12   A simple full-screen editor session (part 3 of 7)

```
===>
<<..+....1....+....2....+....3....+....4....+....5....+.. INP=*INPARA*>>..+..FS
        DATA DIVISION.                                               /===/*
      *                                                              *====*
        FILE SECTION.                                                *====*
      *                                                              *====*
        FD  ARTRANS                                                  *====*
            LABEL RECORDS ARE OMITTED                                *====*
            RECORD CONTAINS 80 CHARACTERS.                           *====*
                                                                     D100*
                                                                     *====*
                                                                     *====*
                                                                     *====*
                                                                     *====*
                                                                     *====*
                                                                     *====*
                                                                     *====*
                                                                     *====*
                                                                     *====*
                                                                     *====*
                                                                     *====*
                                                                     *====*
IA                                                    D-D04
```

Figure 3-12   A simple full-screen editor session (part 4 of 7)

```
===) SAVE TRANLST
<<..+....1....+....2....+....3....+....4....+....5....+.. INP=*INPARA*>>..+..FS
        DATA DIVISION.                                                    /===/*
        *                                                                *====*
        FILE SECTION.                                                    *====*
        *                                                                *====*
        FD  ARTRANS                                                      *====*
            LABEL RECORDS ARE OMITTED                                    *====*
            RECORD CONTAINS 80 CHARACTERS.                               *====*
***** END OF FILE *****                                                  *****




I^A                                        □-□04
```

Figure 3-12   A simple full-screen editor session (part 5 of 7)

```
===) QUIT
*MSG=*SAVED        ....2....+....3....+....4....+....5....+.. MEM=TRANLST >>..+..FS
        DATA DIVISION.                                                    /===/*
        *                                                                *====*
        FILE SECTION.                                                    *====*
        *                                                                *====*
        FD  ARTRANS                                                      *====*
            LABEL RECORDS ARE OMITTED                                    *====*
            RECORD CONTAINS 80 CHARACTERS.                               *====*
***** END OF FILE *****                                                  *****




I^A                                        □-□04
```

Figure 3-12   A simple full-screen editor session (part 6 of 7)

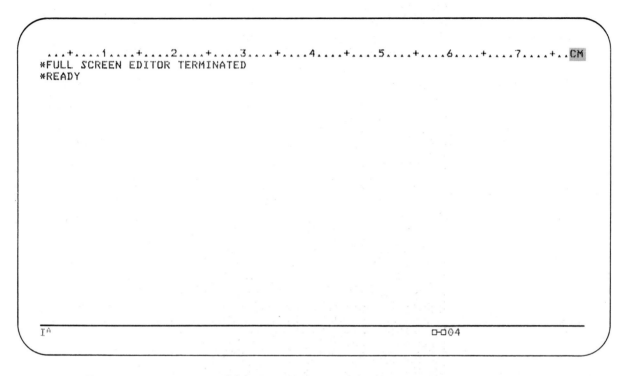

Figure 3-12   A simple full-screen editor session (part 7 of 7)

After I pressed the enter key, ICCF displayed the message in part 7. As the CM in the upper right corner of the screen in part 7 indicates, my terminal is now back in command mode.

This simple editor session illustrates fundamental commands to add and delete text lines, scroll, save text, and end an editor session. Now, I want to present the details of those commands, plus other basic editor commands you need to know.

How to use the basic commands of the full-screen editor

In this section, I'll describe the most important full-screen editor commands: the ones you must know to use the editor effectively. This section presents the basic commands in six groups. First, you'll learn how to use the commands that let you add and delete lines from the member you're editing. Second, I'll show you how to use commands to scroll text. Third, I'll show you how to issue commands to find text strings. Fourth, I'll show you how to issue commands to copy and move text. Fifth, I'll show you how to use commands to manage library members. And sixth, you'll learn how to end the full-screen editor and return to command mode.

Line commands

A n   Insert n lines (up to 999) after the indicated line.

D n   Delete n lines (up to 999) from and including the indicated line.

Editor commands

DELETE $\begin{Bmatrix} n \\ * \\ /string/ \end{Bmatrix}$

n operand: Delete n lines (up to 99999) from and including the current line (indicated by the current line pointer in the line command area).

* operand: Delete all lines from the current position through the end of the member.

/string/ operand: Delete all lines from the current line (indicated by the current line pointer) through the line that contains the text indicated by string. You must enter delimiting slashes on each side of string.

INPUT   Causes lines on the screen beneath the current line to be made available for text entry. After you enter text and press the enter key, the new lines are added to the member where you keyed them in.

LADD n   Insert n lines (up to 1001) after the current line (indicated by the current line pointer).

Figure 3-13   Commands to add and delete lines

When it's appropriate in each group, I'll present both the editor commands and the line commands for the same function. Usually, when a line command is available, it's paralleled by a similar editor command. The editor command is part of the underlying context editor, and the line command is an enhancement made possible by the full-screen editor. I want you to realize that although two different commands are available to perform some functions, you're more likely to use the line command because it's better suited for the full-screen editor environment than its equivalent editor command.

Commands to add and delete lines   Figure 3-13 lists the commands you can use to add and delete lines. In the brief editor session in figure 3-12, I used two of them: the line commands A and D. Of the commands in figure 3-13, I think you'll use these two most often. The other commands in figure 3-13 perform similar functions.

The DELETE command, which is part of the context editor, has three forms you can use. The first,

    DELETE n

parallels the line command D. It causes the specified number of lines to be deleted. It differs, however, in that it deletes lines beginning with the current line, indicated by the current line pointer (/) in the line command area. In contrast, the line command D causes the deletions to begin with the line where the command is entered, whether it's the current line or not.

The second form of the editor command DELETE lets you specify that all lines from the current line through the end of the member be deleted:

```
DELETE *
```

However, I think it's just as easy to use the line command

```
D999
```

to delete 999 lines (the maximum number you can specify). Rarely will you want to delete more lines than 999.

The third form of the DELETE command provides a function that the line command D doesn't. It lets you delete lines from the current position down to, but not including, the first subsequent line that contains a particular text string. For example, to delete all the lines from the current position down to the line that contains the text PROCEDURE DIVISION, you'd enter the command like this:

```
DELETE /PROCEDURE DIVISION/
```

This format of the command can save you time if you don't know exactly how many lines you need to delete, but you know what text string is in the line immediately after the last line you want to delete.

An alternative to using the line command A to add a specific number of blank lines to your member when you want to insert new text is to use the editor command INPUT. When you issue the INPUT command, it causes all the lines on the screen beneath the current line to be made available for text entry. In effect, the existing text that follows the current line is shifted down and off the screen to open up space for you to enter new lines. Then, after you've keyed in one or more new lines and pressed the enter key, they're inserted in the member at that location. Unlike the line command A (or the editor command LADD, which I'll describe in a moment), the INPUT command does not add blank lines to your member; it only adds lines in which you've entered data.

Figure 3-14 shows how you can use the INPUT command. In this example, I want to add several lines of comments at the beginning of the COBOL program I started to enter in figure 3-12. In part 1 of figure 3-14, I've entered the line command / to make the fourth line of the program the current line. Then, in part 2, after the current line pointer has been set at the proper line, I keyed in the INPUT command. Part 3 shows what the full-screen editor screen looks like immediately after I press the enter key to issue the INPUT command. As you can see, the text that followed the current line is shifted down and off the screen,

```
===>
<<...+....1....+....2....+....3....+....4....+....5....+.. INP=*INPARA*>>..+..FS
***** TOP OF FILE *****                                                  /***/
        IDENTIFICATION DIVISION.                                         *====*
      *                                                                  *====*
        PROGRAM-ID.   TRANLST.                                           *====*
      *                                                                  /====*
        ENVIRONMENT DIVISION.                                            *====*
      *                                                                  *====*
        CONFIGURATION SECTION.                                           *====*
      *                                                                  *====*
        SOURCE-COMPUTER.   IBM-370.                                      *====*
        OBJECT-COMPUTER.   IBM-370.                                      *====*
      *                                                                  *====*
        INPUT-OUTPUT SECTION.                                            *====*
      *                                                                  *====*
        FILE-CONTROL.                                                    *====*
            SELECT ARTRANS   ASSIGN TO SYS005-UR-2540R-S.                *====*
            SELECT TRANLIST ASSIGN TO SYS006-UR-1403-S.                  *====*
      *                                                                  *====*
        DATA DIVISION.                                                   *====*
      *                                                                  *====*
        FILE SECTION.                                                    *====*
      *                                                                  *====*
I^                                              □-□04
```

Figure 3-14   How to use the INPUT command (part 1 of 5)

```
===> INPUT
<<...+....1....+....2....+....3....+....4....+....5....+.. INP=*INPARA*>>..+..FS
      *                                                                  /====/*
        ENVIRONMENT DIVISION.                                            *====*
      *                                                                  *====*
        CONFIGURATION SECTION.                                           *====*
      *                                                                  *====*
        SOURCE-COMPUTER.   IBM-370.                                      *====*
        OBJECT-COMPUTER.   IBM-370.                                      *====*
      *                                                                  *====*
        INPUT-OUTPUT SECTION.                                            *====*
      *                                                                  *====*
        FILE-CONTROL.                                                    *====*
            SELECT ARTRANS   ASSIGN TO SYS005-UR-2540R-S.                *====*
            SELECT TRANLIST ASSIGN TO SYS006-UR-1403-S.                  *====*
      *                                                                  *====*
        DATA DIVISION.                                                   *====*
      *                                                                  *====*
        FILE SECTION.                                                    *====*
      *                                                                  *====*
        FD  ARTRANS                                                      *====*
            LABEL RECORDS ARE OMITTED                                    *====*
            RECORD CONTAINS 80 CHARACTERS.                               *====*
***** END OF FILE *****                                                  *****
I^                                              □-□04
```

Figure 3-14   How to use the INPUT command (part 2 of 5)

```
===>
<<...+....1....+....2....+....3....+....4....+....5....+.. INP=*INPARA*>>...+..FS
         *                                                        /===/*
                                                                  *INPUT
                                                                  *INPUT
                                                                  *INPUT
                                                                  *INPUT
                                                                  *INPUT
                                                                  *INPUT
                                                                  *INPUT
                                                                  *INPUT
                                                                  *INPUT
                                                                  *INPUT
                                                                  *INPUT
                                                                  *INPUT
                                                                  *INPUT
                                                                  *INPUT
                                                                  *INPUT
                                                                  *INPUT
                                                                  *INPUT
                                                                  *INPUT
                                                                  *INPUT
 I^                                              □-□04
```

Figure 3-14   How to use the INPUT command (part 3 of 5)

```
===>
<<...+....1....+....2....+....3....+....4....+....5....+.. INP=*INPARA*>>...+..FS
         *                                                        /===/*
         *    TRANLST                                             *INPUT
         *    -------                                             *INPUT
         *    THIS PROGRAM READS INPUT TRANSACTION RECORDS AND    *INPUT
         *    PRODUCES A SIMPLE FORMATTED LISTING OF DATA THEY CONTAIN.  *INPUT
                                                                  *INPUT
                                                                  *INPUT
                                                                  *INPUT
                                                                  *INPUT
                                                                  *INPUT
                                                                  *INPUT
                                                                  *INPUT
                                                                  *INPUT
                                                                  *INPUT
                                                                  *INPUT
                                                                  *INPUT
                                                                  *INPUT
                                                                  *INPUT
                                                                  *INPUT
 I^                                              □-□04
```

Figure 3-14   How to use the INPUT command (part 4 of 5)

```
===>
<<...+....1....+....2....+....3....+....4....+....5....+.. INP=*INPARA*>>...+..FS
       *       PRODUCES A SIMPLE FORMATTED LISTING OF DATA THEY CONTAIN.     /===/*
       ENVIRONMENT DIVISION.                                                 *===*
       *                                                                     *===*
       CONFIGURATION SECTION.                                                *===*
       *                                                                     *===*
       SOURCE-COMPUTER.  IBM-370.                                            *===*
       OBJECT-COMPUTER.  IBM-370.                                            *===*
       *                                                                     *===*
       INPUT-OUTPUT SECTION.                                                 *===*
       *                                                                     *===*
       FILE-CONTROL.                                                         *===*
           SELECT ARTRANS  ASSIGN TO SYS005-UR-2540R-S.                      *===*
           SELECT TRANLIST ASSIGN TO SYS006-UR-1403-S.                       *===*
       *                                                                     *===*
       DATA DIVISION.                                                        *===*
       *                                                                     *===*
       FILE SECTION.                                                         *===*
       *                                                                     *===*
       FD  ARTRANS                                                           *===*
           LABEL RECORDS ARE OMITTED                                         *===*
           RECORD CONTAINS 80 CHARACTERS.                                    *===*
***** END OF FILE *****                                                      *****
IA                                                     0-004
```

Figure 3-14   How to use the INPUT command (part 5 of 5)

and the screen area beneath it is opened for new lines. That's indicated by

        *INPUT

in the line command area. In part 4, I've keyed in four additional comment lines. Then, when I press the enter key, the four lines I entered are added to the text, the unused lines are deleted, and the last line I entered becomes the current line, as you can see in part 5 of the figure.

Another alternative to the line command A or the editor command INPUT is another editor command: LADD. Its effect is more like that of the A command than INPUT. On the LADD command, you specify the number of blank lines to be added to the member immediately after the current line. It's less flexible than the A command because it adds lines only after the current line, while the A command can cause lines to be added after any line on the screen. As a result, I suspect you won't use LADD very often.

(By the way, you might think that the editor command to add lines to a member would be ADD, but it's not. The ADD command is used to append a specified text string to the text string already in the current line. It's a contextual command you'll probably never use because the full-screen editor lets you key in data exactly where you want it.)

Line command

/	Scrolls forward or backward to set the current line pointer at the indicated line.

Editor commands

B̲ACKWARD n	Scrolls to set the current line pointer backward n screens.
B̲OTTOM	Scrolls directly to the end of the text (that is, to set the current line pointer after the last line).
D̲OWN n	Scrolls to set the current line pointer forward n lines. (The same as the NEXT command.)
F̲ORWARD n	Scrolls to set the current line pointer forward n screens.
NEXT n	Scrolls to set the current line pointer forward n lines. (The same as the DOWN command.)
T̲OP	Scrolls directly to the beginning of the text (that is, to set the current line pointer before the first line).
U̲P n	Scrolls to set the current line pointer backward n lines.

Figure 3-15   Commands to scroll text

Commands to scroll text   You've already seen how to scroll the text by using the line command /. You simply enter it on the line you want to become the current line and press the enter key. This is a useful command, but it's limited to relatively short scrolls; you can only scroll up or down to a line that's already displayed on your screen. ICCF includes a variety of other scrolling commands that give you considerable flexibility as you use the full-screen editor. Figure 3-15 lists these commands.

All of the scrolling commands except / are editor commands. In other words, you enter them at the top of the screen. They're easy to understand, so I'm not going to illustrate them with screen images. However, if you want to look back to figure 3-14, you can see that if I had entered

```
DOWN 4
```

instead of the / command in part 1, the result would have been the same in part 2. For short scrolls, it's easier to use the / command because with it, you don't have to count how many lines to scroll and you don't have to think about whether to use UP or DOWN. Those two commands can be confusing because, depending on how you think about them, they seem to work backwards: UP causes the text on the screen to move downward, while DOWN causes it to move upward.

Editor commands

LOCATE text   Moves the current line pointer to the first line after the current line that contains the text you specify.

SEARCH text   Moves the current line pointer to the first line that contains the text you specify, regardless of where the current line is.

Figure 3-16   Commands to find text

Commands to find text   In some editing situations, you want to scroll your display not a particular number of lines or screens, but to a particular line that contains a specific text string. The commands in figure 3-16 let you do that specialized kind of scrolling. To locate the first occurrence of a text string within the member you're editing, you use the SEARCH command. To locate the first line after the current line that contains a particular text string, you use the LOCATE command. For example, to find the first occurence of the text PROCEDURE in the library member you're editing, you'd issue the command

    SEARCH PROCEDURE

These commands are also easy to understand and use in their basic forms. In the next chapter, you'll learn more about specialized find functions you can use.

Commands to copy and move text   The full-screen editor provides five line commands that let you easily copy and move text within a member. Figure 3-17 shows these commands.

The first line command in figure 3-17, ", lets you duplicate a line from 1 to 999 times. The duplicates are added to the member immediately after the original line. This command is particularly useful when you're entering a series of similar lines. Just key in the first, duplicate it as many times as you need, then make minor editing changes to the duplicates. As you can imagine, using the " command can save you plenty of entry time, can help you keep like elements of code aligned, and can help you avoid simple keying errors.

The only editor command in figure 3-17 is DUP, which is the equivalent of the line command ". It makes duplicates of the current line and stores them immediately after the current line. However, since the " command is easier to use and not restricted to the current line, I don't think you're likely to use DUP.

The other four line commands in figure 3-17 all use your punch area (one of the temporary areas allocated for your use out of the ICCF library file when you start a terminal session). Because the punch area isn't otherwise used during a full-screen editor session, ICCF can use it as a scratch pad area for some editor functions. When you do opera-

Line commands

"n	Duplicates the indicated line immediately after the indicated line n times (n must be between 1 and 999).
Cn	Copies n lines (from 1 to 99), beginning with the indicated line, into the editor stack, overlaying whatever is already there. Does not delete the lines from the member.
Kn	Copies n lines (from 1 to 99), beginning with the indicated line, into the editor stack, appending them to what's already there. Does not delete the lines from the member.
Mn	Moves n lines (from 1 to 99), beginning with the indicated line, into the editor stack, overlaying what's already there. Deletes the lines from the member.
I	Inserts the contents of the editor stack after the indicated line in the member being edited. Leaves the contents of the editor stack unchanged.

Editor command

DUP n	Duplicates the current line n times (from 1 to 1000) after the current line.

Figure 3-17   Commands to copy and move text

tions that copy or move lines within a member, ICCF stores those lines in your punch area. When it's used like this, the punch area is called the *editor stack*.

Three of the commands in figure 3-17 cause text lines from the member you're editing to be stored in the editor stack. Both the C and M commands cause the previous contents of the stack to be lost when they transfer lines from your library member into it. They differ in that C leaves the original lines it copied in your library member, while M moves those lines, causing them to be deleted from the library member. The K command is like C in that it leaves the lines it copies in your library member. However, it's different from both C and M in that it does not clear the stack before it transfers lines into it. Instead, the K command appends the lines it copies to what's already in the stack. As a result, you can use the K command to build a series (or "stack") of lines that come from several locations in your library member.

The last command in figure 3-17 is the line command I. You use it to insert the contents of the editor stack into the member you're editing. Simply issue the I command on the line after which you want the contents of the stack inserted. You can use the I command repeatedly without affecting the contents of the stack, as long as you don't issue any intervening C, K, or M commands.

Figure 3-18 illustrates how to use the C and I commands. Here, I've entered a series of statements for a COBOL program. I'm ready to enter the code for the next paragraph, but I realize that it will be similar to the

```
===>
<<..+....1....+....2....+....3....+....4....+....5....+.. INP=*INPARA*>>..+..FS
        130-PRINT-HEADING-LINES.                                    /===/*
    *                                                               *===*
            MOVE HEADING-LINE-1 TO PRINT-AREA.                      *===*
            PERFORM 150-WRITE-PAGE-TOP-LINE.                        *===*
            MOVE HEADING-LINE-2 TO PRINT-AREA.                      *===*
            MOVE 2            TO SPACE-CONTROL.                      *===*
            PERFORM 140-WRITE-REPORT-LINE.                          *===*
            MOVE HEADING-LINE-3 TO PRINT-AREA.                      *===*
            MOVE 1            TO SPACE-CONTROL.                      *===*
            PERFORM 140-WRITE-REPORT-LINE.                          *===*
            MOVE 2            TO SPACE-CONTROL.                      *===*
    *                                                               *===*
        140-WRITE-REPORT-LINE.                                      C6==*
    *                                                               *===*
            WRITE PRINT-AREA                                        *===*
                AFTER ADVANCING SPACE-CONTROL LINES.                *===*
            ADD SPACE-CONTROL TO LINE-COUNT.                        *===*
    *                                                               I===*
***** END OF FILE *****                                            *****

I^                                          □-□04
```

```
===>
*MSG=*END INSERT     ....+....3....+....4....+....5....+.. INP=*INPARA*>>..+..FS
        130-PRINT-HEADING-LINES.                                    /===/*
    *                                                               *===*
            MOVE HEADING-LINE-1 TO PRINT-AREA.                      *===*
            PERFORM 150-WRITE-PAGE-TOP-LINE.                        *===*
            MOVE HEADING-LINE-2 TO PRINT-AREA.                      *===*
            MOVE 2            TO SPACE-CONTROL.                      *===*
            PERFORM 140-WRITE-REPORT-LINE.                          *===*
            MOVE HEADING-LINE-3 TO PRINT-AREA.                      *===*
            MOVE 1            TO SPACE-CONTROL.                      *===*
            PERFORM 140-WRITE-REPORT-LINE.                          *===*
            MOVE 2            TO SPACE-CONTROL.                      *===*
    *                                                               *===*
        140-WRITE-REPORT-LINE.                                      *===*
    *                                                               *===*
            WRITE PRINT-AREA                                        *===*
                AFTER ADVANCING SPACE-CONTROL LINES.                *===*
            ADD SPACE-CONTROL TO LINE-COUNT.                        *===*
    *                                                               *===*
        140-WRITE-REPORT-LINE.                                      *===*
    *                                                               *===*
            WRITE PRINT-AREA                                  /      *===*
                AFTER ADVANCING SPACE-CONTROL LINES.                *===*

I^                                          □-□04
```

Figure 3-18   How to use the C and I commands

previous one. As a result, instead of keying in the next paragraph from scratch, I copy the previous one (which consists of six lines) into the editor stack using the C command. Then, I use the I command to insert the contents of the stack immediately after the copied lines. The top screen shows where I coded the commands, and the bottom screen shows their results. In the new lines in the second screen, I can easily make minor changes to make them read as they should. By the way, it's not necessary to issue the I command immediately after the C (or M or K) command. You can scroll to another section of the member to insert the copied text or even do other editing before you issue the I command.

As you can see in figure 3-18, you can issue more than one command on the same screen. In fact, you can change text in the data display area of the screen, enter an editor command, and issue line commands to perform a variety of operations all with one screen transmission (that is, by pressing the enter key only once). To do that, though, you need to understand how ICCF evaluates the contents of the full-screen editor screen with each terminal I/O operation. I'll describe that at the end of this topic.

Commands to store and retrieve library members   In the simple terminal session I showed you earlier in this topic, you saw that I used the SAVE command to store the contents of the input area in a library member. Now, I want to show you all the basic commands you can use within the full-screen editor to store and retrieve library members. Let me remind you before I describe these commands that when you edit a library member directly (that is, if you specify a library member name when you invoke the full-screen editor), changes you make are recorded immediately in that member.

It's usually wise not to edit a member directly. Instead, you should copy it into your input area, edit it there, then replace the original member when you've finished your editing session. That way, if you decide that you really didn't want to make the changes you entered, you have an unaltered original. Also, in case there's a system failure, the chances are better of recovering your library member if it wasn't in the process of being edited at the time of the failure. As a result, I encourage you to invoke the full-screen editor to edit the input area (by entering @ED without a member name), then use the GETFILE command to copy in the member you want to edit.

Figure 3-19 presents the format of the GETFILE command (which you can abbreviate as GET). To illustrate its use, suppose I wanted to copy the member TRANLST into the member I'm editing. To do that I'd enter

```
GET TRANLST
```

in the editor command area. Then, if I'm editing the input area, I can change the contents of TRANLST without worrying about making unrecoverable changes to the original member.

The GETFILE command

```
GETFILE member-name [password] [start [count]]
```

Figure 3-19   The GETFILE command

The FILE, SAVE, and REPLACE commands

```
FILE     member-name [password] [PRIV|PUBL]
SAVE     member-name [password] [PRIV|PUBL]
REPLACE  member-name [password] [PRIV|PUBL]
```

Figure 3-20   Commands to store data in library members

If you want to copy in only part of a library member, you can issue the GETFILE command with a parameter to specify where to start the copy and another to specify how many lines to copy. For example, the command

```
GETFILE TRANLST 1 75
```

would cause the first 75 lines contained in the member named TRANLST to be copied into the member I'm editing.

You're not restricted to using the GETFILE command only when you start an editing session with the input area; you can use it any time you're editing. So if a library member contains text that you'd like to copy into the member you're editing, just set the current line pointer to the line after which you want the text added, then issue the GETFILE command specifying the proper member name and, if appropriate, start and count values. And, if the member you want to copy from is password protected, you must indicate the password as well.

After you've finished editing text in the input area, you can store it in a new library member with either the SAVE or FILE command. Both have similar syntax, as you can see in figure 3-20. For example, to store the text from the input area in a new member called TRANLST2, I'd enter

```
SAVE TRANLST2
```

The difference between SAVE and FILE is that FILE not only stores the text you're editing, but it also ends the full-screen editor. In contrast, when you issue the SAVE command, your editor session continues. For either command, you must supply a password if you want a new library member to be password protected.

The FILE, QUIT, END, and CANCEL commands

```
FILE member-name [password] [PRIV|PUBL]
QUIT
END
CANCEL
```

Figure 3-21   Commands to end a full-screen editor session

If you want to store the text you've been editing in a library member that already exists, you use the REPLACE command. For example, the command

```
REPLACE TRANLST
```

causes the text from the input area to be stored in the member TRANLST, replacing what was originally there. You must supply a password along with the member name if the member is password protected.

When you use the SAVE, FILE, or REPLACE command, you can specify the protection to be applied to the member. Specify PUBL on the command to make the member a public member, or specify PRIV to make it a private member. You only need to specify these operands to override your user profile. In other words, if your profile indicates that your library members should be created as private members, you need not specify PRIV on these commands.

Once again, remember that if you're editing a library member directly, all changes you make are recorded immediately. When that's the case, you don't issue a command to save your work.

Commands to end the full-screen editor   Figure 3-21 shows the four commands you can use to end a full-screen editor session and return to command mode. For simple full-screen editing sessions, QUIT, END, and CANCEL all have the same effect: They terminate the session. FILE combines the effects of the SAVE command and the QUIT command. For advanced editing sessions in which you're working with more than one active file, the CANCEL command works differently from the others. You'll learn about that when I describe split-screen editing in the next chapter.

OTHER FULL-SCREEN EDITOR INFORMATION YOU NEED TO KNOW

At this point, you've learned how to use all the basic full-screen editor commands. However, there are two other subjects that you need to know about: (1) how to repeat editor commands and (2) how the editor interprets multiple commands on the same screen.

How to repeat commands

Sometimes as you use the full-screen editor, you'll find that you want to issue the same command over and over. For example, you might want to scroll through a long member 15 lines at a time, but you don't want to have to key in

```
DOWN 15
```

for each scroll operation. Or, you might want to examine each occurrence of a particular text string in a member by repeatedly issuing the same LOCATE command.

It's easy to have ICCF repeat an editor command for you. All you have to do is key in an ampersand immediately before the command. Then, ICCF retains the command in the editor command area after it has processed it. All you have to do is press the enter key to issue it again.

For example, to scroll through a member 15 lines at a time, you'd enter this command:

```
&DOWN 15
```

As long as you don't enter another editor command, ICCF processes this DOWN command each time you press the enter key. When you've used this command all you want, just key another command over it or erase the editor command area.

How the full-screen editor interprets the data on the screen

One of the advantages of using the full-screen editor is that you can make more than one change at a time with it. Not only can you key in changes to each text line directly, but you can also enter an editor command and line commands at the same time. To do this effectively, though, you have to understand the sequence ICCF goes through as it evaluates the data from the full-screen editor each time you press the enter key.

The first thing ICCF does when it receives an editor screen is evaluate each line of the data display area for changes. If you did enter changes, they're made to the member you're editing immediately. As a result, if you use commands to copy or move lines that you've changed, realize that the altered, not the original, versions of those lines will be processed.

After ICCF has processed changes you made directly to the text, it processes any line commands you entered. First, all line commands except I are handled. Then, if you did specify any I commands, they're processed. That's why in figure 3-18 I was able to specify both a C command and an I command on the same screen. In that case, ICCF first copied the six lines I specified into the editor stack. Then, it inserted the contents of the stack at the position I indicated with the I command. (The fact that the I command is on a line after the one that contains the C command in figure 3-18 is irrelevant.)

Finally, commands in the editor command area are processed. Keep that in mind if you combine line commands and editor commands on the same screen; the results of the editor command can be affected by the processing ICCF did to satisfy the line commands. Usually, this isn't a problem, and if it is, it's immediately apparent what the difficulty is.

DISCUSSION

The best way to learn the ICCF editing commands is to use them. Once you've used a few, they'll all come easily to you. To enter and edit text, you can certainly get by with the commands you've learned in this topic. However, to take advantage of the power of the full-screen editor, you'll want to learn some of the more advanced features it offers. For example, it's common to set up PF keys to make editor functions like scrolling easier. You'll learn how to do that and how to use a variety of other editor features in the next chapter.

Terminology

full-screen editor
context editor
edit mode
sub-mode
edit sub-mode
current line
line pointer
input sub-mode
full-screen edit sub-mode
macro
scale line
data display area
type I/II command area
editor command area
type I command
type II command
editor command
type III command area
line command area
type III command
line command
scroll
editor stack

Objectives

1. Describe the relationship between the context editor and the full-screen editor and explain why you're better off using the full-screen editor when you're working at a 3270-type terminal.

2. Invoke the full-screen editor to edit either the input area or a library member.

3. Describe the format of the full-screen editor screen and the function of each screen area.

4. Use the full-screen editor commands this topic presented to:
    a. add and delete lines from a member
    b. scroll text
    c. find text
    d. copy and move lines
    e. store and retrieve library members
    f. end an editor session

5. Describe the commands you would use to edit the contents of a library member indirectly through the input area.

6. Describe how to use repeating full-screen editor commands.

7. Describe the steps ICCF goes through as it analyzes a screen of data from the full-screen editor and explain how changes you make and commands you enter can affect other changes and commands.

Chapter 4

Advanced editor commands

This chapter describes advanced full-screen editor commands you may want to use. Each of this chapter's topics is independent of the others, so you can read them in any order you like.

Topic 1 shows you how to use commands for locating and changing text strings. Topic 2 teaches you how to use ICCF commands to control the way a variety of keyboard operations work. Topic 3 presents commands that let you tailor the way your editor display is organized. Topic 4 shows you how to use ICCF's split-screen facility to edit multiple parts of the same member at one time or to edit different members at the same time. Finally, topic 5 presents a few other commands that you may find useful.

This chapter presents most of the commands you can use in the editor, but it doesn't present all of them. However, if you read each of this chapter's topics, you'll learn how to use all of the important editor features; the commands I don't cover are superseded by other more powerful or all-inclusive commands or aren't particularly useful at all.

TOPIC 1 Editor commands for finding and changing text

In this topic, you'll learn how to use all of the ICCF commands to find text. You're already familiar with the basic functions of the SEARCH and LOCATE commands. Now, you'll learn how to use all of their features. In addition, you'll learn how to use the FIND command and two specialized variations of the LOCATE command: the LOCUP and LOCNOT commands. Then, you'll learn how to use the CHANGE command to change multiple occurrences of text strings throughout a member. Finally, you'll learn how to use the ALTER command to enter hexadecimal values for non-printable characters, a function you might have to use on occasion.

Commands for finding text

In this section, I'll show you how to issue commands to locate text strings in the member you're editing; figure 4-1 lists the commands this section presents. In my examples, I'll use the partial COBOL program in figure 4-2. Although you really don't need to use commands to find text in a library member that's this short, it's a good example to show you how the commands work. And it's a realistic example; typical ICCF users spend most of their time working on library members that contain this sort of text.

Basic forms of the LOCATE and SEARCH commands   In the last chapter, you learned how to use basic forms of the LOCATE and SEARCH commands. You should recall that all you have to do to find a text string with one of these commands is to enter the command followed by the text string itself.

For example, suppose you enter the full-screen editor, copy the text in figure 4-2 from a library member into your input area, and enter the TOP command to position the current line pointer at the top of the text. Then, the editor display looks like the screen in the top section of figure 4-3. If you want to go directly to the program's Procedure Division, you could enter either

```
LOCATE PROCEDURE DIVISION
```

or

```
SEARCH PROCEDURE DIVISION
```

The LOCATE, SEARCH, FIND, LOCUP, and LOCNOT commands

```
LOCATE   text
SEARCH   text
FIND     text
LOCUP    text
LOCNOT   text
```

Explanation

text
                          The text string on which the operation will be based. May be bound by
                          delimiter characters for any of these commands except FIND.

Figure 4-1   Commands to find text

After the editor has processed either of these commands, the display looks like the screen in the bottom section of the figure. Here, the current line pointer is at the line that contains the Procedure Division header.

The difference between these two commands is that LOCATE looks forward from your current position, while SEARCH looks forward from the beginning of the text. In figure 4-3, either command would have produced the same result since the current line pointer was at the top of the member when the command was issued.

However, if the current line pointer was already somewhere in the program's Procedure Division, the LOCATE command would not find the division header. Instead, after looking through the remaining lines in the member and not finding the string, the message

```
*EOF
```

would be displayed in the editor scale line, and your current position would be set at the end of the member. (A special case, however, is if your current position is at the end of a member; when that's so, the LOCATE command starts its search at the beginning of the member, just like SEARCH.) On the other hand, the SEARCH command would still find the division header; it would cause your position to be moved *up* in the member.

If you know that the text string you want to find is below your current position, then you should use the LOCATE command. That way, ICCF doesn't have to examine all the lines above your current position for the string you specified. That's why LOCATE is faster and more efficient than SEARCH in the right situation.

```
IDENTIFICATION DIVISION.                                              SUPDATE
*                                                                     SUPDATE
 PROGRAM-ID.   SUPDATE.                                               SUPDATE
*                                                                     SUPDATE
 ENVIRONMENT DIVISION.                                                SUPDATE
*                                                                     SUPDATE
 CONFIGURATION SECTION.                                               SUPDATE
*                                                                     SUPDATE
 SOURCE-COMPUTER.   IBM-370.                                          SUPDATE
 OBJECT-COMPUTER.   IBM-370.                                          SUPDATE
*                                                                     SUPDATE
 INPUT-OUTPUT SECTION.                                                SUPDATE
*                                                                     SUPDATE
 FILE-CONTROL.                                                        SUPDATE
*                                                                     SUPDATE
     SELECT VALTRAN   ASSIGN TO SYS020-AS-VALTRAN                     SUPDATE
                      ORGANIZATION IS SEQUENTIAL                      SUPDATE
                      FILE STATUS IS VALTRAN-STATUS.                  SUPDATE
     SELECT OLDMAST   ASSIGN TO SYS020-AS-OLDMAST                     SUPDATE
                      ORGANIZATION IS SEQUENTIAL                      SUPDATE
                      FILE STATUS IS OLDMAST-STATUS.                  SUPDATE
     SELECT NEWMAST   ASSIGN TO SYS020-AS-NEWMAST                     SUPDATE
                      ORGANIZATION IS SEQUENTIAL                      SUPDATE
                      FILE STATUS IS NEWMAST-STATUS.                  SUPDATE
*                                                                     SUPDATE
 DATA DIVISION.                                                       SUPDATE
*                                                                     SUPDATE
 FILE SECTION.                                                        SUPDATE
*                                                                     SUPDATE
 FD  VALTRAN                                                          SUPDATE
     LABEL RECORDS ARE STANDARD                                       SUPDATE
     RECORD CONTAINS 88 CHARACTERS.                                   SUPDATE
*                                                                     SUPDATE
 01  VALTRAN-RECORD                  PIC X(88).                       SUPDATE
*                                                                     SUPDATE
 FD  OLDMAST                                                          SUPDATE
     LABEL RECORDS ARE STANDARD                                       SUPDATE
     RECORD CONTAINS 256 CHARACTERS.                                  SUPDATE
*                                                                     SUPDATE
 01  OM-AREA                         PIC X(256).                      SUPDATE
*                                                                     SUPDATE
 FD  NEWMAST                                                          SUPDATE
     LABEL RECORDS ARE STANDARD                                       SUPDATE
     RECORD CONTAINS 256 CHARACTERS.                                  SUPDATE
*                                                                     SUPDATE
 01  NM-AREA                         PIC X(256).                      SUPDATE
*                                                                     SUPDATE
```

Figure 4-2   Sample COBOL source program (part 1 of 2)

```
WORKING-STORAGE SECTION.                                     SUPDATE
*                                                            SUPDATE
01   SWITCHES.                                               SUPDATE
*                                                            SUPDATE
     05   ALL-RECORDS-PROCESSED-SW    PIC X     VALUE "N".   SUPDATE
          88   ALL-RECORDS-PROCESSED            VALUE "Y".   SUPDATE
     05   NEED-TRANSACTION-SW         PIC X     VALUE "Y".   SUPDATE
          88   NEED-TRANSACTION                 VALUE "Y".   SUPDATE
     05   NEED-MASTER-SW              PIC X     VALUE "Y".   SUPDATE
          88   NEED-MASTER                      VALUE "Y".   SUPDATE
     05   VALID-TRANS-SW              PIC X     VALUE "Y".   SUPDATE
          88   VALID-TRANS                      VALUE "Y".   SUPDATE
*                                                            SUPDATE
        ^                                                    SUPDATE
        ^                                                    SUPDATE
        ^                                                    SUPDATE
*                                                            SUPDATE
PROCEDURE DIVISION.                                          SUPDATE
*                                                            SUPDATE
000-UPDATE-CUSTOMER-FILE.                                    SUPDATE
*                                                            SUPDATE
     OPEN INPUT   VALTRAN                                    SUPDATE
                  OLDMAST                                    SUPDATE
          OUTPUT NEWMAST.                                    SUPDATE
     PERFORM 100-UPDATE-CUSTOMER-MASTER                      SUPDATE
          UNTIL ALL-RECORDS-PROCESSED.                       SUPDATE
     PERFORM 300-PRINT-TOTAL-LINES.                          SUPDATE
     CLOSE VALTRAN                                           SUPDATE
           OLDMAST                                           SUPDATE
           NEWMAST.                                          SUPDATE
     STOP RUN.                                               SUPDATE
*                                                            SUPDATE
100-UPDATE-CUSTOMER-MASTER.                                  SUPDATE
*                                                            SUPDATE
     IF NEED-TRANSACTION                                     SUPDATE
        MOVE SPACE TO UPDATE-LINE                            SUPDATE
        PERFORM 110-READ-AR-TRANSACTION                      SUPDATE
        MOVE "N" TO NEED-TRANSACTION-SW.                     SUPDATE
        ^                                                    SUPDATE
        ^                                                    SUPDATE
        ^                                                    SUPDATE
```

Figure 4-2   Sample COBOL source program (part 2 of 2)

**How to use the delimiter character with the LOCATE and SEARCH
commands**   If you want to search for a text string that includes one
or more right-most blanks, you can specify that by explicitly delimiting
the string, with its trailing blanks, between two slashes. For example,

SEARCH /NUMBER 3   /

```
===> LOCATE PROCEDURE DIVISION
<<...+....1....+....2....+....3....+....4....+....5....+.. INP=*INPARA*>>..+..FS
***** TOP OF FILE *****                                                  /***/
       IDENTIFICATION DIVISION.                                          *====*
     *                                                                   *====*
       PROGRAM-ID.  SUPDATE.                                             *====*
     *                                                                   *====*
       ENVIRONMENT DIVISION.                                             *====*
     *                                                                   *====*
       CONFIGURATION SECTION.                                            *====*
     *                                                                   *====*
       SOURCE-COMPUTER.  IBM-370.                                        *====*
       OBJECT-COMPUTER.  IBM-370.                                        *====*
     *                                                                   *====*
       INPUT-OUTPUT SECTION.                                             *====*
     *                                                                   *====*
       FILE-CONTROL.                                                     *====*
     *                                                                   *====*
           SELECT VALTRAN   ASSIGN TO SYS020-AS-VALTRAN                  *====*
                            ORGANIZATION IS SEQUENTIAL                   *====*
                            FILE STATUS IS VALTRAN-STATUS.               *====*
           SELECT OLDMAST   ASSIGN TO SYS020-AS-OLDMAST                  *====*
                            ORGANIZATION IS SEQUENTIAL                   *====*
                            FILE STATUS IS OLDMAST-STATUS.               *====*
 I^                                                      □-□04
```

```
===>
<<...+....1....+....2....+....3....+....4....+....5....+.. INP=*INPARA*>>..+..FS
       PROCEDURE DIVISION.                                               /===/*
     *                                                                   *====*
       000-UPDATE-CUSTOMER-FILE.                                         *====*
     *                                                                   *====*
           OPEN INPUT   VALTRAN                                          *====*
                        OLDMAST                                          *====*
                OUTPUT NEWMAST.                                          *====*
           PERFORM 100-UPDATE-CUSTOMER-MASTER                            *====*
               UNTIL ALL-RECORDS-PROCESSED.                              *====*
           PERFORM 300-PRINT-TOTAL-LINES.                                *====*
           CLOSE VALTRAN                                                 *====*
                 OLDMAST                                                 *====*
                 NEWMAST.                                                *====*
           STOP RUN.                                                     *====*
     *                                                                   *====*
       100-UPDATE-CUSTOMER-MASTER.                                       *====*
     *                                                                   *====*
           IF NEED-TRANSACTION                                           *====*
               MOVE SPACE TO UPDATE-LINE                                 *====*
               PERFORM 110-READ-AR-TRANSACTION                           *====*
               MOVE "N" TO NEED-TRANSACTION-SW.                          *====*
                                                                        *====*
 I^                                                      □-□04
```

Figure 4-3   How to use the LOCATE command

causes ICCF to search for the string NUMBER 3, including five trailing blanks. In this case, the string

```
NUMBER 3   NUMBER 4
```

would not satisfy the search because only three blanks follow NUMBER3, but the string

```
NUMBER 3     NUMBER 4
```

would. The slash in the SEARCH command above is the *delimiter character*. In other words, it's the character that's used to delimit the text string explicitly.

The default delimiter character is the slash. As a result, if you want to search for a text string that includes a slash, you have to change the delimiter character to something else. You can do that by issuing the DELIM command, whose only operand is the character you want to use as the new delimiter. The delimiter must be a special character other than the comma, the left parenthesis, or the right parenthesis.

For example, suppose you wanted to find the next line (from your current position) in a library member that contains a JCL statement. The easiest way to find a JCL statement is to issue a LOCATE command for a line that contains two slashes followed by a space (//). To do that, though, you need to change the delimiter character to some character other than a slash. So, I might issue the command

```
DELIM $
```

to change the delimiter character to a dollar sign, then issue this LOCATE command

```
LOCATE $// $
```

In this case, the dollar sign remains the delimiter character until I change it again by issuing another DELIM command.

If you don't remember what the current delimiter character is, you can enter the command

```
SHOW
```

Then, ICCF displays current settings, as in figure 4-4. Among them is the delimiter character, which is shaded in the figure. To return to the editor display from this screen, you simply press the enter key.

How to use column suffixes with the LOCATE and SEARCH commands   Some ICCF editor commands, including SEARCH and LOCATE, let you append a *column suffix* to them to specify a narrower area of each line in which they're to operate. To specify a column suffix, you enter Cnn (where nn is the number of the column where the operation is to begin) immediately after the command name with no intervening spaces. After the column suffix, enter a space and the operand.

Editor command: SHOW

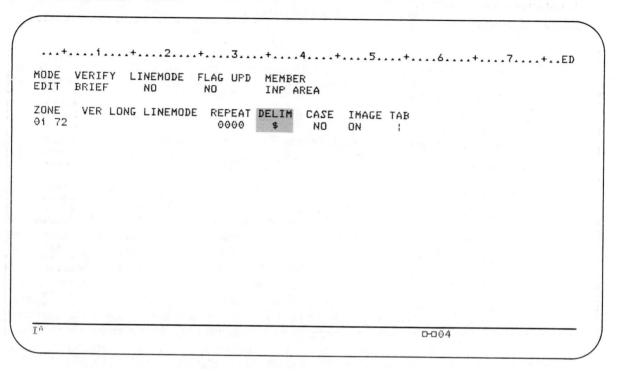

```
 ...+....1....+....2....+....3....+....4....+....5....+....6....+....7....+..ED
MODE   VERIFY   LINEMODE   FLAG UPD   MEMBER
EDIT   BRIEF      NO         NO       INP AREA

ZONE   VER LONG LINEMODE   REPEAT   DELIM   CASE   IMAGE TAB
01 72                       0000      $      NO      ON   ¦
```

```
IA                                                              D-004
```

Figure 4-4   Sample output of the SHOW command, including the current delimiter character

For example, you could enter

SEARCH C16 88

to locate the first occurrence of the text string 88 that begins in *or after* column 16 of a line. Here, the column suffix removes columns 1 through 15 from the part of each line the command evaluates. For example, I might enter this command to try to find the first condition name (88-level item) in my COBOL program. In the sample library member I'm using in this topic, the result of this command is the display in figure 4-5. As you can see, this command did locate the first occurrence of the text string 88 in the member, but it wasn't the occurrence I really wanted: the characters 88 begin in column 28, not column 16. Assuming that all condition names in my program begin in column 16, I should have used the FIND command to force a column-dependent search.

Editor command: SEARCHC16 88

```
===>
<<..+....1....+....2....+....3....+....4....+....5....+.. INP=*INPARA*>>..+..FS
           RECORD CONTAINS 88 CHARACTERS.                          /===/*
      *                                                            *===*
      01   VALTRAN-RECORD              PIC X(88).                  *===*
      *                                                            *===*
      FD   OLDMAST                                                 *===*
           LABEL RECORDS ARE STANDARD                              *===*
           RECORD CONTAINS 256 CHARACTERS.                         *===*
                                                                   *===*
      01   OM-AREA                      PIC X(256).                *===*
      *                                                            *===*
      FD   NEWMAST                                                 *===*
           LABEL RECORDS ARE STANDARD                              *===*
           RECORD CONTAINS 256 CHARACTERS.                         *===*
                                                                   *===*
      01   NM-AREA                      PIC X(256).                *===*
      *                                                            *===*
      WORKING-STORAGE SECTION.                                     *===*
      *                                                            *===*
      01   SWITCHES.                                               *===*
      *                                                            *===*
           05   ALL-RECORDS-PROCESSED-SW   PIC X      VALUE "N".   *===*
                88   ALL-RECORDS-PROCESSED            VALUE "Y".   *===*
 I^                                                  □-□04
```

Figure 4-5   Result of a SEARCH operation with a column suffix

How to force a column-dependent search: the FIND command   If you want to force a search that requires the text you specify to occur in specific columns (rather than in or after a particular column), you can use the FIND command. For example, the command

    FINDC16 88

would result in the display in figure 4-6. Now, the current line *is* the first line that contains an 88-level item. Although the characters 88 occurred earlier in the member in the RECORD CONTAINS clause, that line didn't satisfy the search because the characters 88 weren't in the specified columns.

When you use the FIND command without a column suffix, ICCF assumes you entered column 1. As a result, the command

    FIND 88

would cause ICCF to look for the string 88 in columns 1 and 2 of the source member. And it's almost certain that's not what you'd be looking for. So you'll almost always use the column suffix with the FIND command.

Editor command: FINDC16 88

```
===>
<<...+....1....+....2....+....3....+....4....+....5....+.. INP=*INPARA*>>..+..FS
            88  ALL-RECORDS-PROCESSED              VALUE "Y".        /===/*
        05  NEED-TRANSACTION-SW          PIC X     VALUE "Y".        *====*
            88  NEED-TRANSACTION                    VALUE "Y".        *====*
        05  NEED-MASTER-SW               PIC X     VALUE "Y".        *====*
            88  NEED-MASTER                         VALUE "Y".        *====*
        05  VALID-TRANS-SW               PIC X     VALUE "Y".        *====*
            88  VALID-TRANS                         VALUE "Y".        *====*
     *        '                                                       *====*
              .                                                       *====*
              .                                                       *====*
              .                                                       *====*
     *                                                                *====*
     PROCEDURE DIVISION.                                              *====*
     *                                                                *====*
     000-UPDATE-CUSTOMER-FILE.                                        *====*
     *                                                                *====*
         OPEN INPUT  VALTRAN                                          *====*
                     OLDMAST                                          *====*
                OUTPUT NEWMAST.                                       *====*
         PERFORM 100-UPDATE-CUSTOMER-MASTER                           *====*
             UNTIL ALL-RECORDS-PROCESSED.                             *====*
         PERFORM 300-PRINT-TOTAL-LINES.                               *====*
 I^                                              □-□0̣4
```

Figure 4-6   Result of a FIND operation with a column suffix

You have to be precise when you use the FIND command. You must separate the command (including its column suffix) from the search string by *one* space; any additional spaces are considered to be part of the string. Also, you need to realize that the FIND command treats blanks in the text string you supply differently than LOCATE and SEARCH do. When FIND encounters a blank in your search string, it accepts any character, not just a blank, in that position. For example, if you enter

        FIND   88

(where two blanks separate the operation code from the string), ICCF looks for the first line with 8's in columns 2 and 3, regardless of what the character in column 1 is.

You should also realize that the FIND command works forward from the current position in the library member, like LOCATE; there's no variation of the FIND command that parallels the SEARCH command. As a result, if you want to find the first occurrence of a text string in a specific column position, first issue the TOP command, then follow it with the FIND command. (By the way, the same technique works for LOCATE; you can forget the SEARCH command altogether if you're always willing to precede a LOCATE command with a TOP command when you want to search a library member from the beginning.)

The LOCUP and LOCNOT commands   ICCF includes two other commands that are variations of LOCATE: LOCUP and LOCNOT. LOCUP, like LOCATE, works from the current position in the library member to find the first occurrence of the string you specify. It's different, though, because it works *up* (backward) in the library member instead of down (forward). In the example in this topic, you might use the command

```
LOCUP PROCEDURE DIVISION
```

to move to the start of the Procedure Division when you're editing within the Procedure Division of the program.

Unlike LOCATE and LOCUP, which look for the first line that contains an occurrence of the string you specify, LOCNOT looks for the first line that does *not* contain the string you specify. Although LOCNOT can be useful in some circumstances, I suspect you won't use it very often.

Commands for changing text

The basic way to change text using the full-screen editor is to find the line you're interested in, then key in your change over the existing data. If you only want to change a single occurrence of a text string in a library member, that's almost certainly what you'll do.

However, there will be times when you'll want to make *global changes*. In other words, you'll want to change all occurrences of a particular text string to another value throughout a library member. In this section, I'll show you how to use the CHANGE command to do that. Also, I'll show you how to use the ALTER command to enter characters that aren't printable by specifying their hexadecimal values.

As you can see in figure 4-7, the CHANGE and ALTER commands have similar formats. They differ in that CHANGE lets you substitute one text string for another, while ALTER lets you substitute one character for another. Because you can specify a single character text string on the CHANGE command, their functions overlap. However, CHANGE doesn't let you use hexadecimal values for non-printable characters. As a result, if you need to enter a literal value in hexadecimal, you'll have to use ALTER.

How to make global changes: the CHANGE command   As you can imagine, making global changes explicitly one by one can be a cumbersome, tiring, and error-prone process. You can miss an occurrence of the text string you want to change, or you can make a keying error on one of the changes. When you use the CHANGE command, you don't have to worry about those potential mistakes.

The CHANGE and ALTER commands

```
CHANGE  /old-text/new-text/  [n|*]  [G]
ALTER    old-char new-char   [n|*]  [G]
```

Explanation

/	The current delimiter character, usually a slash by default.
old-text	The text string to be changed.
new-text	The text that will replace old-text. If you omit a value for new-text and code the second and third delimiters next to each other, the result is that old-text is deleted from the line.
old-char	The character to be changed; may be either a single character or the two-digit hexadecimal equivalent of a character.
new-char	The character that will replace old-char; may be either a single character or the two-digit hexadecimal equivalent of a character. If you omit a value for new-char and code the second and third delimiters next to each other, the result is that old-char is deleted from the line.
n	The number of lines from the current position to be searched for old-text or old-char.
*	Specifies that all lines from the current position to the end of the member should be searched for old-text or old-char.
G	Specifies that all occurrences of old-text or old-char in searched lines should be replaced with new-text or new-char. If you omit G, only the first occurrence in the zone will be changed.

Figure 4-7   Commands to change text

Suppose I want to change the name of the file VALTRAN in the member in figure 4-2 to VT1. I can issue a series of LOCATE commands for the string VALTRAN, then key in VT1 over the original name in each line and delete the remaining four characters. However, it's easier to issue this command:

```
CHANGE /VALTRAN/VT1/ * G
```

Here, I specified the original and new strings between delimiters. Then, I entered both of the additional operands available with the command. The asterisk means that all lines that follow the current line in the member should be examined for the specified string (VALTRAN).

Instead of the asterisk, you can specify a number of lines to be searched for the original string. For example,

```
CHANGE /VALTRAN/VT1/ 100 G
```

would cause ICCF to examine only 100 lines beginning with the current line, regardless of how many lines the member contains. If you omit both the asterisk and an explicit number of lines, ICCF defaults to 1, and only the current line is examined. If that's what you want to do, you're better off just to key in the new text over the original text in the current line. To make global changes, you should always enter the asterisk on the CHANGE command, and you should always make sure the current line is before the first occurrence of the string you want to change (or, even safer, at the top of the member).

The G operand indicates that if multiple occurrences of the string you specify occur in a single line, all of them should be changed to the new value. If you don't enter G and a line does contain multiple occurrences of the original string, only its first occurrence in the line will be changed.

How to enter hexadecimal values for non-printable characters: the ALTER command   You're also likely to find times when you want to enter a value that doesn't have a printable character equivalent. ICCF lets you enter non-printable values by using the ALTER command to change one character to another, either of which can be specified in hexadecimal or character format.

For example, part 1 of figure 4-8 is part of a COBOL program that will be used in a CICS system to produce printed output on a terminal printer. This program's output must include a printer new-line character, which is hex 15: a value that doesn't have a printable equivalent.

To get around this problem, I used the ALTER command. First, I entered the text as you see it in part 1 of the figure. In the 05-level item IL-NL, which has to have a value of hex 15, I specified a value of &. Just what that value is doesn't matter at this point (as long as it's unique within the line) because I'm going to change it with the ALTER command.

As you can see in part 1 of the figure, I entered the line command / to make the line that contains IL-NL the current line. Then, in part 2, I entered the command

```
ALTER & 15
```

to change the character & to the hex value 15.

Part 3 of the figure shows the display after the ALTER command was processed. Now, the VALUE clause for IL-NL contains a broken vertical bar. That's what the editor displays when a position contains a non-printable character.

Part 4 of the figure isn't part of the full-screen editor's display. Instead, it's output from the /LISTX command for the text I entered. As you can see, the value of the byte I changed is indeed hex 15. (In the character section of the /LISTX output, the byte whose value is hex 15 is shown with a period; the ICCF list commands use a period to indicate a non-displayable value.)

```
===>
<<..+....1....+....2....+....3....+....4....+....5....+.. INP=*INPARA*>>..+..FS
        01   INVENTORY-LINE.                                              /===/*
        *                                                                 *===*
            05   IL-ITEM-NUMBER      PIC 9(5).                            *===*
            05   FILLER              PIC X(3)         VALUE SPACE.         *===*
            05   IL-ITEM-DESCRIPTION PIC X(20).                           *===*
            05   FILLER              PIC X(3)         VALUE SPACE.         *===*
            05   IL-UNIT-PRICE       PIC ZZ,ZZ9.99.                       *===*
            05   FILLER              PIC X(4)         VALUE SPACE.         *===*
            05   IL-ON-HAND-QUANTITY PIC ZZ,ZZ9.                          *===*
            05   IL-NL               PIC X            VALUE '&'.          /===*
        *                                                                 *===*
        01   INVENTORY-MASTER-RECORD.                                     *===*
        *                                                                 *===*
            05   IM-ITEM-NUMBER      PIC X(5).                            *===*
            05   IM-ITEM-DESCRIPTION PIC X(20).                           *===*
            05   IM-UNIT-PRICE       PIC S9(5)V99     COMP-3.             *===*
            05   IM-ON-HAND-QUANTITY PIC S9(5)        COMP-3.             *===*
        *                                                                 *===*
        PROCEDURE DIVISION.                                               *===*
        *                                                                 *===*
        0000-PRODUCE-INVENTORY-LISTING SECTION.                           *===*
        *                                                                 *===*
 I^                                                    D-004
```

Figure 4-8   How to use the ALTER command (part 1 of 4)

```
===> ALTER & 15
<<..+....1....+....2....+....3....+....4....+....5....+.. INP=*INPARA*>>..+..FS
            05   IL-NL               PIC X            VALUE '&'.          /===/*
        *                                                                 *===*
        01   INVENTORY-MASTER-RECORD.                                     *===*
        *                                                                 *===*
            05   IM-ITEM-NUMBER      PIC X(5).                            *===*
            05   IM-ITEM-DESCRIPTION PIC X(20).                           *===*
            05   IM-UNIT-PRICE       PIC S9(5)V99     COMP-3.             *===*
            05   IM-ON-HAND-QUANTITY PIC S9(5)        COMP-3.             *===*
        *                                                                 *===*
        PROCEDURE DIVISION.                                               *===*
        *                                                                 *===*
        0000-PRODUCE-INVENTORY-LISTING SECTION.                           *===*
        *                                                                 *===*
            PERFORM 1000-START-INVENTORY-BROWSE.                          *===*
            EXEC CICS                                                     *===*
                HANDLE CONDITION ENDFILE(2100-ENDFILE)                    *===*
            END-EXEC.                                                     *===*
            PERFORM 2000-PRODUCE-INVENTORY-LINE                           *===*
                UNTIL INVMAST-EOF.                                        *===*
            PERFORM 3000-SEND-TOTAL-LINE.                                 *===*
            EXEC CICS                                                     *===*
                SEND PAGE                                                 *===*
 I^                                                    D-004
```

Figure 4-8   How to use the ALTER command (part 2 of 4)

```
===)
<<..+....1....+....2....+....3....+....4....+....5....+.. INP=*INPARA*>>..+..FS
            05   IL-NL                PIC X              VALUE ' '.        /===/*
      *                                                                    *===*
      01   INVENTORY-MASTER-RECORD.                                        *===*
      *'                                                                   *===*
            05   IM-ITEM-NUMBER        PIC X(5).                           *===*
            05   IM-ITEM-DESCRIPTION   PIC X(20).                          *===*
            05   IM-UNIT-PRICE         PIC S9(5)V99      COMP-3.           *===*
            05   IM-ON-HAND-QUANTITY   PIC S9(5)         COMP-3.           *===*
      *                                                                    *===*
      PROCEDURE DIVISION.                                                  *===*
      *                                                                    *===*
      0000-PRODUCE-INVENTORY-LISTING SECTION.                             *===*
      *                                                                    *===*
            PERFORM 1000-START-INVENTORY-BROWSE.                          *===*
            EXEC CICS                                                      *===*
                HANDLE CONDITION ENDFILE(2100-ENDFILE)                    *===*
            END-EXEC.                                                      *===*
            PERFORM 2000-PRODUCE-INVENTORY-LINE                           *===*
                UNTIL INVMAST-EOF.                                         *===*
            PERFORM 3000-SEND-TOTAL-LINE.                                  *===*
            EXEC CICS                                                      *===*
                SEND PAGE                                                  *===*
I^                                                        □-□04
```

Figure 4-8   How to use the ALTER command (part 3 of 4)

System command: /LISTX

```
....+....1....+....2....+....3....+....4....+....5....+....6....+....7....+..LS
            05   FILLER               PIC X(3)          VALUE SPACE.
44444444444FF44CCDDCD444444444444444DCC4E4F544444444ECDEC4EDCCC4444444444444444
00000000000050069335900000000000000079307D3D0000000005134502713 5B0000000000000000
            05   IL-UNIT-PRICE        PIC ZZ,ZZ9.99.
44444444444FF44CD6EDCE6DDCCC44444444DCC4EE6EEF4FF4444444444444444444444444444444
00000000000050093045930799350000000079309 9B999B99B000000000000000000000000000000
            05   FILLER               PIC X(4)          VALUE SPACE.
44444444444FF44CCDDCD444444444444444DCC4E4F544444444ECDEC4EDCCC4444444444444444
00000000000050069335900000000000000079307D4D0000000005134502713 5B0000000000000000
            05   IL-ON-HAND-QUANTITY  PIC ZZ,ZZ9.
44444444444FF44CD6DD6CCDC6DECDECEE44DCC4EE6EEF4444444444444444444444444444444444
00000000000050093065081540841539380079309 9B999B00000000000000000000000000000000
            05   IL-NL                PIC X             VALUE '.'.
44444444444FF44CD6DD44444444444444444DCC4E44444444444ECDEC4717444444444444444444
00000000000050093053000000000000000079307000000000000513450D5DB00000000000000000
      *
44444454444444444444444444444444444444444444444444444444444444444444444444444444
000000C00000000000000000000000000000000000000000000000000000000000000000000000000
      01   INVENTORY-MASTER-RECORD.
4444444FF44CDECDEDDE6DCEECD6DCCDDC4444444444444444444444444444444444444444444444
000000001009555536980412359095369 4B00000000000000000000000000000000000000000000000
I^                                                        □-□04
```

Figure 4-8   How to use the ALTER command (part 4 of 4)

When you issue the ALTER command, you can also specify the number of lines through which the command should search and whether all occurrences of the character you specify or just the first occurrence in each line should be changed. However, since you'll use ALTER only for special cases, I suspect you'll be more likely to work on one line and one character at a time, as I did in this example.

By the way, there is one peculiarity of editing lines that contain hex characters you need to be aware of. If you edit a line that contains a hex character and you cause the text to be shifted by using the 3270 delete or insert keys, it's likely that the hex value will be replaced by some other character. As a result, be particularly careful when you edit a line that contains a hex character; you may have to enter the hex character again.

Terminology

delimiter character
column suffix
global change

Objectives

1. Use the LOCATE, SEARCH, FIND, LOCUP, or LOCNOT command, as appropriate, to find a text string in a member.

2. Use the CHANGE command to make a global change in a member.

3. Use the ALTER command to enter a non-printable hex character in a member.

TOPIC 2   Editor commands for controlling keyboard functions

This topic presents several ICCF commands and features you can use to tailor your terminal's keyboard functions. Specifically, you'll learn the concepts and commands you need to know to (1) use tabs and control the cursor, (2) set and use program functions keys, and (3) enter both upper and lower case text.

HOW TO USE TABS AND CONTROL THE CURSOR

Much of the data you enter through ICCF will have a rigid format with standard indentation. An excellent example is a COBOL source program, in which comments must be indicated in column 7, paragraph names must begin in column 8, and statements must begin in column 12 or beyond. And within the program, standard indentation is often used to make the program more readable. Although you can always key in spaces wherever you want text to be indented, it's usually easier to use ICCF's tabbing and cursor control features. That's what this section presents.

Tabbing

If you're used to using a typewriter, you know that the usual way for the tab key to work is to move the carriage to a preset position where you can enter text. For data-entry operations with many fields, the *hardware tabbing* feature of a 3270-type terminal works the same way: it moves the cursor to the start of the next modifiable field on the screen.

However, the way the ICCF full-screen editor screen is formatted, 3270 hardware tabbing isn't particularly useful. That's because there are only two modifiable fields in most of the lines of the editor's display: the part in the data display area and the part in the line command area. As a result, if you press the tab key on your 3270 terminal repeatedly when you're using the full-screen editor, the cursor jumps from column 1 of the first line in the data display area to the line command area in that line, then to column 1 of the second line in the data display area, and so on.

Unfortunately, the kind of tabbing you want to do when you're editing a member is confined to the data display area. Because 3270 hardware tabbing skips over the data display area, you might want to use another feature ICCF provides to let you move to tab positions within a line in the display area: *logical tabbing*.

The TABSET command

$$TABSET \begin{Bmatrix} n \ . \ . \ . \\ ASSEMBLER \\ BASIC \\ COBOL \\ FORTRAN \\ PL1 \\ PLI \\ RPG \\ TENS \\ OFF \\ CLEAR \end{Bmatrix}$$

Explanation

n . . .	Column positions for tab stops.
ASSEMBLER	Sets tab stops at 10, 16, 36, 72, and 73.
BASIC	Sets tab stops at 10, 20, 30, 40, 50, and 60.
COBOL	Sets tab stops at 8, 12, 16, 20, 24, 28, 32, 36, 40, 44, and 73.
FORTRAN	Sets tab stops at 7 and 73.
PL1 PLI	Sets tab stops at 5, 10, 15, 20, 25, 30, 35, 40, 45, and 50.
RPG	Sets tab stops at 6, 20, 30, 40, 50, and 60.
TENS	Sets tab stops at 10, 20, 30, 40, 50, 60, and 70.
OFF CLEAR	Clears all tab stops.

Figure 4-9   The TABSET command

When you use logical tabbing, a special character is defined as the *logical tab character*. Then, whenever ICCF encounters that character in a line, it inserts enough spaces to move the characters that follow to the next tab stop. As a result, to use logical tabbing, you need to know how to do two things: (1) set logical tab stops and (2) specify the logical tab character.

How to set logical tab stops: the TABSET command   You set logical tab stops by issuing the TABSET command within the full-screen editor or the /TABSET system command in command mode. The format of the command is in figure 4-9. You can either specify the column positions of the tab stops you want or you can use one of the other options for a standard set of tab settings for a particular application.

For example, to set the tabs to edit a COBOL source program, I could enter either

```
TABSET COBOL
```

or

```
TABSET 8 12 16 20 24 28 32 36 40 44 73
```

If you want, you can issue the editor command

```
SHOW TABS
```

to display the current tab settings.

How to specify the logical tab character: the SET TAB command
The tab character can be any special character other than the comma, $, @, /, =, *, (, or). The default is for it to be the character generated when you press the *field-mark key* on your 3270 keyboard. (This character displays as a semicolon, but it has a different hexadecimal value.) If you want, you can use the SET command to change the logical tab character. For example, if you wanted to use the less-than sign (<) as the tab character, you'd enter

```
SET TAB=<
```

Then, whenever the full-screen editor encounters the less-than sign in a line, it moves the text that follows to the next tab position, as determined by the values you specified on the TABSET command.

If you want to find out what the current logical tab character is, you can issue either of these commands:

```
SHOW CHAR
```

or

```
SHOW TABCHAR
```

Figure 4-10 shows the output of these commands. Here, the logical tab character is the less-than sign (hex 4C). If the field-mark character were the logical tab character, the hex value would be 1E.

An example of logical tabbing   Figure 4-11 presents an example of how logical tabbing works. In the top section of the figure, I've keyed in the first lines of a COBOL program's Procedure Division using logical tab characters (which here are the character generated when you press the field-mark key). After I press the enter key, each logical tab character is replaced by enough spaces to move the text that follows to the next logical tab stop. Here, I used ICCF's tab settings for COBOL. However, because the first tab stop is set at 8, not 7, I had to key in leading spaces for the comment lines I coded (that is, the lines that contain an asterisk in column 7).

Editor command: SHOW CHAR or SHOW TABCHAR

```
....+....1....+....2....+....3....+....4....+....5....+....6....+....7....+..CM
D T B E E H
E A S N S E
L B   D C X

.  <  .  ¬  .  .
0 4 0 5 0 0
0 C 0 F 0 0
*READY




IA                                                    □-□04
```

Figure 4-10   How to find out what your current logical tab character is

Although logical tabbing can work well in some situations, it's usually difficult to align text properly when you use it. As a result, I think you're more likely to use other ICCF features that let you control the cursor.

Controlling the cursor

Even though the tab key on the 3270 keyboard doesn't provide you with the kind of control you need to move the cursor around within the data display area, you'll still use the cursor control keys heavily when you work with the editor. Figure 4-12 shows the cursor control keys I think you're most likely to use during an editor session. Although you will use these keys frequently, you need to remember that to the 3270, there's a difference between positions that contain spaces and positions that contain null characters.

Basic cursor control and the nulls option   Because one of the design objectives of the 3270 was to make telecommunication line use as efficient as possible, the system was planned so unnecessary characters aren't transmitted to and from the terminal. As a result, "empty" areas on the screen are considered to be just that: Their character positions are said to contain null characters, as I described in chapter 1. That can be a source of confusion for first-time 3270 users because null characters appear to be space characters, but they aren't.

Advanced editor commands   **119**

```
===>
<<..+....1....+....2....+....3....+....4....+....5....+.. INP=*INPARA*>>..+..FS
;PROCEDURE DIVISION.                                                    /===/*
      *                                                                 *===*
;000-UPDATE-CUSTOMER-FILE.                                              *===*
      *                                                                 *===*
;;OPEN INPUT   VALTRAN                                                  *===*
;;;;;OLDMAST                                                            *===*
;;; OUTPUT NEWMAST.                                                     *===*
;;PERFORM 100-UPDATE-CUSTOMER-MASTER                                    *===*
;;;UNTIL ALL-RECORDS-PROCESSED.                                         *===*
;;PERFORM 300-PRINT-TOTAL-LINES.                                        *===*
;;CLOSE VALTRAN                                                         *===*
;;;   OLDMAST                                                           *===*
;;;   NEWMAST.                                                          *===*
;;STOP RUN.                                                             *===*
***** END OF FILE *****                                                 ****
```

```
I^                                              □-□04
```

```
===>
<<..+....1....+....2....+....3....+....4....+....5....+.. INP=*INPARA*>>..+..FS
      PROCEDURE DIVISION.                                               /===/*
         *                                                              *===*
      000-UPDATE-CUSTOMER-FILE.                                         *===*
         *                                                              *===*
         OPEN INPUT   VALTRAN                                           *===*
                      OLDMAST                                           *===*
               OUTPUT NEWMAST.                                          *===*
         PERFORM 100-UPDATE-CUSTOMER-MASTER                             *===*
             UNTIL ALL-RECORDS-PROCESSED.                               *===*
         PERFORM 300-PRINT-TOTAL-LINES.                                 *===*
         CLOSE VALTRAN                                                  *===*
               OLDMAST                                                  *===*
               NEWMAST.                                                 *===*
         STOP RUN.                                                      *===*
***** END OF FILE *****                                                 ****
```

```
I^                                              □-□04
```

Figure 4-11   How to use logical tabbing

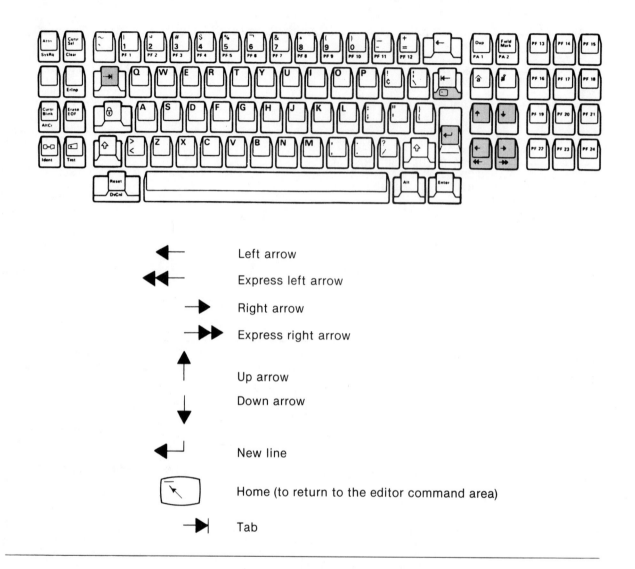

Figure 4-12 The most commonly used cursor-control keys

To understand the practical implications of this, consider figure 4-13. Here, I've keyed in the first lines of a COBOL program using the editor. To indent the lines, I used the cursor control keys to position the cursor at the correct column locations. However, take a look at what happened after I pressed the enter key and ICCF processed the text I entered. The only blank position in the lines I keyed in was between IDENTIFICATION and DIVISION. I didn't actually key in spaces in the other positions that appear to contain blanks, so they continued to contain null characters. As a result, when ICCF processed the screen, it shifted the text I entered to the left.

```
===>
<<..+....1....+....2....+....3....+....4....+....5....+.. INP=*INPARA*>>..+..FS
***** TOP OF FILE *****                                                  /***/
        IDENTIFICATION DIVISION.                                         *====*
      *                                                                  *====*
      PROGRAM-ID.       TSTPROG.                                         *====*
***** END OF FILE *****                                                  *****
```

```
I^
                                        ⌑⌑04
```

```
===>
<<..+....1....+....2....+....3....+....4....+....5....+.. INP=*INPARA*>>..+..FS
***** TOP OF FILE *****                                                  /***/
IDENTIFICATION DIVISION.                                                 *====*
*                                                                        *====*
PROGRAM-ID.TSTPROG.                                                      *====*
***** END OF FILE *****                                                  *****
```

```
I^
                                        ⌑⌑04
```

Figure 4-13   A possible result of using the cursor-control keys when the nulls option is on

There are two ways to avoid this kind of problem, and both solutions raise other problems. One way is to actually key in each embedded space where you want it. In the first line in figure 4-13, I would have keyed in seven spaces, then the text IDENTIFICATION DIVISION. Similarly, embedded spaces would have to be entered in the second and third lines too. Frankly, this isn't as cumbersome as it seems. You only have to hold the space bar down to cause it to produce repeated space characters in sequence. And, when you're editing a large library member (like a source program), many of the lines you'll use will be copied from other parts of the member or from other members. When that's the case, they'll already have embedded spaces in the right positions.

The alternative is to set the full-screen editor *nulls option* off. To do that, you issue this editor command:

```
SET NULLS OFF
```

Then, when ICCF sends data to the screen, all trailing positions in a line are filled with space characters. As you key in data, the characters you type replace spaces instead of nulls.

On first impression, this seems like the ideal way to handle this problem. However, when the nulls option is off, you can't use the insert feature of your 3270 terminal easily. That's because the insert feature depends on the presence of nulls—not spaces—at the end of a line. When null characters are present, as new characters are inserted in the middle of a line, characters to their right are shifted right, and the number of null characters at the end of the line decreases. When there are no more nulls left, inserts can't continue. Then, the keyboard locks, and you must press the reset key before you can continue work. But, if you enter insert mode in the editor when the nulls option is off and try to enter any character, the keyboard immediately locks because there are no trailing nulls at the end of the line.

To do inserts when the nulls option is off, you have to move the cursor to the end of the text in the line, press the ERASE EOF key to remove the trailing space characters; that explicitly makes those positions null. Then, you use the cursor control keys to move the cursor back to the position where you want to do the insert, you key in the data you want, and you press the enter key.

Which technique should you use? That depends on how you use the editor. If you're an excellent typist and you're entering mostly original material that will require little manipulation, I suggest you issue the SET NULLS OFF command and let ICCF pad each line with trailing spaces. (With this technique, you can use the CURSOR command to do tabbing, as I'll describe in a moment.) However, if you're not so good at typing, if telecommunications efficiency is a vital consideration, or if you'll be doing a lot of work that requires inserts in existing lines, I recommend you leave the full-screen editor default (NULLS ON) in effect, and live with keying in embedded spaces where you need them and, where it's appropriate, using logical tabbing.

The CURSOR command

CURSOR $\left\{\begin{array}{l}\text{CURRENT}\\\text{INPUT}\\\text{LINE [n]}\\\text{TABBACK [n]}\\\text{TABFORWARD [n]}\end{array}\right\}$

Explanation

CURRENT   Moves the cursor to the first column of the current line.

INPUT   Moves the cursor to the editor command line.

LINE [n]   Moves the cursor down n lines from its current position and positions it in the first column of that line. Will cause wrap-around if the value you specify for n is off the end of the screen. If you omit n, the default is 1.

TABBACK [n]   Moves the cursor backward n columns from its current position. If you omit n and tab stops have been set, the cursor is moved back to the preceding tab stop.

TABFORWARD [n]   Moves the cursor forward n columns from its current position. If you omit n and tab stops have been set, the cursor is moved forward to the next tab stop.

Figure 4-14   The CURSOR command

You should remember that you aren't tied to one setting for the nulls option for an entire editing session. You can turn the option on and off at will with the SET NULLS command to meet your immediate editing requirements.

Advanced cursor control and the CURSOR command   The CURSOR command lets you move the cursor anywhere on the screen from its current position. Usually, you'll define program function (PF) keys on your terminal to simulate tab functions by associating them with CURSOR commands. For example, you can specify that when you press a particular PF key, the cursor will move forward 12 positions. This would produce the same result as pressing the right arrow key 12 times.

Figure 4-14 gives the format of the CURSOR command. You probably won't use the INPUT option, because you can achieve the same result during a routine editing session by pressing the home key. The CURRENT, LINE, and TABBACK options might be useful in some instances, but the option I think you're most likely to use is TABFORWARD. With it, you can move the cursor to the right any number of character positions. Or, if you don't specify a number of positions for the cursor to be advanced and logical tab stops have been set, the command

```
CURSOR TABF
```

causes the cursor to move forward to the next tab stop. This feature lets you use tabbing in a way that's better suited for the 3270 than basic logical tabbing.

To be able to use the CURSOR command to do tabbing like this, the nulls option must be off, and the CURSOR command needs to be associated with a PF key. Then, whenever you press that PF key, the CURSOR command will move the cursor to the next tab stop. So now, I'll show you how to use PF keys.

HOW TO USE PROGRAM FUNCTION KEYS

As you learned in chapter 1, the program function keys (or PF keys) are attention keys you use to invoke pre-defined ICCF functions. Although a 3270 display station can have up to 24 PF keys, many have only 12. The PF keys are labelled PF1, PF2, and so on up to PF24. (You can look back to topic 1 of chapter 1 to review the functions keys on a typical 3270 keyboard.) When you use the editor you can associate editor commands with function keys to customize your terminal to your needs. (And, as you'll learn in the next chapter, you can associate system commands with PF keys for use in command, list, or execution mode.)

Depending on the release of ICCF you're using, the function keys may or may not invoke the same functions in all ICCF modes. If you're using a newer release of ICCF, there can be a different set of PF key assignments for command mode and edit mode (including the full-screen editor). However, for the information this chapter presents, this distinction isn't important.

How to set program function keys: the SET PFnn command   To set function keys for use within the full-screen editor, you issue the command

```
SET PFnn data
```

where nn is a number from 1 to 24 that identifies the function key you're defining and data is the command you want to associate with the key.

For example, the command

```
SET PF14 UP 15
```

tailors my terminal so that when I press the PF14 key, the full-screen editor will process the editor command UP, with 15 as the number of lines to be scrolled. As a result, I've specified that a key on my terminal will cause the text being edited to be scrolled up 15 lines.

The most common use for PF keys in the full-screen editor (and also in command mode) is to issue frequently used commands so that fewer keystrokes are necessary than if the commands were fully keyed in. Although the exact functions associated with particular function keys will vary for each user, there are some functions that are almost always associated with PF keys. For example, since a large portion of the commands you will enter in the editor are for scrolling backward and forward in a member, these functions are typically associated with PF keys. In addition, as I mentioned a minute ago, the CURSOR TABF command is usually associated with one of the PF keys.

Before I go on, you should realize one thing: Each command associated with a PF key is treated as though it is entered in the editor command area, regardless of where the cursor is positioned on the screen when the PF key is pressed. As you can see, this can save even more keystrokes because not only do you not have to key in the command itself, but it's also unnecessary to move the cursor to the editor command line to issue the command.

How to use the FSEDPF macro   If you want to use PF key settings within the full-screen editor but you don't want to bother with deciding what those settings should be, you can run the ICCF-supplied editor macro FSEDPF. Figure 4-15 shows this macro for VSE/ICCF 1.3 mod-level 0. For mod-level 5 and above, the SET commands specify PFnnED rather than PFnn, but their effects are the same. For now, I just want you to look at the SET commands; you'll learn about the other items that can be in a macro in chapter 6.

To run the FSEDPF macro, all you do is enter

```
@FSEDPF
```

on the editor command line and press the enter key. (If you're using one of the newer releases of ICCF, you don't need to enter the leading @.)

I especially want you to notice the settings in the FSEDPF macro for PF8, PF9, and PF10. All three cause the CURSOR command to be executed to move the cursor left or right. (Remember, for horizontal cursor control to be practical, the nulls option must be off.) PF8 and PF9 cause the cursor to move backward or forward 20 characters from its position when the PF key is pressed. These settings can help you move rapidly from side to side when you're editing a line. The PF10 key's CURSOR command lets you perform tabbing operations. Because it specifies 0, it causes the cursor to move forward not a specific number of columns, but rather to the next tab stop.

If you use the FSEDPF macro, be sure to look carefully at what your PF key settings are after it executes. Your ICCF administrator may have altered the macro for your installation, so it may differ from the version in figure 4-15. To see what your current PF key settings are, you can issue the command

```
SHOW PF
```

System command: /LIST FSEDPF

```
....+....1....+....2....+....3....+....4....+....5....+....6....+....7....+..CM
@MACRO    THE @FSEDPF MACRO SETS PF KEYS FOR THE FULL SCREEN EDITOR
@NOPRINT
SET PF1 BACKWARD 1
SET PF2 DOWN 8
SET PF3 FORWARD 1
SET PF4 CURSOR INPUT
SET PF5 CURSOR LINE 16
SET PF6 CURSOR LINE 5
SET PF7 CURSOR CURRENT
SET PF8 CURSOR TABBACK 20
SET PF9 CURSOR TABFORWARD 20
SET PF10 CURSOR TABFORWARD 0
@PRINT
SHOW PF
*END PRINT
*READY



I^                                                    0-004
```

Figure 4-15   The FSEDPF macro

The output of this command will look something like figure 4-16. This figure shows the editor PF key settings I like to use.

How to use replacable parameters   In some cases, you use the same command over and over, but with different parameters. If you want, you can assign the command to a function key with a replacable parameter. Then, when you issue the command, you key in only the variable value in the editor command area and press the PF key. The full-screen editor combines the data you entered with the function associated with the PF key to create the full command.

To specify a replacable parameter, simply code two ampersands in the PF key assignment. For instance, to set a PF key to issue a LOCATE command with a variable, you enter

```
SET PF9 LOCATE &&
```

Then, to issue a locate command for any text, all you have to do is key in the text in the editor command area and press the PF9 key. For example, to find the text PROCEDURE DIVISION, you might enter

```
PROC
```

Editor command: SHOW PF

```
...+....1....+....2....+....3....+....4....+....5....+....6....+....7....+..ED
13 TOP
14 UP 15
15 UP 1
16 SET NULLS ON
17 SET NULLS OFF
18 CURSOR TABF
22 BOTTOM
23 DOWN 15
24 DOWN 1
*END PF DISPLAY




I^A                                        □-□04
```

Figure 4-16   How to display your current PF key settings

and press PF9. Then, ICCF would process the command

        LOCATE PROC

as if you had entered it just that way.

HOW TO ENTER UPPER AND LOWER CASE TEXT

Most of the text entry you do will use upper case letters. That, combined with the fact that not all terminals allow lower case entry, is the reason ICCF's default is to translate all lower case input into upper case equivalents. However, if your terminal allows lower case input, you can override the default by using the SET CASE or CASE commands. You might want to do that to enter literals for some source programs.

Commands to change case settings   The CASE command lets you specify within the editor that you want to enter either mixed case data or only upper case data. It's in effect only for your current editing session. If you want to enter lower case data, you issue this command:

    CASE M

where M stands for mixed. To switch back to ICCF's default translation to upper case, you issue the command

    CASE U

where U stands for upper case.

If you want to change how ICCF will handle case translation for your entire terminal session, you can issue the SET CASE editor command. If you enter

    SET CASE INPUT MIXED

you can enter upper and lower case data both within the current editor session and afterward too.

For output, ICCF's default is to display text in mixed case. Usually, that's what you want because if a section of text contains lower case letters, you want to see them. However, you can change the current output case translation setting by issuing the command

    SET CASE OUTPUT UPPER

or

    SET CASE OUTPUT MIXED

Although you can change the output translation settings, I don't encourage you to do so.

If you want to see what the current translation settings are, you can issue the command

    SHOW CASE

from within the editor. When you do, the output looks like figure 4-17. Here, the editor is set up to display both upper and lower case data, but to translate lower case input to upper case.

Problems you might have with mixed case text   Keep in mind that factors other than ICCF's case setting can affect how data you enter is translated and how it appears. One factor is the case switch on 3270 terminals. The switch determines how data appears on your screen. If it's in the upper case position, data is displayed as upper case, even if it contains some lower case letters. As a result, even if you key in lower case letters, they appear as upper case. And although they appear as upper case, they're stored as lower case. So if you're doing mixed case entry, be sure the case switch on your terminal is in the mixed position: (A,a).

Editor command: SHOW CASE

```
...+....1....+....2....+....3....+....4....+....5....+....6....+....7....+..ED
  TYPE   TABLE   CASE   CTLCHAR
OUTPUT    00     MIXED    NOCTL
INPUT     00     UPPER    N/A




















I A                                               ▭▭04
```

Figure 4-17   How to find out what your current case translation settings are

A second factor that can affect case translation is how your terminal is defined to CICS. If upper case translation is specified for your terminal, any lower case data you enter will be translated to upper case by CICS before it's passed along to ICCF, regardless of the case setting you've made within ICCF. So if your terminal is defined to CICS with upper case translation, you can fiddle with the SET CASE command all you want, but you'll never be able to enter lower case data. If you can't make the CASE or SET CASE commands do what you think they should, check with your ICCF administrator to see how your terminal is defined.

DISCUSSION   Much of the information in this topic concerns features that you probably won't change often as you use ICCF. I suspect that you'll develop the habit of editing with the same options in effect by default from session to session. For example, you might always work with the nulls option on and with the same PF key settings.

Since you'll usually work with the same settings in effect, you might want to create a personalized editor macro (modeled on one like FSEDPF) that you can execute for each editor session to set up your editor processing environment just the way you want it. Or, you might want to have your ICCF administrator modify your logon procedure so it includes the commands necessary to tailor your editor environment. Then, you don't even have to run a macro to set your editor options the way you want them: That's done automatically for you when you log on to ICCF.

Because many of the functions this topic presents can be performed automatically from a macro or logon procedure, much of the material in this topic can serve as reference. However, it's useful to know how to set and use these advanced functions for those special situations in which they're appropriate.

Terminology

hardware tabbing
logical tabbing
logical tab character
field-mark key
nulls option

Objectives

1. Explain why 3270 hardware tabbing isn't appropriate for the full-screen editor.

2. Describe how to use the TABSET and SET TAB commands to set your tab stops and your logical tab character.

3. Compare the advantages and disadvantages of editing with the nulls option off and with it on.

4. Set your terminal's program functions keys so they're associated with commands you frequently issue. The commands may use replacable parameters.

5. Issue the appropriate commands to change your case translation options.

6. Describe the problems you can encounter when you use mixed-case text.

TOPIC 3 Editor commands for controlling the screen's editing area

When you use the editor, you can control two settings that determine what data you can use and what data you can see in the text you're editing: zone and view. In this section, I'll show you how to use the ICCF commands to adjust both.

Controlling the editing zone

The *editing zone*, or just *zone*, is the range of positions (columns) in which the editing commands and the changes you key in directly in the data display area can take effect. When you start an editing session, the default zone is from column 1 through either column 72 or column 80. You can tell what the zone is by looking for the paired less-than and greater-than signs in the editor's scale line; they mark the zone's boundaries. (If the right boundary of the zone is column 80, only one greater-than sign appears.)

How to change the editing zone: the ZONE command   If you want to change the zone, you issue the ZONE command in this format:

```
ZONE left-column-limit right-column-limit
```

For example, consider the series of screens in figure 4-18. As you can see in part 1 of the figure, the zone is originally in its default position: columns 1 through 72. In part 1, I've keyed in the command

```
ZONE 10 20
```

After I press the enter key, ICCF displays the screen in part 2 of the figure. Here, the pointers indicate the zone is columns 10 through 20. Now, any changes I make to data on the screen or any commands I enter will affect only columns 10 through 20. Changes I make outside the zone are ignored.

To understand, consider parts 3 and 4 of the figure. In part 3, I used the Erase-EOF key to delete all of the text in the data display area. Although it seems that all of the data will be lost, that's not the case. As you can see in part 4, which is the screen ICCF displays after I press the enter key, only data in the editing zone was actually deleted; data in columns 1 through 9 and from column 21 on was retained because it was outside the zone.

If you want to enter data in columns 73 through 80 of a line with the full-screen editor, you have to be sure that the editing zone includes those columns. In addition, you have to be able to see those columns to enter data into them. You can do that in three ways: (1) you can temporarily remove the line command area from the screen, (2) you can

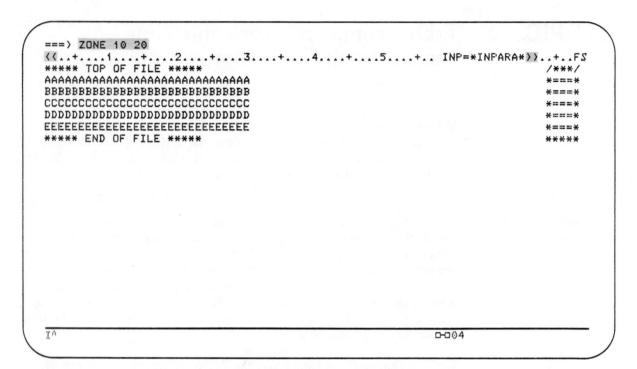

Figure 4-18   How to use the ZONE command (part 1 of 4)

Figure 4-18   How to use the ZONE command (part 2 of 4)

```
===>
....+....《《...+...》》....+....3....+....4....+....5....+.. INP=*INPARA* ...+..FS
                                                                        /***/
                                                                        *===*
                                                                        *===*
                                                                        *===*
                                                                        *===*
                                                                        *===*
***** END OF FILE *****                                                 *****




I^
                                                    □-□04
```

Figure 4-18   How to use the ZONE command (part 3 of 4)

```
===>
....+....《《...+...》》....+....3....+....4....+....5....+.. INP=*INPARA* ...+..FS
                                                                        /***/
AAAAAAAAA            AAAAAAAAAA                                          *===*
BBBBBBBBB            BBBBBBBBBB                                          *===*
CCCCCCCCC            CCCCCCCCCC                                          *===*
DDDDDDDDD            DDDDDDDDDD                                          *===*
EEEEEEEEE            EEEEEEEEEE                                          *===*
***** END OF FILE *****                                                 *****




I^
                                                    □-□04
```

Figure 4-18   How to use the ZONE command (part 4 of 4)

shift the data you're viewing to the left, or (3) you can specify another "view" of your data that includes what's actually in columns 73 through 80 in another screen position.

By the way, if columns 73 through 80 contain sequence numbers, you can view them by issuing the SET command to turn the numbers option on. Then, the characters that normally indicate the line command area are replaced by sequence numbers from the member. You can type line commands right over the sequence numbers, but you can't change the sequence numbers directly. Because the data in those columns can't be edited when you use this technique, I'm not going to describe it here. Instead, I'll show you how it works in topic 5 when I present line numbering.

How to remove the line command area: the FORMAT command　　If you want to remove the line command area from the screen, you can use the FORMAT command. I'll have more to say about it in the next topic when I describe the full-screen editor's split-screen capabilities. For now, I just want to show you how to use the FORMAT command to remove and restore the line command area. All you enter is

        FORMAT *1

to remove the line command area and

        FORMAT 1

to restore it. The asterisk means there should not be a line command area, while its absence means there should be one. The 1 indicates that one line should be used to display each record in the member being edited. Figure 4-19 uses the simple COBOL program from figure 4-2 to illustrate how the FORMAT command works. Columns 73 through 80 of each line contain the text SUPDATE.

How to shift the editing zone on the screen: the LEFT and RIGHT commands　　Another way to see the data in columns 73 through 80 is to shift all of the data in the zone to the left eight or more characters. You use the LEFT command to do that, and you use the RIGHT command to return the text to its original position. Their formats are

        LEFT nn

and

        RIGHT nn

where nn is the number of columns the display is to be shifted. When you use these commands, the data in the member is not actually shifted; only your view of it is.

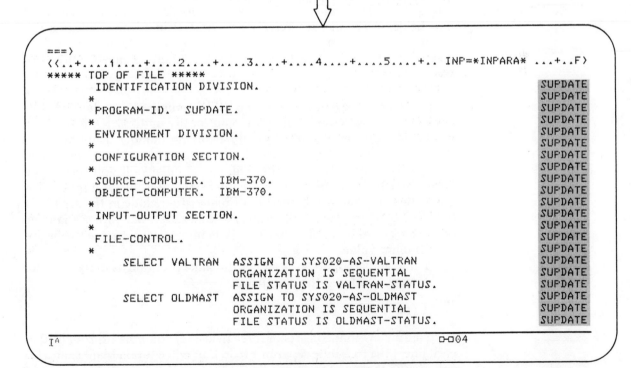

Figure 4-19   How to use the FORMAT command to remove the line command area from the screen

Figure 4-20 shows how the LEFT command works. Here, I'm editing the same data as in figure 4-19. In part 1, I've entered the command

```
LEFT 10
```

to shift the lines 10 columns to the left. Part 2 is the screen ICCF displays after it processes the LEFT command. Notice that columns 73 through 80 have been shifted out from under the line command area. Now, I can make changes to them. Notice in this case that the line command area remains on the screen.

Also, notice in the bottom section of the figure that the message

```
+OFFSET=010
```

in the scale line indicates that the display has been shifted. To return the display to its normal condition, all you have to do is issue a RIGHT command and specify the number of columns indicated in the offset message.

Controlling the editing view

The third and most sophisticated way to access data in columns 73 through 80 is to reconstruct how you see the data in a line, breaking it into fields. You can even resequence those fields. The result is a different *editing view*, or just *view*, than the standard column 1 through 80 view. However, the data in the line isn't actually changed: only your view of it is.

How to change the editing view: the VIEW command   On the VIEW command, presented in figure 4-21, you specify up to 12 fields that you identify by a beginning and an ending column number. Multiple pairs of column numbers are separated from one another with commas. You can specify a separator field that will contain blanks if you specify a 0 for the starting column; then, ICCF interprets the value you specify for the ending column as the number of blanks to include in the separator field. Also, if you want to display the hexadecimal rather than the character values of a field, you specify H immediately before the beginning column value.

For example, figure 4-22 shows the same program as in figure 4-20. In this case, I entered the command

```
VIEW 7 30, 0 5, 73 80
```

to create a view that consists of three fields: (1) columns 7 through 30 of each line, (2) a five-byte separator field that will contain blanks, and (3) columns 73 through 80 of each line. The view ICCF created is shown in the bottom section of the figure.

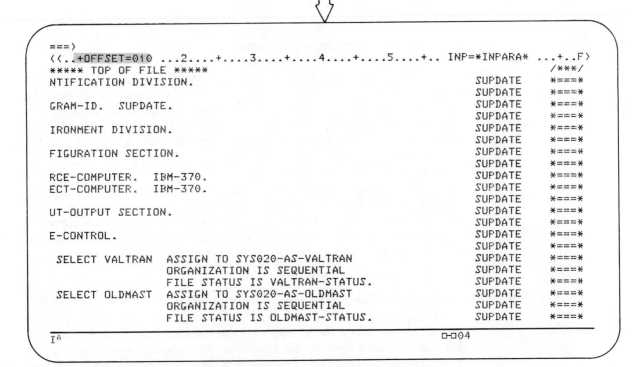

```
===> LEFT 10
<<...+....1....+....2....+....3....+....4....+....5....+.. INP=*INPARA* ...+..F>
***** TOP OF FILE *****                                                 /***/
         IDENTIFICATION DIVISION.                                       *====*
      *                                                                 *====*
       PROGRAM-ID.  SUPDATE.                                            *====*
      *                                                                 *====*
       ENVIRONMENT DIVISION.                                            *====*
      *                                                                 *====*
       CONFIGURATION SECTION.                                           *====*
      *                                                                 *====*
       SOURCE-COMPUTER.  IBM-370.                                       *====*
       OBJECT-COMPUTER.  IBM-370.                                       *====*
      *                                                                 *====*
       INPUT-OUTPUT SECTION.                                            *====*
      *                                                                 *====*
       FILE-CONTROL.                                                    *====*
      *                                                                 *====*
           SELECT VALTRAN  ASSIGN TO SYS020-AS-VALTRAN                  *====*
                           ORGANIZATION IS SEQUENTIAL                   *====*
                           FILE STATUS IS VALTRAN-STATUS.               *====*
           SELECT OLDMAST  ASSIGN TO SYS020-AS-OLDMAST                  *====*
                           ORGANIZATION IS SEQUENTIAL                   *====*
                           FILE STATUS IS OLDMAST-STATUS.               *====*
 IᴬA                                                      ▭-▭04
```

```
===>
<<..+OFFSET=010 ...2....+....3....+....4....+....5....+.. INP=*INPARA* ...+..F>
***** TOP OF FILE *****                                                 /***/
NTIFICATION DIVISION.                                     SUPDATE        *====*
                                                          SUPDATE        *====*
GRAM-ID.  SUPDATE.                                        SUPDATE        *====*
                                                          SUPDATE        *====*
IRONMENT DIVISION.                                        SUPDATE        *====*
                                                          SUPDATE        *====*
FIGURATION SECTION.                                       SUPDATE        *====*
                                                          SUPDATE        *====*
RCE-COMPUTER.  IBM-370.                                   SUPDATE        *====*
ECT-COMPUTER.  IBM-370.                                   SUPDATE        *====*
                                                          SUPDATE        *====*
UT-OUTPUT SECTION.                                        SUPDATE        *====*
                                                          SUPDATE        *====*
E-CONTROL.                                                SUPDATE        *====*
                                                          SUPDATE        *====*
 SELECT VALTRAN  ASSIGN TO SYS020-AS-VALTRAN              SUPDATE        *====*
                 ORGANIZATION IS SEQUENTIAL               SUPDATE        *====*
                 FILE STATUS IS VALTRAN-STATUS.           SUPDATE        *====*
 SELECT OLDMAST  ASSIGN TO SYS020-AS-OLDMAST              SUPDATE        *====*
                 ORGANIZATION IS SEQUENTIAL               SUPDATE        *====*
                 FILE STATUS IS OLDMAST-STATUS.           SUPDATE        *====*
 IᴬA                                                      ▭-▭04
```

Figure 4-20   How to shift text within the editing zone

The VIEW command

```
VIEW [[H]first-column last-column] [,[H]first-column last-column] . . .
```

Explanation

H	Specifies that the field should be displayed in hexadecimal rather than character format.
first-column	Specifies the starting column (from 1 to 80) for this field in the view. Alternatively, you can specify 0 to cause a filler field of spaces to be created in the view.
last-column	Specifies the ending column (from 1 to 80) for this field in the view. If you specify 0 as the value of first-column to cause a field of spaces to be created in the view, then last-column is the actual length of that field.

Figure 4-21   The VIEW command

Figure 4-23 shows that you can also resequence data. Here, I entered

```
VIEW 73 80, 0 5, 7 72
```

so the data stored in the last eight columns of each line is presented in the view in the first eight positions.

When you use the H subparameter to cause a field to be displayed in hexadecimal, each character requires two display positions. If you display a field in hex, you can key in data in hex format over existing data. As a result, you can use the VIEW command in place of the ALTER command when you have to work in hexadecimal. However, since the VIEW command affects all lines and hex editing is usually confined to one line, I think you're more likely to use the ALTER command than this feature of VIEW.

I don't encourage you to use the full features of VIEW, except in special circumstances, because it can be easy to lose track of where you are and what you're doing. But, if you do use some of its complex features, you might want to find out what the current VIEW settings are. To do that, you enter the VIEW command with no operands.

Discussion   For normal editing, the standard zone (column 1 through 72 or column 1 through 80) combined with the standard line command area is ideal. However, you need to be aware of the commands this topic presents because you may need to use all of the 80 characters available to you, perhaps to enter test data. Or, you may need to specify different zones to use the editor alignment commands, which you'll learn in topic 5.

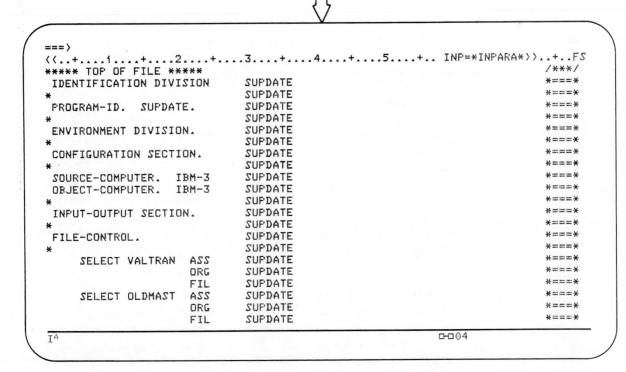

Figure 4-22   How to use the VIEW command to select fields

```
===> VIEW 73 80, 0 5, 7 72
<<...+....1....+....2....+....3....+....4....+....5....+.. INP=*INPARA*>>..+..FS
***** TOP OF FILE *****                                                   /***/
  IDENTIFICATION DIVISION      SUPDATE                                  *====*
*                              SUPDATE                                  *====*
  PROGRAM-ID.  SUPDATE.        SUPDATE                                  *====*
*                              SUPDATE                                  *====*
  ENVIRONMENT DIVISION.        SUPDATE                                  *====*
*                              SUPDATE                                  *====*
  CONFIGURATION SECTION.       SUPDATE                                  *====*
*                              SUPDATE                                  *====*
  SOURCE-COMPUTER.   IBM-3     SUPDATE                                  *====*
  OBJECT-COMPUTER.   IBM-3     SUPDATE                                  *====*
*                              SUPDATE                                  *====*
  INPUT-OUTPUT SECTION.        SUPDATE                                  *====*
*                              SUPDATE                                  *====*
  FILE-CONTROL..               SUPDATE                                  *====*
*                              SUPDATE                                  *====*
      SELECT VALTRAN   ASS      SUPDATE                                 *====*
                       ORG      SUPDATE                                 *====*
                       FIL      SUPDATE                                 *====*
      SELECT OLDMAST   ASS      SUPDATE                                 *====*
                       ORG      SUPDATE                                 *====*
                       FIL      SUPDATE                                 *====*
I^                                              D-D04
```

```
===>
<<...+....1....+....2....+....3....+....4....+....5....+.. INP=*INPARA*>>..+..FS
***** TOP OF FILE *****                                                   /***/
SUPDATE        IDENTIFICATION DIVISION.                                 *====*
SUPDATE        *                                                        *====*
SUPDATE        PROGRAM-ID.  SUPDATE.                                    *====*
SUPDATE        *                                                        *====*
SUPDATE        ENVIRONMENT DIVISION.                                    *====*
SUPDATE        *                                                        *====*
SUPDATE        CONFIGURATION SECTION.                                   *====*
SUPDATE        *                                                        *====*
SUPDATE        SOURCE-COMPUTER.   IBM-370.                              *====*
SUPDATE        OBJECT-COMPUTER.   IBM-370.                              *====*
SUPDATE        *                                                        *====*
SUPDATE        INPUT-OUTPUT SECTION.                                    *====*
SUPDATE        *                                                        *====*
SUPDATE        FILE-CONTROL.                                            *====*
SUPDATE        *                                                        *====*
SUPDATE            SELECT VALTRAN   ASSIGN TO SYS020-AS-VALTRAN         *====*
SUPDATE                             ORGANIZATION IS SEQUENTIAL          *====*
SUPDATE                             FILE STATUS IS VALTRAN-STATUS.      *====*
SUPDATE            SELECT OLDMAST   ASSIGN TO SYS020-AS-OLDMAST         *====*
SUPDATE                             ORGANIZATION IS SEQUENTIAL          *====*
SUPDATE                             FILE STATUS IS OLDMAST-STATUS.      *====*
I^                                              D-D04
```

Figure 4-23   How to use the VIEW command to resequence fields

Terminology   editing zone
zone
editing view
view

Objectives   1.   Use the ZONE command to alter your editing zone.

2.   Issue the appropriate commands to access data in columns 73 through 80 of a member.

3.   Use the VIEW command to select and/or resequence fields in the lines of the member you're editing.

TOPIC 4   Editor commands for using split screens

Most of your full-screen editor time will be spent working on one part of one library member. However, when you use ICCF from a 3270 terminal, you can edit different parts of a member at the same time and you can edit different library members at the same time. To do this, you use the editor's split-screen feature. In the first part of this topic, I'll show you how to work on different parts of the same library member at the same time. Then, in the second part, I'll show you how to edit different library members at the same time.

How to edit different parts of one library member at the same time

Often when you're entering text (as for a source program), you need to scroll up and down to make sure you're using consistent names and formats. To make that kind of work easier, the full-screen editor lets you split the screen into up to eight parts, each of which can display a different part of the library member you're editing. Each of those parts is called a *format area*. Every format area is a "window" into the member you're editing.

Although you'll almost never need to look at eight parts of a single library member at the same time, it's sometimes useful to be able to see two or three parts. For example, if you're entering a COBOL source program, you might want to split the screen into three parts: one to display a record description, one to display other working-storage fields, and a third to enter Procedure Division statements that use fields displayed in the first two areas. To split the screen like this, you use the FORMAT command.

How to create multiple format areas: the FORMAT command   In the last topic, I showed you how to use the FORMAT command to remove the line command area from the editor screen and restore it later. Now, I want to show you how to use all of the FORMAT command's features. Figure 4-24 gives the complete syntax of the FORMAT command. On it, you supply from one to eight parameter groups, each of which corresponds to a format area on the screen.

As you can see in the figure, each parameter group has three subparameters arranged like this:

$$[*] \begin{Bmatrix} 1 \\ 2 \\ 3 \end{Bmatrix} - n$$

The first subparameter, the asterisk, is optional. You enter it only if you do *not* want the format area the parameter group defines to contain a

The FORMAT command

$$FORMAT\ [[*]\ \begin{Bmatrix}1\\2\\3\end{Bmatrix} -n]\ .\ .\ .$$

Explanation

*	Indicates that the format area should not have a line (type III) command area.
$\begin{Bmatrix}1\\2\\3\end{Bmatrix}$	The number of lines to be displayed for each record in the format area being defined.
n	The number of lines in the format area being defined. You may omit this operand for the last area being defined with the command; then, ICCF uses the remainder of the screen for the area.

Figure 4-24   The FORMAT command

line command area. The second subparameter is always required and must be 1, 2, or 3. It specifies how many lines are to be displayed in the format area for each line of text in the member. You'll almost always specify 1. The last parameter, n, is separated from the second by a single hyphen and specifies how many lines the format area you're defining will contain. It's required for all subparameter groups you specify except the last. For the last group, ICCF figures out how many lines are left on the screen and uses that amount as the area size.

To understand how you might use the FORMAT command, consider figure 4-25. In part 1, I've copied a library member that contains a COBOL source program into the input area and keyed in

    FORMAT 1-6 1-6 1-6

This command will split the screen into three format areas, each with six display lines. Because I omitted asterisks on all three subparameter groups, all three format areas will have line command areas.

Part 2 of the figure shows what the screen looks like after it has been divided into three areas. All are displaying the same member, and all are positioned at the same line in the member. Notice that each area has its own editor command area, indicated by

    ===>

I can issue commands for each area in its editor command area and in its line command area. (On the 3270, the editor command area and the current line in each format area are displayed with bright characters. As a result, it's easier to see where format areas are located on the actual display than it is in the figure.)

```
===) FORMAT 1-6 1-6 1-6
<<..+....1....+....2....+....3....+....4....+....5....+.. INP=*INPARA*>>..+..FS
***** TOP OF FILE *****                                              /***/
      IDENTIFICATION DIVISION.                                       *===*
      *                                                              *===*
      PROGRAM-ID.  INV2100.                                          *===*
      *                                                              *===*
      ENVIRONMENT DIVISION.                                          *===*
      *                                                              *===*
      INPUT-OUTPUT SECTION.                                          *===*
      *                                                              *===*
      FILE-CONTROL.                                                  *===*
      *                                                              *===*
          SELECT PRTOUT ASSIGN TO SYS006-UR-1403-S                   *===*
                              ACCESS IS SEQUENTIAL.                   *===*
      DATA DIVISION.                                                 *===*
      *                                                              *===*
      FILE SECTION.                                                  *===*
      *                                                              *===*
      FD   PRTOUT                                                    *===*
           LABEL RECORDS ARE OMITTED                                 *===*
           RECORD CONTAINS 132 CHARACTERS.                           *===*
      *                                                              *===*
      01   PRTOUT-RECORD                    PIC X(132).              *===*
I^                                                     □-□04
```

Figure 4-25   How to use the FORMAT command to create multiple format areas
(part 1 of 4)

```
===)
<<..+....1....+....2....+....3....+....4....+....5....+.. INP=*INPARA*>>..+..FS
***** TOP OF FILE *****                                              /***/
      IDENTIFICATION DIVISION.                                       *===*
      *                                                              *===*
      PROGRAM-ID.  INV2100.                                          *===*
      *                                                              *===*
      ENVIRONMENT DIVISION.                                          *===*
===)
***** TOP OF FILE *****                                              /***/
      IDENTIFICATION DIVISION.                                       *===*
      *                                                              *===*
      PROGRAM-ID.  INV2100.                                          *===*
      *                                                              *===*
      ENVIRONMENT DIVISION.                                          *===*
===)
***** TOP OF FILE *****                                              /***/
      IDENTIFICATION DIVISION.                                       *===*
      *                                                              *===*
      PROGRAM-ID.  INV2100.                                          *===*
      *                                                              *===*
      ENVIRONMENT DIVISION.                                          *===*
I^                                                     □-□04
```

Figure 4-25   How to use the FORMAT command to create multiple format areas
(part 2 of 4)

```
===> LOCATE PROCEDURE DIVISION
<<..+....1....+....2....+....3....+....4....+....5....+.. INP=*INPARA*>>..+..FS
***** TOP OF FILE *****                                                  /***/
        IDENTIFICATION DIVISION.                                         *====*
      *                                                                  *====*
        PROGRAM-ID.  INV2100.                                            *====*
      *                                                                  *====*
        ENVIRONMENT DIVISION.                                            *====*
===> LOCATE INVENTORY-VENDOR-SEGMENT
***** TOP OF FILE *****                                                  /***/
        IDENTIFICATION DIVISION.                                         *====*
      *                                                                  *====*
        PROGRAM-ID.  INV2100.                                            *====*
      *                                                                  *====*
        ENVIRONMENT DIVISION.                                            *====*
===> LOCATE SWITCHES
***** TOP OF FILE *****                                                  /***/
        IDENTIFICATION DIVISION.                                         *====*
      *                                                                  *====*
        PROGRAM-ID.  INV2100.                                            *====*
      *                                                                  *====*
        ENVIRONMENT DIVISION.                                            *====*



I^                                                   □-□04
```

Figure 4-25   How to use the FORMAT command to create multiple format areas
(part 3 of 4)

```
===>
<<..+....1....+....2....+....3....+....4....+....5....+.. INP=*INPARA*>>..+..FS
        PROCEDURE DIVISION.                                              /===/*
      *                                                                  *====*
            ENTRY "DLITCBL" USING INVENTORY-PCB-MASK.                    *====*
      *                                                                  *====*
        000-PREPARE-INV-AVAIL-REPORT.                                    *====*
      *                                                                  *====*
===>
        01   INVENTORY-VENDOR-SEGMENT.                                   /===/*
      *                                                                  *====*
            05   IVS-VENDOR-CODE          PIC X(3).                      *====*
            05   IVS-VENDOR-NAME          PIC X(30).                     *====*
            05   IVS-VENDOR-ADDRESS       PIC X(30).                     *====*
            05   IVS-VENDOR-CITY          PIC X(17).                     *====*
===>
        01   SWITCHES.                                                   /===/*
      *                                                                  *====*
            05   MORE-ITEMS-SW            PIC X     VALUE "Y".           *====*
                 88   MORE-ITEMS                    VALUE "Y".           *====*
            05   MORE-LOCATIONS-SW        PIC X     VALUE "Y".           *====*
                 88   MORE-LOCATIONS                VALUE "Y".           *====*



I^                                                   □-□04
```

Figure 4-25   How to use the FORMAT command to create multiple format areas
(part 4 of 4)

To understand how to use multiple format areas, consider part 3 of the figure. Here, I've entered three different LOCATE commands in the editor command areas of the three format areas. After I press the enter key, the display looks like part 4. Now, I can make changes to data in any or all areas at the same time. What I'm likely to do here is confine my work to the Procedure Division code in the top format area and use the data in the second and third areas to make it easy for me to check on Data Division names I'll use in Procedure Division statements.

Although you can split the screen into up to eight areas, you probably won't want to do that. For a standard 24-line 3270 terminal, that means each area would be so small it would be practically useless. In fact, the three areas in parts 2, 3, and 4 of figure 4-25 are about as small as they can be and still be useful. As you work with the split-screen feature of the editor, you'll develop a feel for what the right area sizes are for your needs and your terminal type.

When you want to return to the normal editor screen after an editing session with multiple format areas, all you have to do is enter

FORMAT 1

This specifies that you want only one format area and that it should use all available lines.

When you use a PF key with multiple format areas, the command associated with a key is processed in the format area where the cursor was located when you pressed the key. Also, you should know that the changes you enter in multiple format areas are processed from top to bottom on the physical screen. As a result, if you enter conflicting changes, the changes from the lowest format area are the ones that remain in effect. However, for typical editing sessions with multiple format areas, you won't be entering changes that result in conflicts.

Just as you might want to use the split-screen feature to edit at more than one location in a single member, you might also want to edit different members at the same time. You can do that with the full-screen editor too.

How to edit different library members at the same time

During normal editor operations, you use the full physical screen of the 3270 terminal for your *logical screen*. When you use the FORMAT command, you're dividing the logical screen into different format areas. However, you can also create multiple logical screens on your terminal's single physical screen. This is how you can edit multiple library members at the same time: Each has its own logical screen.

How to create and use logical screens: the SCREEN and ENTER commands To create multiple logical screens on your display station's physical screen, you issue the SCREEN command. On it, you supply from 1 to 8 numbers to indicate how many lines each logical screen should have. For example, to create two logical screens on your terminal's physical screen, the first with 15 lines and the second with 9, you'd issue this command:

```
SCREEN 15 9
```

As with the FORMAT command, you'll almost never want to use the maximum number of logical screens ICCF supports. If you did, they would all be so small they would be next to impossible to use.

After you've specified how many logical screens you want to use and how large they should be, you can switch from one to another by issuing the ENTER command. On it, you specify the name of the library member you want to edit on another logical screen. (If you issue the ENTER command without a name, you'll be editing the input area.) When you do issue an ENTER command, ICCF opens a logical screen and makes the library member you named the active member. Then, any work you do on that screen will change the member being edited on it. If you specify the name of a member that's already in edit on the ENTER command, ICCF returns you to the logical screen where that member is active; it doesn't open a second logical screen for it.

If you issue the ENTER command and no logical screens are available, the member you specify on the command will appear in the logical screen from which you entered the command. However, the member that you were editing there is still considered to be in edit. When you finish with the editing session for the second member (by issuing the QUIT command), the first member you were editing will reappear.

If you're in the middle of a complex multi-member editing session and you lose track of what members are active, you can enter the command

```
SHOW NAMES
```

Then, the names of all members currently being edited will be displayed. However, for most editing sessions, you'll be editing two or at most three members at the same time, and it shouldn't be difficult for you to keep track of where you are.

When you're doing split-screen editing of two or more library members at the same time, it's easy to copy and move text among them. You use the line commands C, K, M, and I, just as you do when you're working on a single member. Because there's only one editor stack, it's accessible from all logical screens as either the destination of data marked with C, K, or M commands or the source of data to be inserted where you specify the I command.

This can be a preferable alternative to using the GETFILE command to copy text from one member to another because with GETFILE you have to know the line numbers you want to copy (unless you want the entire library member to be copied into the member you're editing). Using copy, move, and insert commands to transfer text between logical screens can be easier than using the GETFILE command because with split-screen editing, you can look directly at the lines you want to copy.

In fact, you can even use the ENTER command to copy text between library members when you're only using one logical screen. Just specify the ENTER command with the name of the member from which you want to copy text, press the enter key, locate the text you want, then use the C, M or K command to transfer the text to the editor stack. Next, enter the QUIT command to finish your work on the member you're copying text from. That returns you to your original member, where you can issue the I command to insert the text from the stack.

After you've finished a multi-member editing session and you want to return the screen to its original format with one logical screen, you enter the command

    SCREEN 24

which indicates that you want only one logical screen and that it should be 24 lines long. (The normal screen length for a 3270 is 24 lines.) However, the format of the screen remains that of the previous, smaller logical screen. To restore it to full-screen size, issue the command

    FORMAT 1

to indicate that the current format area should use all of the available space on the screen.

When you're editing with more than one logical screen, the commands you use to end the full-screen editor—CANCEL and QUIT—have different effects. QUIT ends your editing only for the logical screen on which you issue it. If you're editing more than one member on a single logical screen, the QUIT command ends the edit only for the active member. In contrast, CANCEL ends the entire full-screen editor session, regardless of how many members you're editing. Its effect is the same as if you had entered the QUIT command on all the active logical screens.

A sample editing session that uses multiple logical screens   To understand how all this works, I want you to consider the multiple-member editor session figure 4-26 illustrates. Here, I'll use three logical screens to work on five different library members in a single session.

In part 1 of figure 4-26, I was editing a library member named TESTA. As you can see, this is the standard full-screen editor display. However, in the editor command area, I've keyed in a SCREEN command that will cause my display to be split into three logical screens; each logical screen will use eight lines of the physical screen. After I pressed the enter key, ICCF displayed the screen in part 2.

In part 2, the size of the original logical screen was reduced from full size to just eight lines as a result of the SCREEN command.

```
===> SCREEN 8 8 8
<<...+....1....+....2....+....3....+....4....+....5....+.. MEM=TESTA    >>..+..FS
***** TOP OF FILE *****                                                   /***/
LINE  1 OF MEMBER TESTA                                                   *====*
LINE  2 OF MEMBER TESTA                                                   *====*
LINE  3 OF MEMBER TESTA                                                   *====*
LINE  4 OF MEMBER TESTA                                                   *====*
LINE  5 OF MEMBER TESTA                                                   *====*
LINE  6 OF MEMBER TESTA                                                   *====*
LINE  7 OF MEMBER TESTA                                                   *====*
LINE  8 OF MEMBER TESTA                                                   *====*
LINE  9 OF MEMBER TESTA                                                   *====*
LINE 10 OF MEMBER TESTA                                                   *====*
LINE 11 OF MEMBER TESTA                                                   *====*
LINE 12 OF MEMBER TESTA                                                   *====*
LINE 13 OF MEMBER TESTA                                                   *====*
LINE 14 OF MEMBER TESTA                                                   *====*
LINE 15 OF MEMBER TESTA                                                   *====*
LINE 16 OF MEMBER TESTA                                                   *====*
LINE 17 OF MEMBER TESTA                                                   *====*
LINE 18 OF MEMBER TESTA                                                   *====*
LINE 19 OF MEMBER TESTA                                                   *====*
LINE 20 OF MEMBER TESTA                                                   *====*
LINE 21 OF MEMBER TESTA                                                   *====*
I^                                              □-□04
```

Figure 4-26   How to use the SCREEN and ENTER commands (part 1 of 13)

```
===> ENTER TESTB
<<...+....1....+....2....+....3....+....4....+....5....+.. MEM=TESTA    >>..+..FS
***** TOP OF FILE *****                                                   /***/
LINE  1 OF MEMBER TESTA                                                   *====*
LINE  2 OF MEMBER TESTA                                                   *====*
LINE  3 OF MEMBER TESTA                                                   *====*
LINE  4 OF MEMBER TESTA                                                   *====*
LINE  5 OF MEMBER TESTA                                                   *====*




I^                                              □-□04
```

Figure 4-26   How to use the SCREEN and ENTER commands (part 2 of 13)

```
===>
<<...+....1....+....2....+....3....+....4....+....5....+.. MEM=TESTA    >>..+..FS
***** TOP OF FILE *****                                                   /***/
LINE 1 OF MEMBER TESTA                                                    *====*
LINE 2 OF MEMBER TESTA                                                    *====*
LINE 3 OF MEMBER TESTA                                                    *====*
LINE 4 OF MEMBER TESTA                                                    *====*
LINE 5 OF MEMBER TESTA                                                    *====*
===> ENTER TESTC
<<...+....1....+....2....+....3....+....4....+....5....+.. MEM=TESTB    >>..+..FS
***** TOP OF FILE *****                                                   /***/
LINE 1 OF MEMBER TESTB                                                    *====*
LINE 2 OF MEMBER TESTB                                                    *====*
LINE 3 OF MEMBER TESTB                                                    *====*
LINE 4 OF MEMBER TESTB                                                    *====*
LINE 5 OF MEMBER TESTB                                                    *====*




I^                                              □-□④4
```

Figure 4-26   How to use the SCREEN and ENTER commands (part 3 of 13)

```
===>
<<...+....1....+....2....+....3....+....4....+....5....+.. MEM=TESTA    >>..+..FS
***** TOP OF FILE *****                                                   /***/
LINE 1 OF MEMBER TESTA                                                    *====*
LINE 2 OF MEMBER TESTA                                                    *====*
LINE 3 OF MEMBER TESTA                                                    *====*
LINE 4 OF MEMBER TESTA                                                    *====*
LINE 5 OF MEMBER TESTA                                                    *====*
===>
<<...+....1....+....2....+....3....+....4....+....5....+.. MEM=TESTB    >>..+..FS
***** TOP OF FILE *****                                                   /***/
LINE 1 OF MEMBER TESTB                                                    *====*
LINE 2 OF MEMBER TESTB                                                    *====*
LINE 3 OF MEMBER TESTB                                                    *====*
LINE 4 OF MEMBER TESTB                                                    *====*
LINE 5 OF MEMBER TESTB                                                    *====*
===> SHOW NAMES
<<...+....1....+....2....+....3....+....4....+....5....+.. MEM=TESTC    >>..+..FS
***** TOP OF FILE *****                                                   /***/
LINE 1 OF MEMBER TESTC                                                    *====*
LINE 2 OF MEMBER TESTC                                                    *====*
LINE 3 OF MEMBER TESTC                                                    *====*
LINE 4 OF MEMBER TESTC                                                    *====*
LINE 5 OF MEMBER TESTC                                                    *====*
I^                                              □-□④4
```

Figure 4-26   How to use the SCREEN and ENTER commands (part 4 of 13)

```
    ...+....1....+....2....+....3....+....4....+....5....+....6....+....7....+..ED
*
NAME      TYPE SCREEN
*
TESTA     LIB   YES
TESTB     LIB   YES
TESTC     LIB   YES




















I^A                                              □-□04
```

Figure 4-26   How to use the SCREEN and ENTER commands (part 5 of 13)

```
===>
<<...+....1....+....2....+....3....+....4....+....5....+.. MEM=TESTA   >>..+..FS
***** TOP OF FILE *****                                               /***/
LINE 1 OF MEMBER TESTA                                                *===*
LINE 2 OF MEMBER TESTA                                                *===*
LINE 3 OF MEMBER TESTA                                                *===*
LINE 4 OF MEMBER TESTA                                                *===*
LINE 5 OF MEMBER TESTA                                                *===*
===>
<<...+....1....+....2....+....3....+....4....+....5....+.. MEM=TESTB   >>..+..FS
***** TOP OF FILE *****                                               /***/
LINE 1 OF MEMBER TESTB                                                *===*
LINE 2 OF MEMBER TESTB                                                *===*
LINE 3 OF MEMBER TESTB                                                *===*
LINE 4 OF MEMBER TESTB                                                *===*
LINE 5 OF MEMBER TESTB                                                *===*
===> ENTER TESTD
<<...+....1....+....2....+....3....+....4....+....5....+.. MEM=TESTC   >>..+..FS
***** TOP OF FILE *****                                               /***/
LINE 1 OF MEMBER TESTC                                                *===*
LINE 2 OF MEMBER TESTC                                                *===*
LINE 3 OF MEMBER TESTC                                                *===*
LINE 4 OF MEMBER TESTC                                                *===*
LINE 5 OF MEMBER TESTC                                                *===*
I^A                                              □-□04
```

Figure 4-26   How to use the SCREEN and ENTER commands (part 6 of 13)

```
===>
<<...+....1....+....2....+....3....+....4....+....5....+.. MEM=TESTA    >>..+..FS
***** TOP OF FILE *****                                                /***/
LINE 1 OF MEMBER TESTA                                                 *====*
LINE 2 OF MEMBER TESTA                                                 *====*
LINE 3 OF MEMBER TESTA                                                 *====*
LINE 4 OF MEMBER TESTA                                                 *====*
LINE 5 OF MEMBER TESTA                                                 *====*
===>
<<...+....1....+....2....+....3....+....4....+....5....+.. MEM=TESTB    >>..+..FS
***** TOP OF FILE *****                                                /***/
LINE 1 OF MEMBER TESTB                                                 *====*
LINE 2 OF MEMBER TESTB                                                 *====*
LINE 3 OF MEMBER TESTB                                                 *====*
LINE 4 OF MEMBER TESTB                                                 *====*
LINE 5 OF MEMBER TESTB                                                 *====*
===> SHOW NAMES
<<...+....1....+....2....+....3....+....4....+....5....+.. MEM=TESTD    >>..+..FS
***** TOP OF FILE *****                                                /***/
LINE 1 OF MEMBER TESTD                                                 *====*
LINE 2 OF MEMBER TESTD                                                 *====*
LINE 3 OF MEMBER TESTD                                                 *====*
LINE 4 OF MEMBER TESTD                                                 *====*
LINE 5 OF MEMBER TESTD                                                 *====*
I^                                          □-□04
```

Figure 4-26   How to use the SCREEN and ENTER commands (part 7 of 13)

```
...+....1....+....2....+....3....+....4....+....5....+....6....+....7....+..ED
*
NAME      TYPE SCREEN
*
TESTA     LIB  YES
TESTB     LIB  YES
TESTC     LIB
TESTD     LIB  YES




I^                                          □-□04
```

Figure 4-26   How to use the SCREEN and ENTER commands (part 8 of 13)

```
===)
<<...+....1....+....2....+....3....+....4....+....5....+.. MEM=TESTA    >>..+..FS
***** TOP OF FILE *****                                                /***/
LINE 1 OF MEMBER TESTA                                                 *====*
LINE 2 OF MEMBER TESTA                                                 *====*
LINE 3 OF MEMBER TESTA                                                 *====*
LINE 4 OF MEMBER TESTA                                                 *====*
LINE 5 OF MEMBER TESTA                                                 *====*
===)
<<...+....1....+....2....+....3....+....4....+....5....+.. MEM=TESTB    >>..+..FS
***** TOP OF FILE *****                                                /***/
LINE 1 OF MEMBER TESTB                                                 *====*
LINE 2 OF MEMBER TESTB                                                 *====*
LINE 3 OF MEMBER TESTB                                                 *====*
LINE 4 OF MEMBER TESTB                                                 *====*
LINE 5 OF MEMBER TESTB                                                 *====*
===) QUIT
<<...+....1....+....2....+....3....+....4....+....5....+.. MEM=TESTD    >>..+..FS
***** TOP OF FILE *****                                                /***/
LINE 1 OF MEMBER TESTD                                                 *====*
LINE 2 OF MEMBER TESTD                                                 *====*
LINE 3 OF MEMBER TESTD                                                 *====*
LINE 4 OF MEMBER TESTD                                                 *====*
LINE 5 OF MEMBER TESTD                                                 *====*
IᴬA                                          □-□□4
```

Figure 4-26   How to use the SCREEN and ENTER commands (part 9 of 13)

```
===)
<<...+....1....+....2....+....3....+....4....+....5....+.. MEM=TESTA    >>..+..FS
***** TOP OF FILE *****                                                /***/
LINE 1 OF MEMBER TESTA                                                 *====*
LINE 2 OF MEMBER TESTA                                                 *====*
LINE 3 OF MEMBER TESTA                                                 *====*
LINE 4 OF MEMBER TESTA                                                 *====*
LINE 5 OF MEMBER TESTA                                                 *====*
===)
<<...+....1....+....2....+....3....+....4....+....5....+.. MEM=TESTB    >>..+..FS
***** TOP OF FILE *****                                                /***/
LINE 1 OF MEMBER TESTB                                                 *====*
LINE 2 OF MEMBER TESTB                                                 *====*
LINE 3 OF MEMBER TESTB                                                 *====*
LINE 4 OF MEMBER TESTB                                                 *====*
LINE 5 OF MEMBER TESTB                                                 *====*
===) QUIT
<<...+....1....+....2....+....3....+....4....+....5....+.. MEM=TESTC    >>..+..FS
***** TOP OF FILE *****                                                /***/
LINE 1 OF MEMBER TESTC                                                 *====*
LINE 2 OF MEMBER TESTC                                                 *====*
LINE 3 OF MEMBER TESTC                                                 *====*
LINE 4 OF MEMBER TESTC                                                 *====*
LINE 5 OF MEMBER TESTC                                                 *====*
IᴬA                                          □-□□4
```

Figure 4-26   How to use the SCREEN and ENTER commands (part 10 of 13)

```
===) ENTER TESTE
<<..+....1....+....2....+....3....+....4....+....5....+.. MEM=TESTA    >>..+..FS
***** TOP OF FILE *****                                                /***/
LINE 1 OF MEMBER TESTA                                                 *====*
LINE 2 OF MEMBER TESTA                                                 *====*
LINE 3 OF MEMBER TESTA                                                 *====*
LINE 4 OF MEMBER TESTA                                                 *====*
LINE 5 OF MEMBER TESTA                                                 *====*
===)
<<..+....1....+....2....+....3....+....4....+....5....+.. MEM=TESTB    >>..+..FS
***** TOP OF FILE *****                                                /***/
LINE 1 OF MEMBER TESTB                                                 *====*
LINE 2 OF MEMBER TESTB                                                 *====*
LINE 3 OF MEMBER TESTB                                                 *====*
LINE 4 OF MEMBER TESTB                                                 *====*
LINE 5 OF MEMBER TESTB                                                 *====*




I^                                                     ▭-▭04
```

Figure 4-26   How to use the SCREEN and ENTER commands (part 11 of 13)

```
===)
<<..+....1....+....2....+....3....+....4....+....5....+.. MEM=TESTA    >>..+..FS
***** TOP OF FILE *****                                                /***/
LINE 1 OF MEMBER TESTA                                                 *====*
LINE 2 OF MEMBER TESTA                                                 *====*
LINE 3 OF MEMBER TESTA                                                 *====*
LINE 4 OF MEMBER TESTA                                                 *====*
LINE 5 OF MEMBER TESTA                                                 *====*
===)
<<..+....1....+....2....+....3....+....4....+....5....+.. MEM=TESTB    >>..+..FS
***** TOP OF FILE *****                                                /***/
LINE 1 OF MEMBER TESTB                                                 *====*
LINE 2 OF MEMBER TESTB                                                 *====*
LINE 3 OF MEMBER TESTB                                                 *====*
LINE 4 OF MEMBER TESTB                                                 *====*
LINE 5 OF MEMBER TESTB                                                 *====*
===) CANCEL
<<..+....1....+....2....+....3....+....4....+....5....+.. NEW=TESTE    >>..+..FS
***** TOP OF FILE *****                                                /***/
***** END OF FILE *****                                                *****


I^                                                     ▭-▭04
```

Figure 4-26   How to use the SCREEN and ENTER commands (part 12 of 13)

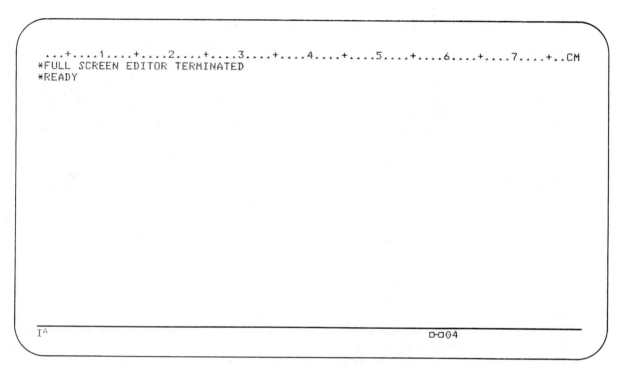

Figure 4-26   How to use the SCREEN and ENTER commands (part 13 of 13)

Although this logical screen is smaller than the original, I can still perform all editing functions within it. The other two logical screens that the SCREEN command created are present in part 2 of the figure, but they're not visible because they're not active; a logical screen is active only when you're editing a member in it. To activate the second logical screen, I keyed in the command

    ENTER TESTB

in the editor command line in part 2.

When I pressed the enter key, the second logical screen was activated, as part 3 shows. It, like the first logical screen, has its own editor command line, editor scale line, data display area, and line command area. You can perform all editor functions independently in both this logical screen and in the first.

Compare this to the split-screen facility the FORMAT command offers. Format areas simply provide different views of a single member. Data in all format areas can be affected by a command you enter in any one format area's editor command area. In contrast, logical screens are always independent: Commands you enter in the editor command area of one logical screen don't affect other logical screens. (An exception is the CANCEL command, which ends editing in all logical screens.)

In part 3 of figure 4-26, the editor scale lines show that I was editing two different library members: TESTA in the first logical screen and TESTB in the second. In the editor command area in the second logical screen, I've keyed in an ENTER command to edit a third member: TESTC. When I pressed the enter key, the third of the three logical screens I created with the SCREEN command was activated, which you can see in part 4. (By the way, the result would have been the same if the ENTER command had been issued in the first logical screen instead of the second. This is true as long as at least one of the logical screens is inactive.)

In the editor command area of the third logical screen in part 4, I entered the SHOW NAMES command to display the names of the members that were currently in edit, and ICCF's response is in part 5. This screen doesn't provide any information that wasn't available from the three logical screens themselves. It tells me that I'm editing three different library members (TESTA, TESTB, and TESTC), that they're all library members (LIB), and that they're all currently displayed on a logical screen.

After I tapped the enter key from the names display in part 5 and returned to the editor logical screens, I keyed in

```
ENTER TESTD
```

in the editor command area in the third logical screen, as you can see in part 6. When I pressed the enter key, ICCF displayed the screen in part 7; at this point, TESTD was the member being edited in the third logical screen.

Because there were no more available logical screens when I entered TESTD, ICCF caused the editing I was doing on TESTC to be suspended (*not* ended). Then, the third logical screen was available for me to work on TESTD. In a situation like this, ICCF suspends editing on the member that was active in the logical screen from which you issued the ENTER command.

To verify that the editing I was doing on TESTC was suspended, not ended, I keyed in SHOW NAMES again in part 7 and pressed the enter key. ICCF's response is in part 8. Here, you can see that four members were indeed being edited, but only three were displayed on logical screens. TESTC was not being displayed, but it was still being edited.

When I finished my work on TESTD in the third logical screen, I entered a QUIT command, as in part 9. Then, when I pressed the enter key, the editing for TESTD ended, and the third logical screen became available again. As a result, ICCF resumed active editing of TESTC, as you can see in part 10. In part 10, I entered the QUIT command again to end editing for TESTC. When the editor processed that command, the third logical screen was no longer needed, so only the first and second remained active, as part 11 shows.

In part 11, I keyed in an ENTER command for another library member: TESTE. Unlike the other four library members I edited in this session, TESTE didn't already exist. However, the ENTER command lets you supply the name of a new member for editing and assumes that it's empty. That's what

```
NEW=TESTE
```

indicates in the scale line in the third logical screen in part 12.

At this point, I decided to stop my editing session for all three active library members (TESTA, TESTB, and TESTE). To do that, I keyed in the CANCEL command in part 12 and pressed the enter key. Then, editing was terminated on all logical screens and the editor itself ended, as part 13 shows.

Discussion

Now, you should be able to use the split-screen editing features ICCF supplies for a variety of editing situations. Even so, I want you to keep the information in this topic in perspective. Most of your editing work will be done on a single screen on a single member; using multiple format areas and multiple logical screens is not typical.

Terminology

format area
logical screen

Objectives

1. Use the FORMAT command to create multiple format areas to edit different parts of the same member at the same time.

2. Use the SCREEN, ENTER, QUIT, CANCEL, and SHOW NAMES commands to manage a split-screen editing session in which you edit different library members at the same time.

TOPIC 5 Other editor commands

In this topic, you'll learn how to use a few other full-screen editor commands. First, you'll learn how to use the editor commands to align text within your editing zone. Second, you'll see how to apply sequence numbers to a library member and how you can edit a member with sequence numbers in columns 73 through 80. Finally, you'll learn how to perform some command mode functions from within the editor.

How to use the editor commands to align text

This section presents commands ICCF provides that let you align text within the editing zone. Because these are commands you'll seldom use, I don't encourage you to spend a lot of time memorizing them. Nevertheless, if you read this section, you'll remember that an appropriate command probably exists when the unusual occasion comes up when you need one of them. Then, you can turn back to this section to refresh your memory about the command and its format.

Figure 4-27 presents the ICCF commands you can use to align text. As you can see, there are both editor command and line command versions for all functions. Unless you specify otherwise, an alignment command applies only to the current line. However, you can cause all of these commands (except the editor command SPLIT and its equivalent line command TS) to affect multiple lines as figure 4-27 shows.

These commands can be confusing, so consider figure 4-28. It gives you an example of each of the line commands in the figure. (The editor commands aren't illustrated, but they work similarly.) If you study parts 1 and 2 of the figure together, you'll see what each of the commands does.

If you use one of the line commands < or >, you need to remember that if you cause data to be shifted outside the zone, that data is lost. In the fourth from the last line in part 1 of figure 4-28, I specified that the text should be shifted to the right five columns. However, the data in that line already filled the zone. To show you that the data was lost, I entered a TL command in part 2. The output the editor displayed is in part 3. As you can see, the last five characters on the line (UMNS:) were lost.

Function	Editor command	Line command
Justify text with both left and right zone limits.	`ALIGN`	`TA[nnn]`
Justify text with left zone limit.	`JUSTIFY LEFT`	`TL[nnn]`
Justify text with right zone limit.	`JUSTIFY RIGHT`	`TR[nnn]`
Center text within the zone.	`CENTER`	`TC[nnn]`
Move text left a specified number of columns (cc) within the zone; data shifted outside the zone is lost.	`SHIFT LEFT cc`	`<cc[,nnn]`
Move text right a specified number of columns (cc) within the zone; data shifted outside the zone is lost.	`SHIFT RIGHT cc`	`>cc[,nnn]`
Split the current line into two lines before the specified column (cc).	`SPLIT cc`	`TS cc`

Notes

To cause an editor (type II) alignment command (other than SPLIT) to be performed repeatedly for a series of lines, issue the command

REPEAT nnnn

immediately before you issue the alignment command. For nnnn, enter the number of lines (up to 9999) that you want to change.

To cause a line (type III) alignment command (other than TS) to be performed repeatedly for a series of lines, enter a number (up to 999) in the nnn position in the command.

Figure 4-27   Commands to align text within the editing zone

How to work with sequence numbers in library members

If you want to add line numbers to a library member, it's easy to do with the editor. All you have to do is issue the RENUM command. If you issue the command with no operands, line numbers begin with 100, are incremented by 100, and occupy positions 73 through 80. However, you can alter these defaults by specifying appropriate operands on the command.

```
===>
<<..+....1....+....2....+....3....+....4....+....5....+.. INP=*INPARA*>>..+..FS
***** TOP OF FILE *****                                                  /***/
THIS LINE WILL BE ALIGNED.                                               TA==*
THIS LINE WILL BE JUSTIFIED TO THE RIGHT.                                TR==*
                  THIS LINE WILL BE JUSTIFIED TO THE LEFT.               TL==*
THIS LINE WILL BE CENTERED.                                              TC==*
THIS LINE WILL BE SHIFTED RIGHT 10 COLUMNS.                              >10=*
                  THIS LINE WILL BE SHIFTED LEFT 10 COLUMNS.             <10=*
THIS LINE WILL BE SPLIT AT COLUMN 15.                                    TS15*
THIS LINE AND THE FOLLOWING THREE LINES WILL BE CENTERED:                TC4=*
     (1) THIS LINE WILL BE CENTERED.                                     *===*
     (2) THIS LINE WILL BE CENTERED.                                     *===*
     (3) THIS LINE WILL BE CENTERED.                                     *===*
THIS LINE AND THE FOLLOWING THREE LINES WILL BE SHIFTED RIGHT 5 COLUMNS: >5,4*
     (1) THIS LINE WILL BE SHIFTED RIGHT 5 COLUMNS.                      *===*
     (2) THIS LINE WILL BE SHIFTED RIGHT 5 COLUMNS.                      *===*
     (3) THIS LINE WILL BE SHIFTED RIGHT 5 COLUMNS.                      *===*
***** END OF FILE *****                                                  *****




_____
I^                                            □-□04
```

Figure 4-28   How to use the line commands to align text within the editing zone (part 1 of 3)

```
===>
<<..+....1....+....2....+....3....+....4....+....5....+.. INP=*INPARA*>>..+..FS
***** TOP OF FILE *****                                                  /***/
THIS           LINE           WILL           BE           ALIGNED.      *===*
                         THIS LINE WILL BE JUSTIFIED TO THE RIGHT.      *===*
THIS LINE WILL BE JUSTIFIED TO THE LEFT.                                *===*
                    THIS LINE WILL BE CENTERED.                         *===*
          THIS LINE WILL BE SHIFTED RIGHT 10 COLUMNS.                   *===*
          THIS LINE WILL BE SHIFTED LEFT 10 COLUMNS.                    *===*
THIS LINE WILL                                                          *===*
 BE SPLIT AT COLUMN 15.                                                 *===*
          THIS LINE AND THE FOLLOWING THREE LINES WILL BE CENTERED:     *===*
                    (1) THIS LINE WILL BE CENTERED.                     *===*
                    (2) THIS LINE WILL BE CENTERED.                     *===*
                    (3) THIS LINE WILL BE CENTERED.                     *===*
        THIS LINE AND THE FOLLOWING THREE LINES WILL BE SHIFTED RIGHT 5 COL TL==*
          (1) THIS LINE WILL BE SHIFTED RIGHT 5 COLUMNS.               *===*
          (2) THIS LINE WILL BE SHIFTED RIGHT 5 COLUMNS.               *===*
          (3) THIS LINE WILL BE SHIFTED RIGHT 5 COLUMNS.               *===*
***** END OF FILE *****                                                  *****




_____
I^                                            □-□04
```

Figure 4-28   How to use the line commands to align text within the editing zone (part 2 of 3)

```
===>
<<..+....1....+....2....+....3....+....4....+....5....+.. INF=*INPARA*>>..+..FS
***** TOP OF FILE *****                                                /***/
THIS             LINE             WILL            BE          ALIGNED. *====*
                                     THIS LINE WILL BE JUSTIFIED TO THE RIGHT. *====*
THIS LINE WILL BE JUSTIFIED TO THE LEFT.                               *====*
                  THIS LINE WILL BE CENTERED.                          *====*
        THIS LINE WILL BE SHIFTED RIGHT 10 COLUMNS.                    *====*
        THIS LINE WILL BE SHIFTED LEFT 10 COLUMNS.                     *====*
THIS LINE WILL                                                         *====*
 BE SPLIT AT COLUMN 15.                                                *====*
        THIS LINE AND THE FOLLOWING THREE LINES WILL BE CENTERED:      *====*
                   (1) THIS LINE WILL BE CENTERED.                     *====*
                   (2) THIS LINE WILL BE CENTERED.                     *====*
                   (3) THIS LINE WILL BE CENTERED.                     *====*
THIS LINE AND THE FOLLOWING THREE LINES WILL BE SHIFTED RIGHT 5 COL    *====*
        (1) THIS LINE WILL BE SHIFTED RIGHT 5 COLUMNS.                 *====*
        (2) THIS LINE WILL BE SHIFTED RIGHT 5 COLUMNS.                 *====*
        (3) THIS LINE WILL BE SHIFTED RIGHT 5 COLUMNS.                 *====*
***** END OF FILE *****                                                *****


I^A                                         □-□04
```

Figure 4-28   How to use the line commands to align text within the editing zone (part 3 of 3)

Figure 4-29 gives the format of the RENUM command. As you can see, you could place line numbers, starting with 10 and incremented by 10 in columns 1 through 6 (the standard positions for line numbers in a COBOL program) by issuing this command:

RENUM 10 1 6 10

If you issue the RENUM command to place sequence numbers in a position that begins before column 73, no numbers will be placed in a line that begins with a slash (/). However, the line will be counted for numbering the lines that follow. If there's data other than a slash in column 1, sequence numbers will overlay data already in the positions the numbers will occupy.

Figure 4-30 illustrates the results this can have. Here, I've numbered a member that contains both COBOL source code and job control and linkage editor control statements. As you can see, the job control statements do not have line numbers applied to them, which is correct, since they begin with a slash. However, line numbers were applied to the linkage editor control statements (lines 000030 and 000040), and that is *not* correct. Also, although the job control statements were not numbered, they were included in determining sequence numbers. As a result, the numbers in the COBOL source program section of the member are not accurate.

The RENUM command

```
RENUM [increment [starting-column [length [starting-number]]]]
```

Explanation

increment	The increment to be used for numbers in the resequencing operation. The default is 100.
starting-column	The column in which the sequence number field is to begin. The default is 73.
length	The length of the sequence number field. The default is 8.
starting-number	The value at which sequence numbering is to begin. The default is the increment value.

Figure 4-29   The RENUM command

If sequence numbers are in columns 73 through 80, you can display them and still use the line command area if you issue the command

```
SET NUMBERS ON
```

For example, consider figure 4-31. Here, a member contains sequence numbers in columns 73 through 80, but they're concealed by the line command area. After I issue the SET NUMBERS ON command, the display looks like part 2 of the figure. You can enter a line command over the sequence numbers as long as you're sure the first character of the command is in column 73 and at least one space follows the last character of the command. For example, to delete 5 lines, I entered the line command in part 3 of the figure, and the result was the display in part 4 of the figure. (To correct the gap in the sequence numbers, you'd have to issue the RENUM command.)

How to get information from outside the editor

The last commands I'm going to present let you get information from outside the editor. In general, they let you invoke some system command functions from within the editor. In this section, I'll show you how to use the LIBRARY, PRINT, SHOW, and MSG commands.

How to display a library directory listing: the LIBRARY command   You might find during an editing session, that you want to retrieve a library member but you can't remember its name. Or, you might want to create a new member but you aren't sure what format to use for its name to make it consistent with other names in your library. To answer questions like these, you can issue the LIBRARY command.

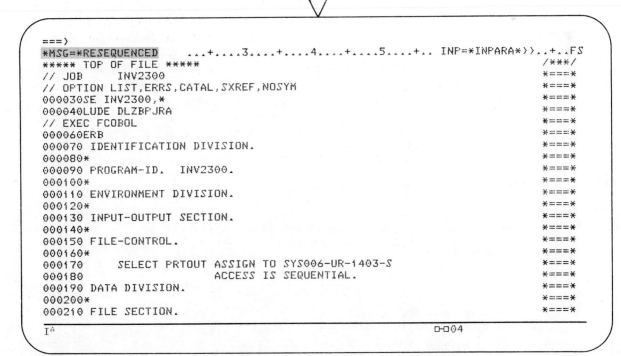

Figure 4-30   The operation of the RENUM command

```
===> SET NUMBERS ON
<<...+....1....+....2....+.....3.....+....4....+.....5....+.. INP=*INPARA*>>..+..FS
***** TOP OF FILE *****                                                     /***/
        IDENTIFICATION DIVISION.                                            *====*
      *                                                                     *====*
       PROGRAM-ID.   INV2300.                                              *====*
      *                                                                     *====*
       ENVIRONMENT DIVISION.                                               *====*
      *                                                                     *====*
       INPUT-OUTPUT SECTION.                                               *====*
      *                                                                     *====*
       FILE-CONTROL.                                                       *====*
      *                                                                     *====*
           SELECT PRTOUT ASSIGN TO SYS006-UR-1403-S                        *====*
                         ACCESS IS SEQUENTIAL.                             *====*
       DATA DIVISION.                                                      *====*
      *                                                                     *====*
       FILE SECTION.                                                       *====*
      *                                                                     *====*
       FD   PRTOUT                                                         *====*
            LABEL RECORDS ARE OMITTED                                      *====*
            RECORD CONTAINS 132 CHARACTERS.                                *====*
      *                                                                     *====*
       01   PRTOUT-RECORD                       PIC X(132).                *====*
I^                                                         □-□04
```

Figure 4-31   How to use the SET NUMBERS ON command (part 1 of 4)

```
===>
<<...+....1....+....2....+.....3.....+....4....+.....5....+.. INP=*INPARA*>>..+..FS
***** TOP OF FILE *****                                                     /***/
        IDENTIFICATION DIVISION.                                           000100
      *                                                                    000200
       PROGRAM-ID.   INV2300.                                             000300
      *                                                                    000400
       ENVIRONMENT DIVISION.                                              000500
      *                                                                    000600
       INPUT-OUTPUT SECTION.                                              000700
      *                                                                    000800
       FILE-CONTROL.                                                      000900
      *                                                                    001000
           SELECT PRTOUT ASSIGN TO SYS006-UR-1403-S                       001100
                         ACCESS IS SEQUENTIAL.                            001200
       DATA DIVISION.                                                     001300
      *                                                                    001400
       FILE SECTION.                                                      001500
      *                                                                    001600
       FD   PRTOUT                                                        001700
            LABEL RECORDS ARE OMITTED                                     001800
            RECORD CONTAINS 132 CHARACTERS.                               001900
      *                                                                    002000
       01   PRTOUT-RECORD                       PIC X(132).               002100
I^                                                         □-□04
```

Figure 4-31   How to use the SET NUMBERS ON command (part 2 of 4)

```
===>
<<..+....1....+....2....+....3....+....4....+....5....+.. INP=*INPARA*>>..+..FS
***** TOP OF FILE *****                                                /***/
        IDENTIFICATION DIVISION.                                       000100
        *                                                              000200
        PROGRAM-ID.  INV2300.                                          000300
        *                                                              000400
        ENVIRONMENT DIVISION.                                          000500
        *                                                              000600
        INPUT-OUTPUT SECTION.                                          000700
        *                                                              000800
        FILE-CONTROL.                                                  000900
        *                                                              001000
            SELECT PRTOUT ASSIGN TO SYS006-UR-1403-S                   001100
                        ACCESS IS SEQUENTIAL.                          001200
        DATA DIVISION.                                                 001300
        *                                                              001400
        FILE SECTION.                                                  001500
        *                                                              001600
        FD  PRTOUT                                                     D5 700
            LABEL RECORDS ARE OMITTED                                  001800
            RECORD CONTAINS 132 CHARACTERS.                            001900
        *                                                              002000
        01  PRTOUT-RECORD                    PIC X(132).               002100
─────────────────────────────────────────────────────────────────────────────
I^A                                              ▭─▭04
```

Figure 4-31   How to use the SET NUMBERS ON command (part 3 of 4)

```
===>
<<..+....1....+....2....+....3....+....4....+....5....+.. INP=*INPARA*>>..+..FS
***** TOP OF FILE *****                                                /***/
        IDENTIFICATION DIVISION.                                       000100
        *                                                              000200
        PROGRAM-ID.  INV2300.                                          000300
        *                                                              000400
        ENVIRONMENT DIVISION.                                          000500
        *                                                              000600
        INPUT-OUTPUT SECTION.                                          000700
        *                                                              000800
        FILE-CONTROL.                                                  000900
        *                                                              001000
            SELECT PRTOUT ASSIGN TO SYS006-UR-1403-S                   001100
                        ACCESS IS SEQUENTIAL.                          001200
        DATA DIVISION.                                                 001300
        *                                                              001400
        FILE SECTION.                                                  001500
        *                                                              001600
        *                                                              002200
        WORKING-STORAGE SECTION.                                       002300
        *                                                              002400
        01  SWITCHES.                                                  002500
        *                                                              002600
─────────────────────────────────────────────────────────────────────────────
I^A                                              ▭─▭04
```

Figure 4-31   How to use the SET NUMBERS ON command (part 4 of 4)

When you issue the LIBRARY command (which you can abbreviate as LIB) from within the editor, you get the same display you would if you exited the editor and issued the /LIBRARY system command. Your terminal enters list mode and displays the directory information you requested. You can specify all the operands available on the /LIBRARY system command on the LIB editor command. When the last screen of library information has been displayed, you tap the enter key and the full-screen editor screen is restored.

How to examine the contents of your user areas: the PRINT command   If you want to look at what's stored in your print area, log area, or editor stack area, you can use the PRINT command. Just issue the command PRINT followed by the name $$PRINT, $$LOG, or $$STACK. For example, to look at the lines you've accumulated in your editor stack area after issuing a series of copy with append (K) line commands, you could enter the command

    PRINT $$STACK

Or, if you've retrieved the output from a batch job from the POWER list queue (which you'll learn how to do in section 3) or just run a job in an ICCF interactive partition (which you'll learn how to do in section 4), you can look at the job's list output by issuing the command

    PRINT $$PRINT

This can be useful when you're correcting diagnostics in a source program.

How to get information on current option settings: the SHOW command   You can issue the editor command SHOW to display a variety of information. In this chapter, you've already seen how to use the SHOW command to look at the current delimiter and tab characters and at the current settings for tab stops, PF keys, and case translation. You can also use any of the operands of SHOW that are available with the /SHOW system command, which I'll describe in the next chapter.

How to get pending messages: the MSG command   In the next chapter, I'll describe the ICCF facilities for message processing. Now, I just want to point out that if messages are pending for you and your terminal isn't set up so you receive them automatically each time you press the enter key, you can issue the MSG editor command to cause them to be displayed.

Objectives

1. Use the full-screen editor commands presented in this topic to align text within your editing zone.

2. Issue the appropriate commands to add sequence numbers to a member or to be able to issue line commands over sequence numbers stored in columns 73 through 80 of a member.

3. Use these commands to get information from outside the full-screen editor:

   a. LIBRARY
   b. PRINT
   c. SHOW
   d. MSG

Chapter 5

Advanced system commands and ICCF-supplied procedures and macros

This chapter's three topics present a variety of features that can help you use ICCF more efficiently. The topics are independent; you can read any or all of them, and you can read them in any order. Topic 1 presents advanced system commands and ICCF-supplied procedures and macros for storing and manipulating library members. Topic 2 presents the commands and macros for handling output directed to your terminal efficiently and easily; it stresses the handling of printer output. Finally, topic 3 presents a variety of other system commands, including commands to set program functions keys and use logging.

TOPIC 1   ICCF facilities for manipulating library members

Although almost all of the work you do to create and change library members will be done with the editor, there are some specialized operations you can only do in command mode. That's what you'll learn in this topic. First, I'll show you how to use advanced system commands to manipulate library members. Then, I'll show you how to use a group of ICCF-supplied procedures and macros that let you perform some functions system commands don't provide.

SYSTEM COMMANDS FOR MANIPULATING LIBRARY MEMBERS

This section presents three ICCF facilities and the system commands you need to know to use them. First, you'll learn how to compress library members to save space and how to expand them later. Second, you'll see how to create and use a generation member group. And third, you'll learn how to change the protection attributes of library members.

How to compress and expand library members

Typically, ICCF library members are stored in *display format*, which means their data is stored in exact card image format. A member must be stored in display format for you to be able to edit it. However, the amount of space available in the ICCF library file is limited, so when you've finished work on a library member you want to keep, you should probably store it in *compressed format*. When you do, unnecessary spaces are removed and the data in the member is stored in a more efficient way. Because many library members (like source language programs) contain large numbers of spaces, it's not uncommon for the space savings to be 70 percent or more when a member is compressed.

As I've already said, you can't edit a compressed member. If you try to edit one directly, ICCF will indicate that the member wasn't found. And if you try to copy a compressed member into your input area using the GETFILE editor command, you'll be advised that the member is compressed. So, if you need to edit a member after you've compressed it, you must first convert it back to display format. Figure 5-1 presents the commands you use to convert members from one format to another. As you'll see, it's simple to convert a member from display to compressed format: All you do is issue the /SQUEEZE command. In contrast, there isn't a single command to "unsqueeze" a member that's stored in compressed format. Instead, you have to issue a series of three commands that cause a compressed member to be converted back to display format.

How to convert a display format library member to compressed format: the /SQUEEZE command   To compress a library member, you use the /SQUEEZE command, whose format is presented in figure 5-1. For example, to compress a library member named INV2100, I'd enter the command

```
/SQ INV2100
```

Then, ICCF displays this message:

```
*INPUT RECS = 00247 OUTPUT RECS = 00067 SAVINGS = 72%
*END COMPRESS
```

(Of course, the specific numbers will vary from one member to another.)

How to convert a compressed format library member to display format: the /INPUT, /INSERT, /REPLACE, and /SAVE commands   The way you convert a member in compressed format back to display format is cumbersome. The key to the process is that you have to transfer the data in the member into your input area, but you can't use the editor to do it. Instead, you have to use system commands that let you access the input area in ICCF's *system input mode* (which is not the same as the editor's input sub-mode). Figure 5-1 lists the commands you're likely to use in this process, and figure 5-2 presents a series of screens that illustrates the process.

To enter system input mode, you issue the system command

```
/INPUT
```

Then, any data you enter on the command line, except a system command, is stored in the input area; system commands are processed normally. Consider parts 1 and 2 of figure 5-2. Part 1 shows a partial library display that includes one member (INV2100) that's stored in compressed format (CPR). In the command line of that screen, I've keyed in the /INPUT command, and when I press the enter key, ICCF displays the screen in part 2 of the figure.

In part 2, my terminal has entered system input mode (indicated by the IN in the upper right corner), and I can key data directly into my input area one line at a time. However, that's *not* what I want to do. Instead, I want to copy the contents of the library member INV2100 into the input area. To do that, I've keyed in the command

```
/INSERT INV2100
```

When I press the enter key, data is transferred from the member to the

**Convert a member from display format to compressed format
(The /SQUEEZE command)**

```
/SQUEEZE member-name [password]
```

**Enter system input mode to begin conversion of a member in compressed format to display format
(The /INPUT command)**

```
/INPUT
```

**Copy a member in compressed format into the input area and, in the process, convert it to display format
(The /INSERT command)**

```
/INSERT member-name [password]
```

**Store text in the input area in a new library member and exit system input mode
(The /SAVE command)**

```
/SAVE member-name [password]
```

**Store text in the input area in an existing library member and exit system input mode
(The /REPLACE command)**

```
/REPLACE member-name [password]
```

Figure 5-1   Commands to convert a library member from one format to another

input area; it's during this transfer that ICCF converts the data from compressed to display format.

After the insert operation has finished, you need to leave system input mode immediately. If you key in other data, it's added a line at a time to the display format text now in your input area, and you almost certainly don't want that to happen. You can leave input mode in three ways; each leaves your newly expanded text in a different place.

One of the three ways to leave input mode is to press the PA2 key to cancel the input operation. In that case, the data is stored in two places: in the original library member in compressed format (INV2100 in this example) and in the input area in display format. The second option is to issue the /SAVE system command to transfer the contents of the input area to a new library member and to return to command mode from system input mode. Then, the data is again stored in two places: in the original library member in compressed format, and in a new library member in display format. The third option, which is the one I'm using in figure 5-2, is to issue the /REPLACE command to cause the display format data in the input area to replace the compressed format data in the library member before system input mode is ended. In part 3 of the figure, I've keyed in the /REPLACE command to do that.

```
/INPUT
...+....1....+....2....+....3....+....4....+....5....+....6....+....7....+..CM
LIBRARY NO. - 0009        05/03/86   16/14/27   DIR ENTRIES = 0201

00026 INV2100  04/30/86 STEV PRIV CPR
00161 INV2100B 06/12/85 STEV PRIV
00169 INV2100C 07/09/85 STEV PRIV
00176 INV2100D 04/25/86 STEV PRIV
00180 INV2100E 06/12/85 STEV PRIV
00200 INV2100A 03/07/86 STEV PRIV
*END PRINT
*READY




I^                                          □-□04
```

Figure 5-2   How to convert a member from compressed to display format (part 1 of 5)

```
/INSERT INV2100
...+....1....+....2....+....3....+....4....+....5....+....6....+....7....+..IN
0001




I^                                          □-□04
```

Figure 5-2   How to convert a member from compressed to display format (part 2 of 5)

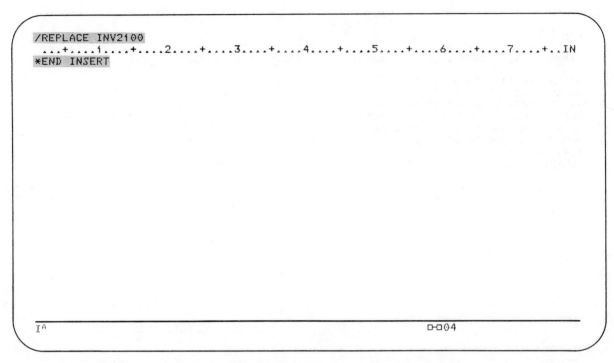

```
/REPLACE INV2100
....+....1....+....2....+....3....+....4....+....5....+....6....+....7....+..IN
*END INSERT




I^

                                                      □-□04
```

Figure 5-2   How to convert a member from compressed to display format (part 3 of 5)

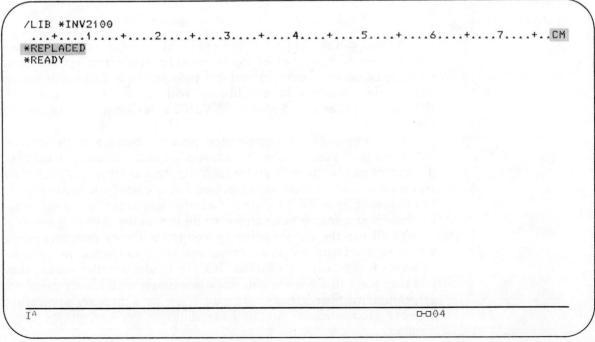

```
/LIB *INV2100
....+....1....+....2....+....3....+....4....+....5....+....6....+....7....+..CM
*REPLACED
*READY




I^

                                                      □-□04
```

Figure 5-2   How to convert a member from compressed to display format (part 4 of 5)

```
...+....1....+....2....+....3....+....4....+....5....+....6....+....7....+..CM
LIBRARY NO. - 0009        05/03/86   16/17/04   DIR ENTRIES = 0201

00026 INV2100  05/03/86 STEV PRIV ▓
00161 INV2100B 06/12/85 STEV PRIV
00169 INV2100C 07/09/85 STEV PRIV
00176 INV2100D 04/25/86 STEV PRIV
00180 INV2100E 06/12/85 STEV PRIV
00200 INV2100A 03/07/86 STEV PRIV
*END PRINT
*READY




I^                                              □-□04
```

Figure 5-2   How to convert a member from compressed to display format (part 5 of 5)

As you can see in part 4, the /REPLACE command was success-fully processed, and it caused my terminal to return from system input mode to command mode. In part 4, I've keyed in a /LIB command to display the members in my library with names that begin with INV2100. And, as part 5 shows, INV2100 is no longer in compressed format.

This sounds like a complicated process, but it's really simple. Nevertheless, if you work with compressed library members regularly, it becomes cumbersome to go through the steps in figure 5-2 each time you want to edit a compressed member. Fortunately, you can make the process easier by writing a macro or a procedure to perform these steps. I'll show you a macro you can use to do this in the next chapter.

You'll use the ICCF facility to compress library members when you've finished working on a member and you don't expect to continue to access it regularly. In contrast, ICCF provides another feature that you may want to use when you work intensively on a library member: generation member groups. As you'll see in a minute, generation member groups allow you to have multiple versions of the same member.

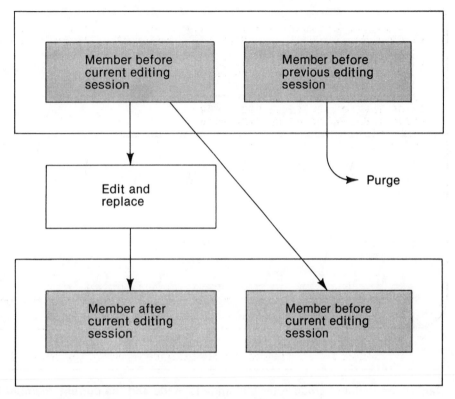

Generation member group before current editing session

Member before current editing session

Member before previous editing session

Edit and replace

Purge

Member after current editing session

Member before current editing session

Generation member group after current editing session

Figure 5-3   A small generation member group

How to create and use generation member groups

In this section, you'll learn how to use generation member groups. First, I'll describe what generation member groups are. Then, I'll show you how to use the /GROUP command to manage them.

What a generation member group is   A *generation member group* consists of the current version of a library member, plus from one to nine old copies of it. To understand how a generation member group works, consider the simple case in figure 5-3. Here, a group has just two members: the current version of the member and one copy that contains what *was* the current version before the last changes were applied to the member.

Generation member group before a change is made

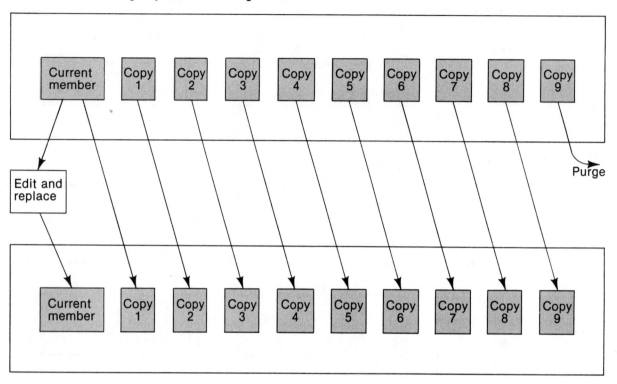

Generation member group after a change is made and the current member is replaced

Figure 5-4   A large generation member group

Now, suppose you make changes to the current version and replace it in your library. Before ICCF actually does the replace, the starting current version becomes the copy (the parent, or older generation), and the old copy is purged. Then, the newly changed version becomes the current member.

You can create a simple generation member group like the one in figure 5-3 or one as complex as the one in figure 5-4, which contains nine generation copies. As you can see, when the current version of a generation member group is replaced, the oldest member of the group is purged, all other generations are moved up one position, and what was the current version is made the most recent generation copy.

A library member that's part of a generation member group has a name in the format

xxxxxx-n

where xxxxxx is a one- to six-character name. The n is a number from 0

The /GROUP command

```
        {CREATE   group-name [password] [PRIV|PUBL] [member-count]}
/GROUP  {UNGROUP  group-name [password]                            }
        {REGROUP  group-name [password]                            }
```

Explanation

CREATE	Causes a new generation data group to be created.
UNGROUP	Disassociates the members of a generation data group from one another.
REGROUP	Reassociates the members of a generation data group with one another after /GROUP UNGROUP.
group-name	The one- to six-character name shared by all members in the generation data group.
PRIV PUBL	Specifies whether the members that will make up the new generation data group will be private or public.
member-count	Specifies how many library members, from 2 to 10, will make up the new generation data group. The default is 3.

Figure 5-5   The /GROUP command

to 9 that indicates the member's position in the group. The member that's numbered 0 is always the current member. For example, if I were to create a generation member group named GMG with four members, their names would be GMG-0, GMG-1, GMG-2, and GMG-3.

How to manage a generation member group: the /GROUP command
To create and manipulate a generation member group, you use the /GROUP command, illustrated in figure 5-5. As you can see, /GROUP has three functions: (1) create a new group, (2) disassociate members of a group so they can be processed independently, and (3) reassociate members of a group so their generation relationships are restored.

Before I describe the /GROUP command, I want you to know that you can't use it unless your user profile specifically authorizes you to do so. As a result, if you need to create and maintain a generation member group and you aren't able to use the /GROUP command, consult your ICCF administrator to have your user profile changed.

To create a group, you issue the /GROUP command in this format:

```
/GROUP CREATE xxxxxx n
```

where xxxxxx is the name for the group and n is the number of members in the group (from 2 to 10). If you omit n, the default is 3. For instance, the command

```
/GROUP CREATE GMG 4
```

creates the generation member group I described above. Four different library members are created, and they're related in a group.

Once the group has been created, you can change the current member (the one with the name that ends with -0), and the previous contents of the -0 member become the -1 member, the previous contents of the -1 member become the -2 member, and so on.

There is a restriction on this, however. You do not edit the -0 member directly. Instead, to cause the generations to be handled correctly, you must use the editor SAVE command to store the input area in the -0 member. This means that you'll invoke the full-screen editor without specifying a member name, then use the GETFILE command to copy the contents of the -0 member into the input area. You can then edit freely. When the editing session is over, you issue the SAVE command to transfer the contents of the input area to the -0 member. Note that in another situation this would result in an error because the -0 member already exists. However, when a generation member group is being used, it's OK. The full-screen editor advises you of what it has done by displaying

```
*MSG=*GENERATION MEMBER SAVED
```

In the four-member generation member group example I'm using, the original contents of GMG-3 are lost, GMG-2 becomes GMG-3, GMG-1 becomes GMG-2, GMG-0 becomes GMG-1, and the contents of the input area become GMG-0.

If you want to break the connections among the members of a generation member group, you can issue the /GROUP command and specify the UNGROUP operand. For example,

```
/GROUP UNGROUP GMG
```

causes the generation relationships among the library members GMG-0 through GMG-3 to be lost. The members still contain the data they held before the command was issued, but now they can be processed independently.

To restore the generation relationships that were disabled with the /GROUP UNGROUP command, issue the /GROUP REGROUP command. For example, the command

```
/GROUP REGROUP GMG
```

would restore the generation relationships among GMG-0, GMG-1, GMG-2, and GMG-3. If one of the members is missing, the group is restored only for the continuous range of names beginning with the -0 member.

The /PROTECT command

```
                                      ⎧ new-password    ⎫
                                      ⎪ NOPASS          ⎪
                                      ⎪ PRIV            ⎪
/PROTECT name [old-password] ⎨ PUBL            ⎬
                                      ⎪ DATE            ⎪
                                      ⎩ USER new-user-id ⎭
```

Figure 5-6   The /PROTECT command

How to change the protection attributes of a library member: the /PROTECT command

As you know, when you create a library member, you can specify a password to protect it from unauthorized access by other ICCF users. Then, when you want to access the member later, you have to supply the password. In addition to member passwords, ICCF provides other facilities to help you secure your data from unauthorized use. In this section, I'll show you how to use the /PROTECT command to alter passwords and the protection attributes of your library members, including (1) the type of data the member contains (public or private), (2) the last modification date, and (3) the user-id associated with the member. Other operands of the /PROTECT command let the ICCF administrator change other attributes of a member, but you probably won't want to use them even if you're allowed to. As a result, I won't describe them here.

For any version of the /PROTECT command, you enter the name of the library member you want to change, followed by its old password, if it has one. Then, you can code one of the options in the figure 5-6.

To understand what these operands do, consider figure 5-7. This figure shows library directory entries for several members, with a variety of protection attributes. For each member, it shows a command I issued to change an attribute, and the result of the command as indicated in a subsequent directory listing.

As you can see, each of the six members displayed is a private member associated with my user-id (STEV). All were last modified on 05/03/86, except PRTICCF, which was last modified on 03/13/86. And only the second and third are password protected.

The first /PROTECT command adds a password (PW2) to a library member that wasn't already password protected (PROTEX1). As you can see, to do this, all you have to do is issue the command, specify the library member name, and then specify the password that's to be applied to it.

The second /PROTECT command removes a password from the member PROTEX2. To be able to do this, of course, you have to know the password that's associated with the member. So you invoke the

Command: /LIB *PR

```
....+....1....+....2....+....3....+....4....+....5....+....6....+....7....+..CM
LIBRARY NO. - 0009        05/03/86    16/38/03    DIR ENTRIES = 0201

00109 PROTEX1  05/03/86 STEV PRIV
00113 PROTEX2 P05/03/86 STEV PRIV
00117 PROTEX3 P05/03/86 STEV PRIV
00121 PROTEX4  05/03/86 STEV PRIV
00125 PROTEX5  05/03/86 STEV PRIV
00190 PRTICCF  03/13/86 STEV PRIV
*END PRINT
*READY
```

I^   □-□04

Figure 5-7   How to use the /PROTECT command to change the protection attributes of
library members (part 1 of 2)

command and supply the library member name followed by the
password, then you enter NOPASS.

The third /PROTECT command changes the password for the
member PROTEX3 from PW1 to PW2. (Again, to be able to make any
change to a member that already has password protection, you must
specify the existing password.) After you do, just enter the value for the
new password.

The fourth /PROTECT command changes the protection attribute
for PROTEX4 from private to public. If you want to change a public
member to private, just code PRIV on the command instead of PUBL.

The fifth command changes the user-id associated with a member.
In this case, I changed the user-id associated with PROTEX5 from STEV
to AAAA. Note that although you can change the user-id associated
with a member, you may not be able to access the member after you
make the change. That will happen if the member is private and your
user profile prevents you from accessing other users' library members.

The last example changes the last modification date of the library
member PRTICCF to the current date. This can be useful if you want to
keep a member that hasn't been used for some time when your shop's
practice is to delete inactive members from certain libraries.

Commands: /PROTECT   PROTEX1   PW2

                /PROTECT   PROTEX2   PW1   NOPASS

                /PROTECT   PROTEX3   PW1   PW2

                /PROTECT   PROTEX4   PUBL

                /PROTECT   PROTEX5   USER   AAAA

                /PROTECT   PRTICCF   DATE

                /LIB   *PR

```
...+....1....+....2....+....3....+....4....+....5....+....6....+....7....+..CM
LIBRARY NO. - 0009         05/03/86    16/39/25    DIR ENTRIES = 0201

00109 PROTEX1 P05/03/86 STEV PRIV
00113 PROTEX2  05/03/86 STEV PRIV
00117 PROTEX3 P05/03/86 STEV PRIV
00121 PROTEX4  05/03/86 STEV
00125 PROTEX5  05/03/86 AAAA PRIV
00190 PRTICCF  05/03/86 STEV PRIV
*END PRINT
*READY




IA                                                    D-004
```

Figure 5-7   How to use the /PROTECT command to change the protection attributes of library members (part 2 of 2)

ICCF-SUPPLIED PROCEDURES AND
MACROS FOR MANIPULATING LIBRARY MEMBERS

In this section, I'll show you how to use the ICCF supplied procedures and macros that let you manipulate library members. Four of them let you copy and move library members; I'll describe them first in this section. One other lets you resequence records in a library member; I'll present it last.

How to copy and move library members

Although the editing facilities of ICCF are extensive, there are no editor or system commands to copy one library member directly to another or to copy or move members between libraries. However, since those are common functions, all current versions of ICCF provide a macro (COPYFILE) and two procedures (CPYLIB and MVLIB) to perform them. In addition, the most recent release of ICCF (version 2, release 1) provides another procedure (COPYMEM) that can perform all of the functions of COPYFILE, CPYLIB, and MVLIB. Figure 5-8 presents the command lines for all four.

The COPYFILE macro   The COPYFILE macro lets you make a duplicate copy of a library member. The output member is stored in your primary library, but the input member may come from your primary or secondary library or the common library. To run the macro, all you have to do is enter a command line like

```
@COPYFILE INV2100 INV2100C
```

Here, I'm copying the member named INV2100 to another member that will be named INV2100C. (If you're using ICCF 1.3 mod-level 5 or above, the leading @ isn't required.)

The password parameter is required if the input member is password protected; when that's the case, the output member is automatically protected with the same password. If you specify the password parameter and the input member isn't protected, the password is applied to the output member.

You can do the same thing the COPYFILE macro does using the full-screen editor. First, you invoke the editor to edit the input area. Then, you issue the GETFILE command to copy the contents of the source member into your input area. Finally, you issue the SAVE command to store that data in a new library member. Although this isn't a difficult process, it's easier to use the COPYFILE macro.

The COPYFILE macro only lets you copy a member from one of your current libraries to your primary library. If you want to copy a member from a library that's not one of your current libraries or you want to copy a member to a library other than your primary library, you can use the CPYLIB procedure.

The CPYLIB procedure   To copy a library member from one library to another, you invoke the CPYLIB procedure like this:

```
CPYLIB COBTEST 9 83
```

Here, the member COBTEST will be copied from library 9 to library 83.

Make a copy of a member stored in any of your current libraries and store the copy in your primary library (The COPYFILE macro)

```
COPYFILE in-name out-name [in-password]
```

Copy a member from one library to another (The CPYLIB procedure)

```
CPYLIB in-name [in-password] in-lib out-lib
```

Move a member from one library to another (The MVLIB procedure)

```
MVLIB in-name [in-password] in-lib out-lib
```

Invoke the multi-function COPYMEM procedure to copy or move a library member (The COPYMEM procedure)

```
COPYMEM in-name [in-password] in-lib
        out-name [out-password] out-lib [PURGE]
```

Explanation

in-name	The name of the source library member to be copied or moved.
in-password	The password associated with the library member in-name. For the COPYFILE macro and the CPYLIB and MVLIB procedures, this password will also be associated with the output member out-name.
in-lib	The number of the library in which the source library member in-name resides.
out-name	The name of the new library member to be created.
out-password	The password to be applied to the new library member out-name. Valid only for the ICCF 2.1 procedure COPYMEM.
out-lib	The number of the library in which the new library member out-name will reside.
PURGE	Indicates that the source library member in-name will be deleted after the copy operation has been completed. Lets the ICCF 2.1 procedure COPYMEM perform move as well as copy operations.

Figure 5-8 Command lines to invoke the COPYFILE macro and the CPYLIB, MVLIB, and COPYMEM procedures

For the CPYLIB procedure to work, both of the libraries you name must be accessible to you. In other words, each must be a public library or a private library which you're authorized to use. Also, if either the source or destination library is your secondary library, you have to issue the command

```
/CONNECT OFF
```

to disconnect it before you invoke the CPYLIB procedure.

Depending on the release of ICCF you're using and the program fixes that have been applied to it, it may not be possible to copy *from* your primary library using the CPYLIB procedure. If you try it and it doesn't work, tell your ICCF administrator. Then, she can make the change necessary to the procedure so it will work properly; it's a relatively simple fix.

The MVLIB procedure   If you want to transfer a member from one library to another, you can use the MVLIB procedure. It works the same way as the CPYLIB procedure, except it deletes the member from the source library after it has copied it to the destination library. For example,

```
MVLIB COBTEST 9 83
```

would cause COBTEST to be copied from library 9 to library 83, then deleted from library 9.

The same restrictions that apply to CPYLIB also apply to MVLIB. You must be authorized to use both libraries you name and if either is connected, you must disconnect it before you invoke the procedure.

The COPYMEM procedure   If you're using VSE/ICCF version 2, release 1, another procedure is available that can perform all the functions provided by COPYFILE, CPYLIB, and MVLIB; it's called COPYMEM, and its format is in figure 5-8. For example, to move the member COBTEST from library 9 to library 83, I'd enter

```
COPYMEM COBTEST 9 COBTEST 83 PURGE
```

As you can see, you need to supply the name for the output member, even if it's the same as the input member. By specifying PURGE on this command line, the procedure will delete the original member after it completes the copy operation.

For inter-library transfers, the restrictions that apply to CPYLIB and MVLIB also apply to COPYMEM. You must be authorized to use the libraries you name, and you may not be connected to either of them.

How to sort a library member: the SORT procedure

Sometimes, you might want to resequence the records in a library member. This is unlikely for typical ICCF library members that contain program source code or VSE job streams. However, if you're creating a

The SORT procedure

```
SORT in-name [in-password] [SEQ sort-specs] [PUNCH out-name]
```

Explanation

in-name	The name of the library member to be sorted.
in-password	The password associated with the library member to be sorted.
SEQ	Indicates that sort specifications follow. If you omit SEQ and sort-specs, the member is sorted into ascending sequence based on the contents of columns 1 through 15.

sort-specs

A single string that defines from one to four sort fields. For each field, you supply three specifications:

1. One letter to indicate the sort sequence for the field:
    A for ascending sequence
    D for descending sequence
2. Two digits to indicate the starting column of the sort field.
3. Two digits to indicate the length of the sort field.

For example,

SEQ A0110A1505A1104D2010

specifies four sort fields. The first is 10 bytes long and begins in column 1; the second is 5 bytes long and begins in column 15; the third is 4 bytes long and begins in column 11; and the fourth is 10 bytes long and begins in column 20. Sequencing is to be in ascending order for all sort fields except the last.

PUNCH out-name

This parameter identifies a new library member that will contain the sorted records: out-name. If you omit this parameter, the sorted records will replace the data in the input member.

Figure 5-9   Command line to invoke the SORT procedure

member that contains test data for an application program, it might be useful to be able to sort its records.

To resequence the records in a library member, you use the SORT procedure, whose command line is presented in figure 5-9. To use the SORT procedure, you specify three groups of parameters: input, sort sequence, and output. First, you identify the library member to be sorted. You enter its name and, if required, its password; this is just like what you'd specify for a system command.

Second, you can specify the sort sequence you want to use. If you omit this parameter group, the sort is in ascending sequence on the data in columns 1 through 15 of each record. It's more likely that you'll override this by specifying from one to four sequence fields for the sort. To start the group, enter SEQ and a space, then a string that contains the data the procedure will use to identify the sequence fields. For each sequence field, enter A or D to indicate whether the field should be sorted in ascending or descending sequence. Then, enter a two-digit number to indicate the starting position of the field and follow it with another two-digit number to indicate the field's length. All of these items should be entered without separating spaces.

Third, you specify where the procedure should store its output. Although there are options for this parameter other than those the figure shows, I suggest you either specify a name for a new library member or omit the parameter altogether. If you don't specify the output for the procedure, the sorted data replaces the data in the input member.

Here's an example of how you might invoke the SORT procedure:

```
SORT TESTDATA SEQ A0108 PUNCH TESTDATA
```

Here, the data in library member TESTDATA will be sorted into ascending sequence based on the contents of the eight-byte field that begins in position 1 of each record. The output of the sort will be punched back into the original library member: TESTDATA.

In this case, you could probably depend on the defaults for the sort sequence and output parameter groups. The command

```
SORT TESTDATA
```

would cause the records in TESTDATA to be sorted into ascending sequence based on the data in positions 1 through 15, which includes 1 through 8. (Of course, records with the same data in positions 1 through 8, but different data in positions 9 through 15 might be sequenced differently than if the sort were done specifically on positions 1 through 8; however, the records will still be in sequence based on positions 1 through 8.) And because no output member was specified, the sorted records are stored in the input library member, replacing the records that were there before the sort.

For a more complicated sort that uses more than one sequence field, the sort sequence parameter group is more complicated. For example, the command

```
SORT TESTDATA SEQ A5004A0149D5410 PUNCH TDSORT
```

would cause the records in TESTDATA to be sorted on three fields. First, they'd be sorted into ascending sequence based on the four-byte field that begins in column 50. If any duplicate keys were found in that field, they'd be sequenced in ascending order based on the contents of the 49-byte field beginning in column 1. And if there were still duplicate records after that, they'd be sequenced in descending order according to the values in the 10-byte field that begins in column 54. And because the command specified PUNCH TDSORT, the output would be stored in a new library member with that name. The contents of TESTDATA wouldn't be changed.

One warning about the SORT procedure: Don't try to sort a member that contains a VSE end-of-data statement (/ *). That's because / and * in columns 1 and 2 signal end of data to the program the SORT procedure invokes.

Terminology

display format
compressed format
system input mode
generation member group

Objectives

1. Use the /SQUEEZE command to convert a library member stored in display format to compressed format and use the /INPUT, /INSERT, /REPLACE, and /SAVE commands to restore a member stored in compressed format to display format.

2. Use the /GROUP command to create a generation member group, disassociate the members of a generation member group from one another so they can be processed separately, and reassociate them.

3. Use the /PROTECT command to change the protection attributes of a library member.

4. Use the COPYFILE macro to copy a member from your primary, secondary, or common library into your primary library.

5. Use the CPYLIB and MVLIB procedures to transfer members from one library to another.

6. Use the COPYMEM procedure to copy a member from your primary, secondary, or common library into your primary library or to transfer a member from one library to another.

7. Use the SORT procedure to resequence the records in a library member.

TOPIC 2   ICCF facilities for controlling terminal output

In this topic, I'll describe the advanced system commands you can use to manage output produced as a result of an ICCF system command or output stored in your temporary areas. Frankly, you'll be able to satisfy most of your output management needs with the /DISPLAY and /LIST commands, which you learned in chapter 3. However, you'll find times when the advanced commands this topic presents will be helpful.

HOW TO PRODUCE A SUMMARY LISTING: THE /SUMRY COMMAND

A variation of the /DISPLAY command is /SUMRY. When you issue it, you can focus more easily on lines that contain job control statements or job entry statements (statements that are used to control the execution of jobs in ICCF interactive partitions). That's because the command only displays lines that begin with a slash (/) and suppresses lines that don't. In place of the suppressed lines, the /SUMRY command displays a count of the number of continuous lines that it doesn't display. For example, figure 5-10 compares the output produced by the /DISPLAY and /SUMRY commands for a library member that contains a job stream that will compile a COBOL program.

HOW TO CAUSE OUTPUT DISPLAY TO BE CONTINUOUS: THE /CONTINU COMMAND

Typically, when ICCF displays output on a 3270 terminal, it pauses between each screen of data and waits for you to press the enter key before it displays the next screen. However, you can change this default so output is displayed continuously. To do that, you issue the /CONTINU command in this format:

```
/CONTINU nnn
```

where nnn is the number of seconds you want ICCF to pause between screens; nnn must be between 1 and 255; if you omit nnn, ICCF pauses for six seconds for 3270 terminals. Unlike most of the other system commands you've seen, /CONTINU is not valid in command mode. You can issue it only in list and execution modes. Its effect ends when you return to command mode. The abbreviation for the /CONTINU command is /C.

During the pause between screen displays, you can turn off continuous display by entering

```
/C OFF
```

Command: /DISPLAY DCTST

```
....+....1....+....2....+....3....+....4....+....5....+....6....+....7....+..LS
00001 // JOB     DCTST
00002 // OPTION  LIST,NOLISTX,NOXREF,NOSYM,ERRS,CATAL
00003    INCLUDE DLZBPJRA
00004 // EXEC    FCOBOL
00005  CBL APOST,LANGLVL(1),NOTRUNC,NOSYM,VERB
00006         IDENTIFICATION DIVISION.
00007       *
00008        PROGRAM-ID.  DLIIINQ.
00009       *
00010        ENVIRONMENT DIVISION.
00011       *
00012        DATA DIVISION.
00013       *
00014        WORKING-STORAGE SECTION.
00015       *
00016        01   SWITCHES.
00017       *
00018            05   VALID-DATA-SW          PIC X     VALUE 'Y'.
00019                 88  VALID-DATA                   VALUE 'Y'.
00020            05   INVOICE-FOUND-SW       PIC X     VALUE 'Y'.

I^                                              □-□04
```

Command: /SUMRY DCTST

```
...+....1....+....2....+....3....+....4....+....5....+....6....+....7....+..CM
00001 // JOB     DCTST
00002 // OPTION  LIST,NOLISTX,NOXREF,NOSYM,ERRS,CATAL
     CARD IMAGE COUNT = 00001
00004 // EXEC    FCOBOL
     CARD IMAGE COUNT = 00231
00236 /*
00237 /&
*END PRINT
*READY




I^                                              □-□04
```

Figure 5-10   Sample output of the /DISPLAY and /SUMRY commands

Then, ICCF returns to its default method of handling screens of data. Alternatively, you can end the display by entering the /CANCEL command or pressing the PA2 key, which has the same effect as /CANCEL.

The commands /LIB, /LIST, and /DISP have special forms that let you automatically enter continuous display mode: /LIBC, /LISTC, and /DISPC. These commands first set continuous display mode on with an interval of six seconds (the default for 3270 terminals), then display the requested output. If you want to use a pause interval other than six seconds, you'll need to issue the /CONTINU command explicitly after you've used the basic form of the command you want.

HOW TO HANDLE PRINTER OUTPUT

Although you'll be able to use your 3270 terminal to display output much of the time, you'll still want to get printed output often. There are a variety of ways you can get printed output from ICCF. In this section, I'll describe how to route printed output to a local terminal printer like a 3287 matrix printer. But first, you need to know how ICCF stores and identifies print-type data.

How ICCF stores and identifies print-type data

You can use the facilities I describe in this section to print library members that contain standard data or to print members with data that's specially formatted for printing; these specially formatted members are called print-type members. In a print-type member, each print line, which can be as long as 132 characters, can be stored in two 80-byte card image records. ICCF uses the first two bytes of each record in a print-type member to store control information. To identify a print-type member, be sure the last-two characters of its name are .P. Even if a member contains data in print-type format, ICCF won't treat it as such unless the name ends with the .P suffix.

To help you understand this, I want to show you an example. Part 1 of figure 5-11 shows a screen displayed by ICCF after I compiled a COBOL program in an interactive partition. (I'll show you how to run programs in interactive partitions in section 4.) For now, just realize that the compiler listing—including the information in this display—is stored in the print area. (Data in your print area ($$PRINT) is stored in print-type format.)

Notice here that lines longer than 80 characters are wrapped around to use two lines on the screen. That's an indication that this is print-type data. Now, to show you how ICCF stored this data, I want you to take a look at part 2 of the figure. To get to this point, I invoked the full-screen editor to edit an empty input area (@ED), and issued the command

```
    ...+....1....+....2....+....3....+....4....+....5....+....6....+....7....+..SP
    * * * * * START OF PROCEDURE (CLIST) * * * * *
    K867I  GETVIS SET TO  48K
    K859I  ALLOCATION FOR IKSYS11 - SERIAL=DOSRES UNIT=SYS013 LOC= 94780,640
    K859I  ALLOCATION FOR IKSYS12 - SERIAL=DOSRES UNIT=SYS013 LOC= 95420,640
    K859I  ALLOCATION FOR IKSYS13 - SERIAL=DOSRES UNIT=SYS013 LOC= 96060,640
    K859I  ALLOCATION FOR IKSYS14 - SERIAL=DOSRES UNIT=SYS013 LOC= 96700,640
        1  IBM DOS/VS COBOL                              REL 3.0              PP NO.
    5746-CB1            17.10.20  05/03/86


    *STATISTICS*          SOURCE RECORDS =    230       DATA ITEMS =    109      PRO
    C DIV SZ =      41
    *STATISTICS*          PARTITION SIZE = 735856       LINE COUNT =     56      BUF
    FER SIZE =     2048
    *OPTIONS IN EFFECT*    PMAP RELOC ADR =   NONE       SPACING     =      1     FLO
    W      =     NONE
    *OPTIONS IN EFFECT*    NOLISTX      QUOTE       NOSYM      NOCATALR      NOLIST
        NOLINK     NOSTXIT      NOLIB
    *OPTIONS IN EFFECT*    NOCLIST      FLAGW       ZWB        NOSUPMAP      NOXREF
        ERRS     NOSXREF      NOOPT
    I^                                                    □-□04
```

Figure 5-11   How ICCF stores and handles print-type data (part 1 of 4)

```
    ===>
    <<...+....1....+....2....+....3....+....4....+....5....+.. INP=*INPARA*>>..+..FS
    ***** TOP OF FILE *****                                              /***/
    1 * * * * START OF PROCEDURE (CLIST) * * * * *                       *====*
    1 K867I  GETVIS SET TO  48K                                          *====*
    1 K859I  ALLOCATION FOR IKSYS11 - SERIAL=DOSRES UNIT=SYS013 LOC= 94780,6 *====*
    1 K859I  ALLOCATION FOR IKSYS12 - SERIAL=DOSRES UNIT=SYS013 LOC= 95420,6 *====*
    1 K859I  ALLOCATION FOR IKSYS13 - SERIAL=DOSRES UNIT=SYS013 LOC= 96060,6 *====*
    1 K859I  ALLOCATION FOR IKSYS14 - SERIAL=DOSRES UNIT=SYS013 LOC= 96700,6 *====*
    1     1  IBM DOS/VS COBOL                              REL 3.0         *====*
    2 . 5746-CB1            17.10.20  05/03/86                            *====*
    1                                                                     *====*
    1                                                                     *====*
    1 *STATISTICS*          SOURCE RECORDS =    230       DATA ITEMS =    10 *====*
    2 ROC DIV SZ =      41                                                *====*
    1 *STATISTICS*          PARTITION SIZE = 735856       LINE COUNT =     5 *====*
    2 UFFER SIZE =     2048                                               *====*
    1 *OPTIONS IN EFFECT*    PMAP RELOC ADR =   NONE       SPACING     =   *====*
    2 LOW      =     NONE                                                 *====*
    1 *OPTIONS IN EFFECT*    NOLISTX      QUOTE       NOSYM      NOCATALR  *====*
    2 T      NOLINK     NOSTXIT      NOLIB                                *====*
    1 *OPTIONS IN EFFECT*    NOCLIST      FLAGW       ZWB        NOSUPMAP  *====*
    2 F      ERRS     NOSXREF      NOOPT                                  *====*
    1 *OPTIONS IN EFFECT*    NOSTATE      TRUNC       SEQ        NOSYMDMP  *====*
    I^                                                    □-□04
```

Figure 5-11   How ICCF stores and handles print-type data (part 2 of 4)

```
*HARDCOPY MODE SET
*READY
*HARDCOPY MODE SET
*READY
****************** HARDCOPY LIST OF MEMBER CF.P    **************
*READY
* * *  * START OF PROCEDURE (CLIST) * * * * *
K867I  GETVIS SET TO 48K
K859I  ALLOCATION FOR IKSYS11 - SERIAL=DOSRES UNIT=SYS013 LOC= 94780,640
K859I  ALLOCATION FOR IKSYS12 - SERIAL=DOSRES UNIT=SYS013 LOC= 95420,640
K859I  ALLOCATION FOR IKSYS13 - SERIAL=DOSRES UNIT=SYS013 LOC= 96060,640
K859I  ALLOCATION FOR IKSYS14 - SERIAL=DOSRES UNIT=SYS013 LOC= 96700,640
   1   IBM DOS/VS COBOL                REL 3.0                 PP NO. 5746-CB1    17.10.20   05/03/86

*STATISTICS*       SOURCE RECORDS =    230        DATA ITEMS =   109        PROC DIV SZ =        41
*STATISTICS*       PARTITION SIZE = 735856        LINE COUNT =    56        BUFFER SIZE =      2048
*OPTIONS IN EFFECT*   PMAP RELOC ADR = NONE       SPACING =        1        FLOW =           NONE
*OPTIONS IN EFFECT*   NOLISTX        QUOTE        NOSYM     NOCATALR        NOLIST    NOLINK    NOSTXIT
*OPTIONS IN EFFECT*   NOCLIST        FLAGW        ZWB       NOSUPMAP        NOXREF    ERRS      NOSXREF
*OPTIONS IN EFFECT*   NOSTATE        TRUNC        SEQ       NOSYMDMP        DECK      NOVERB    NOSYNTAX
*OPTIONS IN EFFECT*   LANGLVL(2)     NOCOUNT      ADV       NOVERBSUM       NOVERBREF
*LISTER OPTIONS*         NONE
CARD   2   DLIIINQ        17.10.20      05/03/86

CARD   ERROR MESSAGE

00172  ILA4072I-W    EXIT FROM PERFORMED PROCEDURE ASSUMED BEFORE PROCEDURE-NAME .
00180  ILA4072I-W    EXIT FROM PERFORMED PROCEDURE ASSUMED BEFORE PROCEDURE-NAME .
00196  ILA4072I-W    EXIT FROM PERFORMED PROCEDURE ASSUMED BEFORE PROCEDURE-NAME .

END OF COMPILATION
*END PRINT
*READY
***************************************************************
*READY
```
                                                                                        NOLIB
                                                                                        NOOPT
                                                                                        NOLVL

Figure 5-11   How ICCF stores and handles print-type data (part 3 of 4)

```
*HARDCOPY MODE SET
*READY
*HARDCOPY MODE SET
*READY
****************** HARDCOPY LIST OF MEMBER  CP         ***********
*READY
1.* * * * * START OF PROCEDURE (CLIST) * * * * *
1.K867I  GETVIS SET TO  48K
1.K859I  ALLOCATION FOR IKSYS11 - SERIAL=DOSRES UNIT=SYS013 LOC= 94780,640
1.K859I  ALLOCATION FOR IKSYS12 - SERIAL=DOSRES UNIT=SYS013 LOC= 95420,640
1.K859I  ALLOCATION FOR IKSYS13 - SERIAL=DOSRES UNIT=SYS013 LOC= 96060,640
1.K859I  ALLOCATION FOR IKSYS14 - SERIAL=DOSRES UNIT=SYS013 LOC= 96700,640
1-    1 IBM DOS/VS COBOL                           REL 3.0          PP NO
2.. 5746-CB1            17.10.20  05/03/86
1.
1.
1.*STATISTICS*          SOURCE RECORDS =    230    DATA ITEMS =    109    P
2.ROC DIV SZ =     41
1.*STATISTICS*          PARTITION SIZE = 735856    LINE COUNT =     56    B
2.UFFER SIZE =    2048
1.*OPTIONS IN EFFECT*   PMAP RELOC ADR =   NONE    SPACING      =     1    F
2.LOW      =     NONE
1.*OPTIONS IN EFFECT*   NOLISTX     QUOTE     NOSYM     NOCATALR     NOLIS
2.T     NOLINK     NOSTXIT     NOLIB
1.*OPTIONS IN EFFECT*   NOCLIST     FLAGW     ZWB     NOSUPMAP     NOXRE
2.F     ERRS     NOSXREF     NOOPT
1.*OPTIONS IN EFFECT*   NOSTATE     TRUNC     SEQ     NOSYMDMP     DEC
2.K     NOVERB     NOSYNTAX     NOLVL
1.*OPTIONS IN EFFECT*   LANGLVL(2)  NOCOUNT     ADV              NOVERBSU
2.M  NOVERBREF
1.*LISTER OPTIONS*          NONE
1-    2    DLIIINQ         17.10.20         05/03/86
1. CARD   ERROR MESSAGE
1.
1. 00172  ILA4072I-W    EXIT FROM PERFORMED PROCEDURE ASSUMED BEFORE PROCEDURE-
2.NAME .
1. 00180  ILA4072I-W    EXIT FROM PERFORMED PROCEDURE ASSUMED BEFORE PROCEDURE-
2.NAME .
1. 00196  ILA4072I-W    EXIT FROM PERFORMED PROCEDURE ASSUMED BEFORE PROCEDURE-
2.NAME .
1.
1.END OF COMPILATION
*END PRINT
*READY
*****************************************************************
*READY
```

Figure 5-11   How ICCF stores and handles print-type data (part 4 of 4)

GETFILE $$PRINT

to copy the contents of the print area into the input area; then, I issued the TOP command to move the current line pointer to the top of the data.

In this figure, you can see the control information ICCF stores in the first two bytes of each record in a print-type member. ICCF uses the value in the first byte to reconstruct complete print lines. The first part of each print line is stored in a record identified with a 1 in the first byte. If the line has to be stored in two records, the second record immediately follows the first and is identified by a 2 in the first byte. The second byte in each record contains printer carriage control information.

Next, I saved the data in a library member named CP.P. Because the member's name ends with the print-type suffix .P, ICCF will handle it properly when it's printed. In part 3 of the figure, you can see what the printed output of this member looks like. It contains full print lines, as it should. (I'll show you how to produce printed output in just a moment.)

However, suppose I had saved the print data in a standard library member with the name CP. Then, although the data itself is formatted for printing, ICCF doesn't know that because the member name doesn't end with the .P suffix. If I were to print the member CP, the result would be the output in part 4 of the figure. Here, the print control characters that are stored in the first two bytes of each record aren't interpreted as such; they're treated as ordinary data.

How to route output to a printer: the /HARDCPY command

Now that you've learned how ICCF stores and identifies print-type data, you're ready to learn how to route it to a printer to produce a permanent copy. To do that, you use the /HARDCPY command which causes your terminal to enter *hardcopy mode*. Then, data is sent to your terminal printer; it's still displayed on your screen, but in a compressed form. When you've finished your printing job, you use the /HARDCPY command to turn hardcopy mode off and return to normal operations.

The way you use the /HARDCPY command varies depending on how your system is set up. Quite frankly, the easiest way for you to find out for sure how to get printed output is to ask someone in your shop who already knows how. In this section, I'll show you how to produce hardcopy output for two situations: (1) when you can send output directly to your terminal printer and (2) when you have to send output indirectly to the printer through a CICS transient data destination.

How to print a hardcopy listing directly   It's possible that the printer attached to your terminal controller can receive print data directly. If so, you go through four steps to send output to it, as listed in figure 5-12.

First, you have to specify where print output will go. You do that by issuing the /HARDCPY command and specifying as its operand the terminal-id of the printer. For instance, if the printer terminal-id is L86P, you'd enter

```
/HARDCPY L86P
```

Of course, you'll have to find out what your printer's terminal-id is to issue a command like this.

Second, after you've named the destination for the print data and you're ready to begin hardcopy printing, you enter

Step 1   **Specify your printer-id**

```
/HARDCPY printer-id
```

Step 2   **Enter hardcopy mode**

```
/HARDCPY ON
```

Step 3   **Clear your screen and produce your print output in continuous form**

```
/LISTC member-name
        or
/DISPC  member-name
```

Step 4   **Exit hardcopy mode**

```
/HARDCPY OFF
```

Figure 5-12   The four steps for producing print output directly on a terminal printer

```
/HARDCPY ON
```

From this point, all data that would normally display on your screen is routed to the printer.

Third, you clear your screen and issue a continuous output command (like /DISPC or /LISTC) at your terminal for the library member you want to print. For example, if you enter

```
/LISTC INV2100
```

the contents of library member INV2100 will be routed to the printer with the terminal-id L86P. As I've already said, the data is also echoed on the screen, but in a compressed format. It's displayed as a verification that the hardcopy operation is taking place.

Finally, you turn hardcopy mode off after your listing has printed. To do that, you enter

```
/HARDCPY OFF
```

For small groups of users who share a printer, this can work well. However, it's possible for two users to send hardcopy data to the same printer at the same time. When that happens using this printing technique, data for the two users can be mixed on the printer. A way to avoid this problem is to use private CICS destinations for hardcopy output.

How to print a hardcopy listing through a private CICS destination
One of the functions of CICS is *transient data management*. In other
words, CICS can store data from a source temporarily in a *transient
data destination* before it routes it to its final destination. The data is
"transient" because it's stored, but only on a temporary basis while it's
moving through the system. The final destination can be a program or a
device; in this case, it's a terminal printer.

In fact, CICS uses a transient data destination to process hardcopy
output that you send directly to your printer, although that's
transparent to you. However, when you use the hardcopy facility
through a *private destination*, you have to be more aware of what's
happening. To use this printing technique, a private destination must
have been defined for you within CICS and it must have been linked
with the final destination: your printer. So check with your ICCF
administrator to find out if your shop uses this facility and, if so, what
your private destination and printer terminal ids are.

To produce a hardcopy listing via a private destination, you go
through *five* steps instead of four (although the first four are similar to
the process for routing output directly to a printer). Figure 5-13 lists
those steps. First, you specify your private destination with a
/HARDCPY command like:

```
/HARDCPY STEV
```

Here, the name of my private destination is STEV. (As I've mentioned,
this name must have already been defined to CICS.) Issuing this command is equivalent to specifying the terminal-id for direct printing; it
specifies where ICCF will route the data.

The second, third, and fourth steps are just like those for direct
printing. When you're ready to print, you enter hardcopy mode by
issuing the command

```
/HARDCPY ON
```

Then, you issue an appropriate output command like

```
/DISPC INV2100
```

and fourth, you issue the command

```
/HARDCPY OFF
```

to return your terminal to normal operations.

At this point, CICS has stored the data you want printed in a
private destination. In this example, it's in the destination called STEV.
However, it's still not printing. To cause the output to be transferred
from the destination to the printer, you enter still another form of the
/HARDCPY command:

Step 1   **Specify your private destination id**

`/HARDCPY dest-id`

Step 2   **Enter hardcopy mode**

`/HARDCPY ON`

Step 3   **Clear your screen and produce your print output in continuous form**

```
/LISTC member-name
         or
/DISPC  member-name
```

Step 4   **Exit hardcopy mode**

`/HARDCPY OFF`

Step 5   **Start the printer associated with your private destination**

`/HARDCPY START printer-id dest-id`

Figure 5-13   The five steps for producing print output through a CICS private destination

`/HARDCPY START printer-id dest-id`

In this example,

`/HARDCPY START L86P STEV`

is the command I'd enter. Only after you finish this step does the printer start to produce your listing.

Although this seems like a more cumbersome technique than direct printing, it prevents your output from being mixed with other users' output. That's because each user has his or her own private destination. And when data is actually printed, CICS doesn't mix lines from different destinations.

How to use the ICCF macros for printing library members

ICCF provides three macros that can be useful for getting data to a printer. Two of them, HC and PRINT, use the /HARDCPY facility I've just described. The third, RELIST, causes data to be printed on the system printer.

The HC and PRINT macros   The HC macro causes your terminal to enter hardcopy mode, processes a command you enter as a parameter on the macro's command line, then returns the terminal to normal mode. For example,

```
@HC /LISTC COBTEST
```

would cause my terminal to enter hardcopy mode, list the library member COBTEST with continuous display (that's why I specified /LISTC instead of /LIST), then return my terminal to normal mode. You can specify up to eight parameters on the command line for the macro; the first is the command you want to execute, and those that follow are its operands.

The PRINT macro is much like the HC macro. It differs, though, because it doesn't let you specify a command you want to be processed in hardcopy mode. Instead, it assumes the command you want to execute is /LISTC, so the only operand you specify is the member to be printed. For instance,

```
@PRINT COBTEST
```

will have the same result as the sample HC macro command line I just showed you. You can also print the contents of the print area with the PRINT macro. To do so, you invoke the macro with this command:

```
@PRINT $$PRINT
```

Both the HC and the PRINT macros require you to have already specified the destination to which the output will be routed with a /HARDCPY command and may require that you issue a subsequent /HARDCPY command with START to begin printing. However, it's possible that special versions of these macros may have been created in your shop that also perform these functions for particular CICS destinations and printers. It's easy to make special versions of the PRINT and HC macros to simplify printing, as you'll see in the next chapter.

The RELIST macro   You can also use the RELIST macro to get a printed listing of a library member. However, the process it goes through differs from PRINT and HC. To put it simply, the RELIST macro causes a VSE job stream to be built that contains the contents of the library member you want to print. Then, that job stream is passed to VSE/POWER to be scheduled for execution in a VSE batch partition. The program that the RELIST macro runs is an ICCF utility called DTSRELST, and the output it produces is printed on the central site system printer, not a terminal printer.

To run the RELIST macro, all you do is enter a command line like

```
@RELIST COBTEST
```

If you want to list the contents of the print area, you can invoke the macro and omit the member name. When you use the RELIST macro, be patient, because it will take a moment for ICCF to create the job stream to invoke DTSRELST and transfer it to VSE/POWER. To monitor and control the POWER job after it has been submitted, you'll have to use the commands I describe in section 3.

Terminology	hardcopy mode
	transient data management
	transient data destination
	private destination

Objectives

1. Use the /SUMRY command to produce a summary listing of a library member.

2. Use the /CONTINU command (or the /LISTC, /LIBC, or /DISPC commands) to cause output to be displayed continuously.

3. Use the /HARDCPY command to cause output to be routed to a terminal printer directly or through a CICS private destination.

4. Use the HC and PRINT macros to route output to a terminal printer.

5. Use the RELIST macro to route output to the central site system printer.

TOPIC 3   Other system commands

This topic presents several other system commands you may want to use. It shows you how to (1) use PF keys, (2) activate logging and access information stored in your log area, (3) use the commands associated with ICCF's message-handling facilities, (4) use commands to get general information from ICCF, and (5) use commands to get information from your user profile.

How to use program function keys

If you've read the section in the last chapter on how to set and use the PF keys, this material will mostly be review. However, because this section presents some additional information about setting and using PF keys that supplements what you learned in chapter 4, I encourage you to read it even if some of the information is review.

As you learned in chapter 1, the program function keys are attention keys you can use to invoke pre-defined ICCF functions. A 3270 display station can have up to 24 PF keys, but most have 12. The PF keys are labelled PF1, PF2, and so on up to PF24. When you use ICCF, you can associate commands with function keys to customize your terminal to meet your needs.

Depending on the release of ICCF you're using, the function keys may or may not invoke the same functions in all ICCF modes. If you're using a release of ICCF that is older than release 1.3 modification level 5, you can have only one group of PF key settings that's in effect for all modes. However, from release 1.3 mod-level 5 on, you can have different groups of PF key settings for command mode, list mode, edit mode, and execution mode.

Even if your ICCF version supports multiple PF key settings, one group of settings is probably enough for most users. (If you don't define edit, list, or execution mode settings, the command mode settings are used.) As a result, I'll describe how to make general settings first. Then, I'll show you how to make mode-dependent settings.

How to assign the same PF key settings for all ICCF modes   To set a function key for use in command mode (and, if no mode-dependent settings are in effect, for all modes), you issue the command

```
/SET PFnn data
```

where nn is a number from 1 to 24 that identifies the function key you're defining and data is the command you want associated with the key. For example, the command

```
/SET PF19 /LIB CONN
```

tailors my terminal so that when I press the PF19 key, the directory entries in my current connected library are displayed.

To make PF key settings more flexible, ICCF lets you specify a replacable parameter in a PF key assignment. You indicate the replacable parameter with a double ampersand in the command you assign to the function key. Then, before you press the function key, you enter the specific value you want the command to process. ICCF combines the data you entered with the function specified by the PF key setting to form the complete command.

For example, suppose you issue this /SET command:

```
/SET PF20 /LIST &&
```

Here, the name of the library member you want to list is indicated with &&. As a result, you key in just the name of the member you want to list and press PF20 rather than enter the entire command. So to list the contents of the punch area, you enter

```
$$PUNCH
```

and press PF20. Otherwise, you'd have to enter the complete command

```
/LIST $$PUNCH
```

and press the ENTER key.

This /LIST command example is easy to understand, but frankly, I don't think you're likely to use a PF key setting with a replacable parameter for such a simple command. Replacable parameters are more useful for long, complicated commands. For example, consider this command:

```
/CP A RDR,COBTEST,CLASS=0,DISP=D
```

Its purpose is to change the attributes of an entry in VSE/POWER's reader queue so it will be eligible to be scheduled for execution in a VSE batch partition. Don't worry for now about the syntax of the command; I just want to use it as an example of a complicated command I use often. Each time I issue the command, it's the same except for the queue entry name (in this case, COBTEST). As a result, I set a PF key with the command

```
/SET PF6 /CP A RDR,&&,CLASS=0,DISP=D
```

Now, I can issue the command above by just entering

```
COBTEST
```

and pressing PF6. (By the way, only ICCF users who have administrator privileges can use the /CP command, so it's likely that you won't be able to issue it.)

How to assign different PF key settings for different ICCF modes   As I've already mentioned, with ICCF release 1.3 mod-level 5 and above, you can make separate PF key settings for edit, list, and execution mode. If you don't make PF key settings in any of these modes, the command mode settings will be in effect by default.

To make a mode-dependent setting, you issue a command like

```
/SET PF8ED LOCATE &&
```

As you can see, this is just like the basic /SET command to make a command mode setting, only I immediately followed the number of the PF key with the letters ED. That indicates that this setting is for edit mode. To make a setting for list mode, you issue a similar /SET command, only you specify LS instead of ED right after the number of the PF key you're assigning. And for execution mode, you specify EX instead of ED.

Assigning different functions to PF keys in different modes can be confusing, particularly if you use them for a variety of functions. My recommendation then, is if you use mode-dependent settings, that you assign similar functions to the PF keys used in different modes. For example, you might want to use different settings for PF keys in edit and list modes to control scrolling. Then, you might associate UP, DOWN, TOP, and BOTTOM editor commands with particular keys in edit mode and equivalent /SKIP commands with the same keys in list mode.

How to see what the current PF key settings are: the /SHOW PF command   If you want to see what your current PF key settings are in command mode, you can issue the command

```
/SHOW PF
```

The output of this command looks much like the output of the SHOW PF editor command I presented in the last chapter.

Also, you can issue a more specific version of this command to display the setting of a particular PF key. For instance, the command

```
/SHOW PF12
```

would display only the setting for PF12. However, you can get the same information from the simpler version of the command. As a result, I don't think you're likely to use the more specific version often.

If you're using mode-dependent settings, you can display the settings for a particular mode by specifying LS, ED, or EX as an extension of PF. For instance, if you enter

```
/SHOW PFED
```

the current PF keys settings for edit mode will be displayed.

Command: /SHOW LOG

```
...+....1....+....2....+....3....+....4....+....5....+....6....+....7....+..CM
IMPEX LOGGING PFON VERIFY LINESIZ CTRL.BYPASS  COM.LIB  DTANL
ON    OFF     ON   ON     72      OFF          ON       OFF
*READY




```

I A   ⊡⊡04

Figure 5-14   Sample output of the /SHOW LOG command

**How to
use logging**

In some cases, you might want ICCF to record, or log, the commands you issue. Then, if you're in the middle of issuing a long series of commands that have to be processed in sequence, you can look at the log to know which ones you've already issued. Because logging usually isn't necessary and because it uses additional ICCF resources, the chances are that it's not automatically in effect for your terminal. To find out if it is, you enter this command:

```
/SHOW LOG
```

Figure 5-14 shows the output of this command. As you can see, it displays several option settings; the second indicates whether or not logging is active.

To activate logging in command mode, you issue the /SET command like this:

```
/SET LOG ON
```

(To activate logging in the editor, you issue the same command, but you leave the slash off.) After you issue this command, commands you enter are stored in one of your temporary user areas: the log area. You can look at the contents of the log area by issuing the command

/LIST $$LOG

in command mode or

PRINT $$LOG

in the editor.

For example, suppose I activate logging, then issue two commands:

/CONN 83

to make library 83 my connected library and

/SHOW LIBS

to display my current libraries. After issuing these commands, I issue the command

/LIST $$LOG

to display the log. The output is in figure 5-15. The I in the first column indicates that the line was input. The time the command was logged and the mode in which it was issued are next, followed by the command itself. Notice that the last command issued is at the top of the listing and the first command issued is listed last. The number of lines stored in the log area during typical operations is 100; if more lines need to be logged, the oldest line in the log is deleted.

Although the information in figure 5-15 can be useful, it doesn't tell you if the commands logged were processed as expected. For example, if I made an error in one of the commands, the invalid command would appear in the log just like valid ones. Figure 5-16 shows what the log might look like if I entered the /LIST command for the log area incorrectly, then correctly.

There is a way around this problem. If you want, you can have ICCF record not only the commands you issue, but the system responses to them as well. To do that, you issue the command

/SET LOG ON INOUT

Then, logging is activated for both input and output. If I had issued this command for the example in figure 5-16, the log display for the commands recorded would look like figure 5-17. Notice now that lines are indicated as either input (I in column 1) or output (O in column 1). Here, it's clear that one of the commands I entered was wrong. Notice that only system replies to commands are logged; command output (like the output of the /SHOW LIBS command) is *not* logged.

```
....+....1....+....2....+....3....+....4....+....5....+....6....+....7....+..CM
I 17/31 CM ' /LIST $$LOG
I 17/31 CM ' /SHOW LIBS
I 17/31 CM ' /CONN 83
*END PRINT
*READY




                                              

 Iᴬ                                               □-□04
```

Figure 5-15   Basic input log records

```
....+....1....+....2....+....3....+....4....+....5....+....6....+....7....+..CM
I 17/33 CM ' /LIST $$LOG
I 17/33 CM ' /LIST $LOG
I 17/33 CM ' /SHOW LIBS
I 17/33 CM ' /CONN 83
*END PRINT
*READY




                                              

 Iᴬ                                               □-□04
```

Figure 5-16   Basic input log records give no indication of whether or not commands were successfully completed

```
....+....1....+....2....+....3....+....4....+....5....+....6....+....7....+..CM
I 17/34 CM ' /LIST $$LOG
0 17/34       *FILE NOT IN LIB
I 17/34 CM ' /LIST $LOG
0 17/34       *READY
I 17/34 CM ' /SHOW LIBS
0 17/34       *CONNECTED
I 17/34 CM ' /CONN 83
0 17/34       *CONTROL SET
*END PRINT
*READY




IA                                               □-□04
```

Figure 5-17   Input and output log records

ICCF message-handling facilities

ICCF provides three ways to deliver messages: (1) broadcast, (2) mail, and (3) notification. As a typical terminal user, you can receive all three kinds of messages, but you can only send notification messages.

How the broadcast facility works   The ICCF administrator can use the *broadcast facility* to send a message to all terminal users. The broadcast message is automatically displayed at a user's terminal when he logs on. To issue a broadcast message, the ICCF administrator has to run an ICCF utility program to store the message in the library file.

For the most part, messages sent by the broadcast facility are brief, general, and of interest to all system users. For example, information about new system procedures or the system schedule are good candidates for a broadcast message. However, if a message contains more than a few lines of data or is of interest only to some ICCF users, the ICCF administrator is likely to use the mail facility.

How to get messages from the mail facility: the /MAIL command
The *mail facility* is similar to the broadcast facility in that the ICCF administrator creates a message that can be accessible to all users. However, it's different in two ways.

First, a mail message differs from a broadcast message in that it can have, in addition to a general message for all users, specific sub-messages associated with particular user-ids. As a result, one user can get a different mail message than another.

Second, mail messages are not displayed automatically when the user logs on. Instead, the user issues the /MAIL command to display them. However, it's likely that each user has a logon procedure that includes the /MAIL command. When that's the case, the user automatically sees his mail without actually keying in the /MAIL command.

How to use the notification facility: the /SEND, /MSG, and /SET MSGAUTO commands   The third message processing facility ICCF provides is the *notification facility*. With it, *any* user can send messages to any other user. In contrast, only the system administrator can use the broadcast and mail facilities. To send a message using the notification facility, you issue the /SEND command like this:

```
/SEND user-id message
```

The user-id can be a specific user-id like STEV or AAAA. Or, you can use two special values. If you want to send a message to all system users, you specify ALL. And if you want to send a message to the system console operator, you specify COPER.

Depending on your user profile, you may or may not receive messages automatically. To find out, you issue the command

```
/SHOW MSG
```

If ICCF's reply is

```
AUTOMATIC MESSAGE DISPLAY
```

any messages that are pending for you are displayed without any intervention. In contrast, if the reply to /SHOW MSG is

```
NON-AUTOMATIC MESSAGE DISPLAY
```

you have to issue the command

```
/MSG
```

to get your messages. There are two exceptions. If any notification messages are pending for you when you log on, they're displayed automatically. And messages from the system console operator are also displayed automatically.

If you want to change your terminal's message mode, you can use the /SET MSGAUTO command. To enable automatic message reception, you enter

```
/SET MSGAUTO ON
```

and to disable it, you enter

```
/SET MSGAUTO OFF
```

How to get ICCF system information: the /SHOW, /USERS, and /TIME commands

This section presents several commands that let you get basic information from ICCF. In it, you'll see how to use some additional options of the /SHOW command as well as the /USERS and /TIME commands.

If you want to work at a terminal and find that another user is logged on, you can always log him off and continue with your own work. However, in some instances, you might want to find out who was using the terminal. To do that, you issue the command

```
/SHOW USER
```

If I am logged on and issue this command, ICCF displays

```
USER ID CODE  = STEV
```

You might also want to find out what your terminal's CICS identification is. (The CICS operator might want to know your term-id if you're having problems using the system.) To find out your term-id, you issue the command

```
/SHOW TERM
```

For my terminal the output is

```
TERMINAL CODE = L1T0
```

If you want to find out how many other users are active on the system, you issue the command

```
/USERS
```

with no operands. ICCF's output is

```
NUMBER OF TIME SHARING USERS LOGGED ON = 0001
```

Here, only one user (me) is logged on the system. You might want to do this if your response times are long and you're interested in seeing how intensively the system is being used. Or, if you're authorized to shut the system down, you'd issue this command before doing so to make sure no other users are working. However, this probably doesn't apply to you because chances are you won't have access to the CICS commands necessary to shut down the system.

You can also use ICCF as a clock. ICCF provides two ways to find out what the current date and time are. First, you can issue the /SHOW command with the DATE option like this:

```
/SHOW DATE
```

The output of this command looks like this:

```
DATE=03/10/86 TIME=08/36/43
```

A shorter command is

```
/TIME
```

which displays the the same information as /SHOW DATE, plus information related to interactive partition use:

```
DATE=03/10/86 TIME=08/36/44
EXEC UNITS=00000 PARTN TIME=00000
```

You'll learn what execution units and partition time mean in section 4. (By the way, there is a /SHOW TIME command, but it only displays information related to interactive partition options, so you wouldn't use it to find out what the current system date and time are.)

How to get information from your user profile: the /USERS PROFILE and /USERS STATS commands

You can issue two variations of the /USERS command to get detailed information on defaults in your user profile and on your system usage. If you issue the command

```
/USERS PROFILE
```

ICCF displays a screen like the one in figure 5-18. This display contains the defaults recorded in your user profile for the indicated items. The ones that are directly relevant to the material you know about so far are shaded in the figure; the others relate to processing in interactive partitions, so I'll describe them in section 4.

In order to have logged on, you must have known your user-id, so the first item in the display isn't particularly useful. The second item is your default primary library. You should probably remember it too.

The next three items (MAXST, MAXPU, and MAXPR) indicate how large your input, punch, and print temporary areas can be.

Command: **/USERS PROFILE**

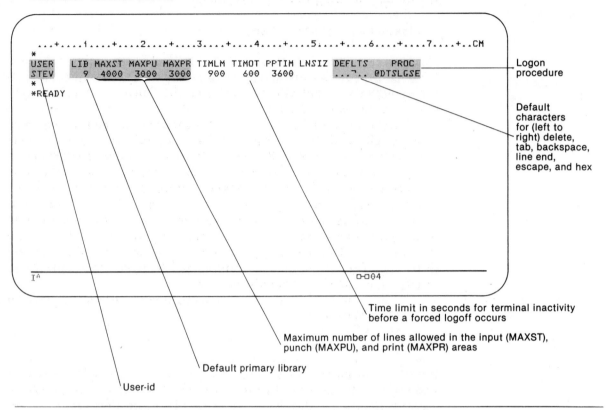

Figure 5-18 Sample output of the /USERS PROFILE command

Because these are actually areas of the ICCF library file, their sizes need to be controlled. As a result, the ICCF administrator specifies their maximum sizes in your user profile.

The next shaded item, TIMOT, specifies how long ICCF will let your terminal be inactive before it forces a log off. Even if you aren't working, when you're logged on you're using system resources. Therefore, it's sensible for a time-out interval to be specified. The value in figure 5-18 is 600 seconds, or 10 minutes. If you want, you can alter the default by issuing the command

    /SETIME TIMEOUT nnnn

where nnnn is the number of seconds (between 60 and 3600) you want the timeout interval to be. For example,

```
/SETIME TIMEOUT 3600
```

changes my timeout interval to 1 hour. Realize, though, that some ICCF users' profiles are set up so they aren't necessarily subject to forced log offs. If that's the case for you, the timeout interval that's in effect for you is meaningless.

I don't think you're likely to use the information the last two items provide. DEFLTS shows what values are currently associated with six ICCF control characters. Of the six, I think you'd only be interested in the current value for the tab character (the second of the six). However, because periods are used to represent non-printable values here, the DELFTS display isn't very useful. The last item, PROC, names your logon procedure. Although you might need to use this name if you want to list your logon procedure, chances are that's all you'd be able to do with it. That's because logon procedures are stored in the common library and typical users aren't authorized to update common data; usually only the ICCF administrator can.

If you want to display information about your system use, you can issue the command

```
/USERS STATS
```

(Don't let the name of this command confuse you: It displays statistics just for the current user, not for all users.) Its output is displayed in figure 5-19. Again, the shaded sections relate directly to information you're already familiar with, while the other items relate to processing in interactive partitions.

The statistics maintained are current from the last time an ICCF accounting run was made. When an accounting run is made, totals are reset to zero. In the example in figure 5-19, it's been a long time since the last accounting run, so the numbers are high. The chances are that on your system, accounting runs are more frequent and, therefore, your cumulative statistics values will be lower.

The first item in the display, LOGONS, is self-explanatory: it's the total number of logon requests made since the last accounting run. REQSTS indicates the number of keyboard requests made; it's the number of times the ENTER key has been pressed. LOGTIM is the total number of seconds you've been logged on. The last item, SPACE, is the number of logical records that are used by library members associated with your user-id.

Terminology   broadcast facility
mail facility
notification facility

Command: /USERS STATS

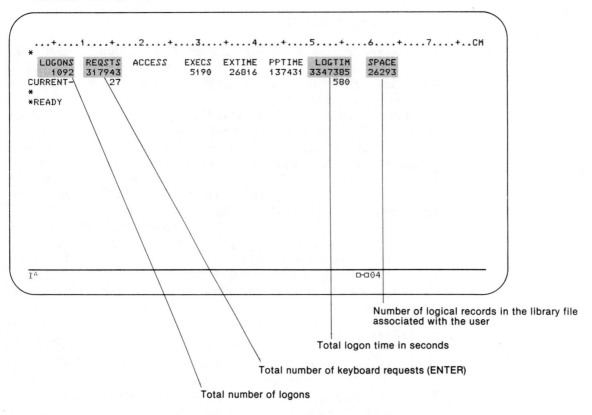

...+....1....+....2....+....3....+....4....+....5....+....6...+....7....+..CM

Figure 5-19   Sample output of the /USERS STATS command

Objectives

1. Use the /SET PF command to associate program function keys with commands for all modes or, if your version of ICCF supports this feature, specifically for command, edit, list, or execution mode.

2. Use the logging features presented in this topic to record your terminal activity.

3. Describe the three message-handling facilities ICCF provides.

4. Use the /SET MSGAUTO, /SEND, and /MSG commands to send and receive notification messages.

5. Use the /SHOW, /USERS, and /TIME commands to get general system information.

6. Use the /USERS command to get information from your user profile.

Chapter 6

How to write macros

A *macro* is a series of commands, stored in an ICCF library member, that you can execute by entering a single command line. Macros are processed in ICCF's foreground, just as if you'd entered the commands they contain one after another. (That's in contrast to a procedure, which can also contain a series of commands, but which is executed in the background.) You can run a macro either in command mode or in edit mode.

You already know how to run a macro: You specify its name like you do a command. However, there are two restrictions you need to be aware of when you run a macro. First, when you invoke a macro, you can't abbreviate its name like you can most ICCF commands. ICCF needs the full name of the library member that contains the macro to be able to retrieve it. And second, you may have to use the @ prefix on the macro name when you run it. If you run a macro in edit mode, you *must* use the prefix; if you run a macro in command mode, the prefix is required only if you're using a release of ICCF before 1.3 modification level 5. You've already seen how to use a variety of macros that are supplied with ICCF, like ED, COPYFILE, HC, and PRINT.

In addition to system and editing commands, macros also contain *macro orders* or just *orders*. Macro orders are special statements that identify macros as such and let you control how they execute. As you'll learn in a moment, all macros have to begin with the @MACRO macro order, but all the other macro orders are optional.

How to write simple macros

Frankly, there's no reason to be intimidated by the idea of writing macros. As you'll see, they're straightforward. For example, consider figure 6-1. This is the ICCF-supplied macro FSEDPF that you can use in

213

Command: /LIST FSEDPF

```
....+....1....+....2....+....3....+....4....+....5....+....6....+....7....+..CM
@MACRO    THE @FSEDPF MACRO SETS PF KEYS FOR THE FULL SCREEN EDITOR
@NOPRINT
SET PF1 BACKWARD 1
SET PF2 DOWN 8
SET PF3 FORWARD 1
SET PF4 CURSOR INPUT
SET PF5 CURSOR LINE 16
SET PF6 CURSOR LINE 5
SET PF7 CURSOR CURRENT
SET PF8 CURSOR TABBACK 20
SET PF9 CURSOR TABFORWARD 20
SET PF10 CURSOR TABFORWARD 0
@PRINT
SHOW PF
*END PRINT
*READY



I^                                                    □-□04
```

Figure 6-1   The FSEDPF macro

the editor to make PF key settings; if you've read chapter 4, it should be familiar to you.

How to identify a macro: the @MACRO macro order   Every macro has to start with the @MACRO macro order. @MACRO doesn't have any operands, but you can include a comment after the order, like the text

`THE @FSEDPF MACRO SETS PF KEYS FOR THE FULL SCREEN EDITOR`

in the @MACRO macro order in figure 6-1.

How to control macro display output: the /SET DELAY command and the @NOPRINT and @PRINT macro orders   When you use macros, two characteristics of the way ICCF works come into conflict. First, ICCF's default is to process the commands in a macro in sequence as fast as it can. After all, if that's not what you wanted, you probably wouldn't have combined them in a macro to begin with. But second, ICCF normally displays a system message after it processes each command to let you know what happened. The result is that when you use a macro, you might see a series of system messages flashed quickly on the screen, one for each command in the macro. They're displayed so fast, they seem to flicker; you don't have enough time to read them.

You can alter either of these characteristics by changing your screen's *delay* with the /SET command. To cause ICCF to pause between message displays long enough for you to read those messages (and thus, in effect, to slow down the execution of the macro), you can issue the command

/SET DELAY nnn

where nnn is the number of seconds ICCF should pause between each message display; nnn can be between 0 and 255. For example, the command

/SET DELAY 3

sets the screen delay to three seconds. Because three seconds is enough time to read most command output, ICCF uses it as its default. To set this defualt, you can use another option on the /SET DELAY command: TIME. So, if you issue the command

/SET DELAY TIME

the delay interval is also set to three seconds.

Although there may be times when you'll want to slow down a macro's output display to review the messages its commands generate, it's more likely that you'll want to suppress message display altogether. To do that, you issue the /SET DELAY command like this:

/SET DELAY BYPASS

When *delay bypass* is in effect, messages from commands in a macro aren't displayed except for the last one generated. As you'll see in a minute, the ED macro uses this command to suppress message displays.

If you aren't sure what delay setting is in effect, you can issue the command

/SHOW DELAY

If ICCF indicates delay bypass is in effect and you don't want it to be, you can turn it off by resetting the screen delay with this command:

/SET DELAY RESET

Another way to alter the display of system messages that are displayed from commands in a macro is to use the @PRINT and @NOPRINT macro orders. (Like @MACRO, these orders don't have any operands.) After @NOPRINT is encountered, screen output that the following commands produce is not displayed. And @PRINT causes output produced by commands that follow it to be displayed. (You'll use @PRINT only to counteract the effect of a preceding

Command: /LIST ED

```
...+....1....+....2....+....3....+....4....+....5....+....6....+....7....+..CM
@MACRO    THE @ED MACRO INVOKES THE FULL SCREEN EDITOR DIRECTLY
/SET DELAY BYPASS
/ED &&PARAM1 &&PARAM2
VERIFY FULL 1
VERIFY FULL 1 1
*END PRINT
*READY
```

I^   □-□04

Figure 6-2   The ED macro

@NOPRINT; if you want all command output to be displayed, you
don't need to code @PRINT.) Note that if delay bypass is in effect,
messages aren't displayed, regardless of the @PRINT and @NOPRINT
macro orders you code.

When you use the @PRINT and @NOPRINT macro orders, be
careful that the @PRINT order isn't the last one in a macro. If it is, it
will be interpreted as a *chained macro* (that is, a macro invoked as a
result of the last command in another macro). Then, the ICCF-supplied
macro PRINT will be invoked, and that's almost certainly not what you
want.

Figure 6-2 presents the ED macro used to invoke the full-screen
editor. As I've already mentioned, it uses the /SET DELAY BYPASS
command to suppress the display of system messages. In addition,
notice that the ED macro contains a couple of peculiar looking names:
&&PARAM1 and &&PARAM2. These are variable parameters.

How to use variable parameters   When you write a macro, only the
simplest will be like the one in figure 6-1, where all the commands use
the same values all the time. More often, you'll want to use a macro to
perform the same function, but with different values. For example,

you'll often run the ED macro to invoke the editor, but sometimes you'll want to edit the input area and other times you'll want to edit a library member. With variable parameters, you can do that.

As you know, the complete command line to invoke the ED macro is

```
@ED [member-name [password]]
```

If you want to edit the input area, you don't code any parameters. If you want to edit a library member that isn't password protected, you supply one parameter. And if you want to edit a password-protected member, you supply two parameters. So the ED macro accepts two variable parameters: member-name and password.

It's possible to code a macro that can process up to nine variable parameters. Instead of coding a literal in the macro, when you want to use a variable parameter you use the names &&PARAM1, &&PARAM2, and so on up through &&PARAM9. These variable parameter names correspond to data that's keyed in on the command line you use to invoke the macro. The first parameter the user keys in after the macro name becomes the variable parameter &&PARAM1, the second becomes &&PARAM2, and so on. In the ED macro, the member-name the user keys in becomes &&PARAM1 and the password becomes &&PARAM2.

As you can see in figure 6-2, these variable parameter names are specified in the /ED command that causes the terminal to enter edit mode:

```
/ED &&PARAM1 &&PARAM2
```

So if you invoke the ED macro and don't specify any parameters, both &&PARAM1 and &&PARAM2 contain spaces. Then, the /ED command that's processed in the macro is simply

```
/ED
```

which causes the input area to be edited. On the other hand, if you invoke the ED macro with the command line

```
@ED COBTEST PW1
```

the member-name COBTEST is stored in &&PARAM1 and the password PW1 is stored in &&PARAM2; the resulting /ED command that's processed is

```
/ED COBTEST PW1
```

After the /ED command has been processed, your terminal is in edit mode, but not full-screen sub-mode. The editor command

```
VERIFY FULL 1
```

causes the editor to enter full-screen sub-mode. The 1 indicates that the current line should be displayed on the first line of the data display area.

The first VERIFY command in the macro is a context editor command that causes the terminal to enter full-screen edit mode. After it has done so, the second VERIFY command in the macro is processed:

```
VERIFY FULL 1 1
```

This is a type I full-screen editor command that sets the size of the editor (type I/II) command area. The first 1 duplicates the setting in the preceding VERIFY command (that is, it causes the current line to be displayed on the first line of the display area). The second 1 causes the size of the editor command area to be set at one line, which is appropriate for almost all full-screen editor work; if this command isn't issued, the editor command area uses two lines instead of one.

A customized macro to invoke the full-screen editor   Now that you know how to code a basic macro and how the ED macro works, you're in a position to write your own ED macro to set up your editor environment just the way you want it. Then, you won't have to depend on the defaults of the standard ICCF macro.

Because the ED macro that comes with ICCF is available to all users, it's stored in the common library. However, if you create your own macro named ED and store it in your primary library, ICCF will process it instead of the ED macro in the common library. That's because ICCF looks in your primary library for a macro you name before it looks elsewhere. If it doesn't find the macro you named there, it looks in your connected library. Then, if it still hasn't found the member, it looks for it in the common library.

Because of this, it's a good idea not to create library members that have the same names as ICCF-supplied macros unless you want them to replace the ICCF versions. For example, if you create a library member that contains standard text and name it ED, ICCF displays

```
*MEMBER IS NOT A MACRO
```

when you try to run the ED macro. That's because it's trying to execute the data stored in the member named ED in your primary library, not the commands in the ED macro in the common library. However, in the example I'm using, it's OK to create a macro named ED that you'll store in your primary library because you *do* want it to be processed instead of the ICCF-supplied ED macro.

Figure 6-3 shows one way you might set up a customized ED macro. Here, I've simply combined the statements from the ICCF-supplied ED macro to enter the full-screen editor with the statements from the FSEDPF macro to set PF keys for the full-screen editor environment. Also, I added a TABSET command and an INPUT command to cause the editor to open up the display area automatically and let me key in new lines.

```
===>
<<...+.....1.....+.....2.....+.....3.....+.....4.....+.....5.....+.. INP=*INPARA*>>...+...FS
***** TOP OF FILE *****                                                         /***/
@MACRO                                                                          *===*
/SET DELAY BYPASS                                                               *===*
/ED &&PARAM1 &&PARAM2                                                           *===*
VERIFY FULL 1                                                                   *===*
VERIFY FULL 1 1                                                                 *===*
SET PF1 BACKWARD 1                                                              *===*
SET PF2 DOWN 8                                                                  *===*
SET PF3 FORWARD 1                                                               *===*
SET PF4 CURSOR INPUT                                                            *===*
SET PF5 CURSOR LINE 16                                                          *===*
SET PF6 CURSOR LINE 5                                                           *===*
SET PF7 CURSOR CURRENT                                                          *===*
SET PF8 CURSOR TABBACK 20                                                       *===*
SET PF9 CURSOR TABFORWARD 20                                                    *===*
SET PF10 CURSOR TABFORWARD 0                                                    *===*
TABSET COBOL                                                                    *===*
INPUT                                                                           *===*
***** END OF FILE *****                                                         *****


I^                                                    □-□04
```

Figure 6-3   Creating a new macro that combines and extends the functions of the ED and FSEDPF macros

Figure 6-4 shows another variation that's a little more specialized. Here, I didn't specify &&PARAM1 and &&PARAM2 on the /ED command. As a result, this macro will always cause the input area to be edited. However, I did add a GETFILE command that specifies these two parameter names. As a result, this macro causes the editor to edit the input area and to copy the contents of an existing library member into it for editing. The last command in the macro, TOP, causes the editor to set the current line pointer at the top of the text after it has copied it into the input area. A macro like this can be useful for many editing situations.

These two variations of the ED macro are basic examples of how you can use ICCF's macro processing features to make using the system easier and less error-prone. If you realize how easy macros are to create and use, I think you'll recognize a variety of situations in which you can use them. One example might be a macro to perform the steps I described in the last chapter to convert a library member stored in compressed format to display format.

A macro to convert a library member in compressed format to display format   If you do much work with compressed library members, it can be an aggravation to have to perform the steps necessary to convert members to display format whenever you want to edit them. Fortu-

```
===>
<<...+....1....+....2....+....3....+....4....+....5....+.. INP=*INPARA*>>..+..FS
***** TOP OF FILE *****                                                   /***/
@MACRO                                                                     *====*
/SET DELAY BYPASS                                                          *====*
/ED                                                                        *====*
VERIFY FULL 1                                                              *====*
VERIFY FULL 1 1                                                            *====*
SET PF1 BACKWARD 1                                                         *====*
SET PF2 DOWN 8                                                             *====*
SET PF3 FORWARD 1                                                          *====*
SET PF4 CURSOR INPUT                                                       *====*
SET PF5 CURSOR LINE 16                                                     *====*
SET PF6 CURSOR LINE 5                                                      *====*
SET PF7 CURSOR CURRENT                                                     *====*
SET PF8 CURSOR TABBACK 20                                                  *====*
SET PF9 CURSOR TABFORWARD 20                                               *====*
SET PF10 CURSOR TABFORWARD 0                                               *====*
TABSET COBOL                                                               *====*
GETFILE &&PARAM1 &&PARAM2                                                  *====*
TOP                                                                        *====*
***** END OF FILE *****                                                    *****


I^                                               □-□04
```

Figure 6-4   Creating another macro that combines and extends the functions of the ED and FSEDPF macros

nately, it's easy to write a macro to do the conversion; figure 6-5 presents this macro.

I've stored this macro in a library member named UNSQ. To run it, all I have to do is enter a command line like

@UNSQ INV2100

Here, the value INV2100 is substituted for the variable parameter &&PARAM1 in the commands in the macro. (If the member I'm converting is password protected, I enter its password after the member name on the command line; it's the second variable parameter, &&PARAM2.) I think you'll agree that if you work with compressed library members regularly, this simple macro will save you plenty of time.

Although the basic macro facilities I've presented so far can help you use ICCF more efficiently, there are still other macro orders you can use to control the way macros execute. Now, I want to describe them.

How to write complex macros

In this section, I'll show you how to use four other macro orders that let you exercise logical control over macro execution. At the outset, I want you to know that these features are relatively unsophisticated; ICCF's

Command: /LIST UNSQ

```
...+....1....+....2....+....3....+....4....+....5....+....6....+....7....+..CM
@MACRO
/INPUT
/INSERT &&PARAM1 &&PARAM2
/REPLACE &&PARAM1 &&PARAM2
*END PRINT
*READY




I^                                                  □-□□4
```

Figure 6-5   A macro to convert a library member in compressed format to display format

procedure processing facilities are more extensive. As a result, if you need to group a series of statements and control how they're processed, I encourage you to consider using a procedure instead of a macro. (Section 4 presents the concepts and details you need to know to write procedures.)

How to change the current position in a macro: the @FOR and @BACK macro orders   Normally, the statements in a macro are processed from beginning to end in the sequence they're coded. However, when you use the @FOR and @BACK macro orders, you can branch from one point in a macro to another. On both of these orders, you code a number that indicates how many lines forward or backward in the macro the current position should be moved. For example,

    @FOR 12

causes the current position to be moved forward 12 lines. As a result, the 11 lines immediately following the @FOR order would be skipped. You'll use @FOR and @BACK along with the @IF macro order, which I'll describe in a moment, to do conditional processing in a macro.

The @IF macro order

ICCF releases below 1.3 modification level 5

```
@IF &&RETCOD {EQ}  comparison-value  {@BACK nn}
                NE                     @FOR  nn
```

ICCF release 1.3 modification level 5 and above

```
        &&RETCOD                               @BACK nn
@IF     &&PARMCT  {EQ}  comparison-value       @FOR  nn
        &&PARAMn   NE                          @EXIT command
```

Figure 6-6   The @IF macro order

How to end a macro: the @EXIT macro order   The @EXIT macro order causes the macro to end when it's encountered. Normally, the statements in a macro are processed until they've all been read. As with @FOR and @BACK, @EXIT is usually used in combination with the @IF macro order. However, unlike @FOR and @BACK, @EXIT is available only with ICCF release 1.3 modification-level 5 and above.

When you use the @EXIT order, you code it like this:

```
@EXIT command
```

where command is a system command to be executed after the macro is terminated. A typical command you'd use in this situation is /ECHO, which simply causes a message to be displayed at the terminal screen. For example,

```
@EXIT /ECHO *LIBRARY MEMBER NOT FOUND
```

would cause the macro to end and the message

```
*LIBRARY MEMBER NOT FOUND
```

to be displayed.

How to perform conditional processing: the @IF macro order
Although the three orders I've just described let you move the current position in a macro or end a macro, they're meaningless by themselves. To use them effectively, you have to use them with the @IF macro order; figure 6-6 shows its format. The features the @IF order provides depend on the release of ICCF you're using. The condition checking you can do is particularly limited under ICCF releases before 1.3 modification level 5.

As you can see, the @IF macro order has two parts that correspond to the "if" and "then" components of a conditional statement in a high-level programming language. The "if" component has four parts: the @IF macro order itself, a variable, a relational operator (either EQ for equal or NE for not equal), and a comparison value. In the "if" component, you specify a condition that can be either true or false. If the condition is true, the "then" component of the order is processed. The "then" component is one of the three macro orders I've just described: @FOR, @BACK, or @EXIT. (Again, for ICCF releases below 1.3 modification level 5, @EXIT isn't supported.)

The only value you can test under older releases of ICCF is called &&RETCOD. You can use it to determine if a command was executed properly. It contains the first eight characters of the system message generated as a result of the preceding system command. If the command only produced the ICCF message *READY, that's what &&RETCOD will contain, but if it also produced a preceding message, that message's first eight characters will be stored in &&RETCOD instead.

As you can imagine, doing condition checking in this way requires that you be thoroughly familiar with the messages your commands produce. The best way to learn what to check for is to test the commands interactively to see what messages they yield. Notice that if any of the first eight bytes of a message contains a blank, you'll have to code your comparison value between single quotes; otherwise, ICCF considers the blanks to be delimiters.

If you're using ICCF release 1.3 modification level 5 or above, you can evaluate variables other than &&RETCOD in @IF macro orders. As you can see in the lower part of figure 6-6, you can evaluate any of the variable parameters the operator can specify when the macro is invoked (&&PARAMn, which can be &&PARAM1, &&PARAM2, and so on).

Also, you can evaluate &&PARMCT to find out if the operator entered any variable parameters when the macro was invoked. If you code the macro order

```
@IF &&PARMCT EQ 0 . . .
```

the condition is true (and the following @FOR, @BACK, or @EXIT macro order is executed) if the operator did *not* enter any variable parameters. If the operator did enter variable parameters, the condition is false, and the "then" component of the order is not executed. Of course, you could achieve the reverse effect by using the NE relational operator instead of EQ. Then, if the operator did not enter variable parameters, the "then" component of the order would be executed. When you use &&PARMCT, you can compare it only to 0. Although the name (which suggests "parameter count") seems to indicate you can determine how many parameters were entered, that's not the case. &&PARMCT only lets you determine whether or not variable parameters were used at all.

Command: /LIST STEVPRT

```
....+....1....+....2....+....3....+....4....+....5....+....6....+....7....+..CM
@MACRO
/SET DELAY RESET
/HARDCPY STEV
/HARDCPY ON
/ECHO ****************** HARDCOPY LIST OF MEMBER &&PARAM1 ************
/LISTC &&PARAM1 &&PARAM2
/ECHO *****************************************************************
/HARDCPY START L86P STEV
/HARDCPY OFF
/ECHO *MEMBER &&PARAM1 ROUTED TO PRINT
*END PRINT
*READY
```
```
Iᴬ                                              □-□04
```

Figure 6-7   A personalized version of the PRINT macro

A customized macro to route output to a printer   Just to give you an idea of the sort of processing you can do with a complex macro, I want to show you an example. Figure 6-7 is a variation of the PRINT macro ICCF supplies. I've changed it so, in addition to turning hardcopy mode on and off, it also (1) specifies my private print destination and (2) starts the printer.

In this example, I want to modify the macro in figure 6-7 so if I invoke it with no variable parameters, it will route the contents of my print area ($$PRINT) to the printer, instead of the contents of my input area (which is the /LISTC command's default). Figure 6-8 shows the version of my macro that does this. In this figure, I've shaded the two lines I particularly want you to notice. The first is an @IF macro order that checks to see if the operator entered variable parameters. If the number of parameters entered is not zero, the operator specified a library member name and perhaps a password. As a result, the @IF macro order's "then" component causes a branch to the section of the macro that routes a library member to the print destination (@FOR 9).

Command: /LIST STEVPRTX

```
...+....1....+....2....+....3....+....4....+....5....+....6....+....7....+..CM
@MACRO
/SET DELAY RESET
@IF &&PARMCT NE 0 @FOR 9
/HARDCPY STEV
/HARDCPY ON
/ECHO ****************** HARDCOPY LIST OF $$PRINT ******************
/LISTC $$PRINT
/ECHO *********************************************************
/HARDCPY START L86P STEV
/HARDCPY OFF
@EXIT /ECHO *$$PRINT ROUTED TO PRINT
/HARDCPY STEV
/HARDCPY ON
/ECHO ****************** HARDCOPY LIST OF MEMBER &&PARAM1 ***********
/LISTC &&PARAM1 &&PARAM2
/ECHO *********************************************************
/HARDCPY START L86P STEV
/HARDCPY OFF
/ECHO *MEMBER &&PARAM1 ROUTED TO PRINT
*END PRINT
*READY
```
```
I^                                                        ▯-▯▯4
```

Figure 6-8   An enhanced personalized version of the PRINT macro

On the other hand, if the operator did not enter any parameters (in other words, if PARMCT NE 0 tests false), control passes normally to the next statement in the macro. The statements that immediately follow the @IF order cause the print area ($$PRINT) to be routed to the print destination. After the last of these statements has been executed, an @EXIT macro order (which is shaded in figure 6-8) causes the macro to end immediately and to display a message advising the user that the print area was routed to the printer. If I hadn't included this @EXIT order, the statements for a named member would have been processed. And since no member-name was provided as &&PARAM1, the contents of the input area would have been printed.

Discussion   As you can see, even with the macro processing extensions provided with the later versions of ICCF, writing complex macros can be difficult to do because the functions ICCF provides are limited. As a result, if you think you need to write a complex macro, I again encourage you to consider developing it as a procedure instead. And that's particularly true if you're using an earlier version of ICCF.

Terminology   macro
                macro order
                order
                delay
                delay bypass
                chained macro

Objectives   1. Write a simple macro that uses no macro orders other than
                    @MACRO, @PRINT, and @NOPRINT.

                2. Write a complex macro that uses any of the macro orders presented
                    in this chapter.

Section 3

VSE job management

In this section, I'll describe how to use the facilities of VSE/POWER from ICCF. You should recall from chapter 1 that POWER is an IBM software product that provides spooling services for VSE systems. In a typical ICCF environment, job streams are entered using the ICCF full-screen editor, then submitted to POWER to be executed in a VSE partition. Once a job is submitted, you can communicate with POWER to monitor and control it.

This section has two chapters. Chapter 7 describes the POWER concepts you must understand to be able to submit jobs. Chapter 8 describes ICCF's submit-to-batch facility, which lets you transfer jobs to POWER, and the ICCF commands you can use to monitor and control the execution of POWER jobs.

Chapter 7

VSE/POWER concepts

This chapter introduces the features and facilities of VSE/POWER. If you're already familiar with how POWER works, either from job experience or previous study, you can probably skip this chapter. Particularly, if you've read the chapters on VSE/POWER in *DOS/VSE JCL*, all of the information in this chapter will be review. To find out if you should read this chapter, review the terminology list and objectives at the end of the chapter. If you're not comfortable with them, you should read this chapter before you go on.

VSE/POWER has two main functions: spooling and job scheduling. As you'll see in a moment, spooling and job scheduling are related functions. *Spooling* is a feature that improves the overall efficiency of systems that execute programs requiring unit record input and output. Because card and printer devices are usually far slower than application programs, much processing time is wasted when a program accesses them directly. With spooling, unit record input and output data are stored temporarily on faster DASDs.

HOW POWER PERFORMS SPOOLING AND JOB SCHEDULING FUNCTIONS

Job execution under POWER involves several steps: input spooling, job scheduling, execution management, and output spooling. Although these steps happen in this sequence, they don't necessarily happen in immediate succession. There may be a delay between any of the steps, depending on system usage and how POWER's options are set.

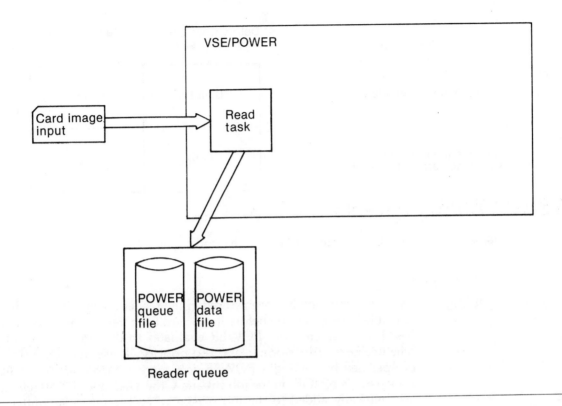

Figure 7-1   How POWER manages input spooling

Input spooling   Figure 7-1 shows how POWER handles a job submitted to it. The input stream is in card-image format, but the job doesn't have to come from a card reader. In fact, it's likely that it comes from ICCF using the facility the next chapter presents. For now, though, assume the basic case: The input job stream is a physical deck read by a card reader.

As you can see in figure 7-1, a *read task* within the POWER partition reads the input stream and stores the card images on disk. Actually, POWER uses two files to store spooled data. The card images are stored in the *POWER data file,* and another file, the *POWER queue file,* contains pointers to the entries in the data file.

Although POWER uses two files to record spooled data, it's more important from your point of view to know that those files are logically divided into three sections called *queues.* A queue is a list formed by items waiting in line for some sort of system service. As figure 7-1 shows, spooled card input resides in the *reader queue.* (You'll see shortly that spooled output resides in either the *punch queue* or the *list queue,* depending on whether it's card or printer output.) I want you to realize that the three queues are not distinct physical entities; they all share space in the POWER queue and data files.

	Delete from queue after processing	Retain in queue after processing
Schedule the job automatically	D(elete)	K(eep)
Schedule the job only after the system operator releases it	H(old)	L(eave)

Figure 7-2   Disposition values for items in the reader queue

Job scheduling   Once the entire job has been stored in the reader queue, POWER has to schedule it for execution before it can run. Each item in the reader queue has three characteristics POWER evaluates to determine what job to schedule next: disposition, class, and priority. These characteristics can be specified by coding a POWER *job entry control language (JECL) statement*, ✳ $$ JOB, in the job stream. Otherwise, the JOB statement is automatically added to the job stream when the job is submitted for execution. When that's the case, the characteristics are determined by the ICCF defaults and the parameters specified on the command line used to submit the job. You'll see examples of this in the next chapter. (Keep in mind as you read about disposition, class, and priority that entries in the punch and list queues have the same three characteristics.)

Disposition   A reader queue item's *disposition* indicates two things: (1) whether it's available for immediate execution and (2) whether it should be deleted from or retained in the reader queue after it has executed. An item's disposition is one of the four values in figure 7-2. As the figure indicates, if a reader queue item's disposition is D or K, it's available for immediate scheduling by POWER. But if its value is H or L, the system operator must explicitly release the job before POWER will schedule it.

Class   Before POWER schedules a job, an "appropriate" partition must be available. The reader queue item's *class* determines what an appropriate partition is. When a VSE system is started, partitions are set up with different options and device assignments to meet the requirements of particular jobs. For some jobs to run properly, they must execute in a specific partition; if they don't, they fail. Under POWER, both jobs and partitions are characterized with class codes that may be single letters of the alphabet or digits. An appropriate partition for a job is one that has a class that matches the job's class.

Classes that are digits are called *partition-specific classes*. For example, class 2 is unique to F2, 3 to F3, and so on. In other words, you can't specify class 3 for F2. Although up to four classes may be associated with one partition, only one may be the partition-specific class.

The other classes that may be associated with a partition are letters. The partition classes on your system depend on the specifications your systems programmer coded in the procedure that starts the POWER partition. On my system, for instance, the background may execute jobs with class I, 0 (zero), or J; F2 may execute jobs with class L or 2; and F3 may execute jobs with class M, N, or 3. The order in which the systems programmer coded the class values for each partition determines the preference POWER gives jobs of different classes. For example, if other factors I'll describe in a moment are equal, a job in the reader queue with class M will be executed in F3 before one with class N.

For POWER to schedule a job, the job's class must match one of the classes specified for a free partition. If you submit a job without specifying a class, POWER assigns it class A. On my system, that means the job can't be scheduled, regardless of its disposition, because no partition allows class A jobs. The system operator would have to change the job's class to one specified for one of the system's partitions before POWER would schedule it. Just when the job is scheduled depends on how many other jobs with the same class have been submitted ahead of it and, more important, on its priority.

Priority   The third characteristic of a reader queue entry POWER evaluates as it schedules jobs is *priority*. Although the term is the same, don't confuse this with partition priority, which is a VSE feature. POWER queue entry priorities can range from 0 (the lowest) to 9 (the highest); the default is 3.

When a partition becomes available, POWER checks the reader queue for jobs that are eligible to execute in it. For example, on my system, an eligible job for the background partition would have disposition D or K and would have class I, 0 (zero) or J. If POWER finds more than one job in the queue that meets these requirements, it schedules the one with the preferred class. If it finds two with the same class, it schedules the one with the higher priority. And if two have the same priority and the same class, POWER schedules the one that was in the reader queue first. So POWER's scheduling sequence (for jobs with dispositions D or K) is class first, priority second, and time in the reader queue third.

Execution management   Once the scheduled job starts to run, it's under the control of VSE, but POWER services its unit record I/O requests. The three POWER tasks in figure 7-3 perform these functions. The *execution read task* retrieves records from the reader queue and passes them to the application

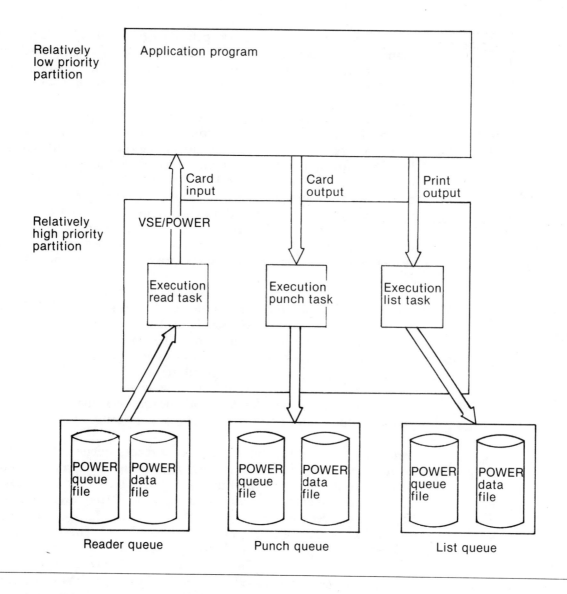

Figure 7-3   How POWER services unit-record I/O requests from application programs

program running in the POWER-controlled partition when it executes a
read instruction for a card reader. Similarly, when the application
program executes a write instruction for a card punch, an *execution
punch task* intercepts the request and writes the data to the POWER
punch queue. And when the program executes a write instruction for a
printer, an *execution list task* intercepts that request and writes the data
to the POWER list queue.

When the job has finished, POWER deletes it from the reader
queue if its disposition is D or H; if its disposition is K or L, POWER
retains it in the reader queue. Retaining jobs in the reader queue is an

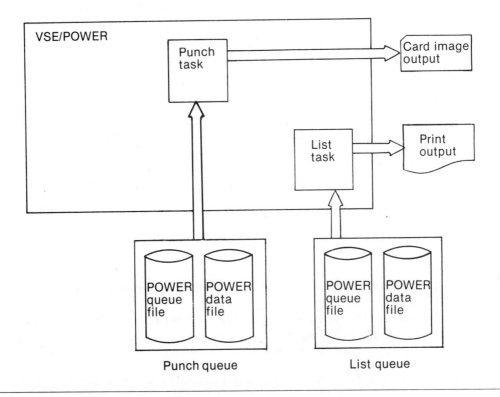

Figure 7-4   How POWER processes spooled output

efficient way to manage jobs that are executed regularly. For example, a job that's run each week to back up the system's DASDs might be stored in the reader queue so the system operator can easily release it when it's needed. This is a practical alternative to using procedures cataloged in VSE procedure libraries.

Output spooling   Figure 7-4 illustrates how POWER processes data stored in the punch and list queues. A *punch task* and a *list task* write data from the punch and list queues to the output devices. Just as jobs in the reader queue are scheduled and handled based on their class, disposition, and priority, so are items in the punch and list queues. And, as with job scheduling, these characteristics are determined by JECL statements coded in the job stream or added to the job stream when the job is submitted. There are two JECL statements used to control output spooling: ★ $$ LST directs the processing of printed output and ★ $$ PUN directs the processing of punched output. You'll have a better idea of how these statements work after you read the next chapter.

Disposition   As a general rule, output is automatically punched or printed, then deleted from its queue. In some cases though, you may

	Delete from queue after processing	Retain in queue after processing
Punch or print item automatically when an appropriate device is available	D(elete)	K(eep)
Punch or print item only after the system operator releases it	H(old)	L(eave)

Figure 7-5   Disposition values for items in the punch and list queues

want to hold output from automatic punching or printing and/or retain it in its queue after processing. Any combination of these functions is possible, as long as you set the item's disposition to the proper value, indicated in figure 7-5. These disposition values parallel those for reader queue entries in figure 7-2.

Class   To punch or print spooled output, POWER has to know what physical device to use. Recall that POWER uses classes to associate jobs in the reader queue with partitions where they can execute. It also uses classes to associate spooled output items in the punch and list queues with the devices on which they can be punched or printed.

Priority   It's possible to specify a priority for output from 0 to 9, where 9 is the highest. As for reader queue entries, the default priority for items in the punch and list queues is 3. Output is processed on a first-in, first-out basis, unless another queue item has a higher priority.

HOW POWER SPOOLS INPUT AND OUTPUT ON A CARDLESS SYSTEM

To let users migrate away from card-based processing, VSE, POWER, and other system components let *card image files* be processed just like physical card decks. For example, POWER can write spooled punch output not only to a card punch, but also to a tape drive. The punch data is recorded on the tape in card image format. Similarly, POWER can read a tape containing card image job streams, called a *SYSIN tape*. The jobs on it appear as if they'd been submitted from a card reader.

However, it's more common to use *inter-partition communication* to transfer spooled items between the POWER partition and another partition. In fact, that's how an ICCF user can submit a job to POWER for scheduling. Figure 7-6 illustrates what happens when an ICCF user submits a job to POWER. First, ICCF retrieves the job stream from its

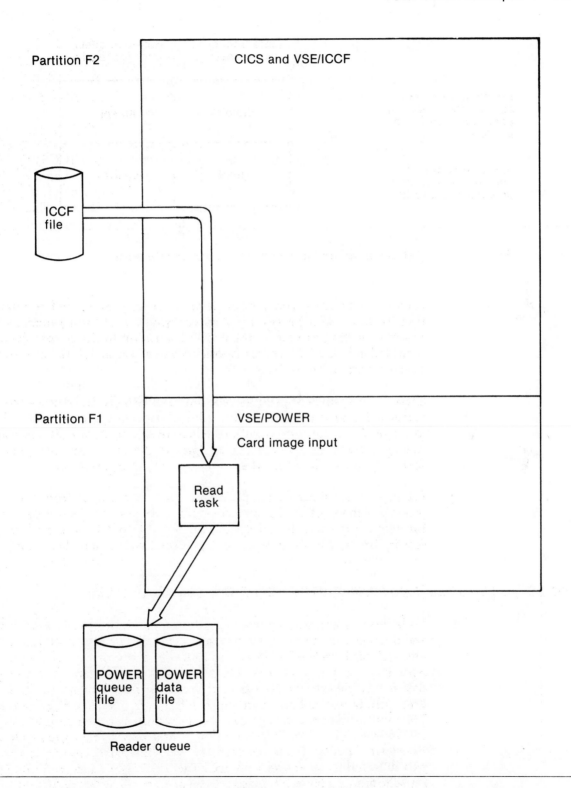

Figure 7-6   How POWER manages input spooling from another partition

library file. Then, inter-partition communication between the CICS/ICCF partition (F2) and the POWER partition (F1) lets the card images that make up the job stream be transferred to POWER. POWER stores the card images in the reader queue just as if they'd come from a card reader. At this point, POWER can schedule the job for execution in an available, eligible partition (probably BG). When the job begins to execute, POWER manages its unit record I/O requests as in figure 7-3.

What happens to the output of a job submitted from ICCF depends on the output's class. For instance, a listing may be printed on a system printer if it's created with the proper class. On the other hand, the item may be held in the list queue for retrieval by the ICCF user. Figure 7-7 shows how this works. When the user enters the proper command, a list or punch output item is transferred by POWER from its queue to ICCF in F2, where ICCF stores it in its library file. In the next chapter, you'll learn how to use ICCF to perform these functions.

DISCUSSION

This chapter is just a brief overview of the basic POWER functions and how they relate to ICCF. As a general VSE user, you should also understand how POWER is able to coordinate spooling and application program I/O requests and how to control POWER functions from within batch jobs using statements from its JECL. For detailed information on these subjects, you can refer to chapters 7 and 8 in *DOS/VSE JCL*.

Terminology

spooling
read task
POWER data file
POWER queue file
queue
reader queue
punch queue
list queue
job entry control language statement
JECL statement
disposition
class
partition-specific class
priority
execution read task
execution punch task
execution list task
punch task
list task
card image file
SYSIN tape
inter-partition communication

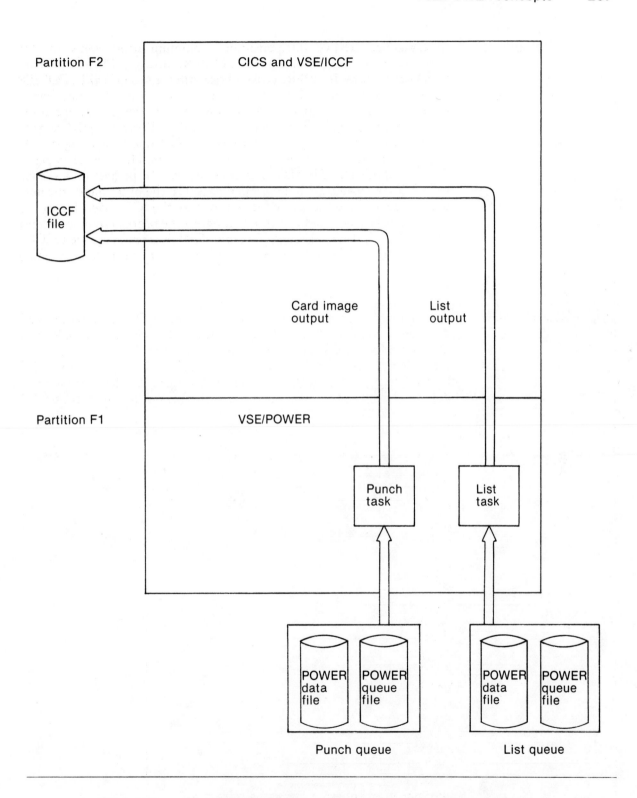

Figure 7-7   How POWER manages output spooling to another partition

Objectives
1. Describe how POWER performs its spooling functions.

2. Describe how POWER works on a system with no card devices.

Chapter 8

How to submit jobs to VSE/POWER, monitor them, and manage their output

Once a VSE job stream has been stored as an ICCF library member, you can use the *submit-to-batch facility* to transfer it to POWER for scheduling in a VSE partition. The key to the process is using the ICCF-supplied procedure SUBMIT. In this chapter, I'll describe how to use the SUBMIT procedure and give you some background so you can understand what it does. Also, after your job has been submitted to POWER, you can use a set of ICCF commands to monitor its progress and manage its output. You'll learn those commands in this chapter too.

How to submit a job to VSE/POWER

To transfer a job to VSE/POWER, you invoke the ICCF SUBMIT procedure. In most shops, the SUBMIT procedure is stored in the common library and, as a result, is available to all users. However, some installations restrict the use of the SUBMIT procedure. When that's the case, it might be stored in a private library that only certain users are authorized to access. As a result, if you try to use SUBMIT and can't find it, check with another ICCF user or your ICCF administrator to find out why.

What the SUBMIT procedure does   When the SUBMIT procedure runs, it brackets your job stream with VSE/POWER job entry control language (JECL) statements to specify how POWER should schedule your job and how it should handle your job's output. The SUBMIT procedure uses parameters that you specify on its command line along with data in the procedure itself to generate the appropriate statements. I presented three of these statements in the last chapter: * $$ JOB, * $$ LST, and * $$ PUN. In addition, the statement * $$ EOJ is used to mark the end of a POWER job.

239

I also mentioned in the last chapter that you can code your own JECL statements in your jobs. However, many installations tightly control how VSE jobs are scheduled and how output is handled. As a result, it's usual for job entry control statements in a typical user's job to be replaced by statements generated by the SUBMIT procedure. But, that depends on your user profile; some users are allowed to submit jobs that are not subject to overrides imposed by SUBMIT. If you code a job that contains JECL and the job doesn't execute the way you think it should, your job entry control statements were probably replaced by SUBMIT's. Again, consult the ICCF administrator if this is a problem. She can either submit the job herself (the ICCF administrator isn't subject to overrides) or change your user profile so your JECL isn't overridden.

After SUBMIT has bracketed your job stream with POWER JECL, it transfers the entire job stream to POWER. To POWER, this is essentially the same as receiving a job from a card reader. After all, the records in the member are in card image format. But let me back up for a minute. As I've already said, the job entry control statements added to your job stream are determined in part by the parameters you code on the command line you use to invoke the SUBMIT procedure. So now, I want to describe those parameters.

Parameters you can supply on the command line that invokes the SUBMIT procedure   You use one of the command lines in figure 8-1 to invoke the SUBMIT procedure. As you can see, the features SUBMIT supports vary slightly depending on your ICCF release.

Regardless of the ICCF release you're using, you must specify the name of the member that contains your job as the first parameter on the command line that invokes the SUBMIT procedure. As the procedure constructs the job stream it will transfer to POWER, it uses the member name as the POWER job name in the * $$ JOB JECL statement it generates. If the ICCF library member is password protected, you supply the password as the second parameter.

Next, you can supply a parameter that specifies what POWER will do with output your job produces. Under all releases of ICCF, you specify DIRECT if you want POWER to route the output directly to appropriate print and punch devices. (If you omit this parameter, the SUBMIT procedure uses DIRECT as its default.) With DIRECT, * $$ LST and * $$ PUN JECL statements are generated to cause list and punch output to be created with disposition D and a class that's associated with a physical device (usually, class A).

In contrast, if you'd prefer that POWER retain your job's print and punch output in its queues, you specify RETURN for this parameter. Then, you can use the ICCF commands and procedures I'll present in a moment to examine the output or to copy it into the ICCF library file for further processing. When you specify RETURN, your print and punch output is usually created with disposition K and class Q. On a typical system, class Q isn't associated with physical devices, so the out-

The SUBMIT procedure

ICCF releases below 2.1

```
                                   ┌─────────┐
                                   │ DIRECT  │
                                   │ DIRECTBG│
SUBMIT member-name [password]      │ RETURN  │      [PRINT] [PWD=power-password]
                                   │ RETURNBG│
                                   └─────────┘
```

ICCF release 2.1

```
                                   ┌────────┐
SUBMIT member-name [password]      │ DIRECT │  [PRINT] [PWD=power-password] [ICCFSLI]
                                   │ RETURN │
                                   └────────┘
```

Figure 8-1   Command lines to invoke the SUBMIT procedure

put will remain in the POWER queues until it's deleted. And, when you retrieve the print and punch output, you won't need to specify its class because the ICCF facilities expect it to be Q.

When you use the DIRECT and RETURN options, it's likely that the job POWER receives will be eligible for execution in any batch partition. To accomplish this, the SUBMIT procedure generates a * $$ JOB JECL statement that specifies a job class that's been specified for all the partitions on the system. Often, that's class A, but this depends on how your shop's system is initialized.

Under releases of ICCF before 2.1, you can also specify DIRECTBG and RETURNBG for this parameter, as you can see in the top section of figure 8-1. When you use either of these values, the job is scheduled to execute only in the background partition. That's because SUBMIT generates a * $$ JOB statement that specifies the partition-specific class 0, which forces your job to run in the background.

Keep in mind that these options are defaults only. Your shop may use a customized version of the SUBMIT procedure that lets you specify other values as well. For example, you might be able to specify values like RETURNF5, RETURNF6, and RETURNF7 to cause your jobs to be executed only in the foreground 5, 6, and 7 partitions.

Another parameter you can specify for the SUBMIT procedure that's available under all ICCF releases is PRINT. If you enter PRINT, the JCL and the JECL that's in the job stream SUBMIT transfers to POWER will be displayed on your screen. If you omit PRINT, those control statements won't be displayed.

The last parameter you can specify for the SUBMIT procedure that's available under all ICCF releases is PWD. On it, you specify the POWER password that you want applied to the output your job produces.

Recall that the basic way SUBMIT works is to construct a job stream that contains the JECL it generates, plus all of the lines in the member you name. Then, it passes all of that data to POWER, where it's stored in the POWER reader queue. For long jobs, this can involve a lot of unnecessary data transfer. As a result, ICCF release 2.1 includes a facility that lets POWER read input data directly from the ICCF library file at execution time. To cause this to happen, you specify ICCFSLI on the command line that invokes the procedure.

The SLI in ICCFSLI stands for source library inclusion. When you specify the ICCFSLI parameter, the SUBMIT procedure generates a * $$ SLI JECL statement in the job that's actually stored in the POWER reader queue. Then, when the job is executed and POWER encounters the * $$ SLI statement, it retrieves the member that contains the job from your library. This is an efficiency consideration more than anything else.

Don't let this discussion of the parameters you can specify when you use the SUBMIT procedure intimidate you. After you've used the procedure a few times, you'll realize that you'll invoke it the same way almost all of the time, varying only the name of the member you want to transfer to POWER. To help you understand how to use the SUBMIT procedure, I want to show you an example.

An example using the SUBMIT procedure   Figure 8-2 presents five screens that illustrate a typical use of the SUBMIT procedure. In part 1 of the figure, I've used the full-screen editor to enter a short job stream. This job is only seven lines long: four lines are VSE JCL and three are control statements for the multi-function utility program VSE/DITTO. In this case, VSE/DITTO is being used to print a volume table of contents (VTOC) listing for one of the DASD units on my system. As you can see in the editor scale line, the name of the member that contains this job is LVTOCD. Notice, however, that the VSE job name (from the // JOB statement) is DISKMAP, not LVTOCD. Although the commands and procedures presented in this chapter generally refer to a job by the member that contains it, you'll see in a minute that this isn't always the case.

After I've finished my editing session for the member, I can submit it to POWER. In part 2 of figure 8-2, I've keyed in this command line to invoke the SUBMIT procedure:

```
SUBMIT LVTOCD RETURN PRINT
```

The first parameter is the name of the library member that contains the job: LVTOCD. Because LVTOCD isn't password protected, I didn't need to supply a password on the command line. The second parameter I specified, RETURN, tells the procedure to generate job entry control statements that will cause the job's output to be held on the POWER list queue. (And if this job had created punch output, it would be held on the punch queue.) Finally, the PRINT parameter tells the procedure to

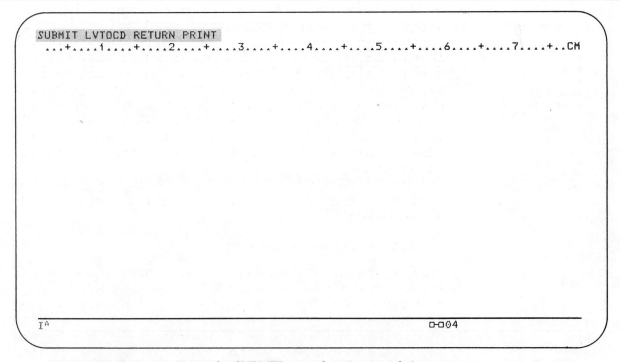

```
===> QUIT
<<..+....1....+....2....+....3....+....4....+....5....+.. MEM=LVTOCD  >>..+..FS
***** TOP OF FILE *****                                            /***/
// JOB DISKMAP                                                     *====*
// UPSI 1                                                          *====*
// EXEC DITTO                                                      *====*
$$DITTO SET DATAHDR=NO,PAGESKIP=YES                                *====*
$$DITTO DVT INPUT=250,SORTBY=EXTENT                                *====*
$$DITTO EOJ                                                        *====*
/&                                                                 *====*
***** END OF FILE *****                                           *****
```

```
I^                                              □-□□4
```

Figure 8-2   Using the SUBMIT procedure (part 1 of 5)

```
SUBMIT LVTOCD RETURN PRINT
...+....1....+....2....+....3....+....4....+....5....+....6....+....7....+..CM
```

```
I^                                              □-□□4
```

Figure 8-2   Using the SUBMIT procedure (part 2 of 5)

```
....+....1....+....2....+....3....+....4....+....5....+....6....+....7....+..EX
*RUN REQUEST SCHEDULED FOR CLASS=A
```
```
I^                                            □-□04
```

Figure 8-2   Using the SUBMIT procedure (part 3 of 5)

```
....+....1....+....2....+....3....+....4....+....5....+....6....+....7....+..SP
* * * * * START OF PROCEDURE (CLIST) * * * * *
* $$ JOB   JNM=LVTOCD,DISP=D,CLASS=I
* $$ LST   DISP=K,CLASS=Q,RBS=0
* $$ PUN   DISP=K,CLASS=Q,RBS=0
// JOB DISKMAP
// UPSI 1
// EXEC DITTO
/&
* $$ EOJ
K889I  JOB LVTOCD   03317 SUCCESSFULLY SUBMITTED -- CARDS OUT=   11
*PARTIAL END PRINT
```
```
I^                                            □-□04
```

Figure 8-2   Using the SUBMIT procedure (part 4 of 5)

```
....+....1....+....2....+....3....+....4....+....5....+....6....+....7....+..CM
**** JOB TERMINATED - RETURN CODE 00 NORMAL EOJ
*READY
```

```
I^A                                                    □-□04
```

Figure 8-2   Using the SUBMIT procedure (part 5 of 5)

display the control statements (both JECL and JCL) that it transfers to POWER.

After I press the enter key, ICCF schedules the SUBMIT procedure to execute in one of its interactive partitions. Part 3 of figure 8-2 shows that my terminal has entered *execution mode.* (That's what the EX in the upper right corner of the screen indicates.) The terminal remains in execution mode until the ICCF job is finished. (For the SUBMIT procedure, that's probably only a moment, although the longer a job stream is, the longer it will take to submit it.) While the terminal is in execution mode, you can't do other ICCF work. During this time, it displays the message

*RUN REQUEST SCHEDULED FOR CLASS=A

But don't let the message confuse you. It means the SUBMIT procedure has been scheduled to run within ICCF; it does *not* mean that your POWER job has been scheduled yet. (In chapters 9, 10, and 11, you'll learn more about how jobs are run in interactive partitions and how procedures work.)

After the ICCF interactive partition job that builds the complete POWER job stream and transfers it to POWER has finished, your terminal enters *spool print mode* and displays completion messages. (In spool print mode, print output from an interactive partition execution is displayed.) That's what part 4 of the figure shows. At the bottom of the screen is a message that advises me that the job was successfully submitted to POWER. The message shows the number of card images transferred to the POWER reader queue (11) and the POWER job number assigned to the job (3317). As you can see, the job name POWER uses is the name of the ICCF library member that contains the job stream (LVTOCD), not the VSE job name (DISKMAP).

Because I entered PRINT on the command line that invoked the SUBMIT procedure, the JCL and JECL transferred to POWER were displayed. You can see that SUBMIT added three JECL statements at the beginning of the job stream to specify the classes that correspond to the processing I requested by entering RETURN. The VSE JCL the screen displays is what I keyed in and stored in the library member LVTOCD. Finally, SUBMIT inserted a POWER * $$ EOJ statement at the end of the job stream. If you add the number of lines that were in the original job (7) and the number of POWER JECL statements the SUBMIT procedure added (4), you'll see that the total is the number of card images that were transferred to POWER (11).

At this point, the job has been submitted to POWER and is stored in the POWER reader queue. When it's executed depends on how busy the entire system is and on the disposition and class specified in the * $$ JOB JECL statement the SUBMIT procedure generated. Do not assume that because the SUBMIT procedure finished that your job is executing: It probably isn't.

When you tap the enter key to leave spool print mode, ICCF displays the message in part 5 of figure 8-2:

**** JOB TERMINATED – RETURN CODE 00 NORMAL EOJ

Again, this applies to the ICCF job run in an interactive partition to construct your POWER job stream and transfer it to the POWER partition. It does not mean that your POWER job has finished, or even that it has started.

How to monitor VSE/POWER jobs

In this section, I'll show you how to use the ICCF commands that let you monitor the progress of jobs after you've submitted them to POWER. First, I'll show you the /STATUSP command, which you can use to track a particular job. Then, I'll show you how to run a special program in an ICCF interactive partition that displays the current activity in VSE's partitions: DTSDA. Finally, I'll show you how to use another ICCF command that lets you look at the contents of the POWER queues: /DQ.

How to monitor your job's progress: the /STATUSP command   The LVTOCD job submitted in figure 8-2 has been transferred to the POWER reader queue. To find out what POWER is doing with it, you can use the /STATUSP system command, whose format is presented in

The /STATUSP command

```
/STATUSP job-name [job-number]
```

Figure 8-3   The /STATUSP command

figure 8-3. As you can see, the command is simple. All I have to do to display the status of my job is enter the command like this:

```
/STATUSP LVTOCD
```

(You can abbreviate the command /SP.) If you want to know the status of a particular job and there are multiple queue entries with the same job name, you should also specify the job number on the command. For example,

```
/SP LVTOCD 3317
```

would display the status of the job I submitted in figure 8-2, even if other queue entries named LVTOCD were present on the system. If you don't specify the job number and there are multiple queue entries with the same job name, the first entry in the queue (the one with the lowest job number) is displayed. The same is true for the rest of the commands and procedures presented in this chapter.

Figure 8-4 shows the output you can receive from the /STATUSP command at different stages in a job's life cycle. For each of the three screens, I entered

```
/SP LVTOCD
```

to display the status of my job.

Part 1 of the figure shows the result of my first inquiry. RD means the job is in the POWER reader queue (R) and that its disposition is D. The job is awaiting execution because the background partition is currently executing another job. The second line of the display shows the POWER reader queue entry for the job: job name LVTOCD, job number 3317, priority 3, disposition D, class I, and 11 card images.

Part 2 of the figure shows the display that indicates the job is running. Notice that the D for disposition has changed to an asterisk: That indicates the job is executing.

After the job had been running for a moment, I entered the /STATUSP command again, and the result is displayed in part 3. Now the job has finished. The status entry indicates that the output is in the list queue (L) and that its disposition is K. The second line is the list queue entry: job name LVTOCD, job number 3317, priority 3, disposition K, class Q, 6 pages, and 1 copy.

Command: /SP LVTOCD (before POWER has scheduled the job for execution)

```
....+....1....+....2....+....3....+....4....+....5....+....6....+....7....+..CM
*STATUS = RD - JOB AWAITING EXEC
1R46I  LVTOCD   03317 3 D I      11
*OK
*READY




















I^A                                                    ▭-▭04
```

Figure 8-4   Output of the /STATUSP command (part 1 of 3)

Command: /SP LVTOCD (while the job is executing)

```
....+....1....+....2....+....3....+....4....+....5....+....6....+....7....+..CM
*STATUS = R* - JOB EXECUTING
1R46I  LVTOCD   03317 3 * I      11
*OK
*READY



















I^A                                                    ▭-▭04
```

Figure 8-4   Output of the /STATUSP command (part 2 of 3)

Command: /SP LVTOCD   (after the job has finished executing)

```
...+....1....+....2....+....3....+....4....+....5....+....6....+....7....+..CM
*STATUS = LK - JOB COMPLETED
1R46I  LVTOCD   03317 3 K Q        6  1
*OK
*READY




I^
                                                    □-□⊖4
```

Figure 8-4   Output of the /STATUSP command (part 3 of 3)

**How to monitor the steps within a job that's executing: the DTSDA
program**   When a job is executing, that's all you can find out from
the /SP command; you can't tell what *part* of your job is running at any
given time. As a result, you might want to use another ICCF facility
that does let you monitor the progress of an executing job: the DTSDA
program.

You run DTSDA in an interactive partition. It, in turn, communicates with VSE to find out what jobs and programs are active in all
of the system's VSE partitions and displays that information for you.
To run DTSDA, all you have to do is enter

    $DA

The $ tells ICCF that you want to load a program directly in an
available interactive partition and execute it; DA is the phase name you
must specify for DTSDA. (You'll learn more about running programs in
interactive partitions in the next chapter.)

Figure 8-5 presents the output of the DTSDA program. When this
screen is displayed, you can tap the enter key repeatedly to display
current data. That way, you can see the transitions from step to step in
your job and how much time each step takes. Here, only three VSE partitions are active: POWER is running in F1, CICS and ICCF in F2, and
my LVTOCD job in the background. In this display, the job name

Command line: $DA

```
...+....1....+....2....+....3....+....4....+....5....+....6....+....7....+..RD
ID PIB  JOB NAME  PHASE NAME    **CPU** **ELAPSED** **SIO** TIME: 13:00:49
BG 00   DISKMAP   DITTO            1.28  00:00:05      183
FB 80   PARTITION UNBATCHED         .00      *          0
FA 80   PARTITION UNBATCHED         .00      *          0
F9 80   PARTITION UNBATCHED         .00      *          0
F8 80   PARTITION UNBATCHED         .00      *          0
F7 80   PARTITION UNBATCHED         .00      *          0
F6 80   PARTITION UNBATCHED         .00      *          0
F5 80   PARTITION UNBATCHED         .00      *          0
F4 80   PARTITION UNBATCHED         .00      *          0
F3 00   **WAITING FOR WORK**        .02      *          3
F2 00   CICSDLI   DTSINIT        576.07  05:00:40   19,235
F1 00   DTRPOWER  DTRPOWER        73.12  05:24:43    8,719
*ENTER DATA?
```

Figure 8-5   Output of the DTSDA program

given is the VSE job name, not the POWER job name. For example, my job, which is running in the background, is identified with the name DISKMAP, not LVTOCD. The phase name column identifies the program that was invoked by an // EXEC statement in the partition. For the background in figure 8-5, the phase is DITTO; for the F2 partition, its DTSINIT, the ICCF initialization program.

The two time values shown for each partition can be useful to diagnose whether or not a program is executing properly. CPU time is total processor time in 1/100ths of a second, and elapsed time is total clock time. If the elapsed time continues to increase while the CPU time has stopped, chances are there's a problem with your job that requires operator intervention, such as a JCL error. On the other hand, if the CPU time increases well beyond what you think is reasonable, there is a chance that your program is executing abnormally (for instance, in a loop). Admittedly, these indicators take some experience to judge, but they can be helpful when you're trying to manage a troublesome batch job from your ICCF terminal.

To end the DTSDA program, all you have to do is enter the command

/CANCEL

The /DQ command

$$/DQ \text{ [queue]} \begin{Bmatrix} \text{HOLD} \\ \text{FREE} \\ \text{class} \\ \text{*abcdefg} \\ \text{job-name [job-number]} \end{Bmatrix}$$

Explanation

queue	The POWER queue whose entries you want to display. You may specify RDR, LST, or PUN. (For ICCF releases at and above 1.3 modification level 5 you can also specify XMT.) If you omit a specification for queue, entries in all queues are displayed.
HOLD	Specifies that only queue entries that are not dispatchable (dispositions L and H) are to be displayed.
FREE	Specifies that only queue entries that are dispatchable (dispositions K and D) are to be displayed.
class	Specifies that only queue entries with the indicated class are to be displayed.
*abcdefg	Specifies that only queue entry names beginning with the specified characters are to be listed. For abcdefg, specify from one to seven characters.
job-name	The exact job name whose queue entries you want to display.
job-number	The POWER job number associated with a particular queue entry that has the job name you specify.

Figure 8-6   The /DQ command

or, simpler, press the PA2 key. I don't encourage you to use the DTSDA program regularly because it ties up ICCF resources and may prevent other ICCF operators from using the submit-to-batch facility. So use it only when you really think there might be a problem with an executing job.

How to display the POWER queues: the /DQ command   Another command you can use to monitor a batch job is /DQ. It lets you display the contents of the POWER queues. As a result, it can be more useful than the /STATUSP command for some situations.

Figure 8-6 illustrates the format of the /DQ command. As you can see, you can request information about the status of specific groups of queue entries with /DQ. Although the options for /DQ look imposing, they're simple to use. For example, to display all the jobs in the POWER reader queue that have class D or K, I'd enter

```
/DQ RDR FREE
```

To display all the jobs in the reader queue that begin with the letter L, I'd enter

```
/DQ RDR *L
```

In fact, after I submitted the LVTOCD job but before it was scheduled, I issued this command, and its output is shown in part 1 of figure 8-7. As you can see, there are three jobs in the reader queue whose names begin with L. Two have been in the queue for some time: LSERV and LVTOC. You can tell that because they have low job numbers. These jobs are retained in the queue so the operator can release them at any time. The third job is the one I just submitted. Its characteristics agree with what ICCF advised me after I submitted the job: job name LVTOCD, number 3317, with 11 cards. Also, the job's disposition (D) and class (I) are what you'd expect based on the JECL * $$ JOB statement the SUBMIT procedure generated for the job. (You can look back to part 4 of figure 8-2 to see it.)

In part 1 of figure 8-7, the display only shows reader queue entries because I specified RDR on the command. However, if you omit the queue operand from the /DQ command, the output shows the entries you request in all queues. In part 2, I entered the command

```
/DQ *L
```

after my LVTOCD job had finished executing. This command caused all entries with names whose first letter is L in all queues to be displayed. If you examine the display in part 2, you'll see that information for the reader, punch, and list queues was provided. Only two reader queue items whose names begin with L remain; LVTOCD was deleted after it had executed because its disposition was D. There are three list queue entries that begin with L; one is my job's output. There are no punch queue items whose names begin with the letter L.

I find the /DQ command to be particularly valuable. If you experiment with it, you'll find the combinations of operands that are most useful for you, and you'll develop a sense of when it's better to use /SP than /DQ.

How to manage the output of VSE/POWER jobs

Typically, when a VSE job has finished executing, you'll need to do something with its output. Most often, that means viewing it at your terminal, then deleting it. Sometimes, you'll want to route the output to the central site printer (or, less often, card punch). And other times, you'll want to copy the data stored in a POWER queue item into your ICCF library for further processing. For example, you might copy in the punch output of a library maintenance job to edit a copy book, or you might want to retrieve a batch program's list output so you can print it

Command: /DQ RDR *L

```
....+....1....+....2....+....3....+....4....+....5....+....6....+....7....+..CM
1R46I    READER QUEUE    P D C S   CARDS          FROM
1R46I    LSERV     00248 3 L 0        5
1R46I    LVTOC     00257 3 L 0        7
1R46I    LVTOCD    03317 3 D I       11
*END PRINT
*READY
```

I^   ▭-▭04

Figure 8-7   Output of the /DQ command (part 1 of 2)

Command: /DQ *L

```
....+....1....+....2....+....3....+....4....+....5....+....6....+....7....+..CM
1R46I    READER QUEUE    P D C S   CARDS          FROM
1R46I    LSERV     00248 3 L 0        5
1R46I    LVTOC     00257 3 L 0        7
1R46I      LIST QUEUE    P D C S   PAGES CC FORM FROM TO
1R46I    LOADVS2   03252 3 K Q        7  1
1R46I    LOADVS2   03254 3 K Q        4  1
1R46I    LVTOCD    03317 3 K Q        6  1
1R46I    PUNCH QUEUE NOTHING TO DISPLAY
*END PRINT
*READY
```

I^   ▭-▭04

Figure 8-7   Output of the /DQ command (part 2 of 2)

The /LISTP command

```
/LISTP job-name [job-number] [class] [PWD=password]
```

The /LOCP command

```
/LOCP /string/
```

Explanation

job-name	The job name associated with the list queue entry you want to display.
job-number	The POWER job number associated with a particular queue entry that has the job name you specify.
class	The class associated with the list queue item you want to display. This operand is required if the list queue entry you want to view does not have class Q. (The standard SUBMIT procedure causes list output to be created with class Q if you use the RETURN parameter.)
password	The one- to eight-character VSE/POWER password associated with the list output.
/	The current delimiter character. Not required if the search string does not contain embedded blanks.
string	The text for which the /LOCP command will scan the VSE/POWER list queue member. If string includes embedded blanks, it must be bracketed by delimiter characters.

Figure 8-8   The /LISTP and /LOCP commands

at a nearby terminal printer. In this section, you'll learn how to use the ICCF commands and procedures for all of these functions.

All of the commands and procedures this section presents require that the output your job produced be stored in one of the POWER queues. Output that's produced with a disposition and class that cause it to be routed immediately to a printer and then deleted is not a likely candidate for processing with the commands and procedures this section presents.

How to view your job's print output: the /LISTP and /LOCP commands   To view printer output produced by your POWER job, you use the /LISTP (or just /LP) command. Figure 8-8 gives its format along with that of the /LOCP command; /LOCP lets you locate text strings in the POWER output you display with /LISTP.

To view the output, you enter /LISTP (or the abbreviation /LP) followed by the job name. In part 1 of figure 8-9, I've keyed in the

```
/LP LVTOCD
....+....1....+....2....+....3....+....4....+....5....+....6....+....7....+..CM
1R46I   READER QUEUE    P D C S  CARDS           FROM
1R46I   LSERV    00248 3 L 0        5
1R46I   LVTOC    00257 3 L 0        7
1R46I    LIST QUEUE     P D C S  PAGES CC FORM FROM TO
1R46I   LVTOCD   03317 3 L Q        6  1
1R46I    PUNCH QUEUE NOTHING TO DISPLAY
*END PRINT
*READY




                                                        □-□04
I^A
```

Figure 8-9   Using the /LISTP and LOCP commands (part 1 of 3)

```
/LOCP INPUT=250
...+....1....+....2....+....3....+....4....+....5....+....6....+....7....+..LS
// JOB DISKMAP                                               DATE 05/
06/86,CLOCK 12/27/40
// UPSI 1
// EXEC DITTO



   VSE/DATA INTERFILE TRANSFER, TESTING AND OPERATIONS UTILITY



   VV      VV  SSSSSSSSS    EEEEEEEEEEE        *  DDDDDDDDD    IIIIIIII
 IIII TTTTTTTTTTTT TTTTTTTTTTTTT  0000000000
   VV      VV  SSSSSSSSSSS  EEEEEEEEEEE        *  DDDDDDDDDD   IIIIIIII
 IIII TTTTTTTTTTTT TTTTTTTTTTTTT  000000000000
   VV      VV SS        SS  EE               *  DD      DD      II
        TT         TT     OO        OO
   VV      VV SS          EE               *  DD      DD      II
        TT         TT     OO        OO

                                                        □-□04
I^A
```

Figure 8-9   Using the /LISTP and LOCP commands (part 2 of 3)

```
     ...+....1....+....2....+....3....+....4....+....5....+....6....+....7....+..LS
     $$DITTO DVT INPUT=250,SORTBY=EXTENT
     * * * * DEVICE    250  SYS098, VOLID=SYSWK3,    FBA, WITH  126016 BLOCKS OF   512 B
     YTES EACH        -- SORTED BY EXTENT     * * * *
     ------ FILE NAME ---------------------------------  VOLSER  YY/DDD  EXT TYPE   BEGIN-E
     ND    RELBLK/NUMBLKS
     .*** VTOC EXTENT ***                                               0 PRIME       2
        17   2,16
     " *** FREE EXTENT ***                                              0  FREE      18
       351  18,334
     Z9999994.VSAMDSPC.T9AD898C.TC00B500            SYSWK3    0/  0     0 PRIME      352
      1055   352,704
     Z9999992.VSAMDSPC.T9AD898E.T5BB6F00            SYSWK3    0/  0     0 PRIME     1056
      9855  1056,8800
     PATB.CORE.IMAGE.LIBRARY                        SYSWK3   86/118     0 PRIME     9856
     11855  9856,2000
     PATB.RELOC.LIBRARY                             SYSWK3   86/118     0 PRIME    11856
     12055  11856,200
     PATB.SOURCE.STMT.LIBRARY                       SYSWK3   86/118     0 PRIME    12056
     18055  12056,6000




     IᴬA                                                      ▭▬▭▭4
```

Figure 8-9   Using the /LISTP and LOCP commands (part 3 of 3)

command

    /LP LVTOCD

to view the output of the job I submitted in figure 8-2. After you issue
the /LP command, the terminal enters list mode and the output is
displayed, as in part 2 of figure 8-9. (Here, the scrambled letters at the
bottom of the screen are part of a banner VSE/DITTO produces in its
list output; the letters appear scrambled because two screen lines are
required to display print lines that have non-blank characters beyond
column 80.) You can tap the enter key to page forward through the
output or you can use the /LOCP command to locate a particular text
string within it.

    In part 2 of the figure, I entered /LOCP followed by INPUT=250
to locate the text string INPUT=250 in the output. The result is that the
output is positioned at the section that contains the VTOC listing for
the unit at address 250, as you can see in part 3. From that point, I can
tap the enter key until I reach the end of the job's output. Alternatively,
I can press the PA2 key to end the display and return to command mode
immediately.

**How to dispose of list output: the /ROUTEP, /ERASEP, and /PURGEP
commands**   After you've viewed your list output, you need to get
rid of it so it doesn't remain on the VSE/POWER list queue indefinitely.

The /ROUTEP command

```
/ROUTEP queue job-name [job-number] [CLASS=class] [PWD=password]
```

The /ERASEP and /PURGEP commands

$$\begin{Bmatrix} /ERASEP \\ /PURGEP \end{Bmatrix} \text{ queue job-name [job-number] [PWD=password]}$$

(Use /PURGEP only for ICCF releases before 1.3 modification level 5; for later releases, use /ERASEP.)

Explanation

queue	For the /ROUTEP command, specify either LST or PUN. For the /PURGEP command, specify LST, PUN, or RDR. For the /ERASEP command, specify LST, PUN, RDR, or XMT.
job-name	The job name associated with the queue entry you want to process.
job-number	The POWER job number associated with the particular queue entry you want to process that has the job name you specify.
class	The class to be associated with the queue item you want to route to print or punch. If you omit class, the default is A; in most shops, that's the system printer or card punch.
password	The one- to eight-character VSE/POWER password associated with the queue entry.

Figure 8-10   The /ROUTEP, /ERASEP, and /PURGEP commands

(And although there isn't a direct way to view punch output, you should dispose of it quickly too.) This section shows you how to use the commands to dispose of queued output. Figure 8-10 presents these commands.

If you want a permanent copy of a job's output, you can issue the /ROUTEP (or /RP) command to route the listing to the central site output device (printer for list output, card punch for punch output). On a simple /RP command, you specify two operands: the name of the POWER queue that contains the output item (LST or PUN) and the queue entry name. For example, I'd enter

```
/ROUTEP LST LVTOCD
```

to cause the output of my sample job to print on the central site printer.

You can specify other operands when you invoke /RP. For example, you can specify the item's output class if you want it to be something other than A. Or, if the output has an associated POWER password, you'll need to supply it using the PWD operand.

If you don't want to do anything with output in a POWER list or punch queue, you should delete it. For ICCF releases at and above 1.3 modification level 5, you use the /ERASEP (/EP) command; for earlier releases, you use the /PURGEP (/PP) command. Their formats are just like /ROUTEP's (except with /EP and /PP, there's no facility to specify a class; that's not necessary). For example, I can enter

```
/ERASEP LST LVTOCD
```

to delete the output from LVTOCD from the POWER list queue. (This is the format of the command that you'll probably use most often.)

How to retrieve data from a POWER queue: the GETL, GETP, and GETR procedures   Although the /LISTP command lets you examine the contents of a list queue item, there are times when you might want to copy a queue item into a member in the ICCF library file. For example, you might want to retrieve a list queue entry so you can print it at a terminal printer near your display station rather than route it to the central site printer. In this section, you'll learn how to use the ICCF-supplied procedures to retrieve items from the POWER queues.

Under all current releases of ICCF, you can use the GETL and GETP procedures to retrieve output from the list and punch queues. And with ICCF 2.1, another procedure, GETR, lets you retrieve a job stored in the reader queue. Figure 8-11 presents the formats of all three procedures.

For GETL and GETP, the POWER queue entry you want to retrieve should have class Q; it will if you specified RETURN (or RETURNBG) when you submitted the job. For GETR the job should have class A. If the queue item you want to retrieve doesn't have the right class for the procedure you'll use, you have to specify the item's class on the command line you use to invoke the procedure.

When you use these procedures, you can specify several parameters to control how they work. For instance, to transfer the print output of LVTOCD into a member named LVTOCD.P, I'd enter

```
GETL LVTOCD MEM=LVTOCD.P PRINT
```

Notice here that I specified PRINT on the command line that invoked the procedure; that causes print control characters to be stored in the library member. Also, I included a .P suffix on the name of the member so ICCF can tell that it contains print-type data. As a result, I can route the contents of LVTOCD.P to my terminal printer, and full 132-character lines will print.

Figure 8-12 shows the screens you'll see when you use the GETL procedure. In part 1, I've keyed in the command line to invoke the procedure. When I press the enter key, ICCF schedules the procedure to run in an interactive partition, as part 2 indicates.

When the program the procedure invokes is executed, it causes my terminal to enter *conversational read mode*. That's what the RD in the

The GETL, GETP, and GETR procedures

```
GETL  job-name            GETP  job-name            GETR  job-name
      [job-number]              [job-number]              [job-number]
      [class]                   [class]                   [class]
    [{ NOPRINT }]
    [{ PRINT   }]
    [{ KEEP   }]             [{ KEEP   }]             [{ KEEP   }]
    [{ DELETE }]             [{ DELETE }]             [{ DELETE }]
      [MEM=member-name]         [MEM=member-name]         [MEM=member-name]
      [PWD=password]            [PWD=password]            [PWD=password]
```

Available with all   Available with all   Available only with
ICCF releases.   ICCF releases.   ICCF release 2.1

Explanation

job-name	The job name associated with the queue entry you want to retrieve.
job-number	The POWER job number associated with the particular queue entry you want to retrieve.
class	The class associated with the queue item you want to retrieve. For the GETL and GETP procedures, you may omit class if the item you want to retrieve has class Q. For the GETR procedure, you may omit class if the item you want to retrieve has class A.
NOPRINT	For the GETL procedure, specifies that the print lines to be retrieved will be stored in the ICCF library file without print control characters. NOPRINT is the default.
PRINT	For the GETL procedure, specifies that the print lines to be retrieved will be stored in the ICCF library file with print control characters. Then, you can use ICCF's printing facilities to print lines that are longer than 80 characters. Since NOPRINT is the default, you must specify PRINT if you want to use this facility. Also, you must store the entry in a print-type member (either the print area or a member whose name ends in .P).
KEEP	Specifies that the item will be retained in its POWER queue after it has been retrieved. KEEP is the default.
DELETE	Specifies that the item will be deleted from its POWER queue after if has been retrieved.
member-name	The name of the member in the ICCF library file in which the queue entry will be stored. For GETL, if you specify * for member name or omit the parameter, the queue entry is stored in the print area ($$PRINT). For GETP, if you specify * for member name or omit the parameter, the queue entry is stored in the punch area ($$PUNCH); for GETP, you may specify $$PRINT to cause punch output to be stored in your print area so you can view it. For GETR, you may not specify *; if you omit the parameter, the name of the job in the POWER reader queue is used as the name of the library member that will contain the item.
password	The one- to eight-character VSE/POWER password associated with the queue entry.

Figure 8-11   The command lines to invoke the GETL, GETP, and GETR procedures

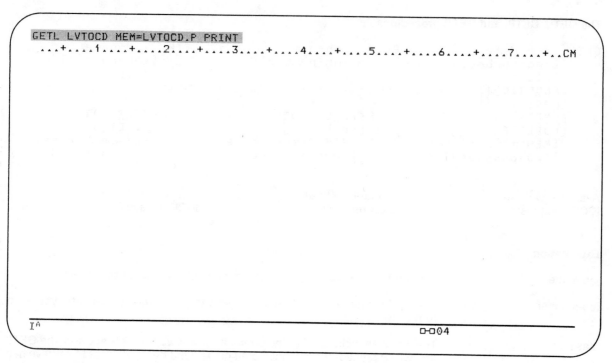

```
GETL LVTOCD MEM=LVTOCD.P PRINT
...+....1....+....2....+....3....+....4....+....5....+....6....+....7....+..CM
```

I ^

□-□04

Figure 8-12   Using the GETL procedure (part 1 of 5)

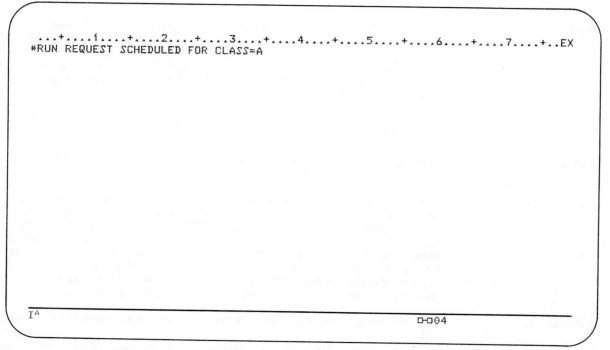

```
...+....1....+....2....+....3....+....4....+....5....+....6....+....7....+..EX
*RUN REQUEST SCHEDULED FOR CLASS=A
```

I ^

□-□04

Figure 8-12   Using the GETL procedure (part 2 of 5)

```
....+....1....+....2....+....3....+....4....+....5....+....6....+....7....+..RD
* * * * * START OF PROCEDURE (CLIST) * * * * *
*
K871D 62 LINES TO BE PLACED IN ICCF LIBRARY MEMBER LVTOCD.P
*
LIST QUEUE: JOB NAME=LVTOCD CLASS=Q DISP=KEEP PRINT
*
DO YOU WISH TO CONTINUE? CANCEL | START POINT AND NUMBER OF LINES | EOB
*ENTER DATA?




















I^                                              □-□04
```

Figure 8-12   Using the GETL procedure (part 3 of 5)

```
....+....1....+....2....+....3....+....4....+....5....+....6....+....7....+..SP
K872I 109 CARD IMAGES PLACED IN ICCF LIBRARY MEMBER LVTOCD.P
*
BY USER: 'STEV' ON TERMINAL: 'L1T1' 05/08/86 10:37:57
*PARTIAL END PRINT

















I^                                              □-□04
```

Figure 8-12   Using the GETL procedure (part 4 of 5)

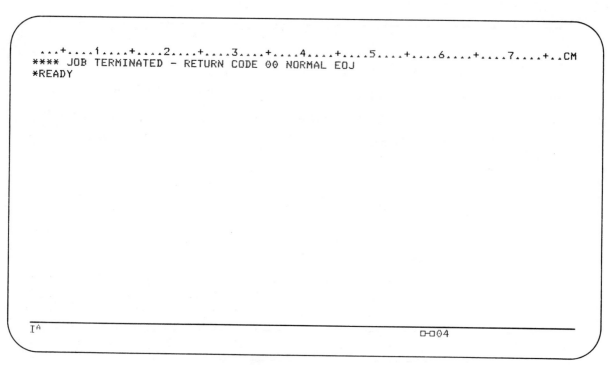

Figure 8-12   Using the GETL procedure (part 5 of 5)

upper right corner of the screen in part 3 means. You'll learn more about this mode in the next chapter. For now, just realize that at this point the program wants me to tell it what to do: proceed and copy in all lines in the queue item by pressing enter (EOB); proceed, but copy in only a certain number of lines beginning at a particular line; or cancel. To copy in only a part of the list output, you just enter the starting line and number of lines at the top of the screen. For example, to copy in 25 lines starting at line 30, you'd key in

    30 25

at the top of the screen and press enter. In this case, I want to copy in the entire item, so I press the enter key without entering any data.

    After the member has been transferred into my library, the screen in part 4 is displayed in spool print mode. Notice that there were 62 print lines in the queue item (shown in part 3), but they were stored in 109 library records (shown in part 4). That's because some print lines required 2 card images when they were stored. After I press the enter key from the screen in part 4, the ICCF job ends, as part 5 shows.

At this point, I can view the member by entering

```
/LIST LVTOCD.P
```

Alternatively, I can route the output to my terminal printer using one of the print macros chapter 5 presented.

If you don't specify a member name when you use the GETL procedure, the output is stored in your print area ($$PRINT). For example, to retrieve the output from the job LVTOCD and store it in my print area, I'd enter

```
GETL LVTOCD
```

Then, to view the output, I'd enter

```
/LIST $$PRINT
```

The GETP procedure works similarly, only it stores output from the POWER punch queue in your punch area ($$PUNCH) if you don't specify a member name. Beware that both $$PUNCH and $$PRINT can be used for other functions, so output you store in them may be lost. If you want to store output permanently, you should use a library member.

With ICCF 2.1, you can use the GETR procedure to retrieve the contents of a POWER reader queue item. Although you'll use GETR less often than GETL or GETP, it can be helpful in some situations.

Discussion

As I've said repeatedly, just how the procedures and commands that make up the complete submit-to-batch facility work for you depend on your installation's unique defaults and on characteristics of your user profile. For example, in my shop, we use a procedure called SUBGO instead of SUBMIT. It performs basically the same functions as SUBMIT, but differs in some details. My point is that you need to talk to other users in your shop to find out just how to use the submit-to-batch facility. And if the facility doesn't work the way you would like it to, discuss it with your system administrator. She can either tailor the SUBMIT procedure to your needs or can explain why you can't do what you want.

Terminology

submit-to-batch facility
execution mode
spool print mode
conversational read mode

Objectives

1. Describe the functions of the SUBMIT procedure.

2. Use the SUBMIT procedure (or your shop's equivalent) to transfer a batch job to VSE/POWER for execution in a VSE partition.

3. Use the /STATUSP and /DQ commands and the DTSDA program to monitor the progress of a VSE/POWER job.

4. Use the /LISTP and /LOCP commands to view VSE/POWER list output at your terminal.

5. Use the /ROUTEP command to route VSE/POWER list or punch output to an appropriate device at your system's central site.

6. Use the /ERASEP or /PURGEP command to delete an entry from one of the VSE/POWER queues.

7. Use the GETL, GETP, and GETR procedures to transfer data from the VSE/POWER queues into your ICCF library.

Section 4

Interactive partition processing

This section's three chapters focus on running programs in interactive partitions. Chapter 9 presents the concepts you need to understand and the control statements you need to know to run programs in interactive partitions. Chapter 10 covers program development in interactive partitions. In it, you'll learn how to use ICCF-supplied procedures to run librarian programs, language translators, and application programs in interactive partitions. Finally, chapter 11 teaches you how to write your own procedures for execution in interactive partitions.

Chapter 9

How to run programs in interactive partitions

In this chapter, you'll learn how to run programs within the ICCF environment in interactive partitions. First, I'll describe the ICCF interactive partition processing concepts you need to know. Then, I'll present the control statements you use to run programs in interactive partitions. Finally, I'll show you four ICCF jobs that use the features this chapter introduces.

To use the features this chapter describes, you need to understand not just ICCF, but also the VSE environment. That's because there are numerous parallels between programs run in ICCF interactive partitions and in VSE batch partitions. As a result, if you're not familiar with DOS/VSE, I encourage you to read my book *DOS/VSE JCL*.

At the outset, I want you to realize that it's possible for the ICCF administrator to set up user profiles to prevent users from running programs in interactive partitions. If that's the case in your shop, it may be that you won't be able to use the facilities this chapter presents. So check with your ICCF administrator or another user to find out if such restrictions are in effect on your system.

USING INTERACTIVE PARTITIONS

In this section, I'll describe what you need to know to understand how processing in interactive partitions works. Also, I'll introduce you to the ICCF system commands you can use to run jobs in interactive partitions and to manage your interactive partition processing environment.

How ICCF interactive partitions compare to VSE batch partitions

For some reason, running programs in interactive partitions can be a source of real confusion. Part of the confusion is due to the fact that there are plenty of parallels between processing in interactive partitions and processing in VSE partitions. However, that can also make it easier to understand running jobs in interactive partitions. In this section, I'll draw on what you should already know about VSE batch processing to help you understand processing in interactive partitions. Specifically, I'll compare storage organization, unit record device usage, control statements, and partition classes for the two environments.

Storage organization   ICCF interactive partitions occupy a part of the virtual storage allocated to the VSE batch partition in which ICCF and its terminal control program (almost certainly CICS) are executing. If you look back to figure 2-7, you'll see that there can be several interactive partitions active at the same time. In fact, the maximum is 35.

An ICCF interactive partition is contained within a VSE batch partition, and it's *similar* to a VSE partition. Most importantly, you need to know that an interactive partition is divided into a program area and a GETVIS area, just like a VSE batch partition. An interactive partition's GETVIS area can be no smaller than 48K, and no larger than the total interactive partition size less 20K. The size of the GETVIS area can affect whether some programs are able to run in an interactive partition. Later in this chapter, I'll show you how to specify what the GETVIS area size should be for a program you want to run in an interactive partition.

Unit record device usage   There are also parallels between interactive partitions and VSE batch partitions with regard to how they support unit record (card and print) operations. For example, you should know that the standard device assignment for print output in a VSE batch partition is made for the system logical unit SYSLST (for most VSE component programs) or the programmer logical unit SYS006 (for most application programs). Then, print output that's directed to one of those logical units by a program is routed to the physical device that was associated with the logical unit. Usually, that's a spooling device managed by VSE/POWER. When you run a program in an interactive partition, SYSLST or SYS006 output is routed to your print area ($$PRINT). Similarly, the VSE default for punch output is SYSPCH (for VSE component programs) or SYS007 (for application programs). In the ICCF environment, write requests for either of these logical units are satisfied by storing the associated data in your punch area ($$PUNCH).

For card input operations in a VSE batch partition, three system logical units can be used. The first, SYSRDR, is assigned to the device from which job control statements are read, and the second, SYSIPT, is assigned to the device from which input data cards are read. Since both control statements and data are often combined in a single job stream, a third system logical unit, SYSIN, can be used to assign both SYSRDR and SYSIPT to the same physical device. Usually, SYSIN input is supplied to a VSE batch partition from a VSE/POWER spooling device. Application programs that read card input typically use the programmer logical unit SYS005 to refer to the device from which it's supplied. For an ICCF interactive partition, control statements and card input data (that is, SYSIN and SYS005 input) are supplied from your input area.

Control statements Job control statements are supplied to VSE batch partitions from SYSRDR (or SYSIN). The equivalent control statements for an interactive partition, supplied from the input area, are called *job entry statements*. If you're familiar with DOS/VSE JCL, you'll recognize some striking similarities between job control and job entry statements. For example, the ASSGN job control statement parallels the /ASSGN job entry statement. The EXEC job control statement function is performed in an interactive partition by the /LOAD job entry statement. And the DLBL and EXTENT job control statements, which describe DASD files, are paralleled in the ICCF environment by the /FILE job entry statement. In fact, job entry statements provide a powerful subset of the features of VSE JCL. Later in this chapter, I'll show you how to code job entry statements and how to combine them in job streams for interactive partitions.

Partition classes If you read chapter 7, you know that VSE/POWER associates classes with each of the VSE batch partitions under its control to determine where to schedule batch jobs. You should remember that a job in the VSE/POWER reader queue has a class that must match that of an available partition before it can be scheduled to execute. As under VSE/POWER, an interactive partition's class determines what jobs can be run in it.

When the ICCF system is set up, the ICCF administrator specifies the characteristics of each interactive partition, including its class. Classes are then used to identify partitions with different characteristics. For example, a class A interactive partition might have 128K of virtual storage and four work files; that's appropriate for running language translators. On the other hand, a class B partition might be tailored for an application program that requires more virtual storage, but no work files.

In the ICCF environment, classes aren't associated with jobs directly, but rather with the users who can initiate jobs. When user profiles are created, the interactive partition classes users can specify are listed. Then, users can run programs in interactive partitions that

Run a job in an interactive partition

```
/EXEC member-name [password]
```

Leave execution mode

```
/ASYNC
```

Return to execution mode

```
/SYNC
```

Display the current status of your terminal relative to an interactive partition job

```
/SHOW EXEC
```

Figure 9-1   Commands for running jobs in interactive partitions

have classes for which they're authorized. For example, all users might be allowed to run programs in class A partitions, while only specific users can use the class B partition. Depending on your user profile, you may be able to change your current execution class to what's appropriate for the programs you want to run. Check with your ICCF administrator to find out what classes you're authorized to use and what kinds of programs they're appropriate for.

ICCF system commands for using interactive partitions

To run a job in an interactive partition, you have to create the job (including its job entry statements), then use the appropriate ICCF system commands to invoke and manage it. This section presents those commands. First, I'll show you the commands that you'll use as you run programs in interactive partitions; they're presented in figure 9-1. Then, I'll describe the system commands you can use to manage your interactive partition processing environment.

How to run a job in an interactive partition: the /EXEC command To run a job in an interactive partition, you have to get the appropriate job entry statements plus any necessary data records into the input area. (Remember, the input area serves the same function as the SYSIN device for a VSE batch partition.) You can do that in a variety of ways, but I'm only going to show you the simplest.

First, you create the job stream (which you'll learn how to do in a moment) using the full-screen editor, and you store the job stream in a library member. Then, to cause the job stream to be transferred to the input area and be executed, you enter the /EXEC command, which has the format

```
/EXEC member-name [password]
```

where member-name identifies the library member that contains the job stream you want to run. If the member is password-protected, you must supply its password as well.

It's also possible to run programs directly without using job entry statements. When that's possible, you simply precede the name of the phase you want to execute in an interactive partition with a dollar sign. (You'll remember from chapter 1 that a phase is an executable module stored in a core image library.) For example, you saw in chapter 8 that entering $DA causes ICCF to run the program DTSDA to display the status of the VSE batch partitions. Actually, the $ causes a job stream to be built in the input area, then executed. For example, entering $DA causes the one-line job stream

```
/LOAD DA
```

to be built and executed. DA is the name of the DTSDA phase in the system core image library. Keep in mind, though, that this method for running programs is appropriate only when a program requires no job entry statements other than /LOAD, which is unusual.

One of the few programs you can invoke directly like this is LSERV, a VSE utility that prints the contents of the label information area. Although you can run LSERV directly, I want to use it in an example of how to run a job. Because LSERV is simple, you only need one job entry statement in a job to run it:

```
/LOAD LSERV
```

If you store this one-line job in a library member named LSJOB, you would run the job by entering the command

```
/EXEC LSJOB
```

As you can see in part 1 of figure 9-2, I've keyed in that command. Then, when I pressed the enter key, ICCF displayed the message in part 2 of the figure. At this point, my terminal had entered *execution mode*. When your terminal is in execution mode, it's synchronized with the execution of a job in the background. In other words, your terminal waits for the job to finish before it lets you do most other work.

How to display your terminal's current execution status: the /SHOW EXEC command   In the command area of the screen in part 2 of figure 9-2, I've keyed in the system command

```
/SHOW EXEC
```

to monitor the progress of the job. The output of the /SHOW EXEC

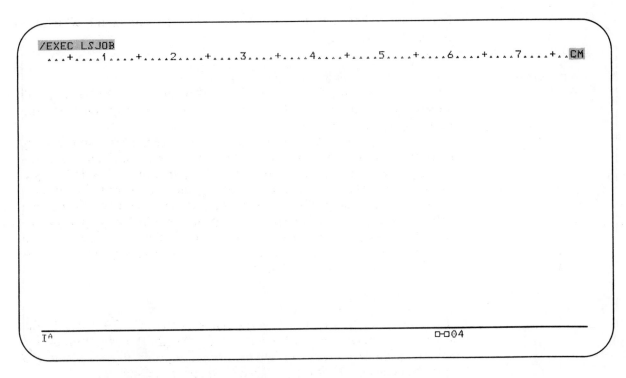

Figure 9-2   Running a program in an interactive partition (part 1 of 4)

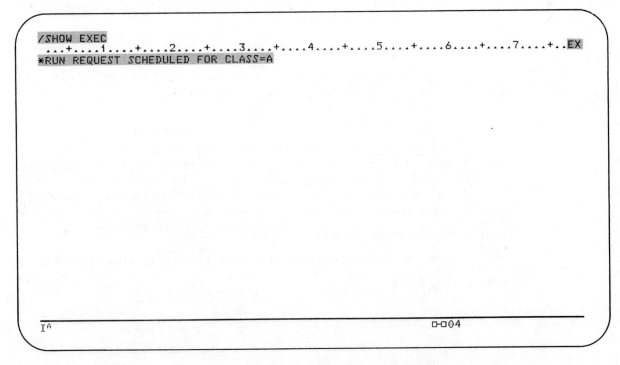

Figure 9-2   Running a program in an interactive partition (part 2 of 4)

```
....+....1....+....2....+....3....+....4....+....5....+....6....+....7....+..EX
*
*EXEC. STATUS =      CLASS EX.UNITS  PP.TIME  RECS:IN/PRINT/PUNCH  PBUFF
EXEC IN PROGRESS       A     11        17            375           3000
*



I^                                                           ⬠-⬠04
```

Figure 9-2   Running a program in an interactive partition (part 3 of 4)

```
....+....1....+....2....+....3....+....4....+....5....+....6....+....7....+..SP
                                          LABEL INFORMATION DISPLAY
- PAGE 001
BG USER LABELS (TEMPORARY PER PARTITION)
   NONE
BG PARTITION STANDARD LABELS (PERMANENT)
   IJSYSLN
           FILE IDENTIFIER                     BG.WORK.LINK
           FILE SERIAL NUMBER                  DOSRES
           VOLUME SEQUENCE NUMBER              01
           CREATION DATE                       OMITTED
           RETENTION PERIOD (DAYS)             0000
           FILE TYPE                           SEQUENTIAL
      EXTENT INFORMATION
           EXTENT SEQUENCE NUMBER              000
           EXTENT TYPE                         1 (PRIME DATA)
           RELATIVE START ADDRESS IN TRACKS/BLOCKS  066676
           NUMBER OF TRACKS/BLOCKS             003088
           SYMBOLIC UNIT                       SYSLNK        LOGICAL UNIT
FORMAT: TYP=00,NUM=05
           VOLUME SERIAL NUMBER                DOSRES


I^                                                           ⬠-⬠04
```

Figure 9-2   Running a program in an interactive partition (part 4 of 4)

command is in part 3 of the figure. It shows my job's class (A) and, as of the moment the command was processed, how many execution units the job has used (11) and how much total elapsed time it has used (17 seconds). Roughly, an *execution unit* is a little less than one second of clock time during which your interactive partition is eligible to receive processor service. When other interactive partitions are active, your partition is not using execution units. The /SHOW EXEC output also shows the number of print records produced so far by the job (375) and the size of my print area (PBUFF: 3000 records).

Although this information is interesting, I particularly want you to notice the execution status (EXEC. STATUS = EXEC IN PROGRESS). This message indicates that my job is actually executing. When the job is finished, my terminal enters *spool print mode* (SP) and displays the job's print output; that's what part 4 of figure 9-2 shows. The output being displayed is stored in the print area. If I wanted, I could retrieve the print output and store it permanently in a library member or route it to a terminal printer.

Although the execution status part of the /SHOW EXEC display isn't very useful when you're idle at your terminal waiting for a job to end, it is valuable information if you use another feature of interactive partition processing: *asynchronous execution*. With asynchronous execution, you can leave execution mode to do command mode work while you're waiting for your job, then return to execution mode when you know (from the /SHOW EXEC display) that your job has finished. Now, I'll show you how to use the commands that let you leave and return to execution mode.

How to leave and return to execution mode: the /ASYNC and /SYNC commands   When your terminal is in execution mode, you can't do other ICCF work. As a result, if you have to wait a long time for your job to be scheduled or if your program is a long-running one, you might want to leave execution mode to do other work in command mode. To do that, you enter the command

    /ASYNC

While a job is executing in an interactive partition, you can monitor its progress by issuing the /SHOW EXEC command. If you issue this command in command mode, the execution status message is

    ASYNC EX IN PROGRS

if your job hasn't finished executing or

    WAITING FOR /SYNC

if it has finished. By using this command then, you'll know when your job has completed executing and when you should return to execution mode. To return to execution mode (and resynchronize your terminal with your job), you can issue the command

> /SYNC

There are some restrictions on what you can do when your terminal is in asynchronous execution mode. First, you can't do anything that changes the contents of the input area. Second, you can't start another job in an interactive partition. In particular, that means you can't run any procedures, either your own or those supplied with ICCF. And third, you can't do any editing; this is the most limiting of the restrictions. However, you can issue other system commands.

How to examine and tailor your interactive partition processing environment: the /USERS PROFILE, /SET, /SHOW, /SETIME, and /TIME commands   Figure 9-3 lists the commands you can use to check and set your interactive partition processing options. Because ICCF resources are valuable, there are limits on how much of particular items you can use. Some of those limits are set as defaults in your user profile, and you can adjust them if necessary for particular requirements. In this section, I'll show you how to find out what your defaults for interactive partition processing are and how to change them.

You can display defaults from your user profile by issuing the /USERS PROFILE command. You've already seen its output, but figure 9-4 presents it again. Here, the values you're interested in are MAXPR, TIMLM, and PPTIM.

MAXPR in the /USERS PROFILE output always indicates the default maximum size of your print area; its current maximum size may be different. If you want to see what your current maximum print area size is, you issue the command

> /SHOW BUFFER

When you issue this command, the maximum print area size is under the heading PRINT.RECS. You can change the current size by issuing the /SET BUFFER command and specifying the new maximum size you want. For example,

> /SET BUFFER 1500

sets the maximum size of my print area at 1500 lines.

The TIMLM and PPTIM defaults in the /USERS PROFILE output are both restrictions on how long a job can run in an interactive partition. If either is exceeded, ICCF cancels your job. TIMLM is the maximum number of execution units your job can use, and PPTIM is the total elapsed time in seconds your job can remain in an interactive partition before it's cancelled.

As with your print area size, your current time limits may differ from the default values in your user profile. To see what the current

Manage your print area size

Display your default print area size

/USERS PROFILE

Display your current print area size

/SHOW BUFFER

Change your current print area size

/SET BUFFER nnnn

Manage your interactive partition processing time limits

Display your default time limits

/USERS PROFILE

Display your current time limits

/SHOW TIME

Display the time used by your last job

/TIME

Change your current time limits

/SETIME timlm [pptim]

Manage your interactive partition processing class

Display your current class

/SHOW CLASS

Change your current class

/SET CLASS n

Figure 9-3   Commands to manage interactive partition processing settings

Command: /USERS PROFILE

```
...+....1....+....2....+....3....+....4....+....5....+....6....+....7....+..CM
*
USER    LIB MAXST MAXPU MAXPR TIMLM TIMOT PPTIM LNSIZ DEFLTS    PROC
STEV     9  4000  3000  3000   900   600  3600         ...⌐..  @DTSLGSE
*
*READY
```

```
I^                                                   ⊡-⊡04
```

Figure 9-4   Sample output of the /USERS PROFILE command

time limits are, you enter

    /SHOW TIME

To alter either time limit, you use the /SETIME command. Its format is

    /SETIME timlm [pptim]

where timlm can be no greater than 32767 and pptim can be no greater
than 65535.

   If you want to see how many execution units and how much
elapsed time a job has used, you can enter the /TIME command. If you
enter it in command mode, it displays, in addition to the current system
date and time, the number of execution units and total elapsed seconds
for the last job run. Figure 9-5 presents its output. Here, the last job
used 26 execution units and was in its partition 24 seconds. Obviously,
the system wasn't busy when I ran that job. Otherwise, the total partition time would be greater than the number of execution units used.

   To find out what your current execution class is, you enter the
command

    /SHOW CLASS

Command: /TIME

```
...+....1....+....2....+....3....+....4....+....5....+....6....+....7....+..CM
DATE=05/10/86 TIME=17/59/20 EXEC UNITS=00026 PARTN TIME=00024
*READY




































IᴬA                                                    ◻◻04
```

Figure 9-5   Sample output of the /TIME command

Then, to change your execution class, you can enter

    / SET CLASS n

where n is the new class value you want to be in effect. The new class value must be one you're authorized to use.

ICCF JOB ENTRY STATEMENTS

Now that you've seen how to use the ICCF system commands to run jobs and manage the interactive partition processing environment, I'm going to show you how to code job entry statements. With what you already know about interactive partitions, this material should be easy for you to understand. As I mentioned earlier, there are some definite similarities between ICCF's job entry statements and VSE's job control statements, so be sure you don't confuse the two.

Syntax of job entry statements

Just as I warn you not to confuse job entry statements with job control statements, you should also be careful not to confuse them with ICCF system commands. That's easy to do because job entry statements and system commands have the same syntax: Both begin with a slash in column 1 that's immediately followed by an operation code. Then, operands usually follow, which may not extend beyond column 72.

Most of the job entry statements are simple; they'll seldom require more than one line. In fact, only two job entry statements can be continued: /LOAD and /FILE. It's only the /FILE statement, which you code to describe a DASD file, that you're likely to need to continue. In VSE JCL, information to define a DASD file is supplied by both the DLBL and EXTENT statements. As you can imagine, then, the data you may have to supply on a /FILE statement can be extensive, and you may need to code it with one or more continuation lines. To continue a job entry statement, simply code a comma as the last non-blank character in the line and continue the statement on the next line. The continuation line should begin with a slash in column 1, followed by at least one space.

How to run a program: the /LOAD statement

As I've already mentioned, the /LOAD job entry statement parallels VSE JCL's EXEC statement. It names the program you want to run and defines a step in your job stream. Its basic format is

```
/LOAD program-name
```

where program-name is the name of a phase in a VSE core image library you want to run.

The /LOAD statement also lets you specify a parameter value that it passes to the application program after it has been loaded. Because that's a feature I don't think you'll use, I'm not going to present it here. If you need to know how to specify a parameter value, refer to the *VSE/ICCF Terminal User's Guide*.

In the example I showed you in figure 9-2, the job I ran contained only one job entry statement:

```
/LOAD LSERV
```

Because the LSERV program doesn't require any specifications for logical units or files, this statement is all that's necessary to run it.

When you need to supply user data in an interactive partition job, it follows the /LOAD job entry statement, just as it follows the //EXEC statement in a VSE batch partition job. ICCF distinguishes between user data and job entry statements by the contents of the first column of each line. If column 1 contains a slash, ICCF interprets the line as a control statement. Otherwise, it interprets the line as user data. If you're running programs in multi-step jobs that require in-line data, you may or may not have to use the end-of-data statement (/*). You'll see examples of both cases later in this chapter.

It's easy to include in-line data in a job that will run in an interactive partition. For example, the job

```
/LOAD PSERV
PUNCH $IPLE
```

causes the library maintenance program PSERV to be loaded into an interactive partition and executed. The second line is a control statement that's read by the PSERV program. There's no need for you to indicate the end of the in-line data here because the job ends immediately.

I used the PSERV program as an example here because it performs a function that's easy to understand and because it uses simple card input. Also, it doesn't require any job entry statements other than /LOAD, which is the only one you're familiar with so far. However, I want you to realize that you'd be likely to use PSERV like this only if your shop runs a release of ICCF that's older than 2.1. You wouldn't use a job like this under ICCF 2.1 for two reasons. First, PSERV is no longer current under VSE/SP 2.1, which includes an entirely new Librarian program, LIBR. And second, ICCF 2.1 includes pre-written procedures that automatically invoke the LIBR program to extract data from VSE libraries. You'll learn how to use those procedures in the next chapter.

How to include other library members in a job stream: the /INCLUDE statement

Instead of coding in-line card-image data directly in a job, like I did in the PSERV job I just showed you, you can use the /INCLUDE statement. When you use /INCLUDE, you specify the name of a library member, like this:

```
/INCLUDE COBPROG
```

Then, when the statement is encountered in the job stream, the contents of the library member it names are processed as input just as if they had been coded directly in the job stream.

For example, suppose a job stream that runs a language translator in an interactive partition is executed. And instead of supplying all the source language statements in the job, I code a single /INCLUDE statement that points to the library member that contains the source program. The results are the same as if I had coded the statements in the job.

You can code any number of /INCLUDE statements in a single job. For example, you might store program source statements in one member and card input test data in another, and then use an /INCLUDE statement for each at appropriate points in your job. Or, if you're working on a long application program, you might store parts of it in different library members to make editing more efficient. Then, you could code a series of /INCLUDE statements, one for each part, in your job stream. Also, /INCLUDE statements can be nested up to eight levels deep, although nesting beyond two levels is unusual.

The /ASSGN job entry statement

```
/ASSGN SYSnnn  {READER  }
               {PRINTER }
               {PUNCH   }
               {UA      }
```

Figure 9-6   The /ASSGN job entry statement

How to manage unit record device assignments: the /ASSGN and /RESET statements

As I mentioned earlier in this chapter, VSE component programs like LSERV and PSERV typically use the system logical unit SYSIN for card input, SYSPCH for punch output, and SYSLST for print output. Similarly, application programs generally use a standard set of programmer logical units for their unit record I/O requests: Card input is usually associated with SYS005, card output with SYS007, and print output with SYS006. If these are the programmer logical units you use, you don't need to do anything special in jobs for interactive partitions to insure that print and punch output go to the print and punch areas and card input comes from the input area.

However, if you use non-standard programmer logical units for unit record files, you need to include /ASSGN job entry statements in your jobs to associate those units with the proper ICCF areas. Figure 9-6 gives the format of the /ASSGN statement. For example, if you've written an application program that writes print output not to the standard logical unit SYS006, but rather to SYS020, you'd include this /ASSGN statement in your job

```
/ASSGN SYS020 PRINTER
```

This will cause SYS020 output to be stored in your print area.

Assignments you make in a job remain in effect for the entire job, so you'll need to change the assignments if subsequent programs in the same job use different logical units for the same functions. To restore all unit record programmer logical unit assignments to their defaults you code

```
/RESET
```

in your job stream. If you want to be more selective about the changes you make, you'll have to go through two steps. First, you need to unassign the unit with an /ASSGN statement in this format:

```
/ASSGN SYS020 UA
```

Then, you code another /ASSGN statement to reassign the unit to the device you want.

Keep in mind that the /ASSGN job entry statement is valid only for unit record device assignments. That's in contrast to VSE JCL, in which the ASSGN statement can also relate a logical unit to other device types, like DASDs. Also, although the default programmer logical unit names I've presented here (SYS005, SYS006, and SYS007) are most commonly used for reader, printer, and punch operations, they may not necessarily be the defaults in your shop. Check with your ICCF administrator if you have any questions about this.

There are other advanced operands you can code on the /ASSGN statement. However, I don't think you're likely to use them, so I'm not presenting them here. If you think you need to use the /ASSGN statement for a function other than reassigning default reader, printer, and punch devices, refer to the *VSE/ICCF Terminal User's Guide.*

How to define DASD files: the /FILE statement

Practically any production job you develop will use files stored on DASD. As a result, to test production programs in interactive partitions, you have to know how to define the files it will use. To do that, you use the /FILE statement. In this section, I'll first describe the syntax of the /FILE statement, then I'll show you how to use it to define four different kinds of files: (1) a VSAM file, (2) a VSE SAM or DAM file, (3) a file in ICCF dynamic space, and (4) a file that's stored as an ICCF library member.

Before I describe how to use the /FILE statement, I want to point out that you don't always have to code it. If a file has already been defined with VSE JCL in the job that was used to start ICCF, you don't have to code a /FILE statement to define it for a program that will run in an ICCF interactive partition. (If you do code a /FILE statement for a file already defined in the ICCF start-up job, the /FILE statement overrides the file definition in the start-up job.) For example, VSE libraries that are defined to the ICCF partition can be accessed by programs running in interactive partitions even though they aren't defined with /FILE job entry statements.

Keep in mind, though, that if a file is defined in the ICCF start-up job, it's probably a production data set that's used by CICS programs that also execute in the ICCF partition. And if that's the case, you're not likely to want to access it, or even be allowed to. As a result, you'll probably use the /FILE statement regularly to define test files, which are not likely to be defined in the ICCF/CICS start-up job.

The syntax of the /FILE statement   Figure 9-7 gives the syntax of the /FILE statement. You always code the NAME operand to supply the name the application program uses to refer to the file; it corresponds to the file-name operand of the VSE DLBL statement. Also, you'll almost always code the IDENT and TYPE operands. IDENT supplies the 1- to

The /FILE job entry statement

```
/FILE   NAME=filename,
/       [IDENT='file-id',]
/       [TYPE=type,]
/       [param1,]
/       [param2,]
          .
          .
          .
/       [paramn]
```

Explanation

NAME = filename	Specifies the name the application program uses to refer to the file. It's equivalent to the file-name operand of the VSE DLBL statement. The NAME operand is required on all /FILE statements.
IDENT = 'file-id'	Specifies the file identification of the file to be accessed. If you omit the IDENT operand, the filename value from the NAME operand is used as file-id.
	You can code &USR, &TRM or &PRT as part of the file-id. &USR is replaced with your user-id, &TRM with your terminal-id, and &PRT with the interactive partition id. These values can be useful if you're creating temporary files in ICCF dynamic space that need to have unique names.
TYPE = type	Specifies the kind of file the /FILE statement is defining. For type, code DIRECT for a VSE DAM file or SEQ for a VSE SAM file, regardless of whether the file is dynamically allocated or not. Code VSAM for a VSAM file or ICCF if the file is an ICCF library member. TYPE = SEQ is the default.

Operand for VSAM data sets

CAT = catalog-name	Specifies the catalog that owns a VSAM data set. The catalog-name you specify should have been specified on the NAME operand of a preceding /FILE statement.

Operands for VSE SAM and DAM files

SERIAL = volser	Specifies the volume serial number of the device on which the SAM or DAM file resides. It's equivalent to the unit operand of the VSE EXTENT statement.
LOC = location,length	Specifies where a VSE SAM or DAM file resides: Location is the CKD relative track number or the FBA block number of the beginning of the file, and length is the number of CKD tracks or FBA blocks the file uses. It's equivalent to the location and length operands of the VSE EXTENT statement.

Figure 9-7   The /FILE job entry statement (part 1 of 2)

Operands for dynamic space allocation

SPACE = storage-units

For CKD devices, storage-units is the number of tracks to be allocated to the file. For FBA devices, storage-units is multiplied by 16 to determine the number of blocks to be allocated to the file.

CYL = YES

Specifies that entire cylinders should be allocated to the file. It causes the allocation specified on the SPACE operand to be rounded up if necessary.

DISP = disp

For disp, code KEEP, DELETE, or PASS. If you specify KEEP, the dynamically allocated file is retained after your job finishes. Both of the other values cause the file to be deleted. With DELETE, the file is deleted at the end of the job step. And with PASS, it's deleted at the end of the entire job. The default is DISP = DELETE.

Operands for TYPE = ICCF files

PASSWORD = pswd

Specifies the four-character password of the password-protected library member to be used as a TYPE = ICCF file.

UNIT = sysunit

For sysunit, code SYSLST, SYSLLG, or SYSPCH. SYSLST causes SYSLST output to be routed to the specified ICCF library member. SYSLLG causes both SYSLST and SYSLOG output to be stored in the member. And SYSPCH causes SYSPCH output to be stored in the member.

Other operands

These operands can be specified for special functions.
For more details, see *VSE/ICCF Terminal User's Guide*.

BLKSIZE	Same as the DLBL BLKSIZE operand.
BUFFER	Same as the DLBL BUFSP operand.
CISIZE	Same as the DLBL CISIZE operand.
DATE	Specifies an expiration date or retention period for the file.
MAXR	Specifies the maximum number of records to be stored in a TYPE = ICCF output file.
RETAIN	Specifies retention for TYPE = ICCF print and punch files.
UNIT	Specifies the logical unit whose associated device will contain the file; SERIAL is easier to use in the ICCF environment for SAM and DAM files.
VOLUME	Used to distribute dynamically allocated space over more than one volume.

Figure 9-7   The /FILE job entry statement (part 2 of 2)

44-character file-id for the file (that is, its VTOC or catalog name). And TYPE specifies what kind of file you're defining.

Depending on the type of file you're defining, the other operands you code vary. I think the easiest way to learn how to code the /FILE statement is to consider how to use it for the four different kinds of files you can define: (1) VSAM files, (2) SAM or DAM files in VSE extents,

(3) SAM or DAM files in ICCF dynamic space, and (4) TYPE=ICCF
files. That's how figure 9-7 is organized, and that's how I'll present the
details of the /FILE statement.

How to use the /FILE statement to define a VSAM file   Most production files are VSAM data sets. To identify a VSAM data set in a job
stream for an interactive partition, you code a /FILE statement like this:

```
/FILE NAME=CUSTMAS,
/       IDENT='CUSTOMER.MASTER',
/       TYPE=VSAM,
/       CAT=DLICAT
```

Here, CUSTMAS is the name the application program you want to run
uses to refer to the data set and CUSTOMER.MASTER is the name that
was given to the file when it was defined. TYPE=VSAM, obviously,
indicates that the file is a VSAM file. And the CAT operand identifies
the user catalog that owns the VSAM file. Here, DLICAT is a file name
that's been associated with a catalog either by another /FILE statement
or by a VSE DLBL statement in the ICCF/CICS start-up job.
    The /FILE statements you code for VSAM data sets are relatively
simple because you don't have to provide extent information on them;
information about a VSAM file's location and length is stored in the
catalog that owns the file. However, to define SAM and DAM files,
you have to supply more information.

How to use the /FILE statement to define a SAM or DAM file   You
can access VSE SAM and DAM (but not ISAM) files from an interactive
partition. When you define a SAM file (indicated in the /FILE statement
by TYPE=SEQ) or a DAM file (indicated by TYPE=DIRECT) you
have to specify the location of the file. To do that, you use the SERIAL
and LOC operands.
    The SERIAL operand provides the volume serial number of the
DASD where the file resides. You can also use the UNIT operand to
specify a logical unit already assigned to the appropriate device, but it's
easier to use SERIAL. (SERIAL corresponds to the volser operand of the
VSE EXTENT statement.)
    The LOC operand serves the same function as the location and
length operands of the VSE EXTENT statement. LOC has two
suboperands that you separate with a comma. The first is the beginning
position of the file. It's either a relative track number (if the file resides
on a CKD device) or a block number (if the file resides on an FBA
device). The second suboperand is the length of the file. For it, you
specify the total number of CKD tracks or FBA blocks the file uses.
    Here's a sample /FILE statement for a VSE SAM output file:

```
/FILE NAME=CUSTTR,
/       IDENT='CUSTOMER.TRANS.FILE',
/       TYPE=SEQ,
/       SERIAL=MMA004,
/       LOC=2760,120
```

In this case, the file the program refers to as CUSTTR will reside on the volume with the serial number MMA004, will begin at relative track 2760, and will use 120 tracks. And the file's id, stored in the VTOC of MMA004, will be CUSTOMER.TRANS.FILE. The /FILE statement for an input file would be similar, only you wouldn't need the LOC operand.

How to use the /FILE statement to define a file in ICCF dynamic space   Because much of the work that's done in ICCF interactive partitions involves program testing, it's often useful to be able to use files that exist only for the duration of a job. When that's the case, it's efficient to create files in a special pool of DASD storage that's allocated to ICCF for that purpose. This technique is called *dynamic space allocation*.

You can create a SAM or DAM file (but not a VSAM file) in ICCF dynamic space. Just specify TYPE=SEQ or TYPE=DIRECT on the /FILE statement. However, to indicate that the file should reside in ICCF dynamic space rather than in its own VSE extent, you specify the SPACE operand rather than the LOC operand.

On the SPACE operand, you code the number of tracks to be allocated to the file, if it's to be stored on a CKD device. If the file is to be stored on an FBA device, you divide the number of blocks you want to be allocated to the file by 16, and specify the result on the SPACE operand.

For CKD devices, if you want the space allocated to the file to be complete cylinders aligned on cylinder boundaries, code CYL=YES. If you specify CYL=YES, the track allocation you specify on the SPACE operand is rounded up to a multiple of the number of tracks per cylinder on the device, if necessary.

Because files created in ICCF dynamic space are usually temporary, it's the default for them to be deleted after they've been processed. That means that unless you specify otherwise, such a file will be deleted after the job step in which it was created. If you want to save a file from one job step to another, you code DISP=PASS on the /FILE statement for the file. For the unusual case in which you want to save a file after your job has ended, you code DISP=KEEP. Then, to access the file after your job has ended, you have to supply location and length information for it. ICCF provides that information in a message it displays when it allocates the file.

A typical /FILE statement for a dynamically allocated file is

```
/FILE NAME=INVMAST,
/      TYPE=DIRECT,
/      SPACE=60,
/      CYL=YES
```

Here, a DAM file named INVMAST is created in ICCF dynamic space. The file will use 60 tracks, aligned on cylinder boundaries. Because I omitted the IDENT operand, the file-id will be INVMAST, the same as the file name I specified on the NAME operand.

ICCF provides two features you can use to manage dynamic file space. You can enter the command line

`$SPACE`

to run the DTSSPACE program in an interactive partition. DTSSPACE displays information on the extents used within the dynamic area. Then, you can use the SCRATCH procedure to delete files created with DISP=KEEP. Later in this chapter, I'll show you how to use both.

How to use the /FILE statement to define a TYPE=ICCF file   The fourth kind of file definition you can make with the /FILE statement is for a TYPE=ICCF file. With this kind of definition, you can let an ICCF library member serve as a unit record I/O area. To use an ICCF library member like this, the member must already exist, even if the program opens the file for output. If the member you want to use is password protected, you must code the PASSWORD operand on the /FILE statement. And if you want to route print or punch output to a library member, you must specify the UNIT operand. See figure 9-7 for the values you can code for the UNIT operand. Later in this chapter, I'll show you how you can use a library member like this.

How to set options: the /OPTION and /UPSI statements

The /OPTION and /UPSI statements correspond to the OPTION and UPSI statements in VSE JCL. On the /OPTION statement, you can code many operands; some are unique to the ICCF environment and some have parallels in VSE JCL. Figure 9-8 lists all the OPTION statement operands and groups them according to how likely you are to use them.

The first group in the figure consists of the operands I think you will use. The situations in which you code them should be obvious after you read the figure. The second group in the figure consists of the operands that control the language translators. You'll probably use these too. The last group in the figure consists of the operands I think you won't use. However, I want to present them so you'll know what options are available.

One of the features of interactive partition processing you can control with the /OPTION statement is whether or not a dump is produced when a program abends. ICCF provides a program you can cause to be invoked automatically if a program that runs in an interactive partition abends. If you specify DUMP on the /OPTION statement in a job, the program DTSCDUMP is invoked. Then, you can use ICCF dump commands to display areas of the program. DTSCDUMP also displays the contents of the PSW and general registers at the time of the abend. Debugging programs is beyond the scope of this book, so if you want more information, refer to the chapter on dump commands in the *VSE/ICCF Terminal User's Guide*.

The /OPTION job entry statement

```
/OPTION param1 [param2 . . .]
```

Explanation

Operand values you're likely to use

NOCONT
CONTINUE

Controls whether or not print output from the job is displayed continuously in spool print (SP) mode or requires the user to tap the enter key to scroll forward.

NODUMP
DUMP

Controls whether or not a dump is displayed if a program you run in an interactive partition abends.

GETVIS = nnnK
GETVIS = P − nnnK
GETVIS = AUTO

Controls the size of your interactive partition's program area and GETVIS area. You'll frequently code this option. If you code nnn, the GETVIS area is set to the size you request. If you code P-nnn, the GETVIS area is set to the size of the partition less the size you specify for nnn. And if you code AUTO, ICCF calculates the proper GETVIS area size based on the largest program phase to be executed in the job step.

GO
NOGO

Controls whether or not a newly compiled application program should be automatically invoked in the partition.

NOINCON
INCON

Controls whether or not card input data can be read in from the terminal in conversational form.

NOLOG
LOG

Controls whether or not job entry statements should be displayed at the terminal as they're processed.

NOOBJECT
OBJECT

Controls whether or not object deck data in a job stream is treated as a module to be loaded and executed (the default) or as data.

NOTRUNC
TRUNC[nn]

Controls whether or not long print lines are truncated for display.   If you specify NOTRUNC, print lines longer than 78 characters are displayed on two lines. If you specify TRUNC without nn, only the first 78 bytes of each line are displayed. If you specify TRUNC with nn, the 78 bytes beginning in column nn are displayed.

Operand values related to language translator execution

| NOALIGN | DECK | NOEDECK | NOLIST | NOLISTX | SUBLIB = AE |
| ALIGN | NODECK | EDECK | LIST | LISTX | SUBLIB = DF |

| NOSYM | NOXREF | RLD |
| SYM | XREF | NORLD |

These operand values correspond directly to the values you can code on the VSE JCL OPTION statement. For more information on their effects, check your JCL reference source.

Figure 9-8   The /OPTION job entry statement (part 1 of 2)

Other operand values you're not likely to use

ANYPHASE = nn	Controls address limits for multi-phase programs.
<u>CLEAR</u> NOCLEAR	Controls whether or not your interactive partition is cleared when your job ends.
<u>EOFPRT</u> NOEOFPRT	Controls when an EOF record is written to the print area.
<u>NOJSDATA</u> JSDATA	Controls whether job entry statements are interpreted as such or treated as data.
<u>NOPERM</u> PERMFILE	Controls whether or not work file names are altered to correspond to ICCF naming conventions.
<u>PROMPT</u> NOPROMPT	Controls whether or not the ICCF prompt ✱ENTER DATA is used to prompt the operator to respond to a program in conversational read mode.
<u>NOSAVE</u> SAVE	Controls, along with NORESET/RESET, how data is accumulated in the punch area.
<u>NORESET</u> RESET	Controls, along with NOSAVE/SAVE, how data is accumulated in the punch area.
<u>NOSPECIAL</u> SPECIAL	Controls whether or not special job-handling features are to be used.
PRCLOSE PUCLOSE	Cancels the effect of a previous /FILE statement that caused SYSLST or SYSPCH output to be stored in a library member and results in that output being routed to the print area (PRCLOSE) or the punch area (PUCLOSE).
TIME = mm[,nn]	Controls time limits for interactive partition use. (Same as the /SETIME system command.)

For details on the effects of these operand values, see the section in *VSE/ICCF Terminal User's Guide* that covers the /OPTION job entry statement.

Figure 9-8   The /OPTION job entry statement (part 2 of 2)

The /UPSI statement is coded just like the VSE JCL UPSI statement. For each of the eight switch bits in the UPSI byte, you can code a 0 to turn the switch off, a 1 to turn it on, or an X to leave it unchanged. For example,

```
/UPSI 100
```

turns on the first switch, turns the second and third off, and leaves the remaining five unchanged. The values of the indicators in the UPSI byte can be evaluated by application programs. However, you'll use the /UPSI statement most often to control VSE programs you run in interactive partitions. You'll see an example of this later in this chapter.

How to use other job entry statements

There are five other job entry statements that you can use: /COMMENT, /TYPE, /DATA, /PAUSE, and /FORCE. They're all easy to understand.

If you want to include comments in a job, you use the /COMMENT (or /COM) statement. It's ignored when a job is processed, so you can include any text with it. The /TYPE statement is similar, only it causes the text you specify to be displayed when the job is executed. Still, it doesn't affect the execution of the job.

The /DATA statement is used only in program development job streams to separate program source code statements, which are processed by the language translator, from in-line data records, which are to be processed by the newly translated program. Because program development functions are typically done using the ICCF-supplied language translator procedures, you'll seldom use the /DATA statement in jobs you write yourself. (In the next chapter, I'll show you how to use the language translator procedures.)

The /PAUSE statement causes execution of a job to stop. This lets you key in additional job entry statements (except /INCLUDE) at execution time. You might use /PAUSE if you want to use the same procedure for different files. Then, when the executing job pauses, you can enter the /FILE statement for the particular file you want to access. To continue with the job, you press the enter key.

The /FORCE statement causes output routed to the print area to be sent directly to your terminal as soon as it's produced. If you don't specify /FORCE, print data is not displayed until the job ends.

SAMPLE ICCF JOB STREAMS

In this section, I want to show you four ICCF job streams that illustrate some of the points I've presented in this chapter. The first two show you how to run the VSE Librarian program PSERV to retrieve data from a VSE library. The second two show you how to define files in the ICCF environment and how to run other VSE utilities and your own application programs.

Before I show you these sample jobs, there's one more thing I want you to realize. When you run a program in an interactive partition using the /LOAD statement, the job entry statements you code to control the execution of the program are coded *after* the /LOAD statement. This is in contrast to a program run in a VSE batch partition in which the job control statements are coded *before* the program is invoked by an EXEC statement. You'll see examples of this in the last three sample jobs.

Sample job 1

Figure 9-9 presents a slightly more complicated version of the PSERV job I showed you when I introduced the /LOAD statement. As you can see in part 1 of the figure, I've keyed in a version of the job that consists

```
===> QUIT
<<..+....1....+....2....+....3....+....4....+....5....+.. MEM=PSERVIPL>>..+..FS
**** TOP OF FILE ****                                                    /***/
/LOAD PSERV                                                              *====*
 PUNCH $IPLE                                                             *====*
 PUNCH $0JCLE                                                            *====*
 PUNCH $1JCLE                                                            *====*
 PUNCH $2JCLE                                                            *====*
 PUNCH $3JCLE                                                            *====*
**** END OF FILE ****                                                    *****
```
```
IA                                          □□04
```

Figure 9-9   A basic PSERV job (part 1 of 5)

```
/EXEC PSERVIPL
...+....1....+....2....+....3....+....4....+....5....+....6....+....7....+..CM
*FULL SCREEN EDITOR TERMINATED
*READY
```
```
IA                                          □□04
```

Figure 9-9   A basic PSERV job (part 2 of 5)

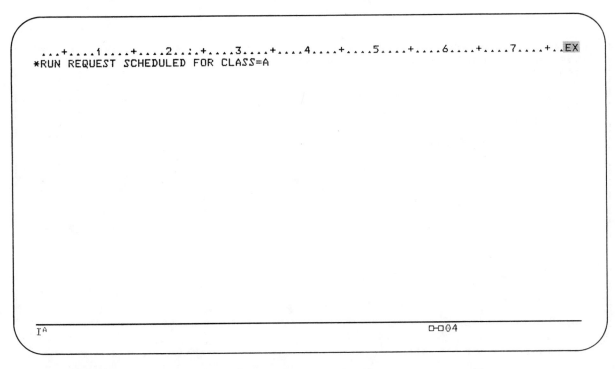

....+....1....+....2..:.+....3....+....4....+....5....+....6....+....7....+..EX
*RUN REQUEST SCHEDULED FOR CLASS=A

I^   □-□04

Figure 9-9   A basic PSERV job (part 3 of 5)

....+....1....+....2....+....3....+....4....+....5....+....6....+....7....+..SP
PUNCH $IPLE
PUNCH $0JCLE
PUNCH $1JCLE
PUNCH $2JCLE
PUNCH $3JCLE
*PARTIAL END PRINT

I^   □-□04

Figure 9-9   A basic PSERV job (part 4 of 5)

```
...+....1....+....2....+....3....+....4....+....5....+....6....+....7....+..CM
**** JOB TERMINATED - RETURN CODE 00 NORMAL EOJ
*READY




                                                                          



                                                                          
I^                                               □-□04
```

Figure 9-9   A basic PSERV job (part 5 of 5)

of five control statements instead of one and I've stored the job in a library member named PSERVIPL. I want to show you this simple job because the next example is an enhancement of it. To invoke the PSERVIPL job, I entered the command line shown in part 2 of figure 9-9.

After I pressed the enter key, ICCF displayed the message in part 3 of the figure. As you learned earlier in this chapter, I could have entered the /ASYNC command at this point to return to command mode while my job is waiting to run and while it is executing. In this case, though, the job was scheduled immediately and it ran quickly. When the job had finished, the print output it produced (which ICCF stored in my print area) was displayed at my terminal, as in part 4 of figure 9-9. Here, the print output is minimal, but for other jobs it can be substantial.

After the job's output had been displayed, my terminal returned to command mode, as you can see in part 5 of figure 9-9. Also, ICCF displayed the end-of-job (EOJ) message in the figure. After this job had finished executing, the contents of the procedures $IPLE, $0JCLE, $1JCLE, $2JCLE, and $3JCLE from the VSE system procedure library were stored, one after another, in my punch area ($$PUNCH).

Sample job 2   Figure 9-10 presents a more complicated job to run the PSERV program. This example illustrates two advanced job entry statement features. First, it shows you how to use a /FILE statement for an ICCF library member. And second, it shows you how to supply card input to a program interactively.

Normally, the PSERV program's punch output is routed to the device associated with the logical unit SYSPCH. In an ICCF interactive partition, the default for SYSPCH output is for it to be routed to your punch area. That was the case with the job in figure 9-9. It's likely, however, that the reason you're retrieving data from a VSE library is to make changes to it. And it's also likely that you want to store the retrieved data in a permanent member in your library, not in the temporary punch area.

As a result, the enhanced PSERV job in part 1 of figure 9-10 includes a statement to do that automatically. Here, the statement

```
/FILE NAME=IPLPROCS TYPE=ICCF UNIT=SYSPCH
```

tells ICCF to route SYSPCH data to the DASD file identified by the statement. And in this case, the /FILE statement used the TYPE=ICCF operand to indicate that a library member, not a VSE file, is to be used. The name of the member is IPLPROCS. The only restriction you need to remember when you use an ICCF library member like this is that it must already exist when you run the job; ICCF won't dynamically create a library member as a result of a /FILE statement that specifies TYPE=ICCF.

In some cases, it's useful to be able to supply card input to programs one record at a time from your terminal. With ICCF's *interactive interface*, you can do that for a program that's running in an interactive partition. Any program that normally reads card input and produces printer output can be run under the interactive interface. To invoke the interactive interface, you code

```
/OPTION INCON
```

in your job stream.

To make it easier for the user to run this job, it includes several /TYPE statements that cause instructions to be displayed when it is run. It's easiest to understand how these elements work together when you look at a typical terminal session that runs this job. That's what the screens in figure 9-10 show.

In part 1 of figure 9-10, I've used the editor to key in the job and store it in a member named PSERVINT. Part 2 of figure 9-10 shows the command line I entered to invoke the job. As with the simpler PSERV job in figure 9-9, the terminal then enters execution mode, as you can see in part 3 of figure 9-10.

```
===> QUIT
*MSG=*SAVED    ....2....+....3....+....4....+....5....+.. MEM=PSERVINT>>..+..FS
***** TOP OF FILE *****                                              /***/
/LOAD PSERV                                                          *====*
/FILE NAME=IPLPROCS TYPE=ICCF UNIT=SYSPCH                            *====*
/OPTION INCON                                          /             *====*
/TYPE ****************************************************************  *====*
/TYPE *                                               *             *====*
/TYPE *     PSERV JOB                                 *             *====*
/TYPE *                                               *             *====*
/TYPE *     THIS JOB PUNCHES SPECIFIED PROCEDURES STORED IN    *    *====*
/TYPE *     THE SYSTEM PROCEDURE LIBRARY AND STORES THEM IN    *    *====*
/TYPE *     A LIBRARY MEMBER NAMED IPLPROCS.          *             *====*
/TYPE *                                               *             *====*
/TYPE *     ENTER A PSERV 'PUNCH' CONTROL STATEMENT WHEN       *    *====*
/TYPE *     YOU'RE PROMPTED.                          *             *====*
/TYPE *                                               *             *====*
/TYPE *     ENTER /* TO END THE JOB.                  *             *====*
/TYPE *                                               *             *====*
/TYPE ****************************************************************  *====*
***** END OF FILE *****                                              *****
```
```
I^                                         □-□04
```

Figure 9-10   A PSERV job to store output in an ICCF library member and accept control statements from the terminal user (part 1 of 9)

```
/EXEC PSERVINT
 ....+....1....+....2....+....3....+....4....+....5....+....6....+....7....+..CM
*FULL SCREEN EDITOR TERMINATED
*READY
```
```
I^                                         □-□04
```

Figure 9-10   A PSERV job to store output in an ICCF library member and accept control statements from the terminal user (part 2 of 9)

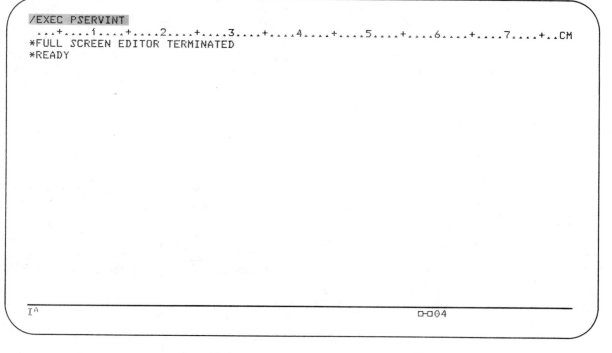

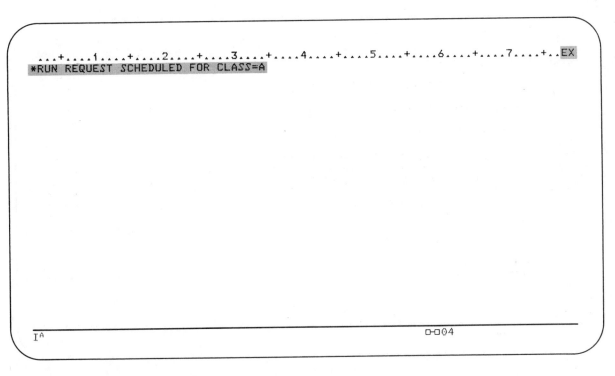

```
...+....1....+....2....+....3....+....4....+....5....+....6....+....7....+..EX
*RUN REQUEST SCHEDULED FOR CLASS=A
```

I^   □-□04

Figure 9-10   A PSERV job to store output in an ICCF library member and accept control statements from the terminal user (part 3 of 9)

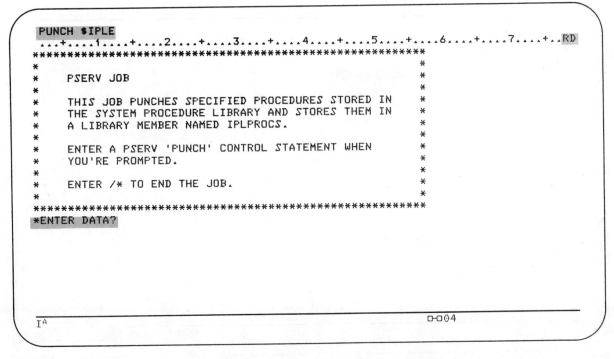

```
PUNCH $IPLE
....+....1....+....2....+....3....+....4....+....5....+....6....+....7....+..RD
******************************************************************
*                                                                *
*    PSERV JOB                                                    *
*                                                                *
*    THIS JOB PUNCHES SPECIFIED PROCEDURES STORED IN             *
*    THE SYSTEM PROCEDURE LIBRARY AND STORES THEM IN             *
*    A LIBRARY MEMBER NAMED IPLPROCS.                            *
*                                                                *
*    ENTER A PSERV 'PUNCH' CONTROL STATEMENT WHEN               *
*    YOU'RE PROMPTED.                                            *
*                                                                *
*    ENTER /* TO END THE JOB.                                   *
*                                                                *
******************************************************************
*ENTER DATA?
```

I^   □-□04

Figure 9-10   A PSERV job to store output in an ICCF library member and accept control statements from the terminal user (part 4 of 9)

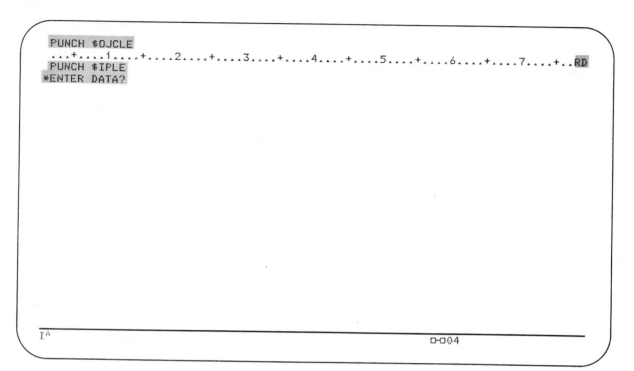

Figure 9-10   A PSERV job to store output in an ICCF library member and accept control statements from the terminal user (part 5 of 9)

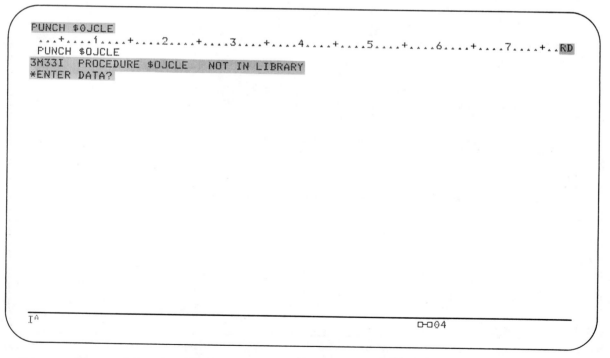

Figure 9-10   A PSERV job to store output in an ICCF library member and accept control statements from the terminal user (part 6 of 9)

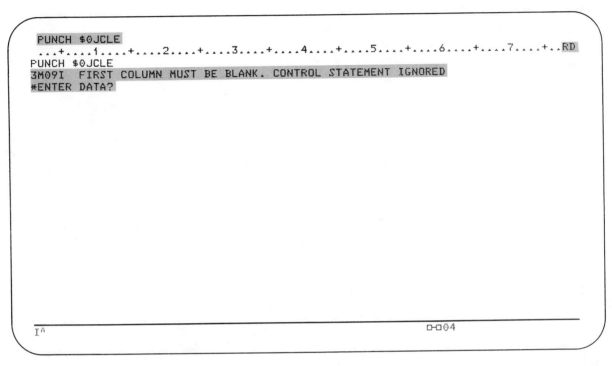

Figure 9-10   A PSERV job to store output in an ICCF library member and accept control statements from the terminal user (part 7 of 9)

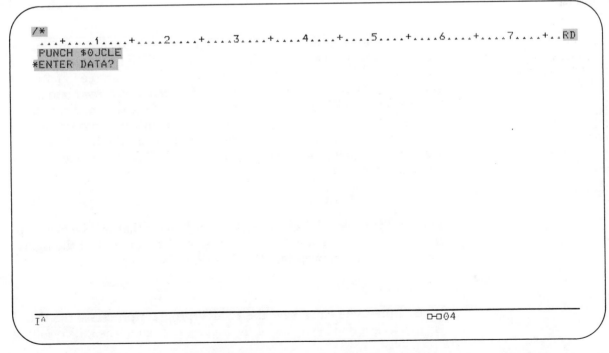

Figure 9-10   A PSERV job to store output in an ICCF library member and accept control statements from the terminal user (part 8 of 9)

```
...+....1....+....2....+....3....+....4....+....5....+....6....+....7....+..CM
**** JOB TERMINATED - RETURN CODE 00 NORMAL EOJ
*READY




















IA                                              □-□04
```

Figure 9-10   A PSERV job to store output in an ICCF library member and accept control statements from the terminal user (part 9 of 9)

However, almost immediately after it enters execution mode, the terminal displays the data associated with the /TYPE statements in the job and prompts the operator to enter data, as you can see in part 4 of the figure. Here, the program is in *conversational read mode*, as indicated by the RD in the upper right corner of the screen. That means that (1) the application program has requested an input card record and (2) input card records are to be supplied not from the job stream but from the terminal as a result of the /OPTION INCON statement. The ICCF prompt

    *ENTER DATA?

requires the terminal user to key in a card image that will be passed to the application program. In the command area in part 4 of the figure, I've keyed in an appropriate PSERV control statement:

    PUNCH $IPLE

When I press the enter key, the PSERV program processes the data I entered as if it had been part of the input job stream. Then, its resulting print output is routed immediately back to the terminal. The line

```
PUNCH $IPLE
```

displayed in part 5 of the figure is print output produced by PSERV. At this point, the program is waiting for another input control statement, as the prompt indicates. This time, I've keyed in a control statement with an error: I've requested the member $OJCLE instead of $0JCLE.

Part 6 of figure 9-10 shows the print output PSERV produced in response to the invalid request. So here, I've keyed in another control statement with the correct name, but I've failed to include a leading space in the control statement. As a result, PSERV indicates that's an error too, as you can see in part 7. Finally in part 7, I've keyed in the correct control statement.

In part 8 of figure 9-10, I've responded to the conversational read prompt by entering the VSE end-of-data statement (/*). The end-of-data statement is required here to cause the PSERV program to end. After the job ends, ICCF displays its standard EOF message, as you can see in part 9. At this point, the library member IPLPROCS contains the contents of the two procedures I successfully retrieved from the VSE system procedure library: $IPLE and $0JCLE.

Sample job 3

Figure 9-11 presents a still more complicated job, this one with several steps. As you can see if you read the comment statements (/COM) in the job, it builds a VSAM data set, loads data into it, prints the contents of the data set, runs an application program that modifies the data set, then prints the data set again, and finally deletes it. The purpose of this job is to test the application program to make sure it executes as expected.

Each of this job's five steps is identified by a /LOAD statement. The first step invokes the VSAM Access Method Services program (IDCAMS) to define the cluster for the test file. Here, I coded

```
/OPTION GETVIS=AUTO
```

to insure that enough GETVIS space would be available in the interactive partition for IDCAMS. As you can see in the in-line data for step 1 of the job, the data set I'm defining will be named ICCF.TEMP.KSDS and will be owned by the user catalog DLI.TEST.USER.CATALOG. To mark the end of the in-line data for IDCAMS, I coded an end-of-data statement (/*).

Step 2 invokes the VSE utility program DITTO to load 50 records into the newly defined data set. Here, I specified

```
/OPTION GETVIS=128K
```

to meet DITTO's storage requirements. Also, I coded two /FILE

```
/COM ***************************************************************
/COM
/COM     THIS JOB BUILDS A TEMPORARY VSAM KSDS, LOADS DATA INTO IT,
/COM     RUNS A TEST APPLICATION PROGRAM, PRINTS THE CONTENTS OF
/COM     THE DATA SET BEFORE AND AFTER THE PROGRAM RUN, AND THEN
/COM     DELETES THE DATA SET.
/COM
/COM ***************************************************************
/COM ***************************************************************
/COM
/COM     STEP 1:  DEFINE DATA SET.
/COM
/COM ***************************************************************
/LOAD IDCAMS
/OPTION GETVIS=AUTO
 DEFINE CLUSTER (NAME       (ICCF.TEMP.KSDS) -
                 VOLUMES    (SYSWK3) -
                 RECORDS    (50) -
                 RECORDSIZE (420 420) -
                 KEYS       (10 0) ) -
        DATA   (NAME        (ICCF.TEMP.KSDS.DATA) ) -
        INDEX  (NAME        (ICCF.TEMP.KSDS.INDEX) ) -
        CATALOG            (DLI.TEST.USER.CATALOG)
/*
/COM ***************************************************************
/COM
/COM     STEP 2:  LOAD DATA SET WITH INITIAL RECORDS.
/COM
/COM ***************************************************************
/LOAD DITTO
/OPTION GETVIS=128K
/FILE NAME=IJSYSUC,
/     IDENT='DLI.TEST.USER.CATALOG',
/     TYPE=VSAM
/FILE NAME=VDSKOUT,
/     IDENT='ICCF.TEMP.KSDS',
/     TYPE=VSAM
/UPSI 1
$$DITTO BVS FILEOUT=VDSKOUT,NLRECS=50,RECSIZE=420,KEYLOC=1,KEYLEN=10,   X
$$DITTO     INCR=3
$$DITTO EOJ
/COM ***************************************************************
/COM
/COM     STEP 3:  PRINT CONTENTS OF DATA SET AFTER LOADING
/COM              INITIAL RECORDS.
/COM
/COM ***************************************************************
/LOAD IDCAMS
/OPTION GETVIS=AUTO
/FILE NAME=DLICAT,
/     IDENT='DLI.TEST.USER.CATALOG',
/     TYPE=VSAM
```

Figure 9-11   A job to test an application program (part 1 of 2)

statements. One defines the data set that will be loaded with data: ICCF.TEMP.KSDS; the file name DITTO will use to refer to it is VDSKOUT. Because DITTO expects a VSAM data set to be owned by the current job catalog, I included a /FILE statement for IJSYSUC that specifies DLI.TEST.USER.CATALOG. This statement temporarily overrides the job catalog in effect for the ICCF partition.

```
/FILE NAME=VKSDS,
/      IDENT='ICCF.TEMP.KSDS',
/      TYPE=VSAM,
/      CAT=DLICAT
               PRINT INFILE (VKSDS) -
                    CHARACTER
/*
/COM ********************************************************
/COM
/COM     STEP 4:  RUN TEST APPLICATION PROGRAM TO ADD MORE RECORDS
/COM              TO THE DATA SET AND MODIFY EXISTING RECORDS.
/COM
/COM              CARD INPUT IMAGES ARE CONTAINED IN THE LIBRARY
/COM              MEMBER DATAVSMP.
/COM
/COM ********************************************************
/LOAD LTSTVEN
/OPTION GETVIS=AUTO
/FILE NAME=DLICAT,
/      IDENT='DLI.TEST.USER.CATALOG',
/      TYPE=VSAM
/FILE NAME=VENDORS,
/      IDENT='ICCF.TEMP.KSDS',
/      TYPE=VSAM,
/      CAT=DLICAT
/INCLUDE DATAVSMP
/COM ********************************************************
/COM
/COM     STEP 5:  PRINT CONTENTS OF DATA SET AFTER RUNNING TEST
/COM              PROGRAM, THEN DELETE THE DATA SET.
/COM
/COM ********************************************************
/LOAD IDCAMS
/OPTION GETVIS=AUTO
/FILE NAME=DLICAT,
/      IDENT='DLI.TEST.USER.CATALOG',
/      TYPE=VSAM
/FILE NAME=VKSDS,
/      IDENT='ICCF.TEMP.KSDS',
/      TYPE=VSAM,
/      CAT=DLICAT
               PRINT   INFILE (VKSDS) -
                    CHARACTER
               DELETE (ICCF.TEMP.KSDS) -
                    CLUSTER -
                    CATALOG (DLI.TEST.USER.CATALOG)
```

Figure 9-11   A job to test an application program (part 2 of 2)

Also, notice in step 2 that I coded

```
/UPSI 1
```

This statement sets the first indicator switch in the UPSI byte on. For DITTO, that means it should look to the job stream for its control statements. And for DITTO, no end-of-data statement was necessary; the DITTO control statement

```
$$DITTO EOJ
```

serves that purpose.

In step 3, I ran IDCAMS again, this time to print the contents of the data set after I'd loaded it with its initial 50 records. To satisfy the requirements of the PRINT function, I coded a /FILE statement to identify the data set. This time, I didn't have to respecify a job catalog, so I coded the CAT operand on the /FILE statement for the data set that points to a preceding /FILE statement for DLI.TEST.USER.CATALOG (file name DLICAT).

Step 4 is the test run for the application program, which is named LTSTVEN. Unlike the utilities (PSERV, DITTO, and IDCAMS) which reside in the system core image library, user programs probably reside in private core image libraries. However, that doesn't present a problem as long as the private library that contains the program you want to run in an interactive partition is named in the core image library search chain for the ICCF partition.

I want you to notice three things about the statements I specified for step 4. First, I coded an /OPTION statement with GETVIS=AUTO. That's typical for programs that process VSAM files. (The utility DITTO is an exception.) Second, I coded a pair of /FILE statements to define the data set and its catalog. Here, the file name I used for the data set is VENDORS. That's because LTSTVEN refers to the data set with that name. And third, I coded an /INCLUDE statement. That causes the contents of the named library member (DATAVSMP, in this case) to be read into the job stream at execution time. DATAVSMP contains card-image data that the program LTSTVEN reads.

Step 5 doesn't present any new job entry statement elements. This step again defines the data set and its catalog and invokes IDCAMS to print the contents of the file. Also, this step includes an AMS DELETE statement to scratch the test data set. Notice that no end-of-data statement is necessary here because no other statements follow in the job.

Sample job 4

The last sample job I want to show you is in part 1 of figure 9-12. This job invokes the utility DITTO to create a VSE SAM file in ICCF dynamic space. The only job entry statement considerations you need to note here are in the /FILE statement. I indicated that the file should be SAM by coding TYPE=SEQ. Because I coded SPACE instead of LOC, ICCF knows that this file will be allocated out of ICCF's dynamic space area. The SPACE operand indicates that six "storage units" should be allocated. "Storage units" are tracks on a CKD device or groups of 16 blocks on an FBA device. In this case, the output device is an FBA DASD, so the file will use 96 blocks.

DISP=KEEP specifies that the file should be retained after my job terminates. Then, I can use the file for other jobs. However, to use the file for subsequent jobs, I have to specify its location using the LOC operand, just as if it were a standard VSE file. That's not a problem, though, because ICCF displays the extent information you need when it allocates the file.

```
===> QUIT
*MSG=*SAVED     ....2....+....3....+....4....+....5....+.. MEM=BLDFILE >>..+..FS
***** TOP OF FILE *****                                                /***/
/LOAD DITTO                                                            *====*
/OPTION TRUNC                                                          *====*
/FILE NAME=NEWSAM,                                                     *====*
/      IDENT='TEST.SEQ',                                               *====*
/      TYPE=SEQ,                                                       *====*
/      SPACE=6,                                                        *====*
/      DISP=KEEP,                                                      *====*
/      CIS=512                                                         *====*
/UPSI 1                                                                *====*
$$DITTO BSQ FILEOUT=NEWSAM,RECSIZE=48,BLKFACTOR=10,NLRECS=25,    X     *====*
$$DITTO      KEYLOC=1,KEYLEN=5,INCR=2,FILLCHAR=X                       *====*
$$DITTO EOJ                                                            *====*
***** END OF FILE *****                                               *****
```
```
I^                                                    □-□04
```

Figure 9-12   A job to build a file in ICCF dynamic space (part 1 of 4)

```
/EXEC BLDFILE
....+....1....+....2....+....3....+....4....+....5....+....6....+....7....+..CM
*FULL SCREEN EDITOR TERMINATED
*READY
```
```
I^                                                    □-□04
```

Figure 9-12   A job to build a file in ICCF dynamic space (part 2 of 4)

```
....+....1....+....2....+....3....+....4....+....5....+....6....+....7....+..EX
*RUN REQUEST SCHEDULED FOR CLASS=A




















I ᴬ                                                   ▭-▭◊4
```

Figure 9-12   A job to build a file in ICCF dynamic space (part 3 of 4)

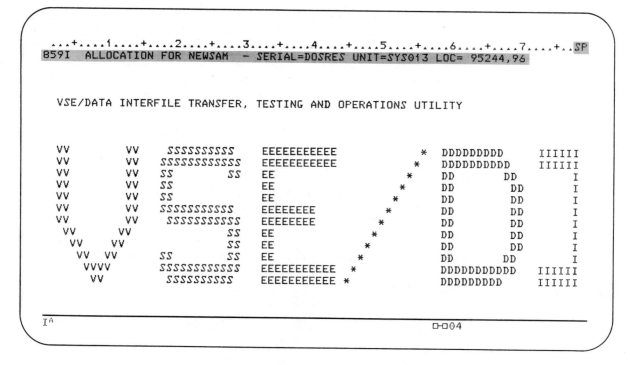

Figure 9-12   A job to build a file in ICCF dynamic space (part 4 of 4)

To understand, consider the series of screens in figure 9-12. After I saved the job in a member named BLDFILE, I invoked it with an /EXEC statement and it was scheduled for execution. Part 4 of the figure shows the beginning of the print output this job produced. As you can see, the first line is the allocation information for the file created in ICCF's dynamic space area. You can use this information later to code /FILE statements for the dynamically allocated file.

Once the job has finished, you can examine how the dynamic space area is being used by entering the command line $SPACE, as in part 1 of figure 9-13. As you know, this causes the ICCF-supplied program DTSSPACE to be loaded into an interactive partition and executed. The output of DTSSPACE is shown in part 2 of the figure. One of the lines here is for the file created by the BLDFILE job in figure 9-12.

If I want to delete this file, I can run the SCRATCH procedure by entering a command line in this format:

```
SCRATCH file-id volser
```

where file-id is the name of the disk file and volser is the volume serial number of the volume that contains the file. In part 3 of figure 9-13, I entered the proper command line to delete the file created by the job in figure 9-12. Part 4 of figure 9-13 shows the message ICCF displayed advising me that the file was deleted.

DISCUSSION

The processing features ICCF provides with interactive partitions and its job entry statements are powerful. However, just how extensively they're used varies from shop to shop. Frankly, for any but the simplest of jobs, I suspect you're more likely to code a VSE job stream and use the submit-to-batch facility to run the job in a VSE—not an interactive—partition. However, a common use for interactive partition processing is program development. For example, you can compile, link, and test a COBOL program entirely in an interactive partition. In the next chapter, I'll show you how to use the ICCF-supplied procedures to do that.

Terminology

job entry statement
execution mode
execution unit
spool print mode
asynchronous execution
dynamic space allocation
interactive interface
conversational read mode

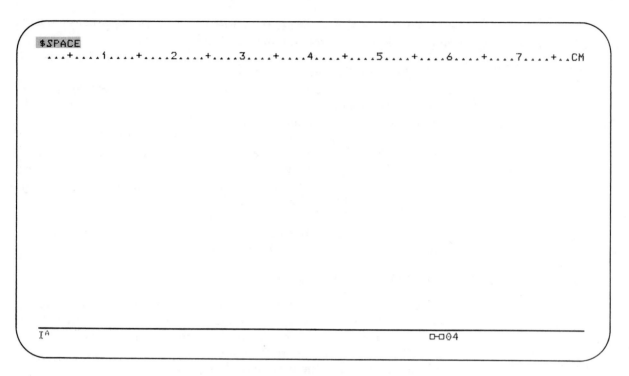

Figure 9-13   Using the DTSSPACE program and the SCRATCH procedure (part 1 of 4)

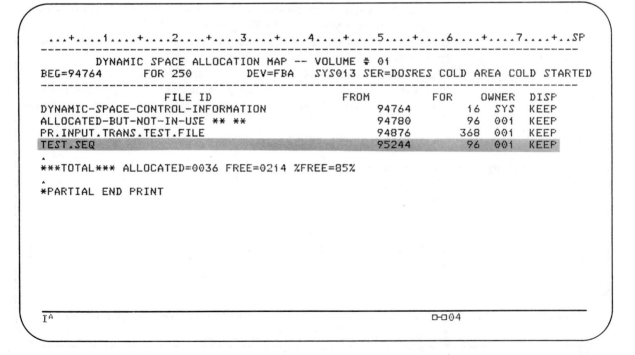

Figure 9-13   Using the DTSSPACE program and the SCRATCH procedure (part 2 of 4)

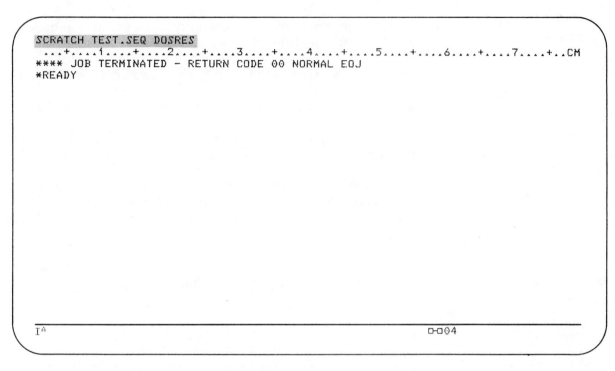

Figure 9-13 Using the DTSSPACE program and the SCRATCH procedure (part 3 of 4)

```
 ...+....1....+....2....+....3....+....4....+....5....+....6....+....7....+..SP
* * * * * START OF PROCEDURE (CLIST) * * * * *
K458I  FILE SCRATCHED
*PARTIAL END PRINT
```

Figure 9-13 Using the DTSSPACE program and the SCRATCH procedure (part 4 of 4)

Objectives

1. Describe the similarities between interactive partition processing and VSE batch partition processing.

2. Use the /EXEC command to run a job in an interactive partition.

3. Use the /SHOW EXEC command to monitor the progress of a job.

4. Use the /ASYNC command to detach your terminal from an executing job and the /SYNC command to reattach it.

5. Use the job entry statements presented in this chapter to write jobs that will run in interactive partitions. The jobs may process VSAM, SAM, or DAM files, files in ICCF dynamic space, or TYPE=ICCF files.

6. Use the DTSSPACE program and the SCRATCH procedure to manage files allocated in ICCF dynamic space.

Chapter 10

How to use ICCF-supplied procedures and macros for program development

In this chapter, I'll show you how to use the ICCF-supplied procedures and macros that let you perform program development functions in interactive rather than VSE batch partitions. First, I'll show you how to use the procedures and macros that let you access members in VSE libraries. Then, I'll show you how to use the procedures to run language translators (for assembler, COBOL, FORTRAN, PL/I, and RPG II programs) in interactive partitions. Finally, I'll show you how to use a procedure (LOAD) to run an application program in an interactive partition. The emphasis in this chapter is on how to use the ICCF-supplied procedures and macros. If you've read chapter 6, you should already have a good idea of how the macros work. In the next chapter, I'll show you what you need to know to understand how the procedures work.

Procedures and macros to access VSE libraries

Often, inactive members from the ICCF library file are stored in VSE libraries to keep them on the system, but they're removed from the ICCF library file. Then, if a change needs to be made to one of these members, it must be extracted from the VSE library and restored to the ICCF library file before the change can be made. Because of this shuffling of members between the ICCF library file and VSE libraries, ICCF provides facilities for accessing VSE libraries.

How extensive those facilities are depends on the release of ICCF you're using. For older releases (that is, before 2.1), the facilities are limited; only two procedures are supplied with those releases of ICCF, and they only let you retrieve data stored in VSE procedure and source statement libraries. I'll show you how to use those procedures (PSERV

309

**Retrieve data from a VSE procedure library
(The PSERV procedure)**

```
        (DSPLY  VSE-member-name
PSERV   {PUNCH  VSE-member-name [INTO ICCF-member-name]}
        (DSPCH  VSE-member-name [INTO ICCF-member-name]
```

**Retrieve data from a VSE source statement library
(The SSERV procedure)**

```
        (DSPLY  VSE-member-name
SSERV   {PUNCH  VSE-member-name [INTO ICCF-member-name]}
        (DSPCH  VSE-member-name [INTO ICCF-member-name]
```

Explanation

VSE-member-name   The name of the member in the VSE procedure or source statement library you want to retrieve.

ICCF-member-name   The name of the ICCF library member in which you want punch data stored. If you omit the INTO clause or specify * for ICCF-member-name, the VSE library member will be stored in your punch area.

Figure 10-1   The PSERV and SSERV procedure command lines

and SSERV) first in this section. Under ICCF release 2.1, the facilities to access VSE libraries are expanded; three macros (LIBRL, LIBRP, and LIBRC) replace the older procedures. These macros not only allow you to retrieve any type of library member; one of them (LIBRC) lets you catalog members in ICCF libraries. I'll show you how to use them second in this section.

Before I show you how to invoke these procedures and macros, I want you to realize that for them to work, the VSE libraries you want to access must be named in a library search chain for the ICCF partition. That means that the ICCF start-up job must have contained a VSE LIBDEF statement that names the library.

How to retrieve data from VSE procedure and source statement libraries under ICCF releases before 2.1: the PSERV and SSERV procedures   The PSERV and SSERV procedures perform functions similar to the variations of the PSERV job I showed you in the last chapter. Figure 10-1 shows the format of the command lines you enter to run the SSERV and PSERV procedures. For example, to run the SSERV procedure, you enter a command line like this:

```
SSERV PUNCH C.INVMAST INTO IMCOPY
```

Here, the contents of the source statement library member INVMAST (stored in sublibrary C) will be copied into the ICCF library member named IMCOPY. If you omit the INTO clause, the source statement book is copied into the punch area ($$PUNCH).

To invoke PSERV, the command line is similar. For example, the command line

```
PSERV PUNCH $IPLE INTO IPLPROC
```

causes the contents of the procedure $IPLE to be copied from the procedure library into an ICCF library member named IPLPROC.

For either SSERV or PSERV, you can specify DSPLY or DSPCH instead of PUNCH. DSPLY causes the contents of the member you specify to be displayed at your terminal; when you specify it, you don't include the INTO clause. (The display output is stored in your print area, and you can list $$PRINT if you want to review it.) DSPCH combines the functions of DSPLY and PUNCH; with it, you *do* include the INTO clause if you don't want the member to be copied into the punch area. (If you're familiar with the VSE Librarian programs, you'll recognize these values as keywords in control statements.)

How to retrieve data from and store data in VSE libraries under ICCF release 2.1: the LIBRL, LIBRP, and LIBRC macros   Under ICCF releases before 2.1, the ICCF-supplied procedures let you print and punch procedures and books stored in VSE libraries. The same functions are available with macros supplied with ICCF release 2.1: The LIBRL macro lets you print a book, object module, procedure or phase, and the LIBRP macro lets you punch one. These macros aren't restricted to particular library types (as, for example, the SSERV procedure is restricted to source statement libraries). With LIBRL and LIBRP, you can retrieve any type of library member. In addition, ICCF 2.1 includes a macro whose function isn't paralleled in earlier ICCF releases: LIBRC. You can use the LIBRC macro to catalog a book, object module, or procedure in a VSE library. (To catalog a phase, you must use the linkage editor in a batch partition.) Figure 10-2 presents the command lines for the LIBRL, LIBRP, and LIBRC macros, and this section shows you how to use them.

To copy (punch) a source statement book into your ICCF library, you enter a command line like this to run the LIBRP macro:

```
LIBRP USRLIB5.STEV INVMAST.C
```

Here, the member I want is contained in the library USRLIB5 and the sublibrary STEV. The member is named INVMAST, and it's a COBOL copy book, indicated by the type specification C. Because I didn't name a member in my ICCF library on this command line, the book will be stored in my punch area. To cause the book to be stored in a member in my library named IMCOPY, I could have entered the command line like this:

**Retrieve data from a VSE library
(The LIBRL and LIBRP macros)**

```
LIBRL VSE-specs ICCF-member-name [password] [REPLACE]
LIBRP VSE-specs ICCF-member-name [password] [REPLACE]
```

**Store data in a VSE library
(The LIBRC macro)**

```
LIBRC VSE-specs {ICCF-member-name} [password] [REPLACE] [DATA=YES] [EOD=xx]
               {$$PUNCH         }
```

Explanation

VSE-specs	Specifications for the VSE library member you want to retrieve or create. A member specification has two components, each with two parts which are separated by periods in this format:
	library.sublibrary membername.membertype
ICCF-member-name	The name of the ICCF library member that will contain the output produced by the LIBRL or LIBRP macro or that will be the source of the input for the LIBRC macro. If you omit this parameter for LIBRL, ICCF uses $$PRINT; if you omit it for LIBRP, ICCF uses $$PUNCH.
password	The ICCF password associated with the ICCF library member to be created (for LIBRL and LIBRP) or read (for LIBRC).
REPLACE	Specifies that the output member (the ICCF library member for LIBRL or LIBRP or the VSE library member for LIBRC) should be deleted if it already exists.
DATA = YES	Valid only when cataloging a procedure into a VSE library with LIBRC. Specifies that the procedure contains in-line data.
EOD = xx	Valid only when cataloging a procedure into a VSE library with LIBRC. For xx, specify two characters that you want to use to mark the end of the procedure. The default is / + .

Figure 10-2   The LIBRC, LIBRL, and LIBRP macro command lines

```
LIBRP USRLIB5.STEV INVMAST.C IMCOPY REPLACE
```

Because I specified REPLACE here, the previous contents of the ICCF library member IMCOPY are lost, if there are any.

To display the contents of a library member, you use the LIBRL procedure. As you can see in figure 10-2, you can store the output in a library member, but it's more likely that you'll want it to be placed in your print area. When that's the case, you don't need to specify an output member. For example, to print the contents of the the procedure $IPLE from the system procedure library, you'd enter this command line:

```
LIBRL IJSYSRS.SYSLIB $IPLE.PROC
```

To invoke the LIBRC macro to catalog a VSE library member from an ICCF library member, you use a command line similar to those for LIBRL and LIBRP. However, the specifications for input and output are reversed: It's the VSE library member (the first one your specify) that's the output, and the ICCF library member (the second one you specify) that's the input. For example,

```
LIBRC USRLIB5.STEV INVMAST.C IMCOPY
```

causes the contents of my ICCF library member IMCOPY to be stored as a COBOL copy book named INVMAST in the STEV sublibrary of USRLIB5. Because I didn't specify REPLACE here, the macro won't cause an existing copy of the VSE library member to be replaced; the macro will only catalog a new member.

Procedures to translate and run programs

To execute a language translator in an interactive partition, you need to cause a job to be run in an interactive partition that will invoke the translator. However, you don't have to code the job yourself. Instead, you can use one of the language translator procedures ICCF supplies. It, in turn, creates an appropriate job stream based on the parameters you provide on the command line that invokes it. In this section, I'll describe in detail how to use the procedures that ICCF provides to let you translate assembler, COBOL, FORTRAN, PL/I and RPG II programs. Then, I'll show you how to use the LOAD procedure to run a newly translated application program.

How to translate source language programs: the ASSEMBLE, COBOL, FORTRAN, PLI, RPG, and RPGIAUTO procedures   Figure 10-3 presents the formats of the command lines you enter to invoke the ICCF language translator procedures. As you can see, the entries you make are similar for each of these procedures.

For each procedure, you specify the name of the library member that contains the source program you want to translate. That's the first parameter after the procedure name. The library member you specify should contain only the source program; it should *not* contain test data, ICCF job entry statements, or job control statements.

The second parameter, OBJ, lets you specify where the translator will store the object module it produces. You can direct the object module to a library member by specifying the member's name. The default, however, is for the object module to be stored in your punch area. That's what happens if you enter OBJ * or omit the OBJ parameter altogether.

Procedures to translate source language programs

```
ASSEMBLE source-member [OBJ object-member] [options]
COBOL    source-member [OBJ object-member] [CBL] [options]
FORTRAN  source-member [OBJ object-member] [FTC] [options]
PLI      source-member [OBJ object-member] [PROCESS] [options]
RPGII    source-member [OBJ object-member] [options]
RPGIAUTO source-member [OBJ object-member] [options]
```

Explanation

source-member	The ICCF library member that contains the program source code.
object-member	The ICCF library member that will contain the object module produced by the language translator. If you omit the OBJ parameter or specify OBJ *, the object module will be stored in the punch area.
options	Any options you can specify on the /OPTION job entry statement (see figure 9-8).

Figure 10-3   ICCF language translator procedure command lines for assembler language, COBOL, FORTRAN, PL/I, and RPG programs

If you're using FORTRAN, COBOL, or PL/I, you can specify that ICCF should prompt you for additional language-specific options. If you want to use language-specific options, enter FTC, CBL, or PRO on the command line. If you don't want to use language-specific options, you can omit this parameter.

For all these language translator procedures, the last parameter you enter consists of any options you want to be in effect for the translation. For this parameter, you can specify many of the values you'd code on the OPTION statement in a batch job. Typically, the ones you enter control list output. The option values you specify are used to generate ICCF /OPTION job entry statements. As a result, you can look back to figure 9-8, which presents the format of the /OPTION statement, to see the values you can use.

An option value you'll probably need to use is GETVIS. To insure that the proper amount of virtual storage is available in the interactive partition to execute the language translator, you should enter

```
GETVIS=0
```

or

```
GETVIS=48
```

Both cause the GETVIS area of the interactive partition to be set at its minimum size: 48K. If you don't code the GETVIS option, it's possible that the program area of your interactive partition won't be large enough to accommodate the language translator program.

Figure 10-4 illustrates a terminal session to compile a COBOL program. The source code is stored in a member called TRANLST. In part 1 of the figure, I specified that the object module should be stored in the punch area (OBJ *) and that the compiler should produce a listing. In addition, I entered GETVIS = 48 to insure that enough storage is available for the compiler in the program area of the interactive partition.

When I press the enter key to start this procedure, the screen in part 2 of the figure is displayed. As you learned in the last chapter, this means that the terminal is in execution mode. As this point, you can enter the /ASYNC command to enter asynchronous execution mode if you wish.

When the job is complete, its list output is stored in the print area and is displayed on the terminal. As you can see in part 3 of the figure, this is the output that would be routed to SYSLST if the compiler had executed in a VSE batch partition: the compiler listing. Part 4 of figure 10-4 shows the end of the compiler listing, which contains diagnostic messages.

After this job has finished, the print area still contains the list output from the compilation, and I can review it by entering /LIST $$PRINT. Alternatively, I can use the hardcopy facility to route the output to a terminal printer or the RELIST macro to send the output to the system printer.

Other procedures for RPG programmers There are two other procedures RPG programmers should know about: RSEF and RPGIXLTR. The RSEF procedure runs the RPG II Source Entry Facility. (If you aren't familiar with RPG II, don't worry about what this facility is used for.) To invoke it, all you do is enter RSEF.

If you're developing a program that will call the DL/I Translator, you can't process it directly with one of the RPG translator procedures. First, you have to process it with the procedure RPGIXLTR. You invoke RPGIXLTR with a command line like

```
RPGIXLTR DBRPT PUNCH DBRPTXLT
```

Here, the contents of the library member DBRPT are processed by the translator and are stored in a new member named DBRPTXLT. If you omit the PUNCH clause, the translator output is stored in the punch area.

How to run a newly translated program: the LOAD procedure
After processing a program using one of the language translator procedures, you can link, load, and execute the object module by invoking

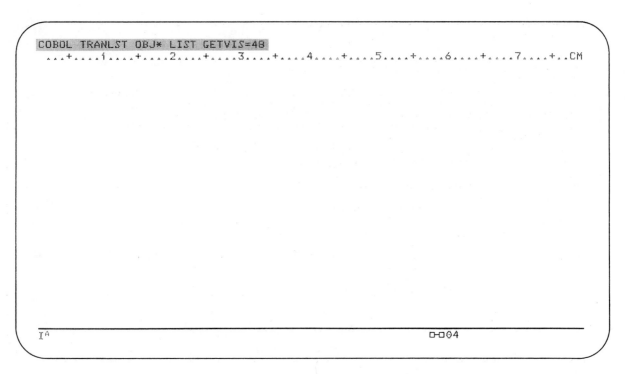

Figure 10-4 Compiling a program in an interactive partition (part 1 of 4)

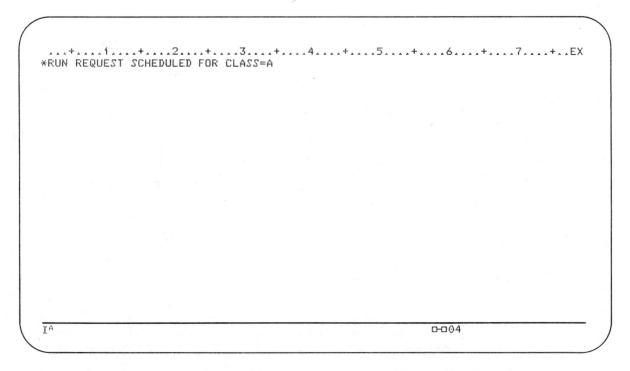

Figure 10-4 Compiling a program in an interactive partition (part 2 of 4)

```
    ....+....1....+....2....+....3....+....4....+....5....+....6....+....7....+..SP
    * * * * * START OF PROCEDURE (CLIST) * * * * *
    K867I  GETVIS SET TO  48K
    K859I  ALLOCATION FOR IKSYS11 - SERIAL=DOSRES UNIT=SYS013 LOC= 95244,640
    K859I  ALLOCATION FOR IKSYS12 - SERIAL=DOSRES UNIT=SYS013 LOC= 95884,640
    K859I  ALLOCATION FOR IKSYS13 - SERIAL=DOSRES UNIT=SYS013 LOC= 96524,640
    K859I  ALLOCATION FOR IKSYS14 - SERIAL=DOSRES UNIT=SYS013 LOC= 97164,640
       1  IBM DOS/VS COBOL                             REL 3.0              PP NO.
    5746-CB1              15.41.18  05/11/86
    00001           IDENTIFICATION DIVISION.
    00002        *
    00003         PROGRAM-ID.  TRANLST.
    00004        *
    00005         ENVIRONMENT DIVISION.
    00006        *
    00007         CONFIGURATION SECTION.
    00008        *
    00009        SOURCE-COMPUTER.   IBM-370.
    00010        OBJECT-COMPUTER.   IBM-370.
    00011        *
    00012        INPUT-OUTPUT SECTION.


    I^                                                  □-□04
```

Figure 10-4   Compiling a program in an interactive partition (part 3 of 4)

```
    ....+....1....+....2....+....3....+....4....+....5....+....6....+....7....+..SP
    *OPTIONS IN EFFECT*    NOSTATE      TRUNC        SEQ    NOSYMDMP        DECK
       NOVERB    NOSYNTAX       NOLVL
    *OPTIONS IN EFFECT*    LANGLVL(2)  NOCOUNT       ADV              NOVERBSUM
       NOVERBREF
    *LISTER OPTIONS*       NONE
        6         TRANLST        15.46.09       05/11/86
     CARD   ERROR MESSAGE

     00155  ILA4072I-W     EXIT FROM PERFORMED PROCEDURE ASSUMED BEFORE PROCEDURE-NA
    ME .
     00163  ILA4072I-W     EXIT FROM PERFORMED PROCEDURE ASSUMED BEFORE PROCEDURE-NA
    ME .
     00203  ILA5011I-W     HIGH ORDER TRUNCATION MIGHT OCCUR.

    END OF COMPILATION
    *PARTIAL END PRINT




    I^                                                  □-□04
```

Figure 10-4   Compiling a program in an interactive partition (part 4 of 4)

The LOAD procedure

```
LOAD [object-member] [JES JES-member] [DATA data-member] [options]
```

Explanation

object-member	The ICCF library member that contains the object module to be processed by the LINKNGO program. If you omit this parameter or specify *, the object module is retrieved from your punch area.
JES-member	The ICCF library member that contains job entry statements to be used for the execution of the application program. If you specify *, you will be prompted for job entry statements.
data-member	The ICCF library member that contains card input data that will be read by the application program. If you specify *, you will be prompted for card input data.
options	Any options you can specify on the /OPTION job entry statement (see figure 9-8).

Figure 10-5   The LOAD procedure command line

the LOAD procedure. Its command line format is presented in figure 10-5. The LOAD procedure invokes a special ICCF program called LINKNGO. LINKNGO replaces the VSE Linkage Editor program, which can't be run in in an interactive partition. Not only does LINKNGO link the object module, but it also loads the resulting phase into an interactive partition and causes it to start executing.

When you invoke the LOAD procedure, you can supply up to four parameters. The first is the name of the library member that contains the object module to be linked and run. If the punch area contains the object module, you can code * or omit this parameter.

The second parameter you can specify tells ICCF where to look for additional job entry statements your program requires. For example, if you want to run a program that uses DASD files, you know that you need to identify them with /FILE job entry statements. If you've already written the /FILE statements and stored them in a library member, you can enter the second parameter like this:

```
JES FILEDESC
```

Here, ICCF looks to the library member named FILEDESC for job entry statements. If you specify

```
JES *
```

ICCF prompts you for job entry statements at execution time. And if you omit this parameter altogether (that is, if you don't code JES in the command line), ICCF assumes that no additional job entry statements are required for your program.

The third parameter you can specify on the command line for the LOAD procedure tells ICCF where to look for in-line card data, if your program requires it. If you code DATA followed by a member name, ICCF supplies input card data to your program from that member. If you specify DATA followed by an asterisk, you can key in card image data one record at a time as your program executes. If you use this technique, you'll need to enter the VSE end-of-data statement (/*) when you've entered all your input data.

The last parameter you can code on the LOAD procedure's command line can be a series of options. As with the options parameter on the language translator procedure command lines, you can specify any options that are valid for an ICCF /OPTION job entry statement. (Look back to figure 9-8 to see what they are.) The one you're most likely to use is the GETVIS option.

Figure 10-6 shows the terminal session to run the program I compiled in figure 10-4. In the command line in part 1 of the figure, the asterisk indicates that the object module to be processed is in the punch area. If I had stored the object module in an ICCF library member, I would have entered the member name instead of the asterisk and the LOAD procedure would have retrieved the object module from that member. In addition, the command line specifies that the program requires card data (DATA) and that the data is contained in a library member named ARTRANS. Because I didn't specify JES, ICCF assumes that no additional job entry statements are required for this program.

When I press the enter key, the job is scheduled for execution, as part 2 of the figure indicates. As with the compile step, if the execution will take a long time, I can use the /ASYNC command to continue with foreground processing while I wait for the job to finish.

When the program execution has finished, its print output is displayed on the terminal, just as in the compile job. Part 3 of figure 10-6 shows the output the program produced. It's stored in the print area, and you can retrieve it if you want to. Note that the output you see on your terminal screen doesn't reflect line spacing—blank lines are omitted from the display. As a result, you'd have to print the output to be sure the spacing is correct.

Discussion   The example in this topic should help you appreciate how convenient ICCF is to use compared with submitting a batch job to develop an application program. However, in some situations, it's not possible to develop a program in an interactive partition. For example, as you develop programs, you'll eventually have to run the VSE linkage editor to add them permanently to a core image library. And you can't do that in an interactive partition.

However, more often than simply not being able to run a job in an interactive partition, you'll choose not to. For system performance

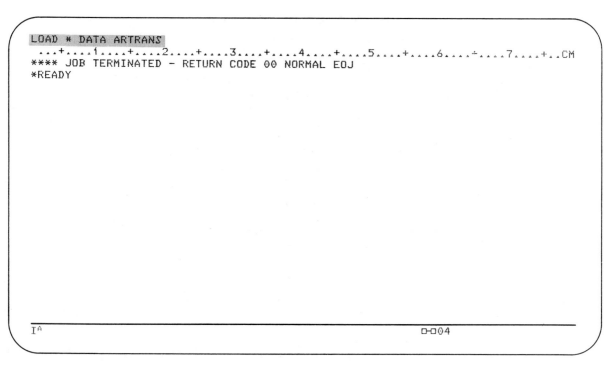

Figure 10-6 Using the LOAD procedure (part 1 of 3)

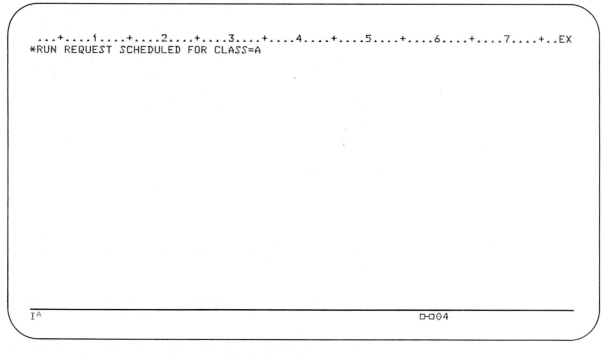

Figure 10-6 Using the LOAD procedure (part 2 of 3)

```
...+....1....+....2....+....3....+....4....+....5....+....6....+....7....+..SP
     * * * * * START OF PROCEDURE (CLIST) * * * * *
** ** ** BEGIN LINKNGO
     14,704 BYTES REQUIRED FOR PROGRAM STORAGE
PGM LOADED AT  8EDC00
XFER ADDRESS   8EDC00
** **
ACCOUNTS RECEIVABLE TRANSACTIONS
BRANCH  REP  CUST     TRAN    INVOICE  TRANSACTION  PAY OR CR
   NO.  NO.  NO.      DATE      NO.       TYPE       AMOUNT
    1   19   01417  0A-20-84   23892   PAYMENT      0435600
    0   00   73280  07-2A-8A   23921   PAYMENT      0000000
    4   41   52339  07-20-84   24830   NEW BILLING
    6   61   49872  07-20-84   24820   NEW BILLING
    8   86   32280  07-20-84   24812   NEW BILLING
    1   14   23052  07-20-84   24802   NEW BILLING
    2   21   16424  07-20-84   2904A   PAYMENT      0089000
    7   74   09822  07-20-84   24792   NEW BILLING
    6   51   02897  07-20-84   24203   CREDIT       0020000
    5   51   02897  07-20-84   23893   CREDIT       0040000
     10 TRANSACTIONS IN FILE
*PARTIAL END PRINT
```

```
 IA                                          0-004
```

Figure 10-6   Using the LOAD procedure (part 3 of 3)

reasons, your shop may have a standard requiring that program development jobs be executed in a VSE batch partition instead of in an ICCF interactive partition. When that's the case, you'll still use ICCF to enter your source program and, *possibly*, to translate it to check for syntax errors. But to test the program, you'll code the proper JCL with the source program and submit the resulting job stream to POWER for execution in a batch partition. You can look back to chapter 8 to refresh you memory about how to use the POWER submit-to-batch facility, if you need to.

Objectives

1. If your shop runs a release of ICCF before 2.1, use the SSERV and PSERV procedures to retrieve books and procedures from VSE libraries.

2. If your shop runs ICCF release 2.1, use the LIBRL, LIBRP, and LIBRC macros to retrieve members from and catalog members in VSE libraries.

3. Use the appropriate language translator procedure(s) to assemble and/or compile programs in interactive partitions.

4. Use the LOAD procedure to run an application program you assembled or compiled in an interactive partition.

Chapter 11

How to write procedures

Throughout this book, I've described how to use ICCF-supplied procedures. For example, you use ICCF procedures to copy and move members from one library to another (CPYLIB, MVLIB, and COPYMEM), to transfer job streams to VSE/POWER for execution in a batch partition (SUBMIT), to retrieve data from VSE libraries (PSERV and SSERV), to translate source programs (ASSEMBLE and COBOL, among others), and to link and run object modules (LOAD). It's easy enough to use these procedures, but to understand how they work and to write your own can be difficult. In this chapter, you'll learn the concepts you need to know to understand just what procedures are and how they operate, and you'll learn how to write procedures of your own.

PROCEDURE CONCEPTS
In the IBM manuals, you'll read that a *procedure* is a library member that can contain ICCF commands, job entry statements, and data. You'll also read that you can invoke a procedure by name to cause its statements to be processed just as if they were entered by the operator. You probably wonder how that's different from a macro (which can contain a series of system or editing commands) or a job (which can contain a series of job entry statements). Frankly, the differences are confusing.

How procedures and macros compare

You should remember from chapter 6 that a macro is a series of ICCF system and/or editing commands that are stored in a library member and that can be processed in sequence just by invoking the macro by name. In addition, macros can contain macro orders used to control, to a limited extent, the processing the macro does. And, perhaps most important, macros can be coded to process variable parameters. When you use variable parameters, you can develop generalized macros that can be run over and over to perform the same function, only under different conditions (most likely, using different library members).

A procedure is similar in many ways to a macro. It can contain a series of ICCF commands, it can be invoked with a single command line, and it can process variable parameters. As a result, both macros and procedures can be generalized. And just as macros can be written with some logic to control how they execute, procedures can too. In a macro, you code macro orders to control its execution; in a procedure, you code *procedure processor orders*. Although procedure processor orders are similar to macro orders, they're more powerful.

The main difference between a procedure and a macro is how they're executed. A macro is executed in foreground mode, just as if you had keyed in each system or editing command yourself. In contrast, a procedure is processed in one of ICCF's interactive partitions by the *procedure processor program* (called *DTSPROCS*). In fact, you can think of the procedure as input data for DTSPROCS. If a line contains a procedure order, DTSPROCS interprets the order and does whatever action the order requires. When it encounters a system command, DTSPROCS passes the command to the appropriate ICCF module, which executes the command immediately. (Often, however, DTSPROCS has first modified the command by adding one or more variable values to it.) Because of this additional processing, procedures typically execute more slowly than macros do.

How procedures and interactive partition jobs compare

Just as it's easy to confuse procedures and macros, it's also easy to confuse procedures and interactive partition jobs. That's because both procedures and jobs execute in interactive partitions. There can also be a more direct relationship between jobs and procedures in that procedures are often used to build and execute jobs. For example, a procedure may contain system commands that cause job entry statements to be stored in the input area, then another system command that causes the job in the input area to be executed. To understand this, take a look at figure 11-1. This is the actual code of the ICCF-supplied COBOL procedure that was invoked in the example in the last chapter. Don't worry for now about the details of the statements; you'll learn exactly how this procedure works later in this chapter. For now, I want you to look at the shaded lines of the procedure. When these statements are processed by DTSPROCS, the shaded /INP (/INPUT) command opens the input area and causes the shaded job entry statements (&/LOAD, /OPTION, /FILE, and &/INCLUDE) to be placed there.

```
*  --  --  --  --  --  --  --  --  --  --  --  --  --  --  --  --  --
*          PROCEDURE TO COMPILE A COBOL PROGRAM
*   COBOL NNNN (OBJ MMMM/*) (CBL) (OPTIONS)
*  --  --  --  --  --  --  --  --  --  --  --  --  --  --  --  --  --
&&OPTIONS 0010001
&&SET &&VARBL1 &&PARAM1                          SAVE NAME OF SOURCE
&&SHIFT 1                                        SHIFT OUT NAME OF PROGRAM
&&IF &&PARAM1 NE OBJ &&GOTO NOOBJ                SKIP TO TEST COMPILER CTL
&&SET &&VARBL2 &&PARAM2                          SAVE NAME OF OBJ MEMBR
&&IF &&VARBL2 EQ '*' &&SET &&VARBL2 ' '          * REQUIRES NO FILE STMT
&&IF &&VARBL2 EQ ' ' &&GOTO +INLIB               SKIP TEST FOR MEM IN LIB
/LIST 1 1 &&VARBL2
&&IF &&RETCOD  EQ *READY &&GOTO INLIB            SKIP IF IN LIB ALREADY
/INP NOPROMPT
DUMMY CARD TO CREATE MEMBER                         AND SAVE IN LIB
/SAVE &&VARBL2
&&LABEL INLIB
&&SHIFT 1                                        SHIFT OUT OBJ
&&SHIFT 1                                        SHIFT OUT NAME
&&LABEL NOOBJ
&&IF &&PARAM1 NE CBL &&GOTO +3                   GO BUILD JOB STREAM
&&SET &&VARBL3 'CBL'                             SET CONTROL CARD DESIRED
&&SHIFT 1                                        SHIFT OUT CBL
/INP NOPROMPT
&/LOAD FCOBOL
/OPTION NOGO RESET
&&IF &&VARBL2 NE ' ' /FILE TYPE=ICCF,UNIT=SYSPCH,NAME=&&VARBL2
/OPTION &&PARAM1 &&PARAM2 &&PARAM3 &&PARAM4 &&PARAM5 &&PARAM6 &&PARAM7
/FILE NAME=IJSYS01,SPACE=40,VOL=0
/FILE NAME=IJSYS02,SPACE=40,VOL=1
/FILE NAME=IJSYS03,SPACE=40,VOL=2
/FILE NAME=IJSYS04,SPACE=40,VOL=3
&&IF &&VARBL3 EQ ' ' &&GOTO +NOCTL               CHECK FOR COMPILER CONTROL
&&TYPE -- ENTER THE '&&VARBL3' CARD IMAGE HERE --
&&IF &&DEVTYP NE '70' &&GOTO +2
&&TYPE .*$$*... CBL
&&READ
&&LABEL NOCTL
&/INCLUDE &&VARBL1
/END
/PEND
/RUN
```

Figure 11-1   A typical ICCF-supplied procedure: the COBOL procedure

Then, the shaded /END command closes the input area, and the shaded /RUN command causes the job that has been built in the input area to be executed.

Figure 11-2 shows the job that was created. As you can see, it contains the job entry statements that the procedure caused to be placed in the input area. Notice that the symbolic variables in the /OPTION and /INCLUDE statements in the procedure were replaced by the parameter values specified on the command line that invoked the procedure (LIST, GETVIS=48K, and TRANLST). You'll see how this works in more detail later in this chapter.

Another point that can confuse you about jobs and procedures is that you can invoke both with the /EXEC command. For example, if you've coded a job stream and stored it in a library member named ICCFJOB, you run the job by entering

```
/LOAD FCOBOL
/OPTION NOGO RESET
/OPTION LIST GETVIS=48K
/FILE NAME=IJSYS01,SPACE=40,VOL=0
/FILE NAME=IJSYS02,SPACE=40,VOL=1
/FILE NAME=IJSYS03,SPACE=40,VOL=2
/FILE NAME=IJSYS04,SPACE=40,VOL=3
/INCLUDE TRANLST
```

Figure 11-2   A job generated by the COBOL procedure

```
/EXEC ICCFJOB
```

Then, the job entry statements in ICCFJOB are transferred to the input area and processed.

To run a procedure, you can enter a similar /EXEC command. For instance, if a procedure is stored in a library member named ICCFPROC, the command

```
/EXEC ICCFPROC CLIST
```

invokes it. Here, the operand CLIST means that the member is not a job stream, but rather a procedure. (CLIST stands for *command list*, another name for a procedure.) The result of this /EXEC command is that this job is placed in the input area and executed:

```
/LOAD DTSPROCS
/INCLUDE ICCFPROC
```

In other words, the procedure processor is executed, and its input is the series of statements contained in the library member ICCFPROC.

This technique for invoking a procedure is new to you. In all the examples you've seen so far in this book, procedures have been invoked simply by entering their names. For example, the command line

```
ICCFPROC
```

is enough to invoke the ICCFPROC procedure. You don't have to key in the full /EXEC statement with the CLIST operand here because of ICCF's *implied execute feature*. When you enter a name that isn't a command (like ICCFPROC), ICCF looks for a library member with the same name. Then, if the member is found and it isn't a macro (that is, if @MACRO isn't its first line), it's considered to be a procedure. As a result, ICCF automatically generates the job I showed you a moment ago to load DTSPROCS and include the statements in the named member in the input area.

Although the implied execute feature is an ICCF default, you can turn the feature off by entering

`/SET IMPEX OFF`

Then, you have to enter the full /EXEC command with the CLIST operand to run a procedure. However, you'll almost never want to do this.

ELEMENTS OF PROCEDURES

If all you want to do is package a series of commands or job entry statements, you're likely to use a macro or an ICCF job. The advantage a procedure offers is that it lets you use a large set of variables and orders to exercise a high degree of control over how the commands and statements in the procedure are handled. If you think of a procedure as a program, variables correspond to data definitions, and procedure processor orders correspond to instructions. In this section, I'll describe both variables in procedures and procedure processor orders. In addition, I'll show you how to use some system commands and job entry statements in procedures.

Variables in procedures

In an application program, you define fields and data structures that contain data elements the program will manipulate. In procedures, data elements are stored in pre-defined variables. As you'll see later, variables can be used to control the execution of a procedure by evaluating and manipulating system data and parameters passed to the procedure. Variables can also be used in system commands and job entry statements in a procedure. When that's the case, DTSPROCS substitutes the actual value for the variable before it passes the command or statement to ICCF to be executed or stored in the input area.

Because variables let you generalize procedures in this way, they're important, particularly for procedures that create ICCF job streams based on user-supplied parameters. You can use three kinds of variables in a procedure: *variable parameters*, *internal variables* (either alphanumeric or numeric), and *special variables*. Figure 11-3 lists the variables in each of these groups.

Variable parameters   If you specify parameters on the command line you use to invoke a procedure (whether it's the /EXEC command with CLIST or just the name of the procedure), they're stored in variable parameter fields. You can use up to 18 variable parameters, and their names are &&PARAM1 through &&PARAM9, followed by &&PARAMA through &&PARAMI. Values are assigned to variable parameters in the sequence they're entered in the command line. In other words, the first parameter is stored in &&PARAM1, the second in &&PARAM2, the tenth in &&PARAMA, and so on. For example, if I

Variable parameters

&&PARAM1	&&PARAMA
&&PARAM2	&&PARAMB
&&PARAM3	&&PARAMC
&&PARAM4	&&PARAMD
&&PARAM5	&&PARAME
&&PARAM6	&&PARAMF
&&PARAM7	&&PARAMG
&&PARAM8	&&PARAMH
&&PARAM9	&&PARAMI

Internal variables

Alphanumeric variables

&&VARBL0	&&VARBLA
&&VARBL1	&&VARBLB
&&VARBL2	&&VARBLC
&&VARBL3	&&VARBLD
&&VARBL4	&&VARBLE
&&VARBL5	&&VARBLF
&&VARBL6	&&VARBLG
&&VARBL7	&&VARBLH
&&VARBL8	&&VARBLI
&&VARBL9	

Numeric variables

&&COUNT0	&&COUNTA
&&COUNT1	&&COUNTB
&&COUNT2	&&COUNTC
&&COUNT3	&&COUNTD
&&COUNT4	&&COUNTE
&&COUNT5	&&COUNTF
&&COUNT6	&&COUNTG
&&COUNT7	&&COUNTH
&&COUNT8	&&COUNTI
&&COUNT9	

Special variables

&&CURDAT	The current date. Six characters, in your system's format.
&&CURTIM	The current time in the format HHMMSS.
&&CURLN	Used for advanced context editor functions from within a procedure. See *VSE/ICCF Terminal User's Guide* for more information.
&&DEVTYP	A two-character code that identifies the kind of terminal device the operator is using.
&&LINENO	The current line being processed in the procedure.
&&PARMCT	The number of parameters the operator specified when the procedure was invoked.
&&RDDATA	The first word of the operator's reply to a &&READ order.
&&RETCOD	The first eight characters (or the first word, if it's less than eight characters) of the ICCF response to the last command processed. See *VSE/ICCF Terminal User's Guide* for details.
&&TERMID	The terminal-id of the user's terminal.
&&USERID	The user-id of the operator who executed the procedure.

Figure 11-3   Variables for procedures

invoke the COBOL procedure with the command line

```
COBOL TRANLST OBJ * LIST GETVIS=48K
```

there are five parameters. Their values are: TRANLST, &&PARAM1;

OBJ, &&PARAM2; *, &&PARAM3; LIST, &&PARAM4; and GETVIS=48K, &&PARAM5. Although ICCF lets you specify 18 variable parameters, it's an unusual procedure that uses more than just a few.

The value of a variable parameter can be no longer than 30 characters. On the command line that invokes the procedure, you separate parameters from one another with delimiter characters, which can be either spaces or commas. If a parameter value contains a delimiter character, you must enclose the entire parameter value between single quotes. And if you want to omit a positional parameter when you invoke a procedure, you can enter an ampersand in the command line in its place.

Parameters from the command line are assembled into a single /PARM control statement that accompanies the /LOAD statement for DTSPROCS. Because all parameter values have to fit on a single /PARM control statement in the DTSPROCS job, the total length of all parameters and the delimiters that separate them cannot be greater than 72 characters.

Internal variables   There are two groups of internal variables you can use in a procedure as a sort of working storage. By coding the appropriate orders, you can move data to these variables and test their contents. The first group can be used to store alphanumeric data. This group contains 19 variables with the names &&VARBL0 through &&VARBL9 and &&VARBLA through &&VARBLI. The second group can be used only to store numeric data. There are also 19 variables in this group, and their names are &&COUNT0 through &&COUNT9 and &&COUNTA through &&COUNTI.

Special variables   There are 10 other variables, called special variables, that you can use in a procedure. The bottom section of figure 11-3 lists them. I think the most useful are &&CURDAT, &&CURTIM, &&PARMCT, &&RETCOD, &&TERMID, and &&USERID. The other four (&&CURLN, &&DEVTYP, &&LINENO, and &&RDDATA) are for specialized functions.

Concatenating variables   If you have an application in which you want to combine data from two or more variables into a single value, you can concatenate variables. All you do is code the names of the variables you want to concatenate with no intervening spaces. For example, if the value of &&PARAM3 is LOGF and my user-id is STEV, the command

```
/LIST &&USERID&&PARAM3
```

would be converted into

```
/LIST STEVLOGF
```

by the procedure processor program. You'll see other examples of concatenated variables later in this chapter.

Procedure processor orders

Now, I want to describe procedure processor orders, which are presented in figure 11-4. As you can see in the figure, I've grouped them by function. First, I'll introduce the orders you use to control how a procedure executes. Second, I'll show you the orders that let you manipulate variables. Third, I'll present the two orders that let a procedure display messages for the user and accept input from him. And fourth, I'll present the remaining orders that don't fit into the other four groups. This section just introduces the functions of the orders; you'll see the details of how they work together in the sample procedures in the next section.

How to control the execution of a procedure: the &&IF, &&GOTO, and &&LABEL procedure processor orders   You use the &&IF, &&GOTO, and &&LABEL orders together to control the execution of a procedure based on conditions you specify. Almost always, those conditions are related to the values of variable parameters supplied by the user. The &&IF order lets you compare a variable (any of those listed in figure 11-3) with another variable or a literal value and, based on the result of the comparison, perform some action. Usually, that action is performed by another order or by a system command.

Often, the action is a branch to another part of the procedure. To branch within a procedure, you use the &&GOTO order. When you code it, you can specify a number of lines to skip, either forward or backward, or the name of a line to which you want to branch. Before you use a name in a &&GOTO order, you must be sure that the name is defined with a &&LABEL order. You use the &&LABEL order to name a point in a procedure. The value you code on the &&LABEL order must begin with a letter and must be no more than eight characters long.

How to manipulate variables in a procedure: the &&SET and &&SHIFT procedure processor orders   The only variables that the user can supply to a procedure are the variable parameters: &&PARAM1 through &&PARAMI. To use the alphanumeric variables (&&VARBL0 through &&VARBLI) and the numeric variables (&&COUNT0 through &&COUNTI), you have to assign values to them with the &&SET order.

To assign a value to one of the alphanumeric variables (&&VARBLn), you specify its name and follow it either with a literal character string or with the name of another variable. Keep in mind, though, that the alphanumeric variables are eight characters long. As a result, if you try to store the contents of one of the variable parameters (&&PARAMn) in an alphanumeric variable and the parameter is longer

Orders to control the execution of a procedure

```
&&IF      variable operator comparison-value then-clause
```

$$\&\&GOTO \quad \left[\left\{\begin{matrix}+\\-\end{matrix}\right\}\right] \left\{\begin{matrix}label\\nn\end{matrix}\right\}$$

```
&&LABEL label
```

Explanation

variable	Any of the variables in figure 11-3.
operator	EQ, NE, LT, GT, LE, GE, or equivalent symbols.
comparison-value	A variable or a literal value.
then-clause	A procedure processor order, a command, or a line of data.
label	Name applied to a procedure line with a &&LABEL order. If a label specified in a &&GOTO order precedes the &GOTO order, then you must code a minus sign before the value.
nn	The number of lines to be skipped forward ($+$) or backward ($-$).

Orders to manipulate variables in a procedure

$$\&\&SET \quad \left\{\begin{matrix} \&\&VARBLn \left\{\begin{matrix}variable\\literal\end{matrix}\right\} \\ \&\&COUNT \left\{\begin{matrix}variable\\ [*] \left[\left\{\begin{matrix}+\\-\end{matrix}\right\}\right] nn\end{matrix}\right\} \end{matrix}\right\}$$

```
&&SHIFT p
```

Explanation

variable	Any of the variables in figure 11-3.
literal	An alphanumeric literal value.
*	Specifies that the current value of the &&COUNTn variable is to be incremented up ($+$) or down ($-$) by the specified amount nn.
nn	Specifies the value to which the &&COUNTn variable is to be set or by which it is to be incremented.
p	The number of the parameter (from 1 to 9) where the shift is to begin. The default is 1.

Figure 11-4   Procedure processor orders (part 1 of 3)

Orders to communicate with the user

```
&&TYPE  text

&&READ  [ {&&VARBLn} ]
        [ {&&COUNTn} ]
        [ {&&PARAMS} ]
```

Explanation

text	The line to be displayed.
&&PARAMS	Specifies that the &&READ order should replace the values of the variable parameters with new values entered by the operator.

Other orders

```
&&EXIT
&&MAXLOOP nn
*         data
&&NOP     data
&&PUNCH   data
&&OPTIONS abcdefg
```

Explanation

nn
The number of &&GOTO orders that may be processed before the procedure is terminated.

data
A text string that serves as a comment (* order), that is not to be subject to procedure processor manipulation (&&NOP order), or that is to be stored in the punch area (&&PUNCH order).

abcdefg
Seven option switch settings; for each position, you may specify 1 or zero. The default for all settings is off (zero), except under ICCF 2.1. With it, the fifth setting (MULTEX) is on by default. The recommended settings for most procedures is 0010001. The effects of the options are:

a   1 (on):   Store output from system commands like /LIST and /DISPLAY in the punch area.

      0 (off):   Do not store output from system commands like /LIST and /DISPLAY in the punch area.

b   Meaningful only if option "a" is on.

      1 (on):   Display output from system commands like /LIST and /DISPLAY as well as store it in the punch area.

      0 (off):   Do not display output from system commands like /LIST and /DISPLAY if the output is stored in the punch area.

c   1 (on):   Do not display normal command output (like messages).

      0 (off):   Display normal command output (like messages).

Figure 11-4   Procedure processor orders (part 2 of 3)

d   1 (on):   Do not remove trailing spaces from variables.
     0 (off):   Remove trailing spaces from variables.

e   The MULTEX option.
     1 (on):   Allow multiple executions to be in effect at the same time from one procedure.
     0 (off):   Do not allow multiple executions to be in effect at the same time from one procedure. If the MULTEX option is off, a /RUN or /EXEC command in a procedure forces the end of the procedure.

f   1 (on):   Maintain control settings (like for tabs) made by the procedure only as long as the procedure is running.
     0 (off):   Maintain control settings (like for tabs) made by the procedure after the procedure ends.

g   1 (on):   Do not force a display of the print area before each /RUN or /EXEC command.
     0 (off):   Force a display of the print area before each /RUN or /EXEC command.

Figure 11-4   Procedure processor orders (part 3 of 3)

than eight bytes, only the first eight bytes will be stored; the remainder of the value is lost.

To assign a value to one of the numeric variables (&&COUNTn), you specify its name and follow it either with a numeric literal or with the name of another variable. If you specify a numeric literal, you can precede it with a minus sign to cause the value of the variable to be set to a negative number. Or, you can cause the current value of the numeric variable to be increased or decreased by specifying an asterisk and then either a plus or minus sign before the numeric literal.

The &&SHIFT order lets you shift variable parameters one position to the left. If you use this order without an operand, it causes the value of &&PARAM1 to be lost and the values of all the other parameters to be shifted to the left; what was &&PARAM2 is then &&PARAM1, what was &&PARAM3 is then &&PARAM2, and so on. Or, you can specify the number of the parameter (from 1 to 9) at which you want the shift to begin. When you do this, parameters before the number you name are unaffected. The ICCF-supplied procedures use the &&SHIFT order extensively; however, I don't find it particularly useful for procedures I write.

How to communicate with the user: the &&TYPE and &&READ procedure processor orders   The &&TYPE and &&READ orders let you write "interactive" procedures. &&TYPE simply writes a line on the screen, and &&READ lets the user key in a new set of parameters that replace those supplied when the procedure was invoked. Later in this chapter, you'll see a sample procedure that uses both of these orders to carry on a "conversation" with the terminal user.

Other procedure orders: *, &&MAXLOOP, &&OPTIONS, &&EXIT, &&NOP, and &&PUNCH   The six remaining orders are either easy to understand or not particularly useful. The * order lets you include comments in your procedures. If you look back to figure 11-1, you'll see that the first four lines in the ICCF-supplied COBOL procedure are comments.

The &&MAXLOOP order lets you control how much processing your procedure can do. Each time a &&GOTO order is processed, an internal counter associated with &&MAXLOOP is increased by one. If that count exceeds 150, your procedure is terminated. If you're developing a complicated procedure that will exceed that default limit, you can specify a higher limit (up to 4096) with the &&MAXLOOP order.

The &&OPTIONS order lets you provide execution instructions to DTSPROCS. On it, you supply values—either 1 or 0—to turn seven options on or off. Figure 11-4 indicates the functions of each option setting. You'll see the &&OPTIONS order in the examples later in this chapter.

The last three orders (&&EXIT, &&NOP, and &&PUNCH) are ones that I suspect you'll never need to use in routine procedures. &&EXIT forces an immediate end to your procedure; it's more useful for error handling than for typical processing. &&NOP causes the procedure processor operations that would be performed on the data in its line to be suppressed. And &&PUNCH causes the contents of the line to be stored in your punch area.

System commands and job entry statements in procedures

In addition to variables and orders, procedures can contain system commands and job entry statements. In this section, I want to point out some considerations you need to keep in mind about commands and job entry statements as you develop procedures.

System commands in procedures   When the procedure processor encounters a system command in its input, it passes it along to ICCF for immediate handling. As a result, even though DTSPROCS executes in the background, some foreground processing functions can be invoked when a procedure is executed. However, because a procedure is written to be executed as a unit, it's not likely that you'll want display output from intermediate system commands to be displayed as the commands execute. For example, in the COBOL procedure you've already seen, a /LIST command is used for the library member you name as the source program. The purpose of that command isn't to display the contents of the file, but rather to let the procedure check to see if the member exists. (I'll explain how that works in the next section when I present sample procedures.)

The most common use for procedures is to build interactive partition jobs based on variable parameters supplied by the operator. In fact, it's so common that all of the sample procedures you'll see in this chapter do that. You know, however, that for a job to be executed, it has to be stored in the input area. And to create a job in the input area, you have to use basic system commands.

If you read the section in chapter 5 about converting library members stored in compressed format to display format, you should remember that doing so involves working in system input mode to transfer the data they contain into the input area. When you build a job stream in the input area from a procedure you use the same technique. To open the input area to build the job stream, your procedure should contain the /INPUT command:

```
/INPUT
```

Then, any lines in the procedure that aren't procedure processor orders and that aren't system commands are transferred into the input area. In this way, your procedures can construct jobs dynamically.

After a procedure has finished building a job stream, it should issue an /END command so no more data is stored in the input area. Then, a /RUN command should follow to cause the newly built job to be executed. You'll see how this works later.

Job entry statements in procedures There's only one consideration you need to keep in mind when you code job entry statements in a procedure that will be used to build a job based on parameter values you supply. Normally, ICCF processes /LOAD and /INCLUDE statements as they're encountered in the job stream. That means that if they're in the DTSPROCS input in their normal form, they're not stored in the input area, but processed immediately as job entry statements. To avoid this problem, you need to code an ampersand before /LOAD and /INCLUDE statements. And, if your input job stream includes an end-of-data statement (/*), you should code an ampersand in front of it too. When DTSPROCS encounters a line in its input data that begins with an ampersand, it removes the ampersand, shifts the remaining characters one character to the left, and treats the result as data. You'll see examples of these *ampersand-coded statements* in the procedures that follow.

SAMPLE PROCEDURES This section presents three procedures that illustrate how to combine variables, procedure processor orders, commands, and job entry statements. First, I'll present a simple procedure that builds a job to run the VSAM multi-function utility program IDCAMS to list the catalog information for a specified entry in a user catalog. Second, I'll show you an enhancement of the LISTCAT procedure that prompts the user for parameters and that lets the user specify up to 9 items whose catalog entries are to be listed. And third, I'll describe in detail the ICCF-supplied COBOL procedure, which you saw in figure 11-1.

```
===)
<<..+....1....+....2....+....3....+....4....+....5....+.. MEM=LC      >>..+..FS
**** TOP OF FILE *****                                              /***/
&&OPTIONS 0010001                                                   *====*
/INP NOPROMPT                                                       *====*
&/LOAD IDCAMS                                                       *====*
&/OPTION GETVIS=AUTO                                                *====*
 LISTCAT CATALOG (&&PARAM1) -                                       *====*
         ENTRIES (&&PARAM2) -                                       *====*
         &&PARAM3                                                   *====*
/END                                                               *====*
/PEND                                                              *====*
/RUN                                                               *====*
**** END OF FILE *****                                             *****


 IᴬA                                                       □-□04
```

Figure 11-5   A simple LISTCAT procedure (version 1)

Sample procedure 1

Figure 11-5 presents a simple procedure to invoke the IDCAMS program to list the catalog information for a single entry. To run this procedure, which is stored in a library member named LC, you'd enter a command line in this format:

```
LC catalog-name entry-name detail-level
```

For example, the command line

```
LC MMA.USER.CATALOG BUYER.INPUT ALLOCATION
```

causes the procedure to build an interactive partition job that will run IDCAMS and produce a catalog listing showing allocation information for the data set BUYER.INPUT owned by MMA.USER.CATALOG.

The first line in the procedure,

```
&&OPTION 0010001
```

specifies options for the procedure processor program. You can look back to figure 11-4 to see what options you can control with this order. Here, the 1's in positions 3 and 7 in the option setting string specify that display output should be suppressed by the procedure processor. You'll normally want to code an &&OPTION order like this.

Remember, the purpose of this procedure is to build an interactive partition job in the input area. As a result, the next statement is an /INPUT command (abbreviated /INP); it causes the data lines that follow to be stored in the input area. The NOPROMPT operand means ICCF will not prompt you for the lines that will be stored in the input area. This is the way you'll usually code the /INPUT command in a procedure that will build a job stream.

The five lines that follow the /INPUT command are data that will be stored in the input area to create the job. However, they'll be stored only after they've been evaluated by the procedure processor. In this case, each of the five lines will be modified in some way by DTSPROCS. The first two lines are job entry statements. To insure that they will not be interpreted immediately as job entry statements, but rather be read by DTSPROCS as data, I coded them with an ampersand in column 1. When DTSPROCS processes these ampersand-coded statements, it will remove the leading ampersands and shift the rest of the data in the lines one position to the left. As a result, proper job entry statements will be stored in the input area.

The next three lines are IDCAMS control statements. Because these lines don't begin with a slash, I didn't have to precede them with ampersands. However, they too are modified by DTSPROCS before they're stored in the input area. DTSPROCS substitutes the parameters entered by the user for the variable parameter names &&PARAM1, &&PARAM2, and &&PARAM3 in these lines.

So if the operator invokes the procedure with the command line

```
LC MMA.USER.CATALOG BUYER.INPUT ALLOCATION
```

the job

```
/LOAD IDCAMS
/OPTION GETVIS=AUTO
 LISTCAT CATALOG (MMA.USER.CATALOG) -
         ENTRIES (BUYER.INPUT) -
         ALLOCATION
```

is stored in the input area.

To end a procedure that builds and executes an interactive partition job, you code the last three lines in the procedure in figure 11-5:

```
/END
/PEND
/RUN
```

The /END command closes the input area. Then, the /PEND statement terminates the procedure processor program, but leaves the contents of the input area intact. Finally, the /RUN command executes the job in the input area. (If you don't end a procedure with /PEND, any data you've built in the input area may be lost unless your procedure has explicitly saved it in a library member with a /SAVE or /REPLACE command.)

You need to terminate the procedure processor before you invoke the job you've built because if you don't, you may use two interactive partitions instead of one: one for DTSPROCS, the other for the program invoked by your newly built job. In some unusual procedures, you might want to use two interactive partitions. For example, if you want to initiate a job but continue to process procedure statements as well, you'll need to use two interactive partitions. That's possible as long as the *multiple execution (MULTEX) option* is on. The fifth setting on the string you code on the &&OPTIONS procedure processor order lets you control the MULTEX option. If the option is on (in other words, if you specify 1 or, for ICCF 2.1, let the default value stay in effect), multiple executions are possible. On the other hand, when the option is off (that is, if you code 0), any /RUN or /EXEC command in the procedure is assumed to mark the end of the procedure.

Before I go on to show you an enhancement of this procedure, I want to point out a possible problem with it. VSAM names can be up to 44 characters long, but the maximum length for a single parameter in a procedure is 30 characters. As a result, the procedure in figure 11-5 won't let you specify names longer than 30 characters. However, you can use concatenated variables to get around this problem.

For example, figure 11-6 presents a second version of the simple LISTCAT job that can let you work around the parameter length restriction. First, I assumed when I wrote this procedure that all user catalog names end with the characters

```
.USER.CATALOG
```

As a result, I coded the procedure so the operator only has to key in the first part of the catalog name and can omit .USER.CATALOG. In the first line of the LISTCAT control statement in the figure, I specified the concatenated variable like this:

```
LISTCAT CATALOG (&&PARAM1.USER.CATALOG) -
```

Then, if the user invokes the procedure and specifies MMA as the first parameter, DTSPROCS adds this line to the input area:

```
LISTCAT CATALOG (MMA.USER.CATALOG) -
```

To let the user key in an entry name longer than 30 characters, I set up the procedure so that value will be the concatenation of two parameters:

```
ENTRIES (&&PARAM2&&PARAM3) -
```

Now, the user can key in two parameters instead of one for the entry name. The problem this introduces is that the two parts have to be separated by a delimiter (usually, a space). Alternatively, if the name is shorter than 30 bytes, the user can key in an ampersand to indicate that the second of the two parameters required to build the name is omitted.

```
===>
<<...+....1....+....2....+....3....+....4....+....5....+.. MEM=LC1    >>...+..FS
***** TOP OF FILE *****                                                  /***/
&&OPTIONS 0010001                                                        *===*
/INP NOPROMPT                                                            *===*
&/LOAD IDCAMS                                                            *===*
&/OPTION GETVIS=AUTO                                                     *===*
 LISTCAT CATALOG (&&PARAM1.USER.CATALOG) -                              *===*
         ENTRIES (&&PARAM2&&PARAM3) -                                    *===*
         &&PARAM4                                                        *===*
/END                                                                     *===*
/PEND                                                                    *===*
/RUN                                                                     *===*
***** END OF FILE *****                                                  *****



IA                                        □□04
```

Figure 11-6   A simple LISTCAT procedure (version 2)

So, assuming the procedure in figure 11-6 is stored in a library member named LC1, you could invoke it with a command line like

LC1 MMA BUYER. INPUT ALLOCATION

where a space separates the two parts of the VSAM entry name or

LC1 MMA BUYER.INPUT & ALLOCATION

where the ampersand indicates that the third parameter is omitted altogether. In either case, the job stream that's built is the same as the one I described for the procedure in figure 11-5:

```
/LOAD IDCAMS
/OPTION GETVIS=AUTO
 LISTCAT CATALOG (MMA.USER.CATALOG) -
         ENTRIES (BUYER.INPUT) -
         ALLOCATION
```

If you were writing a procedure like this for your shop, you'd almost certainly use condition checking to determine how many parameters were entered and then format the control statements for IDCAMS appropriately. The operator shouldn't have to worry about accounting for missing positional parameters. You'll see how you can write procedures that do this when I describe the ICCF-supplied COBOL procedure later in this section.

Sample procedure 2

Before I present the COBOL procedure, I want to present an enhancement of the simple LISTCAT procedures. Figure 11-7, like figures 11-5 and 11-6, is a procedure that builds an IDCAMS LISTCAT job that will be executed in an interactive partition. However, it uses &&TYPE procedure processor orders to prompt the operator for parameters and &&READ orders to accept them. Here, the user can specify up to nine entries for which he wants LISTCAT output; in contrast, the procedures in figures 11-5 and 11-6 let the user specify only one entry. In addition, the enhanced procedure uses condition checking to provide acceptable defaults for all parameters.

If you compare the procedure in figure 11-7 with those in figures 11-5 and 11-6, you'll see that their first four lines and their last three lines are the same. The differences are in how the IDCAMS control statement lines are generated. In the simpler procedures, the control statement lines are built directly from the parameters the user entered on the command line that invoked the procedure. In the enhanced version in figure 11-7, the operator is prompted three times for different parameter values. And each time, the procedure can generate a control statement line using either the value(s) the operator enters or a default that's determined by the procedure. To help you understand how this procedure works, I want to show you how it executes and describe what's happening at each step.

This procedure is stored in a library member named LCINT. To invoke it, I keyed in the command line in part 1 of figure 11-8. As you can see, for this procedure, I didn't supply any parameters on the command line. When I pressed the enter key, ICCF displayed the standard message in part 2.

As a result of the first four lines in the procedure, DTSPROCS opened the input area and stored these two lines in it:

```
/LOAD IDCAMS
/OPTION GETVIS=AUTO
```

So far, this is just like what the procedures in figures 11-5 and 11-6 do.

Next, however, DTSPROCS encountered the first group of &&TYPE orders and caused the lines in part 3 of the figure to be displayed. Because the order that immediately follows the first group of &&TYPE orders is

```
&&READ &&PARAMS
```

DTSPROCS caused my terminal to enter conversational read mode (RD) and wait for my response. Because I specified &&PARAMS on the order, the data I entered here is stored in the variable parameters;

```
&&OPTIONS 0010001
/INP NOPROMPT
&/LOAD IDCAMS
&/OPTION GETVIS=AUTO
&&TYPE --------------------------------------------------------------------
&&TYPE
&&TYPE ENTER THE NAME OF THE CATALOG WHOSE CONTENTS YOU WANT TO LIST.
&&TYPE
&&TYPE THE CURRENT JOB CATALOG IS THE DEFAULT.
&&TYPE
&&TYPE --------------------------------------------------------------------
&&READ &&PARAMS
 LISTCAT -
&&IF &&PARAM1 EQ ' ' &&GOTO LABEL1
      CATALOG(&&PARAM1) -
&&LABEL LABEL1
&&TYPE --------------------------------------------------------------------
&&TYPE
&&TYPE ENTER THE NAMES OF THE CATALOG ENTRIES YOU WANT TO LIST.
&&TYPE
&&TYPE ALL ENTRIES IS THE DEFAULT.  YOU MAY ENTER NO MORE THAN 9 NAMES.
&&TYPE
&&TYPE --------------------------------------------------------------------
&&READ &&PARAMS
&&IF &&PARAM1 EQ ' ' &&GOTO LABEL2
      ENTRIES(&&PARAM1 -
              &&PARAM2 -
              &&PARAM3 -
              &&PARAM4 -
              &&PARAM5 -
              &&PARAM6 -
              &&PARAM7 -
              &&PARAM8 -
              &&PARAM9 ) -
&&LABEL LABEL2
&&TYPE --------------------------------------------------------------------
&&TYPE
&&TYPE ENTER THE LEVEL OF INFORMATION YOU WANT:
&&TYPE      NAME
&&TYPE      VOL        (VOLUME)
&&TYPE      ALLOC      (ALLOCATION)
&&TYPE      ALL
&&TYPE
&&TYPE ALLOCATION IS THE DEFAULT.
&&TYPE
&&TYPE --------------------------------------------------------------------
&&READ &&PARAMS
&&IF &&PARAM1 EQ ' ' &&GOTO LABEL3
        &&PARAM1
&&GOTO LABEL4
&&LABEL LABEL3
        ALLOCATION
&&LABEL LABEL4
/END
/PEND
/RUN
```

Figure 11-7   An interactive LISTCAT procedure

previous data in the variable parameters was replaced. You can also use the &&READ order to accept values from the operator for any one alphanumeric variable (if you specify &&VARBLn), for any one numeric variable (if you specify &&COUNTn), or for a line of data to be stored in the input area.

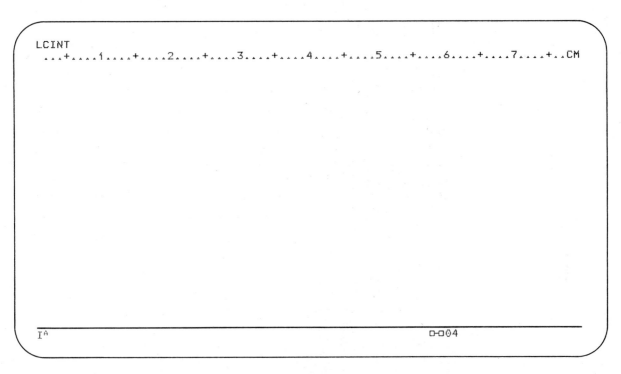

Figure 11-8   Using the interactive LISTCAT procedure (part 1 of 6)

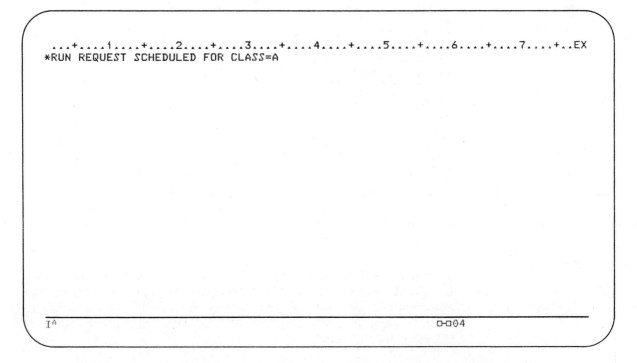

Figure 11-8   Using the interactive LISTCAT procedure (part 2 of 6)

```
MMA.USER.CATALOG
 ...+....1....+....2....+....3....+....4....+....5....+....6....+....7....+..RD
* * * * * START OF PROCEDURE (CLIST) * * * * *
-----------------------------------------------------------------------

ENTER THE NAME OF THE CATALOG WHOSE CONTENTS YOU WANT TO LIST.

THE CURRENT JOB CATALOG IS THE DEFAULT.

-----------------------------------------------------------------------
*ENTER DATA?




I^                                              □-□④4
```

Figure 11-8   Using the interactive LISTCAT procedure (part 3 of 6)

```
BUYER.INPUT INVDB
 ...+....1....+....2....+....3....+....4....+....5....+....6....+....7....+..RD
-----------------------------------------------------------------------

ENTER THE NAMES OF THE CATALOG ENTRIES YOU WANT TO LIST.

ALL ENTRIES IS THE DEFAULT.  YOU MAY ENTER NO MORE THAN 9 NAMES.

-----------------------------------------------------------------------
*ENTER DATA?






I^                                              □-□④4
```

Figure 11-8   Using the interactive LISTCAT procedure (part 4 of 6)

```
NAME
...+....1....+....2....+....3....+....4....+....5....+....6....+....7....+..RD
_____


ENTER THE LEVEL OF INFORMATION YOU WANT:
     NAME
     VOL        (VOLUME)
     ALLOC      (ALLOCATION)
     ALL

ALLOCATION IS THE DEFAULT.

_____

*ENTER DATA?
```

```
Iᴬ                                                  □-□④
```

Figure 11-8   Using the interactive LISTCAT procedure (part 5 of 6)

```
...+....1....+....2....+....3....+....4....+....5....+....6....+....7....+..SP
K867I  GETVIS SET TO  738K
IDCAMS  SYSTEM SERVICES                                    TIME: 14:38:28
        05/20/86      PAGE    1

 LISTCAT -
      CATALOG(MMA.USER.CATALOG) -
      ENTRIES(BUYER.INPUT -
             INVDB -
             -
             -
             -
             -
             -
             ) -
         NAME
IDCAMS  SYSTEM SERVICES                                    TIME: 14:38:28
        05/20/86      PAGE    2
                        LISTING FROM CATALOG -- MMA.USER.CATALOG
CLUSTER ------- BUYER.INPUT
```

```
Iᴬ                                                  □-□④
```

Figure 11-8   Using the interactive LISTCAT procedure (part 6 of 6)

As you can see in the top of the figure, I keyed in the name of a user catalog. When I pressed the enter key, the value MMA.USER.CATALOG was stored in &&PARAM1. Then, the procedure processor stored the line

```
LISTCAT -
```

in the input area.

The next three lines in the procedure are used to supply the proper specification for the catalog to be accessed by the IDCAMS job. If the user did not enter a parameter value, the order

```
&&IF &&PARAM1 EQ ' ' &&GOTO LABEL1
```

causes control to be passed to the line identified with the name LABEL1; it's just two lines down from the &&IF order. If that's the case, no CATALOG specification is included in the IDCAMS job being built in the input area. As a result, the current job catalog will be used as a default by the job.

On the other hand, if the user did specify a value in response to the first &&READ order, the condition in the &&IF order does not test true, and the branch is not performed. Then, the next statement in the procedure is processed by DTSPROCS. Because I entered a parameter value in this example, DTSPROCS caused the line

```
CATALOG (MMA.USER.CATALOG) -
```

to be added to the input area. Notice that the value I supplied in response to the &&READ order was substituted for &&PARAM1 in this line.

Regardless of whether the user keys in a catalog name or not, the next lines processed are the second group of &&TYPE orders and the second &&READ order. Again, in part 4 of figure 11-8, my terminal was in conversational read mode waiting for me to supply parameters. In this case, I was prompted not for a single value, but for up to nine values. In response, I keyed in two data set names (BUYER.INPUT and INVDB). When I pressed the enter key, the value BUYER.INPUT replaced MMA.USER.CATALOG as the value of &&PARAM1, and INVDB became the value of &&PARAM2.

The procedure uses the same technique it did for the catalog to determine whether it should add lines to the input area for the ENTRIES parameter of the LISTCAT control statement. If the user doesn't enter any parameters, an &&IF order causes a branch around the control statement lines. In that case, no ENTRIES specifications are included in the job. As a result, all entries in the catalog will be listed by default. Otherwise, nine lines, each specifying a different variable parameter, are added to the input area. Because I specified only two values, these are the lines that were added to my input area:

```
ENTRIES (BUYER.INPUT -
        INVDB -
        -
        -
        -
        -
        -
        ) -
```

Here, there are seven continuation lines that contain no data; that's not a problem for IDCAMS.

Next, the third and last &&TYPE/&&READ order group is processed to prompt the operator for the level of detail the LISTCAT output should provide. In part 5 of figure 11-8, you can see the display these commands produced and my reply.

The checking the procedure does after these orders is similar to that for the first two operator interactions, only here, if the operator didn't enter any parameters in response to the &&READ order, the procedure adds a line to the input area with a default value (ALLOCATION). In the first two interactions, the procedure simply branched around one or several lines and didn't add anything to the input area if the user didn't enter parameters. Therefore, the procedure used the IDCAMS defaults for CATALOG and ENTRIES. In this case, however, I didn't want to use the IDCAMS default (NAME), so I specified my own default for the procedure (ALLOCATION). For this particular execution of the procedure, I *did* want to use NAME instead of ALLOCATION, so I entered NAME as the parameter. As a result, the line

```
NAME
```

was added to the input area.

When I pressed the enter key for the screen in part 5, the procedure closed the input area with an /END command, terminated DTSPROCS with a /PEND control statement, and caused the newly built job to be executed with a /RUN command. After a moment, the first screen of spooled output was displayed, as you can see in part 6 of the figure. Here, the LISTCAT output shows all the control statement lines the procedure generated. If I pressed the enter key from this screen, the actual catalog data I wanted to see would be displayed.

You might wonder in this example why I coded the procedure so it adds lines to the input area after each screen interaction. The obvious—but wrong—alternative is to store the parameters the operator entered in response to each &&READ order in internal alphanumeric variables; you can use the &&SET order to do that. The reason that wouldn't work here is that &&SET moves only the first eight characters of a variable parameter value to an alphanumeric variable. So if my procedure had included an order like

```
&&SET &&VARBL1 &&PARAM1
```

when &&PARAM1 contained the value MMA.USER.CATALOG, only the characters MMA.USER would have been stored in &&VARBL1. And clearly, that's not acceptable for data like VSAM entry names, which are usually longer than eight characters. However, other data elements, like ICCF library member names, lend themselves well to this kind of treatment, as you'll see in the ICCF-supplied COBOL procedure.

Sample procedure 3

The last procedure I want to describe is the ICCF-supplied COBOL procedure. It's a little harder to understand than the LISTCAT procedures you've seen so far because it uses some obscure procedure processing features to perform some obscure ICCF operations. However, you have enough background now to understand it. And it might give you some ideas for approaches that will be useful in procedures you develop.

Figure 11-9 presents the COBOL procedure, which you've already seen in figure 11-1. In figure 11-9, I've added some spacing to the lines in the procedure so it's easier to study. The first four lines are comment procedure processor orders (★ in column 1). They identify the procedure and present the format of the command line that's used to invoke it. The first parameter (NNNN) is the name of the library member that contains the source code for the compilation; it's required. The other parameters are optional.

The next two lines are straightforward. The &&OPTIONS order suppresses print output, and the &&SET order stores the contents of the first parameter in &&VARBL1. There's no need to worry about losing data due to truncation here because the first parameter, the name of an ICCF library member, can be no longer than eight characters.

The next group of lines contains the orders and commands necessary to prepare the area the COBOL compiler will use to store its output object module. When the procedure is invoked, the user can specify whether the object module should be stored in the punch area or a library member. If the command line does not include the OBJ keyword or specifies

```
OBJ *
```

the punch area is used. Otherwise, the command line must include

```
OBJ member-name
```

to identify the ICCF library member that will receive the object module.

The first line in this group causes the entire set of parameters to be shifted one position to the left. As a result of this order, the value of &&PARAM2 becomes &&PARAM1, &&PARAM3 becomes &&PARAM2, and so on; the value of the original &&PARAM1 is lost. Remember, though, that before the &&SHIFT order was processed, the value of &&PARAM1, the name of the member that contains the source code for the compilation, was saved in &&VARBL1.

```
*  -  -  -  -  -  -  -  -  -  -  -  -  -  -  -  -  -  -  -  -  -  -  -  -  -
*        PROCEDURE TO COMPILE A COBOL PROGRAM
*  COBOL NNNN (OBJ MMMM/*) (CBL) (OPTIONS)
*  -  -  -  -  -  -  -  -  -  -  -  -  -  -  -  -  -  -  -  -  -  -  -  -  -




&&OPTIONS 0010001
&&SET &&VARBL1 &&PARAM1                          SAVE NAME OF SOURCE




&&SHIFT 1                                        SHIFT OUT NAME OF PROGRAM
&&IF &&PARAM1 NE OBJ &&GOTO NOOBJ                SKIP TO TEST COMPILER CTL
&&SET &&VARBL2 &&PARAM2                          SAVE NAME OF OBJ MEMBR
&&IF &&VARBL2 EQ '*' &&SET &&VARBL2 ' '          * REQUIRES NO FILE STMT
&&IF &&VARBL2 EQ ' ' &&GOTO +INLIB               SKIP TEST FOR MEM IN LIB
/LIST 1 1 &&VARBL2
&&IF &&RETCOD  EQ *READY &&GOTO INLIB            SKIP IF IN LIB ALREADY
/INP NOPROMPT
DUMMY CARD TO CREATE MEMBER                       AND SAVE IN LIB
/SAVE &&VARBL2
&&LABEL INLIB
&&SHIFT 1                                        SHIFT OUT OBJ
&&SHIFT 1                                        SHIFT OUT NAME
&&LABEL NOOBJ




&&IF &&PARAM1 NE CBL &&GOTO +3                   GO BUILD JOB STREAM
&&SET &&VARBL3 'CBL'                             SET CONTROL CARD DESIRED
&&SHIFT 1                                        SHIFT OUT CBL




/INP NOPROMPT
&/LOAD FCOBOL
/OPTION NOGO RESET
&&IF &&VARBL2 NE ' ' /FILE TYPE=ICCF,UNIT=SYSPCH,NAME=&&VARBL2
/OPTION &&PARAM1 &&PARAM2 &&PARAM3 &&PARAM4 &&PARAM5 &&PARAM6 &&PARAM7
/FILE NAME=IJSYS01,SPACE=40,VOL=0
/FILE NAME=IJSYS02,SPACE=40,VOL=1
/FILE NAME=IJSYS03,SPACE=40,VOL=2
/FILE NAME=IJSYS04,SPACE=40,VOL=3
```

Figure 11-9   The COBOL procedure (part 1 of 2)

Next, an &&IF order evaluates the new &&PARAM1 (which was
&&PARAM2 on the command line) to see if it contains the keyword
OBJ. If it doesn't, a branch to the line identified with the name NOOBJ
is performed; it's the last line in this group. On the other hand, if the
user *did* specify the OBJ keyword, the next lines are processed. They
cause the new &&PARAM2 (which was &&PARAM3 on the command
line) to be stored in &&VARBL2. Its value is either * or a member
name. If &&VARBL2's value is *, it's reset to space, and a branch is

```
&&IF &&VARBL3 EQ ' ' &&GOTO +NOCTL          CHECK FOR COMPILER CONTROL
&&TYPE -- ENTER THE '&&VARBL3' CARD IMAGE HERE --
&&IF &&DEVTYP NE '70' &&GOTO +2
&&TYPE .*$$*... CBL
&&READ
&&LABEL NOCTL



&/INCLUDE &&VARBL1
/END
/PEND
/RUN
```

Figure 11-9   The COBOL procedure (part 2 of 2)

performed to move down to the line identified with the name INLIB. I'll describe what happens there in a moment.

On the other hand, if the operator did specify member-name as the destination for the object module, the procedure checks to see if that member exists. It does that with the command

/LIST 1 1 &&VARBL2

which causes the first line of the named member to be displayed. The purpose here isn't to display the line for the user (which doesn't happen anyway because display output was suppressed by the &&OPTIONS order), but rather to be able to evaluate the system message generated as a result of the command. If the member exists, the command is processed successfully, and the message generated (which is stored in the internal variable &&RETCOD) is

*READY

The &&IF order that immediately follows the /LIST command evaluates &&RETCOD, and if it determines the command was successfully executed, it too causes a branch to the line with the name INLIB.

However, if the member does not exist (in other words, if the system message generated as a result of the /LIST command is something other than *READY), the member must be created. To do that, the procedure opens the input area with an /INPUT command, stores a single line in it (DUMMY CARD TO CREATE MEMBER), then saves the contents of the input area in a new member with the appropriate name with the command

/SAVE &&VARBL2

Now, the procedure has worked through to the line with the label INLIB. Recall that it may also have branched here if the user specified OBJ ＊ or named a library member for the object member that already existed. Now, the two parameters that specify the destination for the object module (the keyword OBJ and the parameter that follow it) are also shifted; the two &&SHIFT orders accomplish that. At this point, only the CBL keyword and/or any options the user entered on the command line remain as parameters.

The first line in the next group is an &&IF order that evaluates the current &&PARAM1 to see if its value is CBL. If it is, CBL is stored in &&VARBL3 and the remaining parameters are again shifted one position to the left. After the shift, remaining parameters can be nothing other than option values entered by the operator on the command line. If the value in &&PARAM1 isn't CBL, the order

```
&&GOTO + 3
```

causes the next two lines in the procedure to be skipped.

In the next group of procedure lines in figure 11-9, the interactive partition job is finally built. An /INPUT command opens the input area, and an ampersand-coded /LOAD job entry statement to load the COBOL compiler is added to it; it's followed by an /OPTION job entry statement that specifies constant values (NOGO and RESET).

The COBOL compiler routes its punch output (the object module) to SYSPCH; in an interactive partition, that's the punch area. However, because the operator may have specified that the object module be stored in a library member, an &&IF order evaluates &&VARBL2. If it contains a non-blank value, a /FILE job entry statement for a TYPE=ICCF file associated with SYSPCH is added to the input area. As a result, punch output will be stored not in the punch area, but rather in the named library member. In this case, you can see that the "then" part of an &&IF order need not be another order or a system command; it can also supply data.

The next line in the procedure is another /OPTION job entry statement; this one supplies options the operator keyed in on the command line. Because the original parameters were shifted one or more positions to the left, the current parameters contain the first option value in &&PARAM1. As you can see, this /OPTION job entry statement can contain up to seven user-entered options: &&PARAM1 through &&PARAM7. For example, if I invoked the COBOL procedure with the command line

```
COBOL TRANLST OBJ ＊ LIST GETVIS=48K
```

the /OPTION statement created by the procedure would be

```
/OPTION LIST GETVIS=48K
```

Next in the procedure are four /FILE statements that define compiler work files in ICCF dynamic space.

The first line in the next group is another &&IF order. This one evaluates &&VARBL3 to see if it contains spaces. (The only other option is for &&VARBL3 to contain CBL as a result of the &&SET order in the fourth group of lines in the procedure.) If &&VARBL3 does contain spaces, the procedure branches to a line identified with the label NOCTL. However, if &&VARBL3 does not contain spaces, the operator is prompted to enter the data for a CBL control statement. The next &&IF order evaluates the &&DEVTYP variable to see if the user is working at a 3270 type terminal; you don't need to worry about this. Just notice that the procedure contains a &&READ order with no operand. That means that the text entered in response to the &&READ order is treated by DTSPROCS as data; here it's stored in the input area. As a result, the user enters the image of a CBL control statement, and it's positioned properly in the input area.

The first line in the last group is an /INCLUDE job entry statement. Because it's coded with an ampersand, it will be stored in the input area as a job entry statement; it will not be processed immediately. (Since the value in &&VARBL1 is the name of the member that contains the source file to be compiled, this /INCLUDE statement will cause the source file to be included in the job stream when the job is executed.) Finally, like the other procedures you've seen, the COBOL procedure ends with /END, /PEND, and /RUN. As a result, the COBOL compile job that has been built in the input area is executed.

I think you'll agree that although the COBOL procedure is relatively brief, it's complicated. Most of the complexity is due to the fact that it lets the user key in a variable number of parameters. When you write your own procedures, you may decide to make them less flexible from the user's point of view so they won't be so difficult to develop.

DISCUSSION

As I've stressed in this chapter, the most common use for procedures is to generate interactive partition jobs based on variable parameters supplied by a user. If all you want to do is package a group of system commands or job entry statements, a simple macro or job is a better choice than a procedure. However, as you can tell from the COBOL procedure I've just described, procedures give you a relatively high degree of control over how statements are handled, so there are times when you'll want to use them.

Terminology

procedure
procedure processor orders
procedure processor program
DTSPROCS
command list
implied execute feature
variable parameter
internal variable
special variable
ampersand-coded statement
multiple execution option
MULTEX option

Objectives

1. Compare and contrast:

   a. a procedure and a macro
   b. a procedure and an interactive partition job

2. List the elements that can make up a procedure.

3. Given specifications, code a procedure that builds an interactive partition job and causes it to be executed. The procedure may use any of the procedure processor orders presented in this chapter.

Appendix

ICCF reference summary

This appendix presents, in reference format, the syntax of all the (1) system commands, (2) editing commands, (3) ICCF-supplied procedure command lines, and (4) ICCF-supplied macro command lines this book describes. The entries are listed in alphabetical order, with leading slashes and at-signs disregarded. As a result, you should be able to find a particular entry easily. Each entry includes a reference to the chapter (and, if appropriate, the topic) where the command or command line is described. That way, if the brief syntax format this appendix presents for an item isn't enough to refresh your memory, you can turn to the text section where it's described in full.

/	Chapter 3	Topic 2
"n	Chapter 3	Topic 2
<cc[,nnn]	Chapter 4	Topic 5
>cc[,nnn]	Chapter 4	Topic 5
An	Chapter 3	Topic 2
ALIGN	Chapter 4	Topic 5
ALTER old-char new-char [n|*] [G]	Chapter 4	Topic 1
ASSEMBLE source-member [OBJ object-member] [options]	Chapter 10	
/ASYNC	Chapter 9	
BACKWARD n	Chapter 3	Topic 2
BOTTOM	Chapter 3	Topic 2
Cn	Chapter 3	Topic 2
CANCEL	Chapter 3	Topic 2
/CANCEL	Chapter 3 Chapter 8	Topic 1
CASE {M U}	Chapter 4	Topic 2
CENTER	Chapter 4	Topic 5
CHANGE /old-text/new-text/ [n|*] [G]	Chapter 4	Topic 1
COBOL source-member [OBJ object-member] [CBL] [options]	Chapter 10	
/CONNECT {library-number OFF}	Chapter 3	Topic 1
/CONTINU {nnn OFF}	Chapter 5	Topic 2
COPYFILE in-name out-name [in-password]	Chapter 5	Topic 1
COPYMEM in-name [in-password] in-lib out-name [out-password] out-lib [PURGE]	Chapter 5	Topic 1
CPYLIB in-name [in-password] in-lib out-lib	Chapter 5	Topic 1
CURSOR {CURRENT INPUT LINE [n] TABBACK [n] TABFORWARD [n]}	Chapter 4	Topic 2

```
GETP job-name [job-number] [class] [{KEEP  }]                    Chapter 8
                                    [{DELETE}]
           [MEM=member-name] [PWD=password]

GETR job-name [job-number] [class] [{KEEP  }]                    Chapter 8
                                    [{DELETE}]
           [MEM=member-name] [PWD=password]

         ┌CREATE  group-name [password] [PRIV|PUBL]┐
         │          [member-count]                 │
/GROUP  <│UNGROUP group-name [password]            │>            Chapter 5   Topic 1
         └REGROUP group-name [password]            ┘

          ┌ON                      ┐
          │OFF                     │
/HARDCPY <│printer-id              │>                            Chapter 5   Topic 2
          │dest-id                 │
          └START printer-id dest-id┘

@HC command operands                                            Chapter 5   Topic 2

I                                                               Chapter 3   Topic 2

INPUT                                                           Chapter 3   Topic 2

/INPUT                                                          Chapter 5   Topic 1
                                                                Chapter 11

/INSERT member-name [password]                                  Chapter 5   Topic 1

JUSTIFY  LEFT                                                    Chapter 4   Topic 5
         RIGHT

Kn                                                              Chapter 3   Topic 2

LADD n                                                          Chapter 3   Topic 2

LEFT nn                                                         Chapter 4   Topic 3

/LIBC [{CON}] [{FULL      [ALL]}]                               Chapter 5   Topic 2
      [{COM}] [{*abcdefg       }]

LIBRARY [{CON}] [{FULL      [ALL]}]                             Chapter 4   Topic 5
        [{COM}] [{*abcdefg       }]

/LIBRARY [{CON}] [{FULL      [ALL]}]                            Chapter 3   Topic 1
         [{COM}] [{*abcdefg       }]

LIBRC VSE-specs {ICCF-member-name} [password] [REPLACE]         Chapter 10
                {$$PUNCH         }
          [DATA=YES] [EOD=nn]

LIBRL VSE-specs ICCF-member-name [password] [REPLACE]           Chapter 10

LIBRP VSE-specs ICCF-member-name [password] [REPLACE]           Chapter 10

/LIST [start [end]] [member-name [password]]                    Chapter 3   Topic 1

/LISTC [start [end]] [member-name [password]]                   Chapter 5   Topic 2
```

```
/LISTP job-name [job-number] [class] [PWD=password]          Chapter 8

/LISTX [start [end]] [member-name [password]]               Chapter 3   Topic 1

LOAD [object-member] [JES JES-member]
          [DATA data-member][options]                        Chapter 10


LOCATE text                                                  Chapter 3   Topic 2
                                                             Chapter 4   Topic 1

LOCNOT text                                                  Chapter 4   Topic 1

/LOCP /string/                                               Chapter 8

LOCUP text                                                   Chapter 4   Topic 1

/LOGOFF                                                       Chapter 3   Topic 1

/LOGON user-id                                               Chapter 3   Topic 1

Mn                                                           Chapter 3   Topic 2

/MAIL                                                        Chapter 5   Topic 3

MSG                                                          Chapter 4   Topic 5

/MSG                                                         Chapter 5   Topic 3

MVLIB in-name [in-password] in-lib out-lib                   Chapter 5   Topic 1

NEXT n                                                       Chapter 3   Topic 2

PLI source-member [OBJ object-member] [PROCESS]
          [options]                                          Chapter 10

PRINT member-name                                            Chapter 4   Topic 5

@PRINT [member-name [password]]                              Chapter 5   Topic 2

                        ⎛new-password   ⎞
                        ⎜NOPASS         ⎟
                        ⎜PRIV           ⎟
/PROTECT name [old-password]⎨PUBL       ⎬               Chapter 5   Topic 1
                        ⎜DATE           ⎟
                        ⎝USER new-user-id⎠

       DSPLY VSE-member-name
PSERV  PUNCH VSE-member-name [INTO ICCF-member-name]          Chapter 10
       DSPCH VSE-member-name [INTO ICCF-member-name]

/PURGE member-name [password]                                Chapter 3   Topic 1

/PURGEP queue job-name [job-number] [PWD=password]           Chapter 8
```

`QUIT`	Chapter 3	Topic 2
`@RELIST [member-name [password]]`	Chapter 5	Topic 2
`/RENAME old-member-name new-member-name [password]`	Chapter 3	Topic 1
`RENUM [increment [starting-column [length` `        [starting-number]]]]`	Chapter 4	Topic 5
`REPEAT nnnn`	Chapter 4	Topic 5
`REPLACE member-name [password] [PRIV|PUBL]`	Chapter 3	Topic 2
`/REPLACE member-name [password]`	Chapter 5	Topic 1
`RIGHT nn`	Chapter 4	Topic 3
`/ROUTEP queue job-name [job-number]` `        [CLASS=class] [PWD=password]`	Chapter 8	
`RPGIAUTO source-member [OBJ object-member] [options]`	Chapter 10	
`RPGII source-member [OBJ object-member] [options]`	Chapter 10	
`RPGIXLTR source-member [PUNCH translated-member]`	Chapter 10	
`RSEF`	Chapter 10	
`/RUN`	Chapter 11	
`SAVE member-name [password] [PRIV|PUBL]`	Chapter 3	Topic 2
`/SAVE member-name [password]`	Chapter 5	Topic 1
`SCREEN [nn [nn [nn . . .]]]`	Chapter 4	Topic 4

`SDSERV [{*abcdefg}] [{NAME}]`
`       [{CONN   }] [{USER}]`
`       [{COM    }] [{DATE}]`
	Chapter 3	Topic 1

`SEARCH text`	Chapter 3 Chapter 4	Topic 2 Topic 1

`/SEND {user-id}`
`      {COPER  } text`
`      {ALL    }`
	Chapter 5	Topic 3

`/SET BUFFER nnnn`	Chapter 9	
`SET CASE {INPUT } {UPPER}` `         {OUTPUT} {MIXED}`	Chapter 4	Topic 2
`/SET CLASS n`	Chapter 9	
`/SET COMLIB {ON }` `            {OFF}`	Chapter 3	Topic 1

`SHOW NAMES`	Chapter 4 Topic 4
`SHOW PF`	Chapter 4 Topic 2
`/SHOW PF`	Chapter 5 Topic 3
`/SHOW PFED`	Chapter 5 Topic 3
`SHOW TABCHAR`	Chapter 4 Topic 2
`SHOW TABS`	Chapter 4 Topic 2
`/SHOW TERM`	Chapter 5 Topic 3
`/SHOW TIME`	Chapter 9
`/SHOW USER`	Chapter 5 Topic 3

```
          ⎛ n      ⎞
          ⎜ -n     ⎟
          ⎜ S+n    ⎟
          ⎜ S-n    ⎟
/SKIP     ⎨ P+n    ⎬                          Chapter 3    Topic 1
          ⎜ P-n    ⎟
          ⎜ TOP    ⎟
          ⎜ BOTTOM ⎟
          ⎝ END    ⎠
```

`SORT in-name [in-password] [SEQ sort-specs]` `        [PUNCH out-name]`	Chapter 5 Topic 1
`SPLIT cc`	Chapter 4 Topic 5
`/SQUEEZE member-name [password]`	Chapter 5 Topic 1

```
       ⎛ DSPLY VSE-member-name                         ⎞
SSERV  ⎨ PUNCH VSE-member-name [INTO ICCF-member-name] ⎬   Chapter 10
       ⎝ DSPCH VSE-member-name [INTO ICCF-member-name] ⎠
```

`/STATUSP job-name [job-number]`	Chapter 8

```
                                  ⎛ DIRECT   ⎞
                                  ⎜ DIRECTBG ⎟
SUBMIT member-name [password]     ⎨ RETURN   ⎬ [PRINT]     Chapter 8
                                  ⎝ RETURNBG ⎠
             [PWD=power-password] [ICCFSLI]
```

`/SUMRY member-name`	Chapter 5 Topic 2

```
         ⎛ library-number ⎞
/SWITCH  ⎨ RESET          ⎬                    Chapter 3    Topic 1
         ⎝ LIBS           ⎠
```

`/SYNC`	Chapter 9
`TA[nnn]`	Chapter 4 Topic 5

Index

This index doesn't present entry names that begin with special characters in a separate section. Instead, leading special characters are ignored and entries are positioned according to the first letter they contain. However, you can locate some entries with the same initial special characters as follows:

If the entry begins with:	Look under:
/	System command Job entry statement
@	Macro Macro order
&&	Macro variables Procedure processor orders Procedure processor variables
* $$	Job entry control language
//	Job control language

Comment Form

Your opinions count

Your opinions today will affect our future products and policies. So if you have questions, criticisms, or suggestions, I'm eager to get them. You can expect a response within a week of the time we receive your comments.

Also, if you discover any errors in this book, typographical or otherwise, please point them out. We'll correct them when the book is reprinted.

Thanks for your help!

fold

Mike Murach, President
Mike Murach and Associates, Inc.

Book title: DOS/VSE ICCF

Dear Mike: _____

_____

_____

_____

_____

_____

_____

_____

_____

_____

_____

fold

_____

_____

_____

_____

_____

Name and Title _____
Company (if any)_____
Address _____
City, State, Zip _____

Fold where indicated and staple.
No postage necessary if mailed in the U.S.

BUSINESS REPLY MAIL
FIRST CLASS   PERMIT NO. 3063   FRESNO, CA

POSTAGE WILL BE PAID BY ADDRESSEE

Mike Murach & Associates, Inc.

4697 West Jacquelyn Avenue
Fresno, California 93722-9986

Order Form

Our Unlimited Guarantee

To our customers who order directly from us: You must be satisfied. Our books must work for you, or you can send them back for a full refund...no matter how many you buy, no matter how long you've had them.

Name & Title _____

Company (if any) _____

Address _____

City, State, Zip _____

Phone number (including area code) _____

Qty.	Product code and title	Price
DOS/VSE Subjects		
_____ICCF	DOS/VSE ICCF	$25.00
_____VJCL	DOS/VSE JCL	25.00
_____VBAL	DOS/VSE Assembler Language	27.50
VSAM		
_____VSMX	VSAM: AMS and Application Programming	$25.00
_____VSAM	VSAM for the COBOL Programmer	15.00
Data Base Processing		
_____IMS1	IMS for the COBOL Programmer Part 1: DL/I Data Base Processing	$25.00
CICS		
_____CIC1	CICS for the COBOL Programmer: Part 1	$25.00
_____CIC2	CICS for the COBOL Programmer: Part 2	25.00

Qty.	Product code and title	Price
COBOL Language Elements		
_____SAC1	Structured ANS COBOL: Part 1	$20.00
_____SAC2	Structured ANS COBOL: Part 2	20.00
_____RW	Report Writer	13.50
COBOL Program Development		
_____DDCP	How to Design and Develop COBOL Programs	$20.00
_____CPHB	The COBOL Programmer's Handbook	20.00
System Development		
_____DDBS	How to Design and Develop Business Systems	$20.00
OS Subjects		
_____OJCL	OS JCL	$22.50
_____OSUT	OS Utilities	15.00
_____TSO	MVS TSO	22.50
_____ASMO	OS Assembler	22.50

☐ Bill me the appropriate price plus UPS shipping and handling (and sales tax in California) for each book ordered.

☐ Bill the appropriate book prices plus UPS shipping and handling (and sales tax in California) to my
_____Visa _____MasterCard:
Card number_____
Valid thru (month/year) _____
Cardowner's signature _____
(not valid without signature)

☐ I want to **save** UPS shipping and handling charges. Here's my check or money order for $_____. California residents, please add 6% sales tax to your total. (Offer valid in the U.S. only.)

To order more quickly,

Call **toll-free** 1-800-221-5528
(Weekdays, 9 to 4 Pacific Std. Time)

In California, call 1-800-221-5527

Mike Murach & Associates, Inc.

4697 West Jacquelyn Avenue
Fresno, California 93722
(209) 275-3335

BUSINESS REPLY MAIL

FIRST CLASS   PERMIT NO. 3063   FRESNO, CA

POSTAGE WILL BE PAID BY ADDRESSEE

Mike Murach & Associates, Inc.

4697 West Jacquelyn Avenue
Fresno, California 93722-9986